Women, Citizenship and Difference

D1336158

POSTCOLONIAL ENCOUNTERS

A Zed Books series in association with the International Centre for Contemporary Cultural Research (ICCCR), Universities of Manchester and Keele.

SERIES EDITORS: Richard Werbner and Pnina Werbner

This series debates the making of contemporary culture and politics in a post colonial world. Volumes explore the impact of colonial legacies, precolonial traditions and current global and imperial forces on the everyday lives of citizens. Reaching beyond postcolonial countries to the formation of external ethnic and migrant diasporas, the series critically theorises:

- the active engagement of people themselves in the creation of their own political and cultural agendas;
- the emerging predicaments of local, national and transnational identities and subjectivities;
- the indigenous roots of nationalism, communalism, state violence and political terror;
- the cultural and religious counter-movements for or against emancipation and modernity;
- the social struggles over the imperatives of human and citizenship rights within the moral and political economy.

Arising from the analysis of decolonisation and recolonisation, the series opens out a significant space in a growing interdisciplinary literature. The convergence of interest is very broad, from anthropology, cultural studies, social history, comparative literature, development, sociology, law and political theory. No single theoretical orientation provides the dominant thrust. Instead the series responds to the challenge of a commitment to empirical, in-depth research as the motivation for critical theory.

Other titles in the series

Richard Werbner and Terence Ranger, eds, *Postcolonial Identities in Africa* (1996).

Pnina Werbner and Tariq Modood, eds, *Debating Cultural Hybridity: Multicultural Identities and the Politics of Anti-Racism* (1997).

Tariq Modood and Pnina Werbner, eds, *The Politics of Multiculturalism in the New Europe: Racism, Identity and Community* (1997).

Richard Werbner, ed., *Memory and the Postcolony: African Anthropology and the Critique of Power* (1998).

Itty Abraham, *The Making of the Indian Atomic Bomb: Science, Secrecy and the Postcolonial State* (1998).

Women, Citizenship and Difference

edited by

Nira Yuval-Davis and Pnina Werbner

Women, Citizenship and Difference was first published in 1999 by
Zed Books Ltd., 7 Cynthia Street, London N1 9JF, UK and
Room 400, 175 Fifth Avenue, New York, NY 10010, USA

in association with

the International Centre for Contemporary Cultural Research
Universities of Manchester and Keele, UK.

Distributed in the USA exclusively by St Martin's Press, Inc.,
175 Fifth Avenue, New York, NY 10010, USA.

Editorial copyright © Nira Yuval-Davis and Pnina Werbner, 1999
Individual chapters copyright © authors of individual chapters
as indicated on pp. v-vi

Cover design by Andrew Corbett
Set in 10/11½ pt Monotype Garamond
by Long House, Cumbria, UK
Printed and bound in the United Kingdom
by Biddles Ltd, Guildford and King's Lynn

The rights of the authors of this work have been asserted by them
in accordance with the Copyright, Designs and Patents Act, 1988

All rights reserved

A catalogue record for this book
is available from the British Library

US CIP has been applied for

ISBN Hb 1 85649 645 7
Pb 1 85649 646 5

Contents

Notes on Contributors

Aleksandra Ålund is a professor in the Department of Sociology, University of Umeå, Sweden, and also holds a guest professorship at the Danish Centre for Migration and Ethnic Studies, Esbjerg, Denmark. In addition to her general work on ethnicity and multiculturalism in Europe she has, over a number of years, conducted research on multi-ethnic suburban areas in Stockholm with special focus on gender and youth research. In connection with this she has written a number of articles and books published in English and Swedish. Among her books are (with Carl-Ulrik Schierup) *Paradoxes of Multiculturalism* (Avebury 1991) and *Multikultiungdom: Kön, etnicitet, identitet* (Studentlitteratur 1997).

Alison Assiter is Dean of Economic and Social Sciences at the University of the West of England and Professor of Feminist Theory. Her books include *Althusser and Feminism* (Pluto Press 1991) and *Enlightened Women* (Routledge 1998). She lives in London with her partner and their son.

Samia Bano works for Southall Black Sisters. Her previous work includes researching identity among second-generation Pakistanis and Bangladeshis in East London as part of a project directed by Professor Floya Anthias at the University of Greenwich. She has recently been awarded an Economic and Social Research Council doctoral research award at the University of Warwick to study the practice of Islamic personal laws in relation to Asian Muslim women in Britain.

Jacqueline Bhabha is the director of the Human Rights Programme at the University of Chicago. She is an expert in international refugee law and practised immigration and human rights law in London for 15 years before moving to the United States to teach and write. She has published several books, including (with Sue Shutter) *Women's Movement: Women under Immigration, Nationality and Refugee Law* (Trentham Books 1994). She is currently working on questions of inclusion and exclusion in Europe, on child persecution and on mechanisms for improving the implementation of international human rights law. Her most recent article is on the need for child-specific guidelines for adjudicating asylum applications by minors.

Patricia Hill Collins is currently Professor of African-American Studies at the University of Cincinnati. She has just completed her third book, entitled *Fighting Words: Black Women, Critical Social Theory and the Search for Justice*, to be published by the University of Minnesota Press.

Maja Korac received her BA Honours and Masters degrees in Sociology from Belgrade University, in the former Yugoslavia, where she taught for several years. She is currently a doctoral candidate, Graduate Programme, Sociology, at York University, Canada. Since the spring of 1996 she has also worked as a consultant to the Women in Conflict Zones Network project, initiated and hosted by York University.

Ronit Lentin, a feminist sociologist and novelist, is course coordinator of the MPhil in Ethnic and Racial Studies at the University of Dublin, Trinity College, where she also lectures in Sociology and Women's Studies. She is the editor of *Gender and Catastrophe* (Zed Books 1997) and *In from the Shadows: the University of Limerick Women's Studies Collection Vols 1 and 2* (Limerick 1995, 1996). Among her books is *Conversations with Palestinian Women* (Jerusalem: Mifras 1982). She has published extensively in relation to her doctoral research on the gendered relations between Israel and the Shoah (Holocaust) and on feminist research methodologies, gender and racism, feminist auto/biography, women's peace activism, and women and citizenship. Her latest novel is *Songs on the Death of Children* (Dublin: Poolbeg Press 1996).

Judith Monks is a Lecturer in the Department of Sociology and Social Anthropology, Keele University, UK. She is a social anthropologist whose research has been principally in the area of chronic illness and disablement in the UK, a field in which she has also had participatory experience as a nurse and community health worker. She has published articles on personhood, language and personal narrative, and on experiences of locality and belonging. Her forthcoming monograph, based on her doctoral thesis, concerns experiences of personhood and conversation among people with multiple sclerosis.

Cecilia Mauleon Olea is an active veteran Peruvian feminist who works at the Flora Tristan Centre for Peruvian Women and is currently Chair of its Board of Directors. She studied Social Anthropology. During the preparation for the Fourth World Conference on Women at Beijing, she was responsible for the Regional Coordinator's Political Advisory Team. She has published various articles in feminist and political journals and collections, in Spanish and English, about Peruvian and Latin American feminist politics.

Jan Jindy Pettman is reader in Global Politics and Director of the Centre for Women's Studies at the Australian National University in Canberra. She is part of a network of feminists researching connections between identity, culture and political economy in the Asian region. Her most recent book is *Worlding Women: a Feminist International Politics* (Routledge 1996). She is co-editor of the new *International Feminist Journal of Politics.*

Nilofar Pourzand is an Assistant Project Officer with UNICEF Afghanistan. She is also a doctoral student at the University of Greenwich, London, where she is writing a dissertation on 'Gender, Education and Identity among Educated Afghani Refugee Women in Pakistan'. Before working in Afghanistan, she was Gender and Education Officer for UNICEF in Iran. She has published a number of UNICEF documents on gender analysis in that country. Her contacts with Afghanistan go back to childhood.

Birgit Rommelspacher teaches women's studies at the College of Social Work, Alice Salomon Fachhochschule Berlin, and Social Psychology at the Technische Universität Berlin. She has numerous publications on feminist psychology, right-wing extremism, racism and anti-feminism, including *Weibliche Beziehungsmuster. Psychologie und Therapie von Frauen* (Frankfurt: Campus 1987); *Mitmenschlichkeit und Unterwerfung. Zur Ambivalenz weiblicher Moral* (Frankfurt: Campus 1992, with R. Burgard); *Leiden macht keine Lust. Der Mythos vom weiblichen Masochismus* (Frankfurt: Fischer 1992); *Schuldlos-Schuldig? Wie sich junge Frauen mit Antisemitismus auseinandersetzen* (Hamburg: Konkret Literaturverlag 1995); *Dominanzkultur. Texte zu Fremdheit und Macht* (Berlin: Orlanda 1995).

Elaine Unterhalter is a South African woman who is currently a Lecturer in Education and International Development at the Institute of Education, University of London. She has published extensively in journals and collections on themes related to education, gender and international development. Her current research is concerned with gender and curriculum transformation in the Republic of South Africa.

Virginia Valente Vargas is a sociologist who majored in Political Science. Vargas, an active feminist militant, founded the Flora Tristan Centre for Peruvian Women in 1979. Her works, in Spanish or English, include *The Contribution of Women's Rebellion* (1989), *How to Change Development* (1992), *Gender and Development* (co-edited, 1992) and *The Women's Movement and Public Policy in Europe, Latin America and the Caribbean* (co-edited, 1998). Since 1990, Vargas has worked as both an activist and organiser in Latin America, and as a Visiting Lecturer at the Women and Development Programme at the Institute of Social Studies, the Hague, Netherlands. During 1994–96 she was Coordinator of the Latin American and Caribbean Women NGOs for the

World Conference on Women, Beijing. Vargas has been honoured with awards for her work with women by Peruvian, Latin American, Spanish and international bodies.

Pnina Werbner is Reader in Social Anthropology at Keele University and Research Administrator of the International Centre for Contemporary Cultural Research (ICCCR) at the Universities of Manchester and Keele. Her most recent publications are *Embodying Charisma: Locality, Modernity and Emotion in Sufi Cults* (with Helene Basu, Routledge 1998), *Debating Cultural Hybridity* and *The Politics of Multiculturalism in the New Europe*, both co-edited with Tariq Modood (Zed Books 1997). Her monograph is *The Migration Process: Capital, Gifts and Offerings among British Pakistanis* (Berg 1990). Her forthcoming book, *Diaspora, Islam and the Millennium*, is on the political imaginaries of British Pakistanis. Her current research on multiculturalism and on transnational Sufi cults was conducted in Britain and Pakistan.

Nira Yuval-Davis is Professor and Postgraduate Course Leader in Gender and Ethnic Studies at the University of Greenwich, London. She has written extensively on theoretical and empirical aspects of nationalism, racism, fundamentalism and gender relations in Britain, in Israel and in settler societies. Among others, she co-authored *Racialised Boundaries* (Routledge 1992), and co-edited *Women–Nation–State* (Macmillan 1989), *Refusing Holy Orders: Women and Fundamentalism in Britain* (Virago 1992), *Unsettling Settler Societies: Articulations of Gender, Ethnicity, Race and Class* (Sage 1995) and *Crossfires: Nationalism, Racism and Gender in Europe* (Pluto 1995). Her most recent book is *Gender and Nation*, published by Sage (1997).

Preface

During the last few years, citizenship in general, and women's citizenship in particular, has occupied a centre stage in feminism, both theoretically and politically. This book constitutes a contribution to this growing accumulative body of literature on the subject. It is a complementary volume to the special issue of *Feminist Review,* Citizenship: Pushing the Boundaries (*FR* 57, Autumn 1997), of which we were both guest editors, together with the *Feminist Review* Collective members Helen Crowley and Gail Lewis.

The *Feminist Review* special issue, as well as this book, are based on the international conference, 'Women, Citizenship and Difference', which we organised at the University of Greenwich in London on 16–19 July 1996. The 120 participants in the conference came from a wide variety of geographical and professional locations, both academic and activist. What united them all was a recognition of the interdependence of analytical and political commitment, of situated knowledge and of the intersectionality of gender, race and ethnicity, class, ability and other social divisions. Many although not all of the participants felt that the notion of citizenship might be a useful tool to both analyse and promote women's position – however heterogeneous this category may be in contemporary society. A paper written by Nira Yuval-Davis was circulated among the participants before the conference and helped to create a common agenda for the debates that took place there. The paper, which was published in our edited issue of *Feminist Review*, looked at debates concerning citizenship, nationalism and 'the community'; social rights and social difference; the private and the public; active/passive citizenship and citizenship rights and duties. It aimed at constructing a non-sexist, non-racist non-westocentric theory of multi-layered dialogical citizenship.

These issues were discussed at the conference in a series of plenary panels as well as in ongoing, intensive small group discussions, which were randomly composed of the conference participants. The discussions established the possibility of a common language – a transversal dialogue, cross-cutting disciplinary and collectivity boundaries.

More than a hundred women, as mentioned, and some men participated at the conference. The level of contributions, both in the form of papers and as active participants in the discussion, was exceptionally high. Inevitably, only a minority of these papers and panel presentations have found their way into this book and the special issue, although we know that many more participants have continued to develop their standpoints in other forums. The panel presentations and the group discussions in the conference were summed up in the conference report that was circulated later among the participants and also sent to the Wenner Gren Foundation for Anthropological Research and to the members of the European Union Equal Opportunities Commission who sponsored the conference.

The generous support of both bodies ensured that the conference was a truly international and interdisciplinary event. Greenwich University hosted the conference and it was also supported by the International Centre for Contemporary Cultural Research at Keele University. We would like to use this opportunity to thank all participants and sponsors for their contributions to the success of the event, and look forward to the continuation of the dialogue.

Nira Yuval-Davis and Pnina Werbner

CHAPTER 1: INTRODUCTION

Women and the New Discourse of Citizenship

Pnina Werbner and Nira Yuval-Davis

The Modern Aporias of Citizenship

It is widely accepted that citizenship is a contested concept (Lister 1997a: 3). To go beyond that insight, this book begins from a recognition that both as a political imaginary and as a set of commonsense assumptions and practices, modern citizenship is inserted into a social field, an arena of competing, heterogeneous and partially overlapping discourses.[1] Within this field, freedom, autonomy and the right to be different – central credos of democratic citizenship – are pitched against the regulating forces of modernity and the state and subverted by discourses of 'culture and tradition' – of nationalism, religiosity and the family. The aim of this book is to expose the processes that construct these articulations, and the historically specific modalities of citizenship they produce. Such a comparison enables us to theorise the present emergence of a new discourse – one which privileges difference and stresses the dialogical and global dimensions of citizenship. Our particular focus is on the processes that have led to the gendering of citizenship and the counter-movements towards equality and difference these exclusionary forces have produced.

Third World feminists were, in many countries, an integral part of anti-colonial nationalist struggles for independence (Badran 1995; Jayawardena 1986; Mohanty 1991: 10 *et seq.*). For these women, nationalism was an emancipatory movement for autonomy, popular sovereignty and universal citizenship. But after independence women often found themselves excluded from public office and power. The rise of authoritarian regimes and movements in many parts of the Third World and Eastern Europe has, moreover, highlighted some of the tensions which can arise between constructions of nationalism and citizenship. Although historically coexisting within a single social field, democratic citizenship's overt stress on rationality, individuality and the rule of law has frequently been in tension with, and even antithetical to, nationalism's appeals to communal solidarities and primordial sentiments of soil and blood. Rooted in a common (if often invented) history and shared aesthetics, nationalists evoke the sentimental beauty of the landscape, the tastes, sounds and smells of folk cuisines, of music and dance, language and poetry. National subjectivities are embedded in the past, in the sacrifices of national heroes for the sake of communal survival, in collective moments of joy, mourning and extreme danger, even defeat. National communities that privilege origin and culture thus tend to foster much deeper passions than those organised around notions of citizenship.[2]

By contrast, even when its advocates invoke the lost world of the Athenian polis, citizenship remains a thoroughly modern invention. It is, on the surface, jural, cerebral, procedural. Rather than national landscapes of desire, citizenship is defined by residence in an exclusive, homogenised space: an often arbitrarily defined and circumscribed 'territory' which may, and usually does, encompass several self-ascribed nationalities and ethnic groups.

Nonetheless, citizenship has had its foundational moments, from the Magna Carta through the French Revolution to the American Declaration of Independence, the suffragette movement and anti-colonial struggles. Clifford Geertz's original insights on new nation citizenship remain a relevant starting point for a more holistic understanding of citizenship even today: 'Citizenship in the truly modern state', he wrote in 1963, 'has more and more become the most broadly negotiable claim to personal significance' (Geertz 1963: 108). The tensions and contradictions between the 'will to be modern' and the 'demand to exist and have a name' (*ibid.*) have fuelled national politics in the postcolonial world for the past forty years.

Despite its apparent blandness, then, citizenship has been the site of intense struggle, arising from its central locus within modernity itself. As recent debates about the modern versus the late- or postmodern have highlighted, modernity was marked from its inception by contradictory tendencies: towards ordering, control and normalisation, on the one hand, and the toleration of uncertainty, scepticism, disagreement and difference, on the other.[3] Democratic citizenship as a social and political construct encapsulates this modern aporia: it opens up spaces and arenas of freedom – of conflict, unpredictability, intimacy, the right to be different – while restricting and structuring these spaces by procedural hedges about limits. It orders conflict, channels and tames it; it labels and classifies collective differences; it determines how, where and when difference may legitimately be 'represented', and who counts as 'different' in the political arena, itself a social construct. Citizenship defines the limits of state power and where a civil society or the private sphere of free individuals begins. These opposed impulses are part of what makes citizenship, for subjects themselves, such a complex, ambiguous imaginary.

As an unstable political and jural formation, citizenship both compounds and confounds contradictory tendencies: of universalism and particularism, freedom and order, individual rights and collective responsibilities, identity and difference, nation and individual. Because such combinations remain inherently unstable, democratic citizenship is, to echo a favourite Derridean aphorism, always already becoming, a historically contingent social formation, a particular negotiated compromise between forces of normalisation and differentiation. It is therefore always inflected by power and by the commonsense assumptions of hegemonic cultural and political elites.

This inherent instability in both the meaning and limits of identity and difference, we show in this book, is reflected in debates about almost every facet of citizenship as an institution and mode of being. In the contemporary version of these debates, civic republicans and communitarians promote, from their different perspectives, active participation and unitary visions of a common social good. Against these approaches, postliberals and radical democrats argue for the legitimacy of public difference and the need to incorporate plurality within the public sphere. At the same time socialists, reformers, needs activists, multiculturalists and humanists, from a variety of vantage points, stress the responsibilities of the state towards its socially differentiated and divided citizenry.[4]

This leads to a further insight, one which is the starting point of the present volume. Rather than being simply an artificial construct of modernity, citizenship as a subjectivity is deeply dialogical, encapsulating specific, historically inflected, cultural and social assumptions about similarity and difference. The negotiation of these may generate at different times and places quite different sets of practices, institutional arrangements, modes of social interaction and future orientations. This is especially so because unlike nationalism which grounds itself in past myths of common origin or culture, citizenship raises its eyes towards the future, to common destinies. Its politics are aspirational, a 'politics of desire' (Falk 1994: 131, 139–40). As a political imaginary, discourses of citizenship constitute horizons of possibility, a '*telos* to be realised' (Parry 1991: 167), an 'ideal' (Marshall 1950: 29), a 'blueprint' for democracy (Anderson 1983: 81) or, following Toqueville, an 'egalitarian utopia' (Göle 1996: 52; Mouffe 1988: 94). Citizenship is the gold standard against which the negotiated order is measured and, inevitably, found wanting.

This is where citizenship becomes more than itself, both spatially and temporally: implicit within it is a charter for human rights which is uncircumscribed territorially and which envisages, in Claude Levi-Strauss's words, a 'humanity without frontiers' (Levi-Strauss 1966: 166): the ethical, physical and cultural survival of the human species in all its totemic diversity. Against those who regard citizenship as confined to the nation-state, with human rights being applicable only to international or supranational arenas (e.g., Pateman 1996), we argue here that, both historically and ideologically, the discourse of one implies the other, so that national and transnational citizenships constitute two coexisting and interrelated modalities of citizenship. It is in this sense also that the work of citizenship becomes a work for the future, for generations yet to be born. Global citizens have nothing less than the peaceful survival of the planet and its multifarious biological and cultural variety as their *telos*, against the totalising, invasive and homogenising project of Western modernity (Falk 1994: 140).

Hence, the contributors to this volume – as well as to the *Feminist Review* issue (No. 57, 1997) which is its sister collection – despite great differences in focus and approach – are agreed in defining citizenship as much more than simply the formal relationship between an individual and the state presented by an earlier liberal and political science literature. Our alternative approach defines citizenship as a more total relationship, inflected by identity, social positioning, cultural assumptions, institutional practices and a sense of belonging.

Such mediations are addressed in the first part of the book, 'Dialogical Citizenship', which considers the relational dimensions of citizenship against simplistic communitarian and liberal models. The second part, on 'Exclusionary Citizenships', concentrates on the way different positionings of women affect their citizenships in policy areas such as education, population planning and welfare, and how these differences determine both the construction of national collectivities and the boundary between private and public. 'Ambivalent Citizens', the third part of the volume, discloses the predicaments of refugees and asylum seekers on the 'borders' of nations, and interrogates the limits and potential for women of multicultural citizenship. The final part, 'Feminist Citizenships in a Global Ecumene', focuses on women's activism and the explicitly political dimensions of women's citizenship as a local and global force for change. Throughout the book we show that forces of exclusion and inclusion are both played out symbolically while constituting, in Phillips's words (1995), a 'politics of presence', an embodied enactment of toleration or intolerance.

Citizenship and Difference

That citizenship is a contradictory site of, on the one hand, an autonomous subjectivity which envisions and constitutes the political community or communities and, on the other, of subjectification to that very same political community, underlines the fact that any account of citizenship must go beyond a purely formal, jural analysis. Moreover, the degree to which the political agency of subjects determines or is determined by collective forces beyond them is a key issue for investigation. Scholarship on citizenship has exploded the assumption that once suffrage was achieved for women, blacks and other minorities, all citizens became automatically equal subjects of the political community. This is a central topic of the present volume.

A central question in present debates on citizenship is the extent to which 'difference' discriminates between citizens; whether 'the citizen' is an abstract subject with equal access to rights, including the right to participate in democratic politics, or whether discrepancies in the positioning of specific citizens

– both within and between polities – are crucial to the understanding of their citizenship. The contributors to this book are part of a broader trend in the study of citizenship that recognises that the specific location of people in society – their group membership and categorical definition by gender, nationality, religion, ethnicity, 'race', ability, age or life cycle stage – mediates the construction of their citizenship as 'different' and thus determines their access to entitlements and their capacity to exercise independent agency.[5]

T. H. Marshall, the most prominent theorist of citizenship in Britain, defined citizenship as 'full membership in the community' (1950). As Hall and Held have pointed out (1989), such a definition of citizenship opens the way to view citizenship as a multi-layered concept. Even though Marshall himself failed to interrogate the relation between nation and state, it is clear that political subjects are often involved in more than one political community, the boundaries of which can be local, ethnic, national or global, and may extend within, across, or beyond state lines. Moreover, membership in one collectivity can have crucial effects on citizenship in others. This is particularly true of diaspora, migrant and refugee communities, as Werbner demonstrates in her discussion of Pakistani women activists (Chapter 14).[6]

A holistic definition of citizenship goes beyond formal rights such as the right to carry a particular passport. Although that right – or lack of it – is recognised as being often of crucial importance, our general perspective on citizenship points to a more encompassing set of relations than those which can be summed up by formal attributes of voting or passport carrying. It includes not only a focus on intersubjective relations but a consideration of global imbalances of power as these affect migration, an aspect of citizenship discussed here by Pettman (Chapter 13), by Lutz (1997) as well as by Stasiulis and Bakan (1997).

One might argue that by broadening the concept of citizenship in this way we are stretching it so far beyond conventional boundaries as to render it overgeneralised and unworkable. One answer to this is that we need an expansion in the notion of citizenship in order to analyse and understand transformations in formal citizenship as well. No-one observing the debates about the single European currency, the Northern Irish agreement, or lone-mother 'welfare to work' policies, to mention but a few of the salient citizenship-related events in Britain at the turn of the millennium, could fail to notice that previously naturalised assumptions about boundaries and sovereignty are everywhere being challenged and revised, not just analytically and not just elsewhere, in the South or in the Third World, but in the real politics of the metropolis itself. This is an issue to which we return below.

Women and the Moral Pragmatics of Citizenship

Historically, the place of women as both subjectified and subject-making (non)citizens has embodied some of the central aporias of citizenship.

Indeed, one of the great paradoxes of modernity has been that the moment of 'universal' emancipation was also the moment of female subordination and exclusion. Following the French Revolution, for example, women lost their civil, economic and political role in the emergent public sphere and were relegated to the familial, private sphere. It is possible to argue, as many feminist writers have (Pateman 1988; Lister 1997a: 69), that the exclusion of women from citizenship was an intrinsic feature of their naturalisation as embodiments of the private, the familial and the emotional. It was thus essential to the construction of the public sphere as masculine, rational, responsible and respectable. Women became the 'property' that allowed married men, even the working classes, the right to be active citizens in the public sphere.

Like all hegemonic discourses, this particular one was never, however, absolute. From the beginning there were those, both men and women, who stressed the equality of the sexes and hence women's emancipatory rights (see Banks 1981; Eisenstein 1981). Among them Mary Wollstonecraft's *A Vindication of the Rights of Women*, published in 1792, Concordet's 'On the Admission of Women to the Rights of Citizenship' (1790), Olympe de Gouges's *Declaration of the Rights of Women* (1791), and John Stuart Mill's *The Subjection of Women*, published in 1869, were all widely read in liberal circles. This parallel, dissenting discourse gathered pace during the nineteenth century against powerful male opposition. Its existence points to alternative explanations.

Rather than stressing that women's exclusion from citizenship was logically inherent in Enlightenment categories themselves, another way of interpreting the historic emergence of a male–female, public–private, culture–nature divide might begin from a sociological and anthropological theorising of the pragmatics of commonsense reasoning. Ursula Vogel provides an insight into this moral pragmatics when she outlines the ambiguities and internal contradictions produced historically by the threat that Enlightenment principles of egalitarian citizenship posed for the powerful European institution of the bourgeois family, entrenched as a male-headed, corporate unit:

> there has been no coherent pattern of reasons why women as women ... should have been placed outside the boundaries of the political community. To the extent that their exclusion was arbitrary it was bound to distort the meaning of citizenship. (Vogel 1991: 60)

Such distortions, she argues, affected the perceptions both of the privileged and of the excluded. The point is

> that *the resources for perceiving women and men as equals were available in the wider philosophical and moral frameworks of these theories of citizenship*. The egalitarian principles were, however, displaced and overlaid by a predominantly political interest in the hierarchical ordering of marriage. (*ibid.*: 61, emphasis added)

Within this political field of competing discourses, the inconsistencies between the principles upholding family and citizenship led to the kind of *ad hoc* rationalisations and secondary elaborations of belief that anthropologists and sociologists recognise as the hallmark of commonsense reasoning.[7] These sustained gendered inequalities and exclusionary practices while simultaneously continuing to assert the primacy of universal equality and freedom.

Despite her initial insight, Vogel fails ultimately, however, to appreciate the full force of her argument for a sociological theory of citizenship. Instead she asserts – against the grain of her own argument – that 'even the most egalitarian formulations of political rights are predicated upon the gender division between citizens and non-citizens' (*ibid.*: 78). What is elided here is the fact that these formulations are not philosophical or logical. They are the product of a (conscious or unconscious) political manipulation of two contradictory discourses; they disguise their inconsistencies through a rhetoric that seeks to mark women out as subordinate and non-rational.

A phenomenological insight into commonsense reasoning explains why Enlightenment theories of 'abstract' universalism are not *intrinsically* exclusionary *vis-à-vis* women, while at the same time recognising that historically the 'rationality' of the law makers – masculine or otherwise – has itself been a social construction. In response, one route that women used to overcome their construction as 'different' and non-rational was to stress their superior 'maternal' qualities of caring, responsibility and compassion as key constituents of citizenship. They re-imagined citizenship and the public sphere to encompass 'feminine' values. This is the subject of Pnina Werbner's historical and contemporary overview (Chapter 14) of political motherhood as a Euro-American and Third World emancipatory movement that highlights women's empowering 'difference'. But equally important, as Virginia Vargas and Cecilia Olea argue in their chapter on post-democratic, post-Beijing Peru (Chapter 15), and as Pourzand and Bhabha suggest in their discussions of Afghanistan and of human rights discourses (Chapters 5 and 11), is the claim for equality. In different respects these chapters thus stress the way women's struggles become, simultaneously, also struggles for broader, encompassing democratic civil and political rights.

Postcolonial Encounters and the New Discourse of Citizenship

The duality characterising this new discourse on citizenship raises, however, the apparently intractable opposition posed by feminist critical theory between abstract universal egalitarianism (masculine), and particular discourses of needs and care (feminine).

The feminist critique is to be grasped historically as a response to the false universalism of early male citizenship claims. These, we have seen, excluded many classes of potential citizens, including women, indigenous minorities, slaves, colonial subjects, the working classes, on grounds of 'difference'. If so, the argument goes, if abstract universal egalitarianism implies normative homogeneity and the suppression of particularity and difference, it cannot be the basis for a female emancipatory politics. In line with this, Iris Marion Young denies the very possibility of an impartial perspective, 'the view from everywhere' (Young 1990: 103 *et seq.*), a 'monological moral reason' (*ibid.*: 106). Standpoint feminists argue that universals are generated from particular, often hegemonic, vantage points, which impose what is in reality a partial vision on others, placed differentially.

Many of the contributors to this volume examine the issues involved from a rather different position, grounded in Third Worldist and postcolonial women's experience of human rights violations and authoritarianism, and hence of much greater hurdles to be scaled. At the same time we also recognise that, paradoxically, Southern women often command enormous women-specific cultural capital of a kind not readily available to their Western bourgeois counterparts, as Ålund (Chapter 9) and Werbner show (Chapter 14; see also Eisenstein 1997). Here what needs to be stressed is that, as Vargas and Olea highlight (Chapter 15), in the states of the South democracy and universal citizenship are – when they exist at all – relatively recent, often fragile achievements. These are threatened by forces of unregulated capitalism, the subject of Jan Jindy Pettman's chapter (Chapter 13), but also by religious fundamentalism, militarism, ethnic quasi-nationalism and state terror, as well as by endemic bureaucratic incompetence and corruption, global pressures towards structural adjustment and, in late-1990s Asia, economic melt-down and ecological devastation.

In these circumstances the mundane citizenships of European welfare states with their liberal freedoms and comprehensive welfare entitlements seem like distant utopias. For most citizens of Southern states or Eastern Europe, a stable democracy based on universal liberal, civil and political rights is a *precondition* for struggles by women or minorities for particular rights. Constitutional freedoms such as freedom of association, freedom of the press or the right to education in a separate, autonomous sphere, are based on such enlightened principles, as Unterhalter's study of post-apartheid South Africa shows (Chapter 6). Citizenship comes to be embodied symbolically in particular arenas in which state, civil society and individual particularity intersect. Education is one such sphere. Special welfare entitlements for the disabled, the object of the movements discussed by Monks, is another. Within each sphere the negotiation of universalism versus particularism, inclusiveness versus exclusiveness, collective difference versus individual uniqueness, the common good versus personal autonomy, is played out *in practice*, within procedural frameworks set by the wider polity. Such arenas are thus spaces in which subjectivity and subjectivism, individual liberty and governmentality, are *performed* as everyday, pragmatic realities.

A further problem with rejecting 'abstract universalism' and impartiality as false is that this presumes a civil society where all kinds of particularity are allowed to flourish equally. Where this is so, divisions frequently traverse each other: class alliances cut across region or ethnicity; gender alliances cut across nationality or class; religious associations cut across ethnicity or region; political parties or trade unions unite persons otherwise divided by race or religion. There are no particularities which are overarching. Political mobilisation around a particular identity – green, gay, religious, feminist or ethnic – does not exhaust subjects' loyalties. Writing about the new South Africa, Robert Thornton develops Max Gluckman's theory of cross-cutting ties to demonstrate that, despite a multiplicity of intense conflicts and divisions, South Africa does not fall apart because these conflicts create a series of alternative alignments and divisions which *cut across* each other. Paradoxically, then, conflict sustains a wider solidarity (Thornton 1996). For the Taliban studied by Pourzand, by contrast (Chapter 5), religion is all-encompassing: it obliterates alternative alignments and suppresses internal divisions which could generate cross-cutting coalitions. Similarly, essentialised and naturalised, male-designated collectivities in the former Yugoslavia define citizenship in nihilistic terms as purely ethnic, as Maja Korac demonstrates (Chapter 12).

Contributors to this volume thus recognise that particularities can only flourish in the context of shared, broad-based universalist-democratic and socialist-economic equality. Individual and associational freedom and autonomy, and a self-conscious, dialogical respect and toleration of otherness are the soil on which collective differences are nurtured. This is not to say that we think that all citizens must actively, at all times, pursue these goals. It is, however, to posit that activism for particularistic causes or collective recognition of difference needs to be pursued within procedural frameworks. Chantal Mouffe's 'grammar' of democratic conduct (Mouffe 1992: 238) embodies, rather than denies, this abstract universalism. Dialogue across difference requires such ground rules, as does coalition building.

At the same time we are arguing here that these ground rules must allow, as many have stressed (e.g., Young 1990; Phillips 1993 and 1995; Mouffe 1993; Taylor 1994), for the legitimacy of *publicly* articulated difference – of gender, race, sexuality, ability, ethnicity or religion *as well as* class and economic interest. The difficulty, of course, is how to recognise and respect 'difference' without reifying 'it' as perpetual, closed and unchanging. This is the question which debates about multiculturalism and human rights are most concerned with, as Aleksandra Ålund, Samia Bano and Jacqueline Bhabha demonstrate (chapters 9, 10 and 11).

One avenue is to recognise the centrality of transversal dialogue across difference. Nira Yuval-Davis (1997a, Chapter 6) has proposed that transversal politics differs from 'identity' politics in denying that social positioning (for example, being a woman) can automatically be conflated with personal values (for example, being a feminist). Further, while advocating that social differences in location must be recognised and respected, transversal politics presupposes that these must be grasped in all their complex intersections, rather than in terms of a single, prioritised identity. Such a politics, conscious of the partiality of each gaze, aims to use dialogue to reach closer to a shared reality (Collins 1990). It is limited, however, to those who share compatible values. In other words, exclusivist identity politics are not, and cannot be, an *alternative* to abstract universalism as the basis for democracy (Werbner 1991; Yuval-Davis 1994). The need is, therefore, to reflect further on the ontological and epistemological relations between equality and difference and how these may interact in a new discourse of citizenship.

A Logic of Encompassment

In her recent work on citizenship from a feminist perspective (1997b; 1997a) Ruth Lister argues for a dialectical model of citizenship which stresses a middle course of 'differentiated universalism' between false dichotomies: of civic republican or communitarian 'responsibilities' versus liberal 'rights'; of 'masculine' rationality and justice versus 'feminine' ethics of care; of identity versus difference (Lister 1997a). This dialectic, we want to suggest here, can be understood as operating through a logic of encompassment.

Louis Dumont (1972) uses the notion of encompassment to denote a hierarchy of values, the higher value encompassing an opposed value ranked below it. Thus, in the case of the Indian caste system, purity and spiritual authority, represented by Brahman priests, encompass power and temporal authority, represented by the warrior Kshatriya caste; both in turn encompass agricultural and artisan labour which is impure but essential to life, and, finally, all three encompass polluting occupations (such as leather work). The point is that purity at the apex of the hierarchy both depends upon, and limits, temporal power just below it.

A somewhat similar dialectical and hierarchical logic of encompassment works, we suggest, to resolve the apparent contradiction posed by a critical theory of citizenship between abstract universalism and difference. For democracy to work, universalism must transcend difference, defining all subjects in abstract terms as equal before the law. But difference is then *reinstated* as a higher-order value which encompasses equality through a relational and dialogical ethic of care, compassion and responsibility. This higher-order stress upon difference thus encompasses and subsumes universal and inclusive ideas about equality within it, without denying them. Hence, rather than a model which posits an opposition between two diametrically opposed approaches – a 'liberal' individualist and a 'republican' communitarian – feminist scholars seek to formulate models that highlight citizenship and civic activism as dialogical and relational, embedded in cultural and associational life.

The Dialogical Subject of Citizenship

Alison Assiter's essay, which opens the volume, subjects communitarian approaches to critical scrutiny, a critique also taken up by Bano (Chapter 10) in her discussion of multiculturalism and the law. Against communitarian claims, Assiter conceives of citizenship as a moral journey. A subject is born into a moral community but during the course of a lifetime comes dialogically to experience other perspectives and other moralities. There is no fixed moral ground or unitary value that a 'community' shares – only a continuous process of expanding emancipatory politics. Thus, while Assiter, like communitarians and civic republicans, endorses active, participatory and emancipatory citizenship, she regards the objectives of these as continuously evolving through social encounters with unlike 'others'. But she warns against an assumption that all minoritarian discourses are equally emancipatory. In engaging with the Other, the need is to recover those narratives which lead to more inclusive socialities, and ultimately, to human rights as a global discourse. Like Monks (Chapter 4), she highlights the possibility of 'egological' dialogical engagement in expanding the shared horizons of moral knowledge of civic activists.

A further defence of 'relational' or 'traditional' conceptions of citizenship, this time against liberal individualist 'enlightened' claims, is taken up by Birgit Rommelspacher in her study of women who joined the Nazi movement (Chapter 3). For such women, identification with a quasi-national collectivity and its supremacist ideology became the grounds for their self-worth. The key point made by the author is that among the ranks of these women were both individualists and traditionalists, the former finding personal scope in the movement, the latter stressing their gendered role as mothers and wives. Empowered by their sense of destiny as mothers of the race, they sent their sons to die and resisted the orders of their husbands.

Drawing on Norbet Elias, Rommelspacher argues that such right-wing movements provide women with a mode of relational transcendence denied to them in their daily lives. This leads her to criticise liberal feminists who stress individual equality and autonomy while ignoring the relational dimensions of citizenship. Competitive individualist ideologies are, she argues, fundamentally exclusionary, defining norms of success which exclude the disabled and the weak. They can only result, therefore, in widening social inequalities between women. They gloss over the fact that many women prefer to be respected for their roles as mothers and wives, a feature of women's activism also pointed to by Ålund (Chapter 9) and by Werbner in her discussion of emancipatory movements of political motherhood (Chapter 14). Yet the discourse of women as different may be equally marginalising, tending to construct women as heterosexual and 'able,' and excluding those, as Evans (1993) puts it, on the 'marginal matrix' of society, who cannot or would not comply with normative requirements of gendered participation.

Rommelspacher's evidence aims mainly, however, to disprove the view that liberalism and individualism are always progressive whereas family and community-oriented 'traditional' or relational values are regressive. The question clearly is one of ensuring, however, that such a sense of gendered, relational or dialogical difference *encompasses* ideas about human equality and universality rather than *denying them*. A similar danger of particularism without universalism lurks in multicultural and human rights policies and discourses, as Jacqueline Bhabha, Aleksandra Ålund and Samia Bano highlight (chapters 9, 10 and 11; see also Lutz 1997).

The route which emphasises women's difference is not one open to or preferred by all women, even when they are effectively excluded from citizenship, as Meekosha and Dowse point out (1997). Women in the disability movement's self-help groups studied by Judith Monks (Chapter 4) choose to emphasise their underlying similarity and shared humanity in the face of visible, embodied difference. Drawing on Mead and Merleau-Ponty's work on communication and intersubjectivity, Monks shows that identity and difference are produced simultaneously whenever subjects engage in dialogical interaction. In this sense neither commonality nor 'difference' can *in themselves*, Monks argues, be the starting point for an ethos of citizenship, since both are, equally, emergent qualities of intersubjective interaction; of the dialogues which constitute the political community and its subjects both experientially and socially.

Monks's discussion of egological intersubjective communication echoes Yuval-Davis's advocacy of transversal dialogue as a way of resolving difference (Yuval-Davis 1994, 1997a, 1997b). A key feature of such pluralist theories of citizenship is, we suggest, the *premise of agency*. By this we refer to one of the most central assumptions of citizenship, repeatedly stressed by liberal theorists and, most recently, by human rights activists: to be fully a citizen, one must be an autonomous, *conscious* subject (on this see Held 1995: 145–56, especially 151; Gould 1988: 213). Autonomy and consciousness are attributes of the presumed unique, creative individuality of modern subjects, but also of their dialogical engagement with fellow citizens. As we shall see below, these conditions have expanded the definition of global, universal human rights (Gould 1988: 190–214).

A Clash of Discourses: Education, Nationalism and Modernity

The denial of women's role as equal citizens in the public sphere arises not only from their relegation to the familial sphere but also from their simultaneous elevation as reproducers of the nation. Theoretically there can be a clear disjunction, we have seen, between the nation, defined in narrowly cultural terms, and the state – the latter being the political community which both governs and grants its members citizenship. Nationalist anti-colonial struggles for independence were broadly inclusive, overriding internal cultural, class and even gendered divisions. But after independence it became evident that cultural minorities were often effectively excluded from full participation in the political community. This is true of postcolonial states whose boundaries were often the product of imperial administrative accident or convenience (Anderson 1983/1991: 163–85), but it is equally the case for European nation-states which are everywhere complex ethnic formations, the historical product of disintegrating empires, invasions, migrations and wars, as Eastern Europe has so tragically demonstrated.[8]

Despite this emergent disjunction between cultural group identity and citizenship, however, the politics of citizenship are inextricably intertwined with those of cultural nationalism or religiosity. Most saliently, in the face of extreme nationalist or religious movements, women have had to challenge their symbolic function as guardians of their culture, the embodiments and 'borderguards' of national collectivities.[9] Women's ambivalent positioning is expressed in the fact that, on the one hand, they are considered fully fledged members of the political community – often, together with their children, its most precious possessions, the promise of a collective future and the reason why men go to war. On the other hand, they are subjected to special rules and regulations aimed at controlling their behaviour in order to ensure that they conform to this imposed 'burden of representation' (Mercer 1990).

Against this subjectification, the 'emancipation of women' (including their incorporation in national liberation militaries) has come to signify much wider political and social transformations in attitudes towards modernity. It marked a variety of revolutionary and decolonisation projects, from Marxist to democratic (see Kandiyoti 1991). Chatterjee (1990) has pointed out that because the inferiorising colonial gaze focused on the position of women, their emancipation became, symbolically, an anti-colonial declaration of modernity and claim to autonomy. For Chatterjee (1986) this makes post-colonial nationalism a derivative discourse. Against that, Anzaldua (1987) has suggested that anti-colonial nationalist movements were characterised by 'empowered hybridisation'; they appropriated cultural and religious traditions as emblems and symbolic borderguards of identity.

This tendency has impacted on the position of women as postcolonial citizens. On the one hand, their emancipation has come to signify – inwardly and outwardly – a move towards modernisation. But the postcolonial Westernised urban elites who have spearheaded this move nevertheless invoked 'culture' and 'tradition' in an attempt to sustain their links to a rural hinterland. Indeed, in many countries, kinship continues to dominate civil society and the public sphere, as Suad Joseph has argued (1997). Recently, however, a new generation of postcolonial leaders has turned to those same customs and traditions to develop ethnic and national projects of a very different kind. In a counter-move, they reject modernisation as Western mimicry and European cultural imperialism, and invoke a return to an original, 'true' culture, a reinvented tradition (see Hobsbawm and Ranger 1983) which often has limited bearing on the past. This move, too, has been played out over women's bodies and their rights as citizens, as Nilofar Pourzand and Maja Korac show in their studies of women in Afghanistan and Serbia (chapters 5 and 12). This is nowhere more evident than in the field of education, an arena in which private and public, civil and civic, traditional and modern, ambiguously meet.

The nationalist discourse of women as 'mothers of the nation' banishes them, as indeed did bourgeois emancipatory discourses, to the private sphere of the family. There were, nonetheless, real ambiguities apparent in the bourgeois civic discourse: it fostered women's education while denying their rationality and hence their right to act as autonomous agents in the public sphere. The familial space is one where important aspects of the biological and cultural reproduction of collectivities take place. Making a home includes fostering relations across generations, cooking and nurturing, playing and educating. Familial relations thus seem to constitute the 'essence' of national culture, a way of life to be passed from generation to generation. Equally, however, training to be a citizen, to respect the rights of others, begins at home. Women thus bear a double burden of representation: as national cultural icons and as mothers of citizens (see Vogel 1991: 63).

In the Muslim world women's education became the litmus test for modernity and the move towards citizenship. The Young Turks who founded modern Turkey were inspired by the emancipated conduct of European women and sought to abolish purdah and bring Turkish women into the public domain (see Göle 1996). They promoted female education. Similar processes occurred in Afghanistan where, as Niloufar Pourzand shows (Chapter 5), girls' education has been for the past seventy years the focus of ferocious struggles between modernity and tradition, national autonomy and Western dependence. Against modernist discourses on girls' education, introduced by a modernising monarchy in the 1920s, and by Afghan communists during the 1970s and 1980s, traditional and Islamist discourses, introduced most recently by the Taliban, have categorically denied girls' right to education, constructing it as a threat to the integrity of the Afghan nation. In a subtle analysis of the complex structural differences in Afghan society, Pourzand argues that the high-handed coercive bureaucratic methods used by the secularist and modernising state in Afghanistan in order to compel Afghan citizens to send their daughters to school engendered, dialectically, a conservative backlash against the 'West', and also against girls' education. Education thus became the symbolic domain for struggles over citizenship and the authenticity of the nation.

The case of Afghanistan highlights the important role women come to occupy in national projects, the locus of a clash between emancipatory and conservative or fundamentalist discourses. For the fundamentalists veiling, and even widow immolation (*sati*) are a mirror held up defiantly to a Western postcolonial gaze which constructs them as Other.[10] At the same time, traditionalists do not abandon modernity and its tools, using the media or high-tech weaponry to great effect.

Such struggles are grist to the mill of educational theorists of citizenship who, Elaine Unterhalter discloses (Chapter 6), are divided on the role education should play in the making of citizens as equal but different. Against Gellner's view that education is the essential training ground of a homogenised, modern national culture, contemporary educationalists adopt three main positions: the first promotes education for active citizenship and lifelong learning, recognising individual difference and the need for tolerance, but according no space for other forms of collective difference. It thus fails to acknowledge that difference may be either empowering or disempowering. The second approach regards education as itself an acting out, a performance of citizenship, suggesting that citizenship shares many similar terrains and processes with education, or that education is an articulation of citizenship. There is room in this approach, clearly, for the performance and negotiation of difference within the classroom. The third view suggests that citizenship enables education by according it a relatively autonomous institutional and analytical sphere, in which critical narratives can be constructed without state interference. Each view, then, entails a particular notion of how difference, including gender, must figure in education.

Unterhalter's chapter is inspired by transformations in education in post-apartheid South Africa. As in Afghanistan, so too in South Africa education has been a central platform of nationalist versus cosmopolitan struggles for citizenship. During the apartheid era, attempts were made to introduce Afrikaans as a compulsory medium of instruction in black schools. Indeed, the development of Afrikaans as a separate language of poetry and literature was one of the major – and most successful – Afrikaner national projects (Moodie 1975). Attempts to force Afrikaans on black children, however, caused an acute crisis and extreme backlash in the townships. It is against this background, and in the context of the enormous cultural and religious pluralism of the South African polity, that the new South African constitution accords education a 'sphere of its own', having relative autonomy from state interference.

Unterhalter concludes by suggesting that education is best kept separate from state or nationalist projects in order to allow for the possibility of addressing both private and public concerns within a single arena. Yet at the moment of writing the new South African government is intervening in higher education in ways that threaten to undermine the autonomy of the academic community and its universities (Johnson 1998: 16–17).

There are other forms of state interference in the private domain as well, which are invasive of what are normally defined as liberal negative freedoms. Among these are eugenic population policies.

Demographic Discriminations: Biopolitics and Citizenship

In her *Feminist Review* article (1997b: 12), Nira Yuval-Davis highlights inconsistencies in the way the boundaries of private and public have been theorised. Some, like Jayasuriya (1990), and even Marx in his article on the 'Jewish Question' (1975), draw the line between the state and civil society, while others, like Bryan Turner (1990) and Carole Pateman (1988), stress the divide between the family and the public sphere, in which they include both civil and political state arenas. Across these differences, however, what is shared is an adamant insistence that the sphere of citizenship is that of the public domain. Against this broad agreement, Sylvia Walby (1994: 383) argues that Turner's comparative framework of citizenship (1990) adopts a 'male viewpoint' by identifying the family as the space of freedom from state intervention in which individuals can pursue self-enhancement and other leisure or spiritual activities. While the family may or may not be free from intervention by the state, she points out, it is not an autonomous and free space for women, nor does it have a unitary set of interests. Different members of the family – nuclear and extended – occupy different social positions and resources within it. Indeed, Yuval-Davis (1997b) suggests, individual 'private' pursuits routinely take place outside the family, in civil and bureaucratic contexts, while the space of the metropolis offers privacy and anonymity, especially for women of ethnic minorities, to escape from familial controls exerted in the name of 'culture' or 'tradition' (Yuval-Davis forthcoming).

There are also subtle ways in which the state intervenes in the private sphere of the family for the sake of larger, sometimes open and sometimes disguised, national projects. The direct operation on bodies, often supported by the state, is increasing all the time with new medical and reproductive technologies (Plummer 1995). Mothers in particular, as reproducers of the nation, are often the target of biopolitical discourses and eugenics policies. These can vary in their means from gentle persuasion and propaganda to bribes and coercion – from viewing 'people as power' to a Malthusian perspective which constructs every baby born as a threat (Yuval-Davis 1996). More often, different populations are distinguished by their positive or negative biological 'contribution' to the national project.

In her discussion of motherhood and population policies in the United States, Patricia Hill Collins highlights the state's differential attitude to the birth rates of different populations (Chapter 7). Women as mothers and citizens, she shows, are constructed as bearers of either negative or positive futures. To understand why, we need to recognise that the family in the US constitutes, she proposes, the elementary unit of cultural, racial and class difference. Selective population policies are thus applied to middle-class or working-class white women, to African-American women and to undocumented Latinos. This echoes Ronit Lentin's findings that women Travellers are the special targets of Irish population policies (Chapter 8). Hill Collins suggests that these policies are aimed at preserving a white, middle-class American national identity. She considers the implications of this fact for an understanding of the way citizenship rights are constructed *vis-à-vis* diverse groups of women.

In broader terms, Hill Collins's work discloses not only that the familial domain is an important component of the political domain in the United States, but that the relation between these spheres and the state is mediated by race, class and gender. Any notion of citizenship, even a gendered notion, which does not take into account women's additional identifications with various racial and ethnic collectivities, as well as their class, age, religion, sexuality and ability, would fail to understand some of the ways in which a liberal polity organises relations with its individual subjects.

The familial domain is important to the understanding of citizenship in other ways as well. As feminist theorists of the welfare state have commented, comparative frameworks which concentrate solely on the public domain of the state and market, to the exclusion of the family, neglect crucial functions of the welfare state. These include major aspects of daily life, such as consumption, distribution or care.[11] Indeed, the extent to which the welfare state in fact relies on (mostly) women carers to meet the continuous needs of the elderly and handicapped raises the question of what is meant when we speak of 'active' citizenship.

The hidden assumptions of welfare and welfare consumption, along with the normalising tendencies of modern governmentality, are revealed in Ronit Lentin's study of Irish Traveller women (Chapter 8). Lentin shows how such ordering impulses strike with particular force against 'abnormal' populations, denying them the individual rights granted routinely to other citizens. Hence, even though the Irish constitution recognises the central role of women as family and home-makers, Traveller women are vulnerable to housing or site eviction. Lentin speaks of 'sedentary racism' – that is, the biases, both intentional and unintentional, which a nomadic way of life generates: schools, health clinics, law-and-order authorities, are all institutionally organised on the assumption that populations will stay put. Nomadic populations are viewed with suspicion. They need to be managed and, in typical fashion, despite the fact that women play a prominent role in Travellers' internal affairs, the 'masculinised' state turns to Traveller men to represent the community in its external dealings.

Lentin's analysis shows that liberal 'freedoms' are themselves highly organised, ordered and circumscribed for modern citizens. Transgressive life-styles, even those which evoke romantic notions of freedom, are penalised by the subjectivising forces of modernity because they implicitly occupy, from the point of view of the state, disorganised, 'wrong' kinds of spaces. 'Wrong' kinds of cultures, more generally, can also be the target of state policies.

Ambivalent Citizens: the Limits of Cultural Difference

Like other potentially emancipatory discourses, multiculturalism can be used by the state to disguise its failure to address the economic and social predicaments that immigrants and refugees encounter (Schierup 1995), just as culturalist stereotyping can be used to 'explain' their 'failure' to integrate. This is the subject addressed by Aleksanda Ålund (Chapter 9; see also Ålund and Schierup 1991; Ålund 1993).

At its best, multiculturalism is an interruptive rhetoric which destabilises the false homogeneity of the 'nation' and publicly highlights the fact that the political community is a complex cultural and ethnic aggregation of indigenous groups and immigrant settlers (H. K. Bhabha 1994; Werbner 1997b). Multiculturalism creates for the majority population a consciousness of difference, of cultural heterogeneity. Multiculturalism is thus also an important antidote to the assimilationist tendencies of the nation-state, to the interpretation of the equality of citizenship as grounded in cultural, gendered, religious and racial homogeneity.[12]

The danger of multiculturalism is that it can reify cultural communities as internally homogeneous, fixed and bounded collectivities, and thus that it might transfer too many decision-making powers to unelected 'traditional' communal male elders.[13] This type of 'incorporative' multiculturalism is prevalent in several European countries where immigrants do not have full citizenship rights (on Germany see Yalcin-Heckman 1997, for example). The incorporative tendency is far less likely to be practised where the majority of immigrant-settlers are full citizens, whose individual autonomy and freedom is guaranteed by the state, and who participate actively in a wide range of civil and political associations.

Sharing a culture is collectively empowering, and new, hybrid cultures may be invented by immigrant settlers which unite them across different ethnic backgrounds. This was revealed to Ålund in her research on young Swedish women and men living in Stockholm's multi-ethnic suburbs. These youngsters create new cultural narratives, responding to current deprivation and engaging in widespread mobilisation against state policies which marginalise even second-generation settler-citizens. Ålund's argument echoes Abner Cohen's theorisation of political ethnicity as a continuously inventive cultural-political formation, mobilised in response to changing economic and political interests.[14] She points to culturalist explanations deployed even by progressive groups in Sweden, such as trade unions or feminists, which stereotype settlers as backward and responsible for their own marginality. Swedish policy makers and feminists alike fail to recognise that culture is a resource for mobilisation rather than a homogeneous, discrete and unchanging entity. Thus Yugoslav women in Stockholm use cultural resources of social networking and exchange to create connections within and across neighbourhoods and ethnic groups. This leads Ålund to a far-reaching critique of feminist discourses which marginalise Third World feminisms as regressive, a theme raised also by Werbner in her discussion of political motherhood (Chapter 14).

Not all immigrant settlers are engaged in such multi-ethnic hybrid projects. In Britain, there have been calls by a tiny fraction of British Muslims, organised under the grandiose name of the 'Muslim Parliament', for full communal autonomy in matters of personal law. They refer back to Islamic law itself which recognises the right to autonomy of strangers-sojourners, known as *dhimmis,* in Muslim territories (see Shadid and van Koningsveld 1996). Most early Muslim states and empires thus granted religious communities in their territories autonomy in matters of personal law. In the Ottoman empire this came to be known as the millet system, still upheld in some parts of the Middle East such as the Lebanon and Israel. In British India, the colonial powers codified both Hindu and Muslim personal law on the basis of religious texts, glossed with regional customary law. This meant, for example, that Muslim women's rights to inheritance and divorce were far superior to those of their Hindu counterparts, since the Koran grants far more rights to women than do Hindu *shastras* (Aggarwal 1994, Chapter 5).[15] The British were careful, however, not to allow Muslim women property rights to agricultural lands in the Punjab, for example (*ibid.*), thus reflecting also their own bourgeois biases of the time against married women owning property.

In a critique of simplistic communitarian models as these are reflected in debates about multiculturalism and the law (Chapter 10), Samia Bano spells out some of the dangers for Asian and Muslim women of the – hypothetical – possibility that Asian customary law or Islamic personal law be made binding on all British Asians and Muslims. Even though Islam was, for its time, a highly progressive religion in its treatment of women, allowing them a share of inheritance in their own name, the right to divorce their husbands and the right to compensation in case of divorce, Islamic laws are nevertheless discriminatory towards women, measured by the yardstick of present-day liberal democratic standards. Bano also points to the obvious truth that the Asian and Muslim community in Britain is so divided by sect, school, ethnicity and national origin that any attempt to recognise personal law would become an administrative minefield of competing interpretations and multiple jurisdictions. Religious texts can be used for a variety of different, and even opposing, ethnic and political projects, as struggles regarding contraceptive policies in Egypt indicate (Yuval-Davis 1997a: 44). In Britain, the emergence of a hybrid Anglo-Islamic and Anglo-Asian corpus of precedent case law is the most significant development to affect Asian settlers, rather than the institution of separate legal systems.

On the whole, liberal calls for multiculturalism as an embodiment of tolerance rest on two principles: first, that fully self-conscious, creative personal and collective autonomy cannot be achieved without majoritarian cultural and religious recognition and toleration of difference; second, that many minority groups suffer not simply from racism but from *cultural* racism (Modood 1997a and 1997b). Cultural difference can, and often does, evoke disgust, disdain or violence, and people of colour are frequently differentiated according to the degree to which they assimilate Western middle-class values (Ong 1996). This means that multiculturalism has to be understood as one strand in a broader strategy of anti-racism (Blum 1994; Ben-Tovim 1997; Werbner 1997a); hence cultural recognition and respect, 'symbolic citizenship' (Margalit 1996), cannot and should not entail a limiting of individual liberal rights. Indeed, the evidence is that the majority of European Muslims do not want a separate status before the law. As is the case for Rabbinical courts, there is nothing to stop Muslims from institutionalising their own Islamic law courts to be used on a voluntary basis (Shadid and van Koningsveld 1996).

Ambivalent Citizens: Refugees

The discourse of human rights critically influences legal reasoning in particular nation-states, when it comes to judging the cases of women asylum seekers, as Jacqueline Bhabha shows (Chapter 11). Importantly, human rights and citizenship share a common language. This underlines the fact that 'citizenship' is a conception which transcends state boundaries (Lister 1997a: 59). Immanuel Kant envisioned a future 'cosmopolitan society' which would be a 'pacific federation' (in Held 1995: 229), based on the principle of 'universal hospitality' (*ibid.*: 227). Held argues that to achieve this requires no less than a cosmopolitan 'democratic public law' which respects the autonomy of individual subjects as well as nations (*ibid.*).

Human rights have not in fact been a fixed, *a priori* set of universal humanitarian axioms. As notions of citizenship have expanded, in response first to socialist and feminist movements and more recently to environmental, indigenous, cultural, sexual and reproductive movements, so too human rights charters have become more broadly inclusive under the umbrella of the UN. The minimum conditions for human autonomy have been redefined to include the right to economic, cultural and reproductive autonomy and agency. Protection from bodily violence now explicitly addresses not merely protection from state torture, arbitrary arrest, violence, or war, but also protection from violence in the family, and especially violence towards women and girl children. Even a cursory glance at the World Conference on Women in Beijing's Declaration makes the range of what are regarded as universal human rights clear. It includes the eradication of poverty and women's right to economic self-sufficiency (declarations 16, 26, 27, 35, 36), control of fertility (17), promotion of peace (28), non-violence against women (29), education and health (30), the right to freedom of thought, conscience, religion and belief (12), participation in decision-making processes (13) and equal sharing of responsibilities for the family in harmonious partnership between men and women (15) (United Nations 1996: 2–5). The problem, of course, is that only states at present have the institutional means to enforce these rights. Only states can be held fully accountable. Moreover, states are crucial actors in relief and emergency programmes to alleviate the effects of natural disasters or civil war beyond their boundaries (Parry 1991; Soysal 1994).

The broad definition of overarching human rights principles is not, of course, without its internal contradictions. Hence, in Beijing, the Platform of Action on Violence against Women stated that, among other factors, violence against women 'derives essentially from cultural patterns, in particular the harmful effects of certain traditional or customary practices' (United Nations 1996: 49). This includes, for example, female genital mutilation, widely practised and specifically condemned (*ibid.*: 97). At the same time the Global Framework states that 'religion, spirituality and belief play a central role in the lives of millions of men and women' and must be protected (*ibid.*: 11). Similarly, the 'identity, cultural traditions and forms of social organisation [of indigenous women] enhance and strengthen the communities in which they live' (*ibid.*: 13).

These sorts of contradictions create legal loopholes in asylum laws, as Jacqueline Bhabha highlights in her discussion of the legal processing of asylum seekers to the United States, Canada and the UK. The conflict between human rights and state sovereignty is, Bhabha argues, particularly evident in the case of women refugees fleeing gender persecution on grounds of intimate personal violations. Such cases highlight the clash between women's private right to control their own bodies and the rights attached to national, culturally defined public moralities. Requests for asylum are rejected on cultural relativist grounds of respect for a country-of-origin's culture. In arguing thus, adjudicators ignore ideological, gendered and cultural divisions existing within these countries, and effectively endorse the absence of a space where, by right, differences may be articulated.

Initially, Bhabha reports, such arguments were used to deny Westernised Iranian women asylum from Khomeini's regime, but, over time, Islamic fundamentalist coercion came to be recognised as a form of state persecution. Yet this liberalisation was embedded in a rising Western anti-Islamic rhetoric stressing the civilisational clash between an essentialised 'Islam' and the 'West'. Respect for state sovereignty was also entangled in geopolitical considerations in variously and inconsistently denying or granting asylum to Chinese women escaping China's draconian demographic policies, including enforced sterilisation, or West African women seeking to escape forced genital mutilation. Bhabha concludes by criticising blanket endorsements of cultural relativism for failing to recognise that rights must be understood as always contextual, and that in the asylum context the universality of human rights allows women the 'right to differ'.

The right to differ is one which Serb, Croatian and Muslim women refugees in Serbian refugee camps have had to battle for, Maja Korac shows (Chapter 12). The victims of highly masculinised, ethnic-religious ideologies, women refugees have become symbolic markers of ethnically *cleansed* boundaries, a process which continues even in their place of exile. Refugees are particularly vulnerable to bureaucratic state manipulation in which ethno-political considerations take precedence over human rights. Those ambiguously marked, such as partners in 'mixed' marriages, or those who refuse to comply, are stigmatised as traitors. Yet for some women, living together in refugee camps enables them to create counter-narratives and work alongside women's groups in cross-ethnic and religious coalitions which challenge naturalised ethnic separations and open up potential spaces for transformation.

In her interpretation of their personal narratives, Korac highlights the predicament of refugees, caught between different identities, homelands and ethnic or religious communities, that makes them particularly vulnerable to conflicting definitions of subjectivity and autonomy. The women must embark on a quest for meaning in the face of dislocations which disrupt prior assumptions of commonality and difference.

Planetary Disruptions, Global Feminisms, and the Rights of Non-Citizens

Human rights discourses emerged in the postwar era in response to the war trauma of mass extermination. This underlined the need to protect subjects from their own states and to make violators accountable to the international community. Paradoxically, then, the globalisation of the nation-state form in the postwar era has come along with a shift away from the principle of state sovereignty, making it today conditional on the upholding of democratic principles (Held 1995: 104). In reality, however, this globalisation has failed, as yet, to achieve the planetary adoption of democratic values. Instead, the brutal legacies of colonialism and imperialism, the arbitrary definition of the boundaries of newly independent states, underdevelopment, economic conditionality and militarisation have generated multiple forms of religious and ethnic quasi-nationalism; in these, as we saw in the former Yugoslavia and Afghanistan, a single ethnic or religious group captures the state and its monopolistic instruments of violence, unleashing state terror and civil war in the name of national unity.[16] 'Citizenship' in such conditions becomes a travesty and citizens must appeal for support beyond the state. As both Werbner and Vargas and Olea show (chapters 14 and 15), a politics of desire that envisions individual autonomy and democratic freedom of association and expression has survived in these states even in the face of authoritarianism and state terror. In sustaining such a politics, courageous activists such as Women in Black in Serbia (Zajovic 1994), Women Living Under Muslim Laws (Helie-Lucas 1993), or human rights activists in Zimbabwe (R. Werbner 1995), rely on networks of support beyond the nation-state, and on the fact that the state is no longer defined as inviolable and unaccountable to broader, international bodies and charters.

Some of the crises in the South and in Eastern Europe have been caused by forces unleashed by globalising capital which has been dominated in the post-Cold War period by a neoliberal market economy. The movements of finance and venture capital, of consumer goods and people, whether as economic migrants or refugees, have generated huge displaced populations of non-citizens throughout the world. So much so that Jan Jindy Pettman (Chapter 13) argues that a key challenge of feminist politics today is to take seriously the rights of *non-citizens.* Clearly, inclusivist emancipatory and social welfare policies within nation-states create exclusionary tendencies. To achieve the economic welfare and spiritual well-being of citizens requires enormous financial and institutional investments. But these entitlements also serve *ipso facto* to accentuate territorial boundaries by demarcating an exclusive space of privilege for full citizens. Quite obviously, international aid agencies can hardly substitute for full social citizenship.

Globalisation, Pettman suggests, has resulted in the impoverishment of certain populations, particularly women, who form a transnationally exploited class of cheap workers pitched against a new transnational elite. Whatever their prior political ethos, states become facilitators of global capital, pressured into neo-liberal policies. The resultant breakdown of welfare and public services affects women disproportionately. Feminist critics were, Pettman points out, at the forefront of a socialist and human rights movement that urged that active citizenship requires material conditions which support and enable women's participation in the political sphere (see also Lister 1997a: 58–9).[17] Now hard-won feminist gains are being attacked everywhere. This has resulted in an increasingly massive transnational movement of female migrant labour. Such women are often caught between states, defended neither by their home nor by their migration state, subject to policing without recourse to the law. Citizenship has itself become a highly complex, multiple and fluid identity.

What kind of transnational feminist strategies of resistance are necessary to counter such unregulated globalisation forces? Can there be a global civil society? Pettman argues that global feminism has, above all, to expose the myth that governments and states are powerless in the face of global forces, and to insist on notions of public accountability and political responsibility.

Pettman's views echo Alberto Melucci (1993/94) who argues that a key role of both local and planetary activists is to expose the invisible assumptions motivating the political community. Dissent is, of course, built into democratic institutions, but who has the right to dissent and what the acceptable language of dissent may be – what sort of appeals to difference are legitimate – is a set of implicit assumptions embedded in particular political cultures. These discursive assumptions constitute, we want to suggest, a *semantics of difference*. Part of the struggle of activists, then, both in the North and in the South, is to expose this hidden semantics, so that their claims for environmental protection or gendered, ethnic or religious recognition are heeded, even when these are not easily translatable into the cold political language of economic inequality or law and order which politicians are used to address.

In this regard, the global feminist movement has become a powerful force for lobbying governments. It achieves this by bringing together local activists in global arenas. This was evident in recent UN conferences, like the 1992 Rio conference on the environment, the 1993 Vienna conference on human rights, and the 1994 Cairo conference on population policies and development. The Beijing UN World Conference on Women assembled, in the official plenary sessions, representatives of 201 states and observers, five secretariats, 16 United Nations bodies and programmes, 12 specialised international agencies such as the World Bank, 26 intergovernmental organisations, and 4,035 (sic!) non-governmental organisations. Alongside the official sessions an estimated 30,000 NGO representatives came together in a parallel NGO forum (United Nations 1996: 134–8; Lister 1997a: 214). Women are particularly active in this emergent global civil society, perhaps because they are used to engaging in social networking and in a politics from the margins (Ashworth 1995; Waterman 1998; Melchiori 1998).

What is striking here is that a global cosmopolitan society is being constructed through a number of different channels: first, through the United Nations Charter of Human Rights and other international charters, conventions and declarations to which member states are signatories; second, through bilateral or multilateral agreements between states about mutual entitlements of sojourners, permanent residents or denizens, and rights to dual or multiple citizenship (Bauböck 1991); these are supplemented by regional or global trade and security agreements which implicate national citizens (Weale 1991); third, through individual states' asylum bills which draw on human rights discourses as well as national constitutions; fourth, through international and transnational support networks composed of both global and national voluntary associations and non-governmental organisations. These include major actors promoting a large variety of political and moral projects such as the Catholic Church, Amnesty International and Greenpeace, as well as diasporic organisations, and they extend across state boundaries between North and South, First and Third Worlds. Finally, international conferences such as Beijing make manifest and embody a global public sphere and civil society.

Women's Activisms and the Transformation of the Public Sphere

Debates about human rights point to the complexity and heterogeneity of the modern democratic public sphere: it extends globally, beyond the boundaries of nation-states, and reflects the politics of a heterogeneous public. This implies, according to Iris Young, that 'no persons, actions or aspects of a person's life should be forced into privacy; and (b) no social institutions or practices should be excluded *a priori* from being a proper subject for public discussions and expression' (Young 1990: 120; see also 178).

Young refers to the work of feminist political philosophers such as Seyla Benhabib (1986) who draws on Habermas's theory of communicative ethics to construct a 'discursive model' of the public sphere. Like others, Benhabib too starts from the recognition that the women's movement has made issues previously considered private into public matters of justice (1992: 109). It has thus extended egalitarian morality into spheres of life controlled by tradition and custom (*ibid.*: 110). This does not deny rights to privacy. It does, however, imply a critical feminisation of rights discourses and bureaucratic procedures (*ibid.*: 113).

As we saw earlier, the feminist slogan 'the personal is the political' implies that any issue can become the proper subject of public debate. This is so because, as anthropologists too have recognised, all spheres of life, from the family through voluntary associations to the political arena proper, are inflected by competitive power relations, unequal access to human and symbolic capital, and agonistic dialogue (Bourdieu 1977; Werbner 1998; Yuval-Davis 1993). Post-liberal feminists such as Young or Benhabib recognise the fluid boundaries separating private and public, while also stipulating the need to retain foundational human, civil and political rights. Yet even these basic rights, Benhabib argues, can be the subject of moral scrutiny and debate, while being the very condition of such critical dialogue (Benhabib 1992: 107). In similar vein Chantal Mouffe has urged that the private/public distinction can no longer be grasped as corresponding to 'discrete, separate spheres' because both private acts and public performances are framed by 'ethico-political principles' (Mouffe 1993: 84). The further key point is that these foundational principles, the 'grammar' of liberty and equality, are interpreted variously from different perspectives (*ibid.*).

The denial of a substantive divide between public and private means that there are no specific spaces or places which occupy the 'public sphere'. Public participation is engaged in critical dialogue on a range of normative issues, from the local to the transnational. The public sphere comes into existence whenever people engage in practical dialogue, so that 'there may be as many publics as there are controversial general debates ... a plurality of public spaces ... around contested issues of general concern' (Benhabib 1992: 105). Although in many senses this seems merely to redescribe the liberal conception of civil society, its strength is in privileging the dialogical openness and porousness of the public sphere and its responsiveness to inequality and difference.

Much civic participation, especially by women, is local, and Lister defends a broader, more inclusive notion of the political which embraces such grassroots activisms (Lister 1997a: 27–9). For many women, she argues, 'involvement in community organisations and social movements can be more personally fruitful than engagement in formal politics which is often more alienating than empowering' (*ibid.*: 31). Local activism strengthens self-esteem and develops political consciousness and a sense of personal agency, both essential attributes of citizenship (*ibid.*: 39). This is a feature of local activism emphasised also by Parry *et al.,* who add that, in Britain at least, local campaigns often seem actually to work, which reflects well on the responsiveness of the political system (1992: 430).

The spaces from which women's activism is first fostered are theorised by Pnina Werbner as a key to understanding the way women's political consciousness develops (Chapter 14). The chapter draws parallels between first-wave 'motherist' and contemporary peace movements in the Anglo-American West and their counterparts in postcolonial nations – in Latin America, South Asia and Israel, and among diasporic Pakistanis in Britain. Werbner's central argument is that women's active citizenship often starts from pre-established cultural domains of female power and rightful ownership or responsibility. These culturally defined domains, or the attack upon them, create the conditions of possibility for the movement of such women into the public sphere, and their progressive defiance of authoritarian structures of power, usually controlled by men. Although women's activism is locally embedded, it reaches out even beyond the nation to create transnational networks of economic support, peace and human rights.

Historically, Werbner proposes, political motherhood challenged established notions of civic legitimacy and created the conditions for the *feminisation* of citizenship: the reconstitution of citizenship in terms of encompassing qualities associated with women's role as nurturers, carers and protectors of the family and its individual members. Rather than dualistic theories of gendered opposition, these qualities came increasingly to be defined as critical to justice and hence to the continued legitimacy of the wider political community. Although reforms were achieved piecemeal, they came over time to effect a radical transformation in the values of the public sphere and attitudes to it.

Werbner's analysis supports anthropological and sociological accounts which recognise that women in postcolonial nations are not simply victims but active agents of their own destiny; they can exercise their rightful claims *vis-à-vis* male members of their families while sustaining viable female cultural worlds.[18] They can also draw upon indigenous traditions of cultural resistance and a strong sense of concern for family and community (Miles 1996: 88, 135). Analysing global 'integrative feminisms', Angela Miles makes the point that

> many Third World women can call on important resources in their action that we in North America often lack. They often have more intact women's subcultures, identities and organisations; less mystified and romantic notions of male–female relations; and clearer understandings of male power .... (Miles 1996: 86)

Women's subcultural resources have been mobilised to generate the present enormous efflorescence of local, national and global women's organisations. According to Miles, women's global empowerment first became visible at the Nairobi Forum in 1985 where women became the overwhelming presence, setting the pace and breaking down barriers between North and South (*ibid.*: 117). The level of organisation of Third World women at the Fourth World Conference on Women in Beijing in 1995 was so striking as to lead one African-American participant to speak of the 'humbling' experience of confronting Southern women's power, solidarity and vision by comparison with her own fragmented North American delegation (Duff 1996: 520). The women's movement, as Virginia Vargas and Cecilia Olea put it, 'appropriated' the conference. Miles highlights integrative feminists' stress on diversity and dialogue across difference: between North and South, and between traditional women and feminists of various persuasions (Miles 1996: 134, 139).

Many of these issues come together in the subtle analysis by Virginia Vargas and Cecilia Olea of the transformations in the feminist movement in post-democratic Peru (Chapter 15). Vargas is herself one of the leaders of the movement and was coordinator of the Latin American NGOs joint delegation to Beijing. She and Olea write both as scholars and activists.

The present period has been one, they say, in which democracy and citizenship became the banners of the women's movement in Peru, seen as crucial to the development of diversity, the negotiation of different interests and the visibility of social inequalities; a buttress against conservative forces. The two authors reflect on the goals of the movement and its present dilemmas which they describe as 'knots' to be unravelled. These arise from the pluralisation and fragmentation of the movement as it has gained presence and new forms of expression in different public arenas. New laws and institutions have been created specifically for women. There are now visible women leaders. Under the circumstances, the problem has been one of preserving a radical outlook and meaningful autonomy while entering democratic alliances and intervening in state policies. 'Identity' is no longer simply an expression of resistance but a 'project' which needs to be defined. In this regard Vargas and Olea object to a tendency to marginalise women as engaged in an 'ethical politics', not in the 'real' politics of the political arena proper. The goal of the movement should be to expose any politics, they say, that infringes upon women's claims to full citizenship. At present, however, feminist NGOs dissipate their collective power through lack of a coherent overall agenda. The need, Vargas and Olea argue, is to demand from the state clear rules and mechanisms of accountability and participatory democracy. While women should recognise the many advances made, they should aim to achieve further specific reforms in reproductive, social and economic rights, and to open up the movement to new actors and further diversity.

Moreover, as the contributors to this volume have argued in different ways, the very compositeness of modern subjectivities opens up paths towards local, national and even global dialogue across bounded identities, creating the grounds for a new politics of solidarity.

Conclusion: the Way Forward

Both as a political imaginary and as a set of practices citizenship is caught, we have seen, between the normalising forces of modernity and the essentialising forces of nationalism and exclusion. These are played out historically in conjunctures that impact in culturally specific ways on women's membership in their political communities. Yet citizenship, we have argued, holds a promise for the future: of personal autonomy and the protection of collective difference and diversity even beyond the nation-state. The women's movement has played a key role in articulating this future vision of citizenship that combines both equality and difference and is based on more inclusive forms of dialogue. In the conference on 'Women, Citizenship and Difference' – on which this volume, along with its companion *Feminist Review* issue, are based – we reached a series of conclusions which contain policy implications about the way forward for citizenship. In summary, then, we present these conclusions here, inspired and based upon the discussions at the conference (see Yuval-Davis and Werbner 1996):

- Despite its gendered history, it is possible to recast citizenship in a feminist and plural perspective as an important political tool. The language of citizenship provides women with a valuable weapon in the fight for human, democratic, civil and social rights.

- However, we need to be vigilantly aware of the double-edged nature of citizenship – the fact that it is not only emancipatory and socially progressive but simultaneously exclusionary and often tied to essentialising cultural discourses. These need to be challenged if the full potential of citizenship is to be realised.

- In a globalising world in which the economic, political and military power of nation-states is increasingly being eroded, there is a need to re-imagine citizenship from a gendered perspective in progressive terms.

- To the extent that states are deterritorialised, we need to open up our thinking about political accountability. Supranational states such as the European Union have to be evaluated in terms of their gains and losses for women and disadvantaged minorities. Without new forms and procedures of political accountability we cannot contemplate transnational, supranational or global forms of citizenship.

- At the same time, in a globalising world the women's movement cannot be only territorial. The challenge is to create movements that are genuinely international at the grassroots level.

- To the extent that nation-states have been weakened, this has resulted in an attack on their weakest members and this has occurred in the absence of any counter-attack by progressive forces or the Left. Hence the women's movement must fight to defend those vulnerable groups that are most disadvantaged and marginalised in the current political climate.

- A separation of the women's movement and an exclusive focus on women's interests can lead to a privileging of white professional women at the expense of these vulnerable groups. To avoid this we need to bring feminism into conjunction with other social movements and non-governmental organisations, to ensure grassroots participation, and work closely with the labour movement and with other disadvantaged groups, irrespective of gender.

- Women have a proven capacity for transnational networking and for creating alliances across cultural, class and national differences. In building such alliances, women should aim to work with state, suprastate and UN agencies in order to persuade them to incorporate ideas formed in the women's movement. At the same time, the women's movement must guard its own autonomy and retain its innovative and subversive power.

- The private/public division is fluid, historically and contextually determined, contested and constantly struggled over and redefined. It is culture- and gender-specific. Women need to fight to reclaim civil rights to privacy, protection and autonomy *vis-à-vis* the state, while challenging current state welfare reforms that are undermining social citizenship entitlements and a whole range of achievements gained by a prior generation of women activists.

- As public spaces have been democratised and have come to be open to women and minorities there has been a tendency to privatise real decision-making power by shifting it away from the public sphere and to privatise public spaces. Women must struggle to keep power in the public sphere, to retain its openness and to fight against this dual tendency.

- Community-level women's activism is not only a way of raising consciousness and self-confidence, and opening new spaces in which women's voices can be heard. It is the pre-political base for social movements and it has the power to effect real long-term changes in mainstream politics. The importance of this intermediate sphere must therefore not be underestimated.

- Like citizenship, multiculturalism is a double-edged sword that often excludes the interests of women and economically disadvantaged groups by privileging cultural, regional or national divisions. We need to challenge the corporatising tendencies of pluralist policies which obscure class, gendered and racial disadvantages and ignore the predicaments experienced by the disabled, by non-citizens and by stigmatised minorities.

- Women must continue to fight to expose universalist claims that disguise particularist interests and for the right to participate in the determination of the social categories which are deemed relevant in the making of social policy, and the circumstances in which these policies and categories are applicable.

Notes

1. Our use of the notion of a social field draws on Bourdieu's work (1977; 1984).
2. This is always a relative matter, however. See Kapferer (1988); Anthias and Yuval-Davis (1992); Ignatieff (1993); Yuval-Davis (1993; 1997a, Chapter 1).
3. On postmodernism see Lyotard (1986/1977); Bauman (1991 and 1992); on late modernity see Giddens (1991); on the ordering tendencies of modernity see Foucault (1977); on modern uncertainty see Werbner (1996a).
4. On some of these approaches, see Held (1995); Walzer (1995); Lister (1997a); Modood (1997a); Yuval-Davis (1997a and 1997b).
5. There is a vast literature on this subject. On women see, for example, Young (1990), Collins (1990), and Yuval-Davis (1991, 1997a and 1997b); on indigenous and cultural minorities see Kymlicka (1995), Modood and Werbner (1997).
6. See also Tololyan (1996); Anderson (1994); Werbner (1994, 1996b).
7. The pragmatics of 'commonsense', everyday, taken-for-granted moral knowledge have been addressed from various perspectives by Evans-Pritchard in his study of the persistence of witchcraft beliefs (1937); Schutz (1941, and throughout his work); Kuhn (1962) and Gramsci, in his *Prison Notebooks* (see Simon 1982/1991: 64–5). In different ways these authors all show how knowledge and belief are sustained despite internal inconsistencies and contradictory evidence, because they are

applied selectively and situationally, and because they work to uphold entrenched or hegemonic institutions.

8. This is highlighted by Hobsbawm (1990: 33, 155, 174, 185–6); more generally see also H. K. Bhabha (1994), Anthias and Yuval-Davis (1992), Yuval-Davis (1997a, Chapter 1).

9. This may be particularly true in societies which mark their boundaries through endogamous marriages, thus preserving women within the collectivity (see, for example, Boddy 1989; Kandiyoti 1991); it may also be true at times of national conflict. On the role of women as reproducers of the nation more generally see Yuval-Davis (1980, 1996, 1997a); Yuval-Davis and Anthias (1989).

10. See Mani (1989), Chhachhi (1991); on women and fundamentalism see Sahgal and Yuval-Davis (1992).

11. See critiques by Orloff (1993) and O'Connor (1993) of Esping-Anderson (1990).

12. For a detailed discussion and case studies exemplifying this, see the contributions to Modood and Werbner (1997). For some of the paradoxical dimensions of multiculturalism as it reflects back on new racist discourses of culture, see Bauman (1997a) and Wieviorka (1997).

13. On the first point see Yuval-Davis (1997); Caglar (1997); Baumann (1997). On the second, see Sahgal and Yuval-Davis (1992) and Yuval-Davis (1997b, Chapter 3).

14. See, for example, his discussion of the Notting Hill carnival in Cohen (1991) and (1993).

15. We might say ironically, then, that the British were effectively one of the first religious fundamentalist groups in India! They relied in their codification efforts on the advice of Brahman priests and Muslim religious clerics (Aggarwal 1994).

16. Quasi-nationalism is discussed by Richard Werbner (1994 and 1995) in relation to post-independence Zimbabwe where Mugabe's Shona-based ZANU party, having won elections, unleashed state terror against its 'Ndebele' ZAPU opponents in the name of national security. As in Sri Lanka, Rwanda, Burundi, Israel, Iraq, the Sudan, Indonesia or Latin America, ethnic or religious groups controlling the state invoke discourses of popular sovereignty while using the instruments of state power to violently impose their sectional interests.

17. The feminist discourse, at certain times, was also among the narratives that neoliberal globalisation coopted, transformed, commodified and exported (Eisenstein 1996 and 1997).

18. For the anthropological argument see Peters (1990: 243, 262); Richard Werbner (1989: 80); Werbner (1990: 294). These accounts stress that women can make claims against a network of male kin, including the claim to authority over the domestic sphere.

References

Aggarwal, Bina (1994). *A Field of One's Own: Gender and Land Rights in South Asia*, Cambridge: Cambridge University Press.

Ålund, Aleksandra (1993). 'Crossing Boundaries: Notes on Transethnicity in Modern Puristic Society', *Xenophobia and Exile, Rescue* 43: 149–61, Copenhagen: Munksgaard.

Ålund, Aleksandra and Carl-Ulrik Schierup (1991). *Paradoxes of Multiculturalism*, Aldershot: Avebury.

Anderson, Benedict (1983/1991). *Imagined Communities: Reflections on the Origin and Spread of Nationalism*, 2nd edition, London: Verso.

—(1994). 'Exodus', *Critical Inquiry* 20: 314–27.

Anthias, Floya and Nira Yuval-Davis (1992). *Racialised Boundaries: Race, Nation, Gender, Colour and Class and the Anti-Racist Struggle*, London: Routledge.

Anzaldua, Gloria (1987). *Borderlines/La Frontera*, San Francisco: Spinster/Aunt Lute Books.

Ashworth, Georgina (ed.) (1995). *The Diplomacy of the Oppressed: New Directions in International Feminism*, London: Zed Books.

Badran, Margot (1995). *Feminists, Islam, and Nation: Gender and the Making of Modern Egypt*, Princeton NJ: Princeton University Press.

Balibar, Etienne (1990). 'Paradoxes of Universality', in D. T. Goldberg (ed.) *Anatomy of Racism*, Minneapolis, MN: University of Minnesota Press.

Banks, Olive (1981). *Faces of Feminism: A Study of Feminism as a Social Movement*, Oxford: Martin Robertson.

Bauböck, Rainer (1991). 'Migration and Citizenship', *New Community* 18, 1: 27–48.

Bauman, Zygmunt (1991). *Modernity and the Holocaust,* Cambridge: Polity Press.

— (1992). *Intimations of Postmodernity*, London: Routledge.

— (1997). 'The Making and Unmaking of Strangers', in Pnina Werbner and Tariq Modood (eds) *Debating Cultural Hybridity: Multi-Cultural Identities and the Politics of Anti-Racism*, London: Zed Books, pp. 29–45.

Baumann, Gerd (1997). 'Dominant and Demotic Discourses of Culture: Their Relevance to Multi-Ethnic Alliances', in Pnina Werbner and Tariq Modood (eds) *Debating Cultural Hybridity: Multi-Cultural Identities and the Politics of Anti-Racism*, London: Zed Books, pp. 209–25.

Bebhabib, Seyla (1986). *Critique, Norm and Utopia*, New York: Columbia University Press.

— (1992). *Situating the Self: Gender, Community and Postmodernism in Contemporary Ethics*, Cambridge: Polity Press.

Ben-Tovim, Gideon (1997). 'Why "Positive Action" is "Politically Correct"', in Tariq Modood and Pnina Werbner (eds) *The Politics of Multiculturalism in the New Europe: Racism, Identity and Community*, London: Zed Books, pp. 209–22.

Bhabha, Homi K. (1994). *The Location of Culture*, London: Routledge.

Blum, Lawrence (1994). 'Multiculturalism, Racial Justice and Community: Reflections on Charles Taylor's "Politics of Recognition"', in Lawrence Foster and Patricia Herzog (eds) *Defending Diversity,* Amherst: University of Massachusetts Press, pp. 175–206.

Boddy, Janice (1989). *Wombs and Alien Spirits*, Madison: University of Wisconsin Press.

Bourdieu, Pierre (1977). *Outline of a Theory of Practice*, trans. R. Nice, Cambridge: Cambridge University Press.

— (1984). *Distinction*, trans. Richard Nice, Cambridge: Polity Press.

Caglar, Ayse S. (1997). 'Hyphenated Identities and the Limits of "Culture"', in Tariq Modood and Pnina Werbner (eds) *The Politics of Multiculturalism in the New Europe: Racism, Identity and Community*, London: Zed Books, pp. 169–85.

Chatterjee, Partha (1986). *Nationalist Thought and the Colonial World: a Derivative Discourse*, London: Zed Books.

— (1990). 'The Nationalist Resolution of the Women's Question', in K. Sangari and S. Vaid (eds) *Women: Essays in Colonial History*, New Brunswick NJ: Rutgers University Press.

Chhachhi, Amrita (1991). 'Forced Identities: the State, Communalism, Fundamentalism and Women in India', in D. Kandiyoti (ed.) *Women, Islam and the State*, Basingstoke: Macmillan.

Cohen, Abner (1991). 'Drama and Politics in the Development of a London Carnival', in Pnina Werbner and Muhammad Anwar (eds) *Black and Ethnic Leaderships in Britain: the Cultural Dimensions of Political Action*, London: Routledge, pp. 170–202.

— (1993). *Masquerade Politics: Explorations in the Structure of Urban Cultural Movements*, Berkeley: University of California Press.

Collins, Patricia Hill (1990). *Black Feminist Thought: Knowledge, Consciousness and the Politics of Empowerment*, London: Harper Collins.

Cooke, Miriam and Angela Woollacott (eds) (1993). *Gendering War Talk*, Princeton, NJ: Princeton University Press.

Duff, Malika (1996). 'Some Reflections on US Women of Color and the United Nations 4th World Conference on Women and Non-Governmental Organisations Forum in Beijing, China', *Feminist Studies*, special section on Beijing, 22, 3: 519–28.

Dumont, Louis (1972). [1966] *Homo Hierarchicus*, New York: Paladin.

Eisenstein, Zillah R. (1981). *The Radical Future of Liberal Feminism*, New York and London: Longman.

— (1996). *Hatreds*, London: Routledge.

— (1997). 'Women's Publics and the Search for New Democracies', *Feminist Review* 57: 140–67.

Esping-Anderson, Gosta (1990). *The Three Worlds of Welfare Capitalism*, Cambridge: Polity Press.

Evans, David T. (1993). *Sexual Citizenship: the Material Construction of Sexualities*, London: Routledge.

Evans-Pritchard, E. E. (1937). *Witchcraft, Oracles and Magic among the Azande*, Oxford: Clarendon Press.

Falk, Richard (1994). 'The Making of Global Citizenship', in Bart van Steenbergen (ed.) *The Condition of Citizenship*, London: Sage, pp. 127–40.

Foucault, Michel (1977). *Discipline and Punish*, London: Penguin Books.

Geertz, Clifford J. (1963). 'The Integrative Revolution: Primordial Sentiments and Civil Politics', in Clifford J. Geertz (ed.) *Old Societies and New States: the Quest for Modernity in Asia and Africa*, New York: Free Press, pp. 105–7.

Giddens, Anthony (1991). *Modernity and Self-Identity*, Cambridge: Polity Press.

Göle, Nilufer (1996). *The Forbidden Modern: Civilisation and Veiling*, Ann Arbor, Michigan: University of Michigan Press.

Gould, Carol C. (1988). *Rethinking Democracy*, Cambridge: Cambridge University Press.

Hall, Stuart and David Held (1989). 'Citizens and Citizenship', in Stuart Hall and Martin Jacques (eds) *New Times: the Changing Face of Politics in the 1990s*, London: Lawrence and Wishart in association with Marxism Today, pp. 173–88.

Held, David (1995). *Democracy and the Global Order: From the Modern State to Cosmopolitan Governance,* Cambridge: Polity Press.

Helie-Lucas, Marieme (1993). 'Women Living Under Muslim Laws', in J. Kerr (ed.) *Ours By Rights: Women's Rights as Human Rights*, London: Zed Books.

Hobsbawm, Eric J. (1990). *Nations and Nationalism since 1780: Programme, Myth, Reality*, Cambridge: Cambridge University Press.

Hobsbawm, Eric J. and Terence Ranger (eds) (1983). *The Invention of Tradition*, Cambridge: Cambridge University Press.

Ignatieff, Michael (1993). *Blood and Belonging: Journey into the New Nationalisms*, London: BBC/Chatto and Windus.

Jayasuriya, Lakiri (1990). 'Multiculturalism, Citizenship and Welfare: New Directions for the 1990s', paper presented at the 50th Anniversary Lecture Series, University of Sydney.

Jayawardena, Kumari (1986). *Feminism and Nationalism in the Third World*, London: Zed Books.

Johnson, R. W. (1998). 'South Africa's Chaotic Cultural Revolution', *The Higher* 1344, 7 August: 16–17.

Joseph, Suad (1997). 'The Public/Private – the Imagined Boundary in the Imagined Nation/State/Community', *Feminist Review* 57: 73–92.

Kandiyoti, Deniz (1991). 'Identity and Its Discontents: Women and the Nation', *Millennium* 20, 3: 429–44.

Kapferer, Bruce (1988). *Legends of People, Myths of State: Violence, Intolerance and Political Culture in Sri Lanka and Australia*, Washington DC: Smithsonian Institution Press.

Kuhn, Thomas (1962). *The Structure of Scientific Revolutions*, Chicago: Chicago University Press.

Kymlicka, Will (1995). *Multicultural Citizenship: a Liberal Theory of Minority Rights*, Oxford: Clarendon Press.

Levi-Strauss, Claude (1966). *The Savage Mind*, London: Weidenfeld and Nicholson.

Lister, Ruth (1997a). *Citizenship: Feminist Perspectives*, London: Macmillan.

— (1997b). 'Citizenship: Towards a Feminist Synthesis', *Feminist Review* 57: 28–48.

Lutz, Helma (1997). 'The Limits of Europeanness', *Feminist Review* 57: 93–111.

Lyotard, Jean-Francois (1986)[1977] *The Postmodern Condition: a Report on Knowledge*, trans. Geoff Bennington and Brian Massumi, Manchester: Manchester University Press.

Mani, Lata (1989). 'Contentious Traditions: the Debate on Sati in Colonial India', in K. Sangari and S. Vaid (eds) *Women: Essays in Colonial History*, New Brunswick NJ: Rutgers University Press.

Margalit, Avishai (1996). *The Decent Society*, Cambridge MA: Harvard University Press.

Marshall, T. H. (1950). *Citizenship and Social Class,* Cambridge: Cambridge University Press.

Marx, Karl (1975). 'On the Jewish Question', in *Early Writings*, Harmondsworth:

Penguin, pp. 211–42.

Meekosha, Helen and Leanne Dowse (1997). 'Enabling Citizenship: Gender, Disability and Citizenship in Australia', *Feminist Review* 57: 49–72.

Melchiori, Paola (1998). 'Redefining Political Spaces and Concepts of Politics: Migrating Practices of Consciousness-raising', in L. Christiansen-Ruffman (ed.) *The Global Feminist Enlightenment: Women and Social Knowledge*, Madrid: ISA.

Melucci, Alberto (1993/94). 'Paradoxes of Post-Industrial Democracy: Everyday Life and Social Movements', *Berkeley Journal of Sociology: A Critical Review* 38: 185–92.

Mercer, Kobena (1990). 'Welcome to the Jungle: Identity and Diversity in Postmodern Politics', in L. Rutherford (ed.) *Identity: Community. Culture, Difference*, London: Lawrence and Wishart.

Miles, Angela (1996). *Integrative Feminisms: Building Global Visions 1960s–1990s*, New York: Routledge.

Modood, Tariq (1997a). '"Difference", Cultural Racism and Anti-Racism', in Pnina Werbner and Tariq Modood (eds) *Debating Cultural Hybridity: Multi-Cultural Identities and the Politics of Anti-Racism*, London: Zed Books, pp. 154–72.

— (1997b). 'Introduction', in Tariq Modood and Pnina Werbner (eds) *The Politics of Multiculturalism in the New Europe: Racism, Identity and Community*, London: Zed Books, pp. 1–26.

Modood, Tariq and Pnina Werbner (eds) (1997). *The Politics of Multiculturalism in the New Europe: Racism, Identity and Community*, London: Zed Books.

Mohanty, Chandra T. (1991). 'Introduction: Cartographies of Struggle: Third World Women and the Politics of Feminism', in Chandra T. Mohanty, Ann Russo and Lourdes Torres (eds) *Third World Women and the Politics of Feminism*, Bloomington: Indiana University Press, pp. 1–47.

Moodie, Dunbar T. (1975). *The Rise of Afrikanerdom: Power, Apartheid, and the Afrikaner Civil Religion*, Berkeley: University of California Press.

Mouffe, Chantal (1988). 'Hegemony and New Political Subjects: Towards a New Concept of Democracy', in Cary Nelson and Lawrence Grossberg (eds) *From Marxism to the Interpretation of Culture*, Urbana: University of Illinois Press, pp. 89–103.

— (1992). 'Democratic Citizenship and the Political Community', in Chantal Mouffe (ed.) *Dimensions of Radical Democracy: Pluralism, Citizenship, Community,* London: Verso, pp. 225–39.

— (1993). *The Return of the Political*, London: Verso.

O'Connor, Julia S. (1993). 'Gender, Class and Citizenship in the Comparative Analysis of Welfare State Regimes: Theoretical and Methodological Issues', *British Journal of Sociology* 44, 3: 501–18.

Ong, Aihwa (1996). 'Cultural Citizenship as Subject-Making', *Current Anthropology* 37, 5: 737–62.

Orloff, Ann Shola (1993). 'Gender and the Social Rights of Citizenship: the Comparative Analysis of Gender Relations and Welfare States', *American Sociological Review* 58 (June): 303–28.

Parry, Geraint (1991). 'Conclusion: Paths to Citizenship', in Ursula Vogel and Michael Moran (eds) *The Frontiers of Citizenship*, London: Macmillan, pp. 166–201.

Parry, Geraint, George Moyser and Neil Day (1992). *Political Participation and Democracy in Britain*, Cambridge: Cambridge University Press.

Pateman, Carole (1988). *The Sexual Contract*, Cambridge: Polity Press.

— (1996). 'Democratization and Citizenship in the 1990s', Institute for Social Research, Oslo.

Peters, Emrys L. (1990). *The Bedouin of Cyrenaica: Studies in Personal and Corporate Power*, edited by Jack Goody and Emanuel Marx, Cambridge: Cambridge Univesity Press.

Phillips, Anne (1993). *Democracy and Difference*, Cambridge: Polity Press.

— (1995). *The Politics of Presence*, Oxford: Clarendon Press.

Plummer, Ken (1995). *Telling Sexual Stories: Power, Change and Social Worlds*, London: Routledge.

Sahgal, Gita and Nira Yuval-Davis (eds) (1992). *Refusing Holy Orders: Women and Fundamentalism in Britain*, London: Virago Books.

Schierup, Carl-Ulrik (1995). 'Multiculturalism and Universalism in the USA and EU', paper presented to the workshop on Nationalism and Ethnicity, Berne, March.

Schutz, A. (1944). 'The Stranger: an Essay in Social Psychology', *American Journal of Sociology* 49, 6: 499–507.

Shadid, Wasif and Sjoerd van Koningsfeld (1996). 'Loyalty to a Non-Muslim Government: an Analysis of Islamic Normative Discussions and of the Views of Some Contemporary Islamists', in W. A. R. Shadid and P. S. van Koningsveld (eds) *Political Participation and Identities of Muslims in Non-Muslim Countries*, Kampen, the Netherlands: Kok Pharos Publishing House, pp. 84–114.

Simon, Roger (1982/1991). *Gramsci's Political Thought*, London: Lawrence and Wishart.

Soysal, Yasemin (1994). *Limits of Citizenship: Migrant and Postnational Membership in Europe*, Chicago: Chicago University Press.

Stasiulis, Daiva and Abigail B. Bakan (1997). 'Negotiating Citizenship: the Case of Foreign Domestic Workers in Canada', *Feminist Review* 57: 112–39.

Taylor, Charles (1994). 'Examining the Politics of Recognition', in Amy Gutmann (ed.) *Multiculturism*, Princeton: Princeton University Press, pp. 25–74.

Thornton, Robert (1996). 'The Potentials of Boundaries in South Africa: Steps Towards a Theory of the Social Edge', in Richard Werbner and Terence Ranger (eds) *Postcolonial Identities in Africa*, London: Zed Books, pp. 136–62.

Tololyan, Khachig (1996). 'Rethinking Diaspora(s): Stateless Power in the Transnational Moment', *Diaspora* 5, 1: 3–36.

Turner, Bryan S. (1990). 'Outline of a Theory of Citizenship', *Sociology* 24, 2: 189–218.

United Nations (1996). *Report of the Fourth World Conference on Women: Beijing, 4–15 September 1995*, New York: United Nations.

Vogel, Ursula (1991). 'Is Citizenship Gender Specific?', in U. Vogel and M. Moran (eds) *The Frontiers of Citizenship*, Basingstoke: Macmillan.

Walby, Sylvia (1990). *Theorizing Patriarchy*, Oxford: Basil Blackwell.

— (1994). 'Is Citizenship Gendered?', *Sociology* 28, 2: 379–96.

Walzer, Michael (1996). (ed.) *Toward a Global Civil Society*, Oxford: Berghahn Books.

Waterman, Peter (1998). *Globalisation, Social Movements and the New Internationalisms*, London: Cassells.

Weale, Albert (1991). 'Citizenship beyond Borders', in Ursula Vogel and Michael Moran (eds) *The Frontiers of Citizenship*, London: Macmillan, pp. 155–65.

Werbner, Pnina (1990). *The Migration Process: Capital, Gifts and Offerings among British Pakistanis.* Oxford: Berg Publishers.

— (1991). 'Black and Ethnic Leaderships in Britain: a Theoretical Overview', in Pnina

Werbner and Muhammad Anwar (eds) *Black and Ethnic Leaderships in Britain: the Cultural Dimensions of Political Action*, London: Routledge, pp. 15–37.

— (1994). 'Diaspora and Millennium: British Pakistani Local-Global Fabulations of the Gulf War', in Akbar Ahmed and Hastings Donnan (eds) *Islam, Globalization and Postmodernity*, London: Routledge, pp. 213–36.

— (1996a). 'Allegories of Sacred Imperfection: Magic, Hermeneutics and Passion in *The Satanic Verses*', *Current Anthropology* 37, Supplement: S55–86.

— (1996b). 'Public Spaces, Political Voices: Gender, Feminism and Aspects of British Muslim Participation in the Public Sphere', in W. A. R. Shadid and P. S. van Koningsveld (eds) *Political Participation and Identities of Muslims in Non-Muslim States*, Kampen: Kok Pharos Publishing House, pp. 53–70.

— (1997a). 'Afterword: Writing Multiculturalism and Politics in the New Europe', in Tariq Modood and Pnina Werbner (eds) *The Politics of Multiculturalism in the New Europe: Racism, Identity, Community*. London: Zed Books, pp. 261–67.

— (1997b). 'Introduction: the Dialectics of Cultural Hybridity', in Pnina Werbner and Tariq Modood (eds) *Debating Cultural Hybridity: Multi-Cultural Identities and the Politics of Anti-Racism*, London: Zed Books, pp. 1–26.

— (1998). 'Diasporic Political Imaginaries: a Sphere of Freedom or a Sphere of Illusions?' *Communal/Plural: Journal of Transnational and Crosscultural Studies* 1, 1: 11–31.

Werbner, Richard (1989). *Ritual Passage, Sacred Journey: the Process and Organisation of Religious Movements*, Washington DC: Smithsonian Institution Press.

— (1994). [1991] *Tears of the Dead: the Social Biography of an African Family*, 2nd edition, Washington DC: Smithsonian Institution Press.

— (1995). 'Human Rights and Moral Knowledge: Arguments of Accountability in Zimbabwe', in Marilyn Strathern (ed.) *Shifting Contexts*, London: Routledge.

— (1996). 'Introduction: Multiple Identities, Plural Arenas', in Richard Werbner and Terence Ranger (eds) *Postcolonial Identities in Africa*, London: Zed Books, pp. 1–26.

Wieviorka, Michel (1997). 'Is It So Difficult to Be an Anti-Racist?', in Pnina Werbner and Tariq Modood (eds) *Debating Cultural Hybridity: Multi-Cultural Identities and the Politics of Anti-Racism*, London: Zed Books, pp. 139–53.

Yalcin-Heckmann, Lale (1997). 'The Perils of Ethnic Associational Life in Europe: Turkish Migrants in Germany and France', in Tariq Modood and Pnina Werbner (eds) *The Politics of Multiculturalism in the New Europe: Racism, Identity and Community*, London: Zed Books, pp. 95–110.

Young, Iris Marion (1990). *Justice and the Politics of Difference*, Princeton: Princeton University Press.

Yuval-Davis, Nira (1980). 'The Bearers of the Collective: Women and Religious Legislation in Israel', *Feminist Review* 4: 15–27.

— (1991). 'The Citizenship Debate: Women, the State and Ethnic Processes', *Feminist Review* 39: 58–68.

— (1993). 'Gender and Nation', *Racial and Ethnic Studies* 16, 4: 621–32.

— (1994). 'Women, Ethnicity and Empowerment', in K. Bhavnani and A. Phoenix (eds) *Shifting Identities, Shifting Racisms*, special issue of *Feminism and Psychology* 4, 1: 179–98.

— (1996). 'Women and National Reproduction', special issue edited by Barbara Einhorn on 'Links across Difference: Gender, Ethnicity, Nationalism', *Women's*

Studies International Forum 19, 1–2: 17–24.

— (1997a). *Gender and Nation*, London: Sage Publications.

— (1997b). 'Women, Citizenship and Difference', *Feminist Review* 57: 4–27.

— (forthcoming). 'The Spaced-Out Citizen: Collectivity, Territoriality and the Gendered Construction of Difference', in E. Inis (ed.) *Rights to the City: Citizenship, Democracy and Cities in a Global Age*, London: Routledge.

Yuval-Davis, Nira and Floya Anthias (eds) (1989). *Woman – Nation – State,* Basingstoke: Macmillan.

Yuval-Davis, Nira and Pnina Werbner (1996). *Women, Citizenship and Difference: Final Report.* Greenwich and Keele Universities.

Zajovic, Stasa (ed.) (1994). *Women for Peace,* Belgrade: Women in Black.

PART ONE
Dialogical Citizenships

CHAPTER 2

Citizenship Revisited

Alison Assiter

Many writers on the subject of citizenship take it to mean participation in a nation-state. For example, Hobhouse writes: 'the people, or at any rate the citizens, are the state' (1994: 145). The liberal ideal envisages a society of free and equal persons, but, as Kymlicka puts it: 'for most people [society] seems to mean their nation' (1995: 93). There is a reciprocity of obligation between the individual and the state. International law, indeed, does not recognise the distinction between citizenship and nationality. It is arguable that citizenship, as a concept, with its assumption that the world is divisible into nation-states with their inclusionary and exclusionary boundaries, is an inappropriate concept to use if the community is be the world. It is possible to argue further that there cannot be a truly Marxist concept of citizenship, in so far as Marx envisaged, in a fully communist society, the abolition of nation-states.

There could be a broader notion of citizenship, however, one that does not rely on the notion of the nation-state and that is encapsulated in Rousseau's ideal of an association of free and equal persons. In this chapter I consider two traditions of thinking that lie behind current views of citizenship. These are the liberal, on the one hand, and the communitarian, on the other. I then suggest a variant on communitarianism which might offer the basis for a different approach to citizenship which does not take it for granted that individuals are members of nation-states.

The Liberal Conception of Citizenship

For the liberal, individuals are primarily isolated, autonomous, self-sufficient, atomistic selves, possessing rights to such things as life, liberty and, in some versions of liberalism, property. In Mill's version (1962) laws protecting the individual from interference by the state (except where individuals might harm one another) were vital. Freedom from illegitimate interference by another is, for Mill, a crucial value. Indeed, Kymlicka (1989), a prominent modern liberal, defends freedom as a fundamental value, one that is presupposed for any other to be possible. Citizenship, on this classical liberal view, involves the protection by the state of individual liberties. Citizens may use their rights to promote their own self-interest within the constraint of respecting the rights of others to do the same thing. Recently, Kymlicka has extended this notion to incorporate, in the case of minority groups in certain cultures, respect for groups and group rights (Kymlicka 1995).

Communitarian Critiques of Liberalism

I shall begin by summarising, for the uninitiated, the four main strands of certain versions of the communitarian critique of liberalism. First, liberalism is said to rest upon an overly individualistic conception of the self. This notion of the self is viewed by some communitarian critics (e.g., Sandel) as metaphysically flawed. The self outlined by the early Rawls (1971), who 'brackets off' all its values and many of the features that differentiate it from other selves, is said to be incoherent. In contrast, say the communitarians, people's ends and values partially form who they are; as Sandel puts it, people are constitutively attached to their ends (1981). This claim can be described either as a sociological point to the effect that people necessarily derive their self-understandings from the social world, or as a conceptual claim that language and moral life are impossible outside a social setting.

A second criticism made by communitarians of liberalism is that the community or society is significant for a moral theory to have practical force: as Waltzer has argued, it is important that we stay rooted in our traditions in order to interpret to our fellow citizens the meanings that we share (Waltzer 1983).

Third, communitarians question whether the liberal self, even supposing that it were coherent, is a desirable one. MacIntyre puts this point particularly forcefully. In *After Virtue* he describes the post-Enlightenment liberal self, the typically 'modern' self, as an 'arbitrary will' devoid of rational means or criteria for choosing between standpoints (MacIntyre 1984, especially Chapter 3).

Fourth, communitarians have argued that liberals inappropriately universalise from one type of experience: are freedom and justice, critics have asked, appropriate for those who adhere, in fact, to radically different values?

It must be said that some liberals, and notably Kymlicka (1989), have argued that some of these criticisms can be accommodated.

There is another criticism that is not specifically communitarian, but is often made, of certain versions of the liberal conception of citizenship. It has been argued that the individual of classical liberal theory is actually the bourgeois male, and that this liberal individual has relied upon the role of women as wives, mothers and carers (see Pateman 1995; Vogel 1994). Carol Pateman has argued that the third element in the trilogy – liberty, equality, *fraternity* – is often forgotten. She argues, in *The Disorder of Women* (Pateman 1995), that liberalism and the concept of citizenship are forged through the necessary subjection of women – of women's bodies. In the social contract theory, sexual or conjugal right is natural: men's dominion over women is held to follow from the respective natures of the sexes. The individuals who make up the social contract that gives rise to citizenship are men. Women are constructed as naturally deficient in a specifically political capacity, the capacity to create and maintain political right (*ibid.:* 96). Civil society is the sphere of freedom, equality, individualism, reason, contract and impartial law. This sphere is separated in classical liberal theory from the 'private' world – from the world of ties of love, emotion and sexual passions – the world of women, but also the world of the body.

The argument here is two-fold: it says (1) that liberal individualism implicitly, as a theoretical ideal, has excluded women; and (2) that liberalism has relied upon women's role as wives and mothers to hold society together. On this argument liberal theory and liberal conceptions of citizenship effectively exclude the family. An extension of the argument of Pateman and Vogel is that the liberal ideal is founded upon a number of related dualisms – reason/emotion; man/woman; soul/body – each of which denigrates some grouping through defining it as 'other' to the dominant group and through homogenising that negatively characterised grouping (see Plumwood 1993).

The latter type of argument is different from claims that have been made frequently in the literature – that particular nation-states are sexist, racist and founded upon exclusionary boundaries. In these terms several critics have assailed what has passed as citizenship, citing the exclusion of some groups from entering a country or from remaining in it; fear of not being allowed back on visits; the selective denial to individuals of certain aspects of citizenship rights (see, for example, Yuval-Davis 1997). Liberals might argue, though, that these laws (for example, British immigration legislation; the denial of the right of return to Kurdish people) are anti-liberal. It is possible to argue (Bakan and Stasiulis 1994) that hegemonic states that give racialised and gendered definitions of who is and who is not entitled to citizenship rights are states that are insufficiently liberal in their interpretation of citizenship. The argument of Pateman, however, defends the claim that liberalism is necessarily racist and sexist, and that there is no point, therefore, in setting out to defend a liberal feminist or a liberal anti-racist stance.

Communitarianism

In offering a brief outline of communitarianism, I shall not restrict the argument to the civic republican versions of the thesis that have been mentioned in the literature. These are the versions that are often referred to in discussions of citizenship (see, for example, Mouffe 1993, Miller 1992). Communitarianism, however, is broader than this version.

Communitarians argue that we are social beings; that we are embodied agents deriving our self-understandings from the social world. We cannot, *contra* liberals, detach ourselves from our ends and values. Communitarians suggest that political thinking involves interpreting shared understandings bearing upon the political life of a community. This is in contrast to the liberal view that there are universal principles based upon an abstract consideration of an individual's needs and wants. Communities, for the communitarian, can be communities of place or of memory, or they can be grounded in 'psychological sharings' like, for example, friendship. Communities, for the communitarian, are not explicitly identified either with localised collectivities or with any other actual collectivity with specific boundaries. The concept of community purports to be a theoretical ideal, yet communitarians often refer to actual examples such as the family, the nation, the workplace, a person's ethnicity. Communitarians have argued that each of these communities shares a set of meanings that constitute it as a community and that form its central values.

Communitarians, in other words, emphasise that being a citizen involves belonging to a community. Individuals operate within communities. Civic republicans argue that citizens should be concerned about the ethical health of a community as well as with individual rights and duties (Dworkin 1993). They argue in favour of 'active' citizenship. Citizens, they argue, should actively join with others to promote the common good in communities.

I believe, although there is not space to argue the claim here, that the central virtue of the communitarian tradition is its anti-individualism and its commitment to the notion of the individual as being necessarily entangled in communities. In this sense, communitarians are at one with thinkers as diverse as Karl Marx and Emile Durkheim. Some feminists have made a similar kind of point. Benhabib, for example, urges that the autonomous, disembodied individual of classical liberalism ignores social existence and particularity (Benhabib 1992).

One difficulty with communitarianism, though, is that it is not clear what is meant by a community. Communitarians tend to rely on examples like the family, the nation. But then one can ask: what are the commonalities between family, nation, and a collectivity based upon a common ethnicity? What constitutes a community? What are the similarities between these disparate entities? There are some similarities between them, but there are also many differences. One set of similarities and differences pertains to the nature of the various characteristics that are shared by members of the communities. For example, there are aspects of my history as a member of my family – my date and place of birth, and the identity of those who were with me at the time of my birth – which I have no choice but to accept. The same is true of my nationality at birth. Such facts about me constitute what Keith Graham has called 'constraints of necessity' (1996: 139). There is, however, no constraint of such a kind in respect of my workplace – another community mentioned in the communitarian literature. Other qualities pertaining to membership of these communities may be more deep-seated for some people than they will be for others. Thus country of residence will be more significant in relation to the various rights that flow from national citizenship for someone who has crossed borders than it will be for someone who has lived in the same country all their life. The meaning attaching to any one of the constitutive features of any one community may be radically different for any two people.

One further point that is often made in critiques of communitarianism is that some versions of it tend to homogenise groupings – that it does not recognise differences between individuals in communities, or conflicts within them (see, for example, Ramsey 1997: 251; Campbell 1995). It tends to gloss over class, gender, racial and other power differentials between groupings, in the interest of generating a common identity and a common value system.

Even if there is some sense of shared meaning in a collectivity, why should what is shared be constitutive of a person's value system? What sense, for example, of shared meaning do two Jewish people have who have neither upbringing in the same country nor a political and moral outlook in common? To describe a person's Jewishness as being formative of his or her value system seems arbitrary and possibly even pernicious. It could be pernicious because there may be no connection between the deep-seatedness of a set of values and their justice or rightness. Think of the 'constitutive' community of the Nazi Party. In that case, most people would want to argue that, contrary to a community furnishing appropriate moral values, it was, rather, dislocation from it that was the only way of hanging on to any sense of morality. Active involvement, in civic republican terms, in such a community is not one that many people would wish to advocate.

Some Positives and Some Negatives

Many of us were formed in families, in schools, in communities of various kinds. Each of these 'communities' helps form the sorts of people that we are, and the sorts of ends or aims to which we are attached. But to claim this is not at all the same as saying that we are 'constitutively' attached to particular ends, and that these ends are therefore immune from our criticism. On the contrary, our ends may change radically or not so radically as we move in and out of communities. The young lad, for example, who grew up in peacetime Bosnia no doubt has different values and ends from the same person who fought on the Serbian side in the war, and who was forced to participate in crimes against humanity. Even if I am wrong, as I may well be, about this particular case, there are cases where it is quite clear that a person's ends and values have fundamentally altered.

We can accept, therefore, that people are constitutively formed by certain types of community. But it does not follow that they continue, throughout their lives, to uphold the specific values of those particular communities. On the contrary they may choose to opt for a different kind of community, or they may, by chance, find themselves in an entirely new kind of situation, which incorporates radically different kinds of value. It does not follow from what I am saying that I am suggesting a retreat to the liberal position earlier described. If the ends to which someone was once constitutively attached are open to criticism, this does not imply that that person is not constitutively attached to anything, that he or she is detached, with no commitments. MacIntyre (1984) seems to want to have things both ways, in so far as he suggests that the concept of a 'tradition' is vital to the formation of moral concepts, and yet he stresses that that tradition should provide scope for critical reflection on one's values. But what if the tradition in which we are immersed fails to do that? What if it actually encourages us to behave in ways that run counter to any real values?

An Alternative

Each of us is associated with several different communities throughout our lives. Some of them, as I have suggested earlier, are communities we have no choice about whether to belong to. Someone who is born into a particular culture and family in Pakistan where arranged marriage is the norm has not chosen that destiny. There are, however, other communities we become part of in the course of our lives that we may choose to join. Gay and lesbian people, for example, may choose to join a family of gays and lesbians, and once this choice has been made, the family no doubt comes to exercise a significant influence over the values that are held by an individual member. This choice need not involve the exercise of Kantian transcendent rationality. Indeed, we do not have to opt for one or other dimension of a supposed polarity between embodied particularity and Kantian transcendence. Each of us is both embodied, particular and embedded, but each one of us nonetheless has open to us opportunities for choice and value judgment. We may become part of a chosen community as a result of education, socialisation, chance encounter, friendship or work networks. It is possible, I shall now argue, to separate constitutive communities in which a person happens to find herself from those that come about through the exercise of some sort of choice. Furthermore, there is one fundamental community to which we all belong, the importance of which we often forget – that is, the community of all human beings.

In a different context, I developed the notion of an epistemic community (Assiter 1996). I suggested that one feature of such a community is the Aristotelian commitment to certain ends or values. Like communitarians, I drew on Aristotle. But a feature of Aristotle's political thinking that appears to be neglected in some communitarian thinking is his key question: how could the Greek *polis* be justified over its rivals? I would like to suggest that this feature is also neglected in some recent feminist thinking. Much recent feminism has stressed the importance of listening to marginal voices; of allowing these voices to speak; of engaging with radical otherness, rather than assuming that people are all alike (Yuval-Davis 1997; Seller 1994). My reservation about an unqualified acceptance of radical otherness, however, is that there may be some 'others', and indeed some aspects of our own identity and background, which should be challenged and rejected, on moral and political grounds. Listening, on its own, is a vital corrective to those perspectives which would, by failing to listen, project too much onto another (assuming, for example, that white Australian colonials know the voice of and can speak for the Aboriginal). Listening without judgement, however, would allow us to hear the voices of Nazis and others whose ends are counter to the interests of some groupings of people. I would like, then, to begin to ask the question: what makes one constitutive community better than another? I should like to attempt to answer the question: how are we to judge which aspects of our self-identity and of 'otherness' might be unacceptable on moral and political grounds?

I characterised an epistemic community as a group of individuals who share certain interests, values and beliefs in common – for example, that sexism is wrong, that racism is wrong – and who work on the epistemic consequences of those presuppositions. These individuals, I argued, are particularly interested in the truth of their views, and in providing evidence for their truth. Members of one epistemic community may be members of diverse other social, cultural, and political groupings. Epistemic communities may contain people who are unequal in power and status. I suggested that they are 'imagined communities' in something like Anderson's sense (Anderson 1983). They may never communicate with one another, even by e-mail. I then went on to argue that the viewpoint of an epistemic community most committed to what I called 'emancipatory values' provides radical insights into what can be called knowledge, because that community enables us to see the world in new and enlightened ways. I used the concept 'emancipatory' in the following sense: a value will be emancipatory if it contributes to removing oppressive power relations. Emancipatory values are not absolute, nor is it possible to say exactly which values they are. Values will be emancipatory relative to others: so, for example, liberal values are emancipatory relative to Nazism because they help us understand anti-semitism, but not relative to feminism. It may be argued, however, that this claim is not uncontroversial. Gayatri Chakravorty Spivak (Spivak 1988), for example, has written of the difficulty of judging whether white liberal colonial values were emancipatory for Indian women even in the extreme case of their disallowing *sati* – self-immolation on the husband's funeral pyre. Paul Gilroy (1993) has advanced the case that for some black American slaves, death was actually a preferable option to continuing in the kind of extreme subjugation that denied them entirely their freedom as human agents. I would urge us, however, against a relativism of value which induces us to accept that a value system which, under extreme circumstances of total loss of agency, calls for the right of victims to choose death over life is preferable to subjugation. There is a need to accept some limitations on our relativism: as a minimum, a value is more emancipatory than another if it has the effect of removing a person or a group of people from subjugation. For whom is the choice of death preferable to the option of enslavement? It is hard to argue that it is actually preferable for the enslaved person, since he or she would no longer be there to make any kind of choice at all. Is it the chosen route, in order to provide a symbol for others; to point out to them that it is possible to reject the fundamentally dehumanising role of the slave? But death is clearly a tragic and drastic option to be forced to take. As a symbol of the potential emancipation of slaves, no doubt death (and imprisonment, in the case of many black Africans over the years) is valuable. But is it not the perspective of the believer in the possibility of emancipation that allows us to see such deaths as symbolic in this way? Do we not need the perspective of a universal humanity in order to see it in this light? Is it not the notion of a scale of types of emancipatory value – with the preservation of life as the ultimate one – that allows us to see things this way?

At their most extreme, then, policies which subjugate would be those, like Nazism, which lead to the death of the subjugated grouping. A less extreme case would be policies, like those of the apartheid South African government, and many liberal democracies early this century, which denied people certain categories of fundamental right – an obvious example would be the right to vote. I believe that it would be very difficult, except in the case of a grouping who were likely through perversity or irrationality to vote in a government that denied them even more fundamental rights, to defend the view that denying a group the right to vote was actually more emancipatory than offering them that right. The question arises, of course, emancipatory for whom? I am suggesting that a set of values that upholds a particular right for a wider range of people is more emancipatory than a set which does not do this.

I would like to go further than this, however, and in this context I can do no more than sketch out the bare bones of the argument. Whilst liberal values are emancipatory relative, as I have said, to Nazism, I would like to argue that there is a set of values that is more emancipatory than the liberal ones. Following Gewirth, I would like to argue that it is not possible to act at all unless one has certain degrees of freedom and well-being. 'The components of such well being thus fall into a hierarchy of goods, ranging from life and physical integrity to self-esteem and education' (Gewirth 1982: 61). This viewpoint presupposes that there are objectively defined human needs that must be satisfied before any action towards any ends can be pursued. Survival is a fundamental biological need that takes different forms depending on the socioeconomic context in which it is exemplified. Needs, I would argue, can be distinguished from wants (for some spelling out of this argument, see Assiter 1990).

Fundamentally, then, emancipatory values will be those that ensure life, first of all, and then those that enable the satisfaction of objectively defined needs. Following these may be values that advocate the extending of fundamental rights to a wider range of people, and then on to less 'extreme' ones. Less extreme values might include those that help prevent unconscious or institutional discrimination against particular groups. Broadly, though, all emancipatory values help remove some group from subjugation. But the most fundamental values of all involve all of us in recognising our membership of a common humanity, and the role played by that community and its common needs in generating values.

These values will not, of course, emerge from nowhere; they will be linked in various ways to the group or groups that generated them. Lesbian emancipatory values, for example, arose from the writings and the behaviour of politically active lesbians. Radclyffe Hall deliberately wrote of the lesbian as the pervert, drawing on the work of nineteenth-century sexologists. She helped draw attention both to the existence of lesbianism and to the many forms of discrimination lesbian women suffered in the UK at the time. Later lesbian writing has brought to light the heterosexism of much early second-wave feminist writing.

It may be difficult, given that the idea of a universal feminism has been criticised, to see how there can be such things as epistemic communities. How can there be such a thing when there is a contradiction between the policies of different feminist groupings? In the case of abortion, for example, there is a conflict between the views articulated by white Western women and by Chinese feminists wanting the right to have girl children. Nonetheless, dialogue, listening to the voices of others, the notion of 'transversal politics' can help generate better epistemic communities (see Yuval-Davis 1997). I am suggesting, though, that this dialogue, in addition to being informed by a commitment to one's own identity and to hearing the voices of marginalised others, should incorporate a vision that is open to constant revision, but a vision nonetheless of possible emancipation. Without such a vision, some of the voices to which one listens will be committed to closing down communities, closing down opportunities for some people.

Why?

Why should anyone accept any of this? One kind of objection, no doubt, will concern the abstract nature of the purported community. How can the proposal escape the criticism that it is really a version of Kantian rationalism, because the communities described are 'imagined' ones, and therefore not grounded in people's embodied and embedded identity? In response I would like to say that there are many different kinds of embeddedness; we can reconceptualise, for example, the meaning that childhood events have had for us; we can distance ourselves more or less from the values upheld by our parents, our teachers, our politicians, and our fellow workers. We can also choose – as I have suggested some people have done – to adopt values that may have contradicted those that were 'constitutive' for us at certain points in our lives. In this sort of way can epistemic communities be formed.

Emancipatory Values and Knowledge

There is a further partial answer to the question, why should anyone accept the notion of an epistemic community? I argued elsewhere (Assiter 1996) that the idea of a community committed to emancipatory values can be linked to knowledge. Repressive values, I suggested, can blinker the vision of the knower.

A different way of putting the point is as follows: all moral theory is underdetermined by the data. No theory can ever be completely determined by any set of facts. Therefore values will always enter into the determination of the truth of a theory. Since knowers are human agents, a theory that denies some aspect of this agency to some group of possible knowers is less likely to be true than one that does not do this. Any value that limits the capacity of human beings as cognitive agents cannot help advance knowledge.

Community and Citizenship

What might all of this tell us about citizenship? What follows is no more than the briefest of sketches of the basic components of the idea. I would argue that there are several parts to the answer. First, the notion of a hierarchy of types of emancipatory value suggests that there might be levels of citizenship, the most fundamental of which simply involves respecting the right to life. Even this very basic notion of citizenship, however, has rarely been universally upheld in any given nation-state.

Underpinning a set of rights, then, would be something analogous to an Aristotelian commitment to a set of 'virtues'. This would presuppose an active component to citizenship, as in the republican tradition, yet it would not be a commitment to particular local communities. It would involve an active commitment to listening to the voices of marginalised others, but one always underpinned by an evolving vision of emancipation.

The theoretical model of citizenship, then, will involve two components – on the one hand, as an ideal, it presupposes a commitment to a set of values which will be as important as a set of rights – if not more so. Some of these values will be equivalent to rights. It may be, however, that other values could not be realised within the ambit of any existing nation-state. It may be that, for example, a real commitment to free and equal citizens – and to the satisfaction of needs that, I have suggested, is presupposed by this –

involves more fundamental change than would be encompassed by an alteration of government or by a change in legislation. Some individual rights – to enter and leave particular nation-states, to work, to welfare – could be said to apply to communities that have not embedded a commitment to fundamental emancipatory values. Fundamentally, then, citizenship will be global.

The second component of citizenship involved in the model, then, is a process component. This would presuppose formal and informal education in the significance of listening to the voices of marginalised others, of being open to hearing what they are saying, but always within the constraint of the overall vision of emancipation.

Conclusion

It is possible to accept the communitarian point that some characterisations of the liberal conception of the self are flawed, but to deny that it follows that we must identify wholly with the communities of our childhood, our background, our race or our class. The significance of a particular community for a specific individual will not be, as it is from the communitarian perspective, necessarily the fact of its being part of that person's embeddedness, that person's culture and identity, but rather it may be to do with the person's present commitments and values. For example, the white British woman who chooses to reject the values of her nation in favour of taking up the cause of some Bosnian women is choosing a community, a constituency that may well come particularly to define her identity, but it was not originally part of it. Rather than globalisation leading us back into the constitutive communities of our childhood and our history, as the communitarian would have it, let us allow global thinking and culture to enable us to extend our horizons and to widen the communities which come to constitute our identity.

Following this perspective, then, there is neither a value nor a set of values that would be adhered to by disembedded, disembodied selves, nor are there values that are integrally connected with the traditional identity of groups of individuals. Rather, I am suggesting that significant values are those that emancipate some group from a particular type of oppression. Mill partially justified his principle of liberty on the ground that allowing a multiplicity of viewpoints to flourish would enable the truth to emerge. According to the perspective outlined here, it is emancipatory values that encourage a viewpoint close to the truth to emerge.

In the classical liberal perspective, there is a set of rights that individuals are said to possess, and a set of principles governing behaviour and governing the maintenance of the optimal distribution of these rights across social groupings. For the 'classical' communitarian, political thinking involves interpreting the shared meanings that help form the identities of social groupings. Following the perspective I am outlining here, by contrast, political thinking involves interpreting the emancipatory content of the values upheld by particular groupings and considering the relationship of those values to the knowledges that they reveal.

References

Anderson, B. (1983). *Imagined Communities: Reflections on the Origins and Rise of Nationalism*, London: Verso.

Assiter, Alison (1990). 'Althusser and Feminism', London: Pluto Press.

— (1996). *Enlightened Women*, London: Routledge.

Bakan, A. and D. Stasiulis (1994). 'Foreign Domestic Worker Policy in Canada and the Social Boundaries of Modern Citizenship', *Science and Society* 58, 1: 7–33.

Benhabib, Seyla (1992). *Situating the Self: Gender, Community and Postmodernism in Contemporary Ethics*, London: Routledge.

Campbell, B. (1995). 'Old Fogeys and Angry Young Men, a Critique of Communitarianism', *Soundings* 1: 4–65.

Dworkin, Richard (1993). 'Liberal Community', in S. Avineri and A. de-Shalit (eds) *Communitarianism and Individualism*, Oxford: Oxford University Press, pp. 205–25.

Gewirth, A. (1982). *Human Rights: Essays in Justification and Application*, Chicago: University of Chicago Press.

Gilroy, Paul (1993). *The Black Atlantic: Double Consciousness and Modernity*, Cambridge, MA: Harvard University Press.

Graham, K. (1996). 'Coping with the Many-Coloured Dome: Pluralism and Practical Reason', in D. Archard (ed.) *Philosophy and Pluralism*, Cambridge: Cambridge University Press.

Hobhouse, L. T. (1994). *Liberalism and Other Writings*, Cambridge: Cambridge University Press.

Kymlicka, Will (1989). *Liberalism, Community and Culture*, Oxford: Oxford University Press.

— (1995) *Multicultural Citizenship*, Oxford: Oxford University Press.

MacIntyre, Alisdair (1984). *After Virtue*, second edition, Indiana: University of Notre Dame Press.

Mill, J. S. (1962). 'Essay on Liberty', in M. Warnock (ed.) *Utilitarianism*, London: Collins.

Miller, D. (1992). 'Community and Citizenship', in S. Avineri and A. de-Shalit, (eds) *Communitarianism and Individualism*, Oxford University Press, Oxford, pp. 85–101.

Mouffe, Chantal (1993). *The Return of the Political*, London: Verso.

Nozick, R. (1974). *Anarchy, State and Utopia*, Oxford: Blackwell.

Pateman, Carole (1995 [1989]). *The Disorder of Women*, Cambridge: Polity.

Plumwood, V. (1993). *Feminism and the Mastery of Nature*, London: Routledge.

Ramsey, M. (1997). *What Is Wrong with Liberalism? A Radical Critique of Liberal Political Philosophy*, Leicester: Leicester University Press.

Rawls, John (1971). *A Theory of Justice*, Oxford: Oxford University Press.

Sandel, M. (1981). *Liberalism and the Limits of Justice*, Cambridge: Cambridge University Press.

Seller, A. (1994). 'Should the Feminist Philosopher Stay at Home?' in K. Lennon and M. Whitford (eds) *Knowing the Difference: Feminist Perspectives in Epistemology*, London: Routledge.

Spivak, Gayatri Chakravorty (1988). *In Other Worlds: Essays in Cultural Politics*, London: Routledge.

Vogel, Ursula (1994). 'Marriage and the Boundaries of Citizenship', in B. van Steenbergen (ed.) *The Condition of Citizenship*, London: Sage, pp. 76–90.

Waltzer, Michael (1983). *Spheres of Justice*, Oxford: Blackwell.

Yuval-Davis, Nira (1997). *Gender and Nation*, London: Sage.

CHAPTER 3

Right-Wing 'Feminism': a Challenge to Feminism as an Emancipatory Movement

Birgit Rommelspacher

In the past few years there has been a marked increase in incidents of racist violence and radical right-wing activities in Germany. This has led us to ask: What role have women played in this context?

Statistically speaking, the violence was almost entirely a male affair, as 96 per cent of the perpetrators were young men (Willems *et al.* 1993). These statistics do not mean, however, that women were in no way involved. A closer examination reveals that women played the traditional roles of wives and girlfriends, supporters of 'their' men. But we also find another role played by women, the role of the female fighter, who is both self-confident and self-reliant. These women demand the right to fight and raise their voices in the political process. Most men reject their demands, but some doubt if they can afford to exclude these women, particularly because they are strong and might make a substantial contribution to the radical right-wing movement. Consequently, an internal debate has begun on the topic of radical right-wing 'feminism' (Axeli-Knapp and Wenk 1995) and whether it should be accepted by the movement.

Radical right-wing feminism is not a new phenomenon. A look into history shows that even under National Socialism in Germany, there were women to be found who demanded the same rights as men and equal participation at all levels of society: they were called the 'oppositionelle Faschistinnen' (Korotin 1994). They argued that the battle for German supremacy needed every German man and every German woman and founded a magazine called *Die deutsche Kämpferin* ('The German Female Fighter'). Although this magazine and the organisation were soon banned, the case of the 'oppositionelle Faschistinnen' indicates that some women saw a chance for personal success in the Nazi political system. Afterwards, many of the women interviewed by Koonz – at least the ones who dared to speak openly – reported that they had had a good time in Nazi Germany (Koonz 1986). This may seem on the surface quite surprising in the light of the extremely patriarchal Nazi political system, which attempted to force women into traditional roles and constantly celebrated maleness and male chauvinism. How could these women feel comfortable, let alone have feminist goals, within this system?

Radical Right-Wing 'Feminism'

The 'feminist' goals of these women were above all based on racism. Sophie Rogge-Börner, founder of *Die deutsche Kämpferin,* asserted that the Nordic race had a tradition of gender equality, since women were able to attain power in ancient Germany as priestesses and judges, and that it was 'oriental Jewry' which introduced patriarchy and forced women into submission. According to Rogge-Börner, gender equality is a question of race. She demanded equality for men and women of the same origin (Jung 1997). Similarly, some contemporary Norwegian radical right-wing feminists argue that the ancient Vikings also practised gender equality, but that the non-Nordic races destroyed this with patriarchy. Such 'feminist' ideologies not only fit perfectly into the radical right-wing ideology of a biologically based racial hierarchy, but also strengthen this ideology with supplementary arguments.

Racism is not the only significant characteristic of radical right-wing 'feminism', which is also based on elitism. According to the 'oppositionelle Faschistinnen', not every woman of 'Aryan' race should be allowed to participate in power, but only the 'best'. Although racism and elitism are necessarily linked with radical right-wing 'feminism', this is not true of gender segregation. Under National Socialism we also find a liberal type of the female fighter who felt committed only to herself and her nation and/or race, unlike the women who accepted the gender segregation of the Nazi system.

Hence, we can identify at least two different types of women in this system: the 'relational' (Offen 1993) type of woman, who emphasises her role as wife and mother, and the more 'individual' type who stresses self-reliance and gender equality. Similarly, Rebecca Klatch sees a fundamental division among women in her study on 'Women of the New Right' (1987) and characterises these two constituencies as the 'social conservatives' and the 'laissez-faire conservatives'. The former believe in gender as different but equal whereas the latter mainly believe in themselves as individual persons. They are both anti-feminists in the sense that neither believes in gender roles as discriminating aspects: the one by denying that gender roles are important at all, and the other by believing in a natural order in which gender provides no basis for comparison.

Although we do also find these two types of women in the fascist system, the main difference is that here both believe strongly in the mission of their nation and/or race. And this – so my argument goes – is the main reason why women might experience that situation as 'emancipatory' for them. Identification with the collectivity becomes a central basis for their own self-worth. This is true for both the relational and the individual type of woman. The mother is then not only mother of her children but also mother for the whole nation or race. Similarly, the individually oriented woman feels challenged by the nation and race to prove her individual supremacy as a reflection and embodiment of the supremacy of the collectivity.

Numerous records of those times show that many women felt a sense of self-enrichment under the Nazi system because of the wide-scale commitment, encompassing the entire nation and/or race, that it invoked, and the concomitant growth in their own sense of worth and importance. They felt needed, and believed that they had a mission. They experienced a sense of ecstasy in belonging to an enormous community. All of these experiences made them feel liberated and even emancipated. Their husbands and families became insignificant by comparison. That is one reason why so many mothers sent their sons willingly or even enthusiastically to war, because they felt that this was their contribution to the community which made them part of the whole.

This 'emancipation' through identification with and in service of the 'whole' works by different mechanisms: first, it expands the individual's range of activity and responsibility, thus enhancing feelings of self-worth. These women felt that they were fighting for more than just a better position in the family or in the workforce, that they were in fact liberating themselves from the constraints of the family and also from a relatively self-referential existence.

Second, this sense of general commitment offered an alternative to dependence on a family and a concrete husband. The belief that they were serving the *Führer* could give them the strength and the legitimation to resist the orders of their husbands. They identified, as Ulrike Prokop puts it (1995), with male grandiosity and in turn were able to devalue the concrete husband. The man was idealised, but only as the bearer of national values, as hero and fighter, abstract and distant. The women's relation to the authority of the *Führer* was eroticised, which led to the paradox of submission in a general sense and emancipation from male dominance in a concrete sense. Prokop defines this as an 'active authoritarianism', as opposed to a passive authoritarianism in which women delegate their agency to men.

In this respect, the overwhelming power of the state was ambivalent. On the one hand, it intruded into the family with its demands for a proper conduct of life and fascist education of children. On the other hand, it gave the women who fitted into the 'adequate' category of race and social conduct the opportunity to relate to its power. Such women could be worshipped as mothers of the proper race; they were endowed with the power to commit their husbands to the proper ideology, as well as to denounce others.

Finally, assignments for the nation sometimes gave these women the legitimation to transcend traditional roles. This is especially true for the Bund deutscher Mädchen (the Nazi girl organisation). The girls in the BDM were allowed to participate in sports, to go camping, and to experience numerous adventures which they were never before allowed, because they too were supposed to be able to fight for 'Volk und Vaterland'.

In similar vein, Tanikar Sarka and Urvashi Butalia describe how fascinated women are by the radical Hindutva movement today. These women appear stimulated by the strategy of the Hindu right which makes women see themselves as legitimate, equal and valued participants in public and even political demonstrations of Hindu fervour and faith; secondly,

> the careful erasure of boundaries between home and the world, private and public spaces, religion and politics, through ceremonial enactments of familiar household rituals transforms and reinscribes the public Hindu cause as a deeply felt and experienced private wrong that every woman, irrespective of her caste and community origins, will willingly nurse in her heart. (1995: 9)

If this expansion and enhancement of self-worth by identification with a larger social unit is to be deemed 'emancipation', the question remains as to what kind of oppression this said emancipation is directed against, especially because this larger social unit is highly patriarchal in itself. The oppression in this historical case seems to be the constraints and emptiness of a daily life without broader perspectives, be it a life centred around the family, a profession, or both.

In his analyses of the rise of the Nazi system Norbert Elias (1990) mentions that the value and meaning of life is often connected to relations with others, to something which transcends mere personal existence, something which can be real or illusory. Without a social function, human life remains meaningless. If life is too restricted, and the surrounding political and social culture lacks ideals and visions, the need for meaning will be frustrated. It might then express itself in spiritual or political radicalism, because the need for broader perspectives is not integrated in everyday life. It is here that Elias sees the danger of a political culture and mentality which addresses only the basic needs of human existence. This might be especially true for women, who are – according to the well-known analyses of Simone de Beauvoir (1986) – damned to immanence. In her opinion, the need for transcendence is a particularly frustrated one for most women. This might help to explain many women's readiness to participate in religious and spiritual movements, and also in radical right-wing activities.

At the same time, the transcendence offered by such a political system as Nazi Germany is only reached through submission to a totalitarian and highly patriarchal regime. This makes such a form of 'emancipation' illusory. There is no actual emancipation for women as a whole who submit to a patriarchal system and their male leaders, even if only in a general sense. Women under National Socialism were still forced into male-conceived roles for women and although these differed somewhat from traditional roles, especially under the circumstances of war, this was scarcely a liberation which expanded personal freedom. Finally, there was no liberation in the sense of humanity since the system was eagerly creating new, and constantly elaborating old, hierarchies with – as we know – murderous consequences.

To sum up: the paradox that women are committed to chauvinist, patriarchal right-wing movements – and even experience this as emancipatory – has a lot to do with the experience of broadening the narrow female world and enriching women with meaning and self-worth. The line between public and private is redrawn, intruding into the private sphere, on the one hand, but opening it for women on the other. This is especially important for the family-oriented woman.

In contrast, the overwhelming meaning of the collectivity helps the self-oriented women to overcome the loneliness and societal disrespect for self-sufficient women. In view of 'higher' goals, she is not only allowed to give her best; rather, she is required to do so.

In any case, it is important to note that right-wing radicalism cannot solely be identified with concepts of traditionalism and female oppression. It also has its incentives and rewards for women. And it also encompasses different positions concerning gender roles. Whereas right-wing movements are often seen only in terms of gender polarisation, this is – according to my argument in the following section – mainly due to the tendency of dominant Western liberal feminism to identify liberalism with emancipation. This, in turn, obscures the extent to which this liberal type of feminism is implicated in hierarchy and inequality.

Individual Versus Relational Feminism

An example of liberal feminism is that proposed by Julia Anna (1993), who argues that different societies can be positioned on a scale from traditionalism to liberalism. At the one pole, the gender-specific division of labour is polarised whereas, at the other, gender division is weak. Annas points out that women are discriminated against in all known societies with differing gender constructions. This would certainly appear to be true. But the conclusion underlying this argument, that in liberal societies women are more equal, is not necessarily cogent. And it is certainly not true that only a feminism which strives for a liberal society is one which fights against patriarchy and for women's equality.

This is one result of the study by Karen Offen (1993), who utilises historical and comparative methods to seek an adequate definition of contemporary feminism. Offen finds that feminism, defined as the fight against male privilege and dominance as well as patriarchal ideology, is not necessarily connected with the liberal feminism which is currently predominant in Western theory. This liberal feminism is based on the idea of a gender-neutral individual which conceives of itself as independent and free to engage in whatever sort of relations it wants. Offen calls this 'individual feminism' as opposed to 'relational feminism', in which women are primarily seen in relation to others, namely their children, their husbands, their fathers and other women. The former type of feminism is an expression of the situation of non-married women which emerged in the nineteenth century, whereas the latter type is more representative of the condition of married women and mothers. In cultures and times in which women are primarily engaged in family relations, relational feminism is dominant, as was true for the first phase of feminism, particularly in continental Europe, and also for other cultures today (see also Chapter 14 of this volume).

By comparison, Offen argues that contemporary liberal feminism focuses on autonomy and the individual to the point of 'categorical absolutism'. As women's history was mainly formed by relational feminism, an individual feminist monopoly on the definition of feminism devalues large periods of history, as well as the forms of feminist activism in other countries and cultures. Feminism is not identical with liberalism and individualisation, or at least it has not been so until recently.

Individual feminism is legitimised by the argument that gender relations have always been identical with hierarchical orders. This is probably true, but it does not mean that individual feminism can be equated with equality. As the example of radical right-wing 'feminism' clearly shows, personal individualism may act as part of a larger order based on hierarchical principles. This is also true for the core concept of Western feminism – autonomy – as I will demonstrate in the example of the fight for reproductive rights.

Autonomy and Dominant Norms

One of the main issues for the new feminist movement in Western countries has been the fight for self-determination regarding pregnancy, especially in respect to abortion. This fight is directed against husbands, doctors, priests and politicians, who have the authority to decide if a woman should carry a pregnancy to term or not. The pro-choice movement opposes this authority and demands self-determination and autonomy.

A lot has changed since the beginning of these struggles in the late 1960s and early 1970s. Feminists have gained ground in many countries. At the same time, medical technology has developed enormously, with two-fold consequences: on the one hand, this technology has been intruding more and more into the female body and women's decision-making processes. On the other hand, it does offer progressively more options for women. For example, women are today able to decide what sex their child should have, whether or not they want to give birth to a disabled child, and if they want to apply for artificial insemination, which means that they can get pregnant without having to have sexual intercourse with a man. Finally, they have the chance to select from the catalogues of the sperm banks if the father of their child should be white or black, blond, blue-eyed, athletic, intelligent, a Nobel prize winner, etc.

This situation produces contradictions for women at at least two different levels:

- Women are becoming more and more the objects of a 'male' technology and at the same time the range of their options is constantly expanding.
- The increase of women's autonomy in terms of their self-determination involves them more and more in the hegemonic culture and its value system[s]. This is obvious in the choice of a child's sex resulting in feminocide, but it is also true for the question of disability.

When a pregnant women decides against bearing a potentially disabled child, she reproduces a societal value system which says that the life of a disabled person is of less worth. She also reinforces the dominant values of beauty, health and normative functioning. Finally, she supports the idea that there are easy solutions to complex problems and she releases herself and others from the responsibility of striving for a society in which disabled people have chances equal with or comparable to those of non-disabled people.

This situation is conflict-ridden for the pregnant woman. She knows that having a disabled child will most likely result in restrictions for her, because society is prone to placing all responsibility for care on the mother. She is therefore afraid of being forced to change her plans for her own life. Also, such a decision often challenges her narcissistic projections onto the child, which is expected to mirror her own desire for grandiosity, or even only for 'normality'.

Such a decision under the existing circumstances is a moral dilemma, as Laurie Shrage (1994) puts it, in which there is no proper solution. Shrage argues that there is no easy right or wrong in this case. That is why it is necessary to look at all of the different sides of the problem and to try to understand the different perspectives involved. One can only speak of a responsible decision if all of the different aspects have been taken into account. This might look different for different women. The basis for such a decision has to be what Shrage calls 'pluralistic ethics', which allow for the fact that there is no one right way for everyone and for always, but only a specific reaction to a complex situation.

Nira Yuval-Davis (1994) pursues a similar line in her argument for 'transversal politics' which reflect the different and changing standpoints of women and do not give any one woman privileged access to the truth. Neither a universalist nor a relativist view is able to deal adequately with this reality, but rather a process of dialogue which refers to different standpoints and accepts the fact of 'unfinished knowledge' (Collins 1990).

The acceptance of hegemonic norms in the cases discussed also pertains to racism, since racism always has two faces: it is concerned with discriminating against and excluding the Other, on the one hand, and with 'improving' one's own race, the 'proper' one, on the other. According to Foucault (1992), the repressive power of former societies is being replaced more and more with a normative power which trains people to reproduce hegemonic norms, namely those of health, competence and achievement.

'Biopolitics' is his term for this type of oppression, in which life is constantly being altered in order to improve, intensify and multiply it.

The feminist movements are no exception to this. The more established they become the more they mirror the dominant norms of their society. This was one result of a study conducted in Berlin last year about relationships between disabled and non-disabled women. The analysis of the feminist literature showed a very low level of awareness of this subject (Sanders 1995). Current German and Anglo-American feminist literature hardly mentions this topic and instead produces theories which reflect the vision of strong, proud, healthy women. These values are particularly noticeable in feminist utopian literature.

Theory and practice are equally problematic in this case. As the Berlin study shows, feminist projects do not employ more disabled women than other public service institutions. Although there are prescribed quotas for this in Germany, they are usually not met. The main reason that women mentioned in the interviews was that the feminist projects have to struggle so hard to survive that they cannot afford to burden themselves with even more problems. Everyone has to be well trained, highly professional and able to fight. 'We need', as one woman put it, 'absolutely professional women who are super-emancipated. We do not have a position for a doorman' (Sanders 1995 : 74). Disability for these women equals inefficiency, stupidity and backwardness. This means that feminist norms do not differ substantially from the norms of the dominant society.

The liberal male concept of autonomy is based on ownership of property, achievement and the ability to defend oneself. In this concept, the collective is threatening. Freedom then means not being limited or disturbed by others. The feminist critique of this concept has demonstrated that the implied independence is an illusion and that male self-reliance relies heavily on female support. For example, Jessica Benjamin (1990) argues that the illusion of non-attachment is nothing other than the demand for power. The attempt to deny the Other is self-destructive, in so far as it risks losing the Other, the Other which affirms the self.

In this sense, autonomy does more than merely liberate, because it also cuts off the individual from others. The more one learns to rely on oneself, the more one loses the ability to rely on others and maintain trusting and supporting relationships. One loses the ability to knit a network together, to receive support from others, and to accept and appreciate this support as well as offer it oneself. Autonomy which concentrates mainly or only on self-reliance distances and alienates individuals and devalues relationships, as well as the concern for others (Rommelspacher 1992). Feminist theory has formulated this critique, answering it with concepts like the 'self-in-relation' (Baker-Miller 1980) or 'relational autonomy' (Nedelsky 1996), but the question remains if Western ideas of emancipation really do realise these concepts and live up to their own critiques.

The debate on the male concept of liberalism and its feminist critique points to the ambivalence of autonomy, aiming on the one hand to liberate women from the oppression by others, and on the other hand running the risk of losing these others and their support. The two different types of feminist movement I discussed above exactly reflect this ambivalence. Both emphasise one important aspect of emancipation, which cannot be seen as an either/or. Since 'individual feminism' aims to gain more resources and power for the individual woman, this power will always be based on the oppression of other women and men, if a 'relational feminism' is not taken into account, one which emphasises that interpersonal relations are the basis of human life and that we have to fight for mutuality within these relations in order to fight the exploitation in them. This mutuality can only be achieved by respecting all parties involved. But, on the other hand, mutuality is often – especially in contemporary Western cultures – based on unequal access to economic and political resources. The circle is closed again.

In so far as 'individual feminism' reproduces the dominant norms and looks for benefit for individual women, necessarily at the costs of others, it might not be surprising to find this type of 'feminism' also at the radical pole of right-wing women striving for equality with men at the cost of other 'races' and 'incompetent' and 'worthless' others.

In the same way also we find elements of the feminist fight for mutuality in interpersonal relations at the radical-right political pole, when mothers are honoured and fathers are called to honour their family duties: there again, what we find is embedded in racist and elitist concepts.

Conclusions

'Individual feminism', as it is primarily represented by contemporary liberal feminism, is not the only, and not even the predominant, form of feminism. The fight against male dominance can just as easily be connected with a 'relational feminism', in which women are understood in their relation to others. But 'individual feminism' tends to equate liberalism with egalitarianism. In order to do so, it identifies 'relational feminism' with traditionalism and vice versa. Therefore, it assumes that in conservative and especially in right-wing movements one should find exclusively women interested in gender polarisation. This obviously is not the case.

We do find 'feminists' in radical right-wing movements who demand equality for women and men. Indeed even family-oriented women often feel emancipated in conservative and right-wing movements. Among other reasons this is due to the fact that they feel accepted in their role and supported as women, and the collectivity gives the impression of shelter, enhancing the worth and widening the range of contents in which women have agency.

Hence, to judge the emancipatory value of a movement exclusively by the criteria of gender difference versus equality, as the liberal discourse suggests, is to conflate two disparate issues. Rather, the need is to look at the experienced needs of women which these movements meet. These needs often seem, and are, contrary to gender equality in the liberal sense. Nevertheless, they might strengthen women in the short run, for example by giving them more importance in their community or in their family. But in right-wing movements this is always embedded in a patriarchal framework, so even if women gain some ground they do so in the context of male supremacy. In the short run they might also feel stronger in relation to their husbands, they might feel freed from traditional female constrictions by fighting for the aims of a collectivity, but they remain under a male law and gain their benefits always at the cost of others.

The problem is that this is also true for liberal Western feminism in its predominant form. The more successful it becomes, the more it is hegemonically oriented. The more women establish themselves, the more they also participate in the dominant value system, which excludes women and men from discriminated-against groups. Autonomy in the sense of self-determination always includes the determination of others. If these others belong to a discriminated-against group, the probability is high that autonomy will coincide with the oppression of others.

This means that it is no longer enough for feminists to look ahead in their fight for emancipation and to concentrate on the oppression which they are fighting. Rather, they must also look back, in order to see whom they are leaving behind. For one can only speak of feminism if it is simultaneously bound to an egalitarian concept. But what kind of feminism can truly say this about itself?

References

Anna, Julia (1993). 'Women and the Quality of Life: Two Norms or One?' in Martha C. Nussbaum and Amartya Sen (eds), *The Quality of Life,* Oxford: Clarendon Press.

Axeli-Knapp, Gudrun and Silke Wenk (1995). 'Idole, Ideale, Konflikte: Frauen in rechtsradikalen Bewegungen', in Christel Eckart *et al.* (eds) *Sackgassen der Selbstbehauptung: Feministische Analysen zu Rechtsradikalismus und Gewalt,* Kassel: Jenior & Preßler, pp. 17–56.

Baker-Miller, Jean (1980). *Die Stark Weiblicher Schwäche,* Frankfurt: Fischer.

Beauvoir, Simone de (1986). *Das andere Geschlecht: Sitte und Sexus der Frau*, Reinbek: Rowohlt.

Benjamin, Jessica (1990). *The Bonds of Love: Psychoanalysis, Feminism and the Problem of Domination*, London: Virago.

Collins, Patricia Hill (1990). *Black Feminist Thought,* London: Harper-Collins.

Elias, Norbert (1990). *Studien über die Deutschen*, Frankfurt: Suhrkamp.

Foucault, Michel (1992). 'Leben machen und sterben lassen: Die Geburt des Rassismus, Vorlesungen vom March 1976', in Sebastian Reinfeldt and Richard

Schwarz (eds), *Biomacht, Duisberg: Dissertation Text 25*, pp. 27–50.

Jung, Aanne (1997). 'Faschistische Feministinnen – ein Widerspruch?' in Renate Bitzan (ed.), *Rechte Frauen,* Berlin: Elefanten Press.

Klatch, Rebecca E. (1987). *Women of the New Right,* Philadelphia: Temple University.

Koonz, Claudia (1986). *Mothers in the Fatherland,* New York: St. Martin's Press.

Korotin, Ilse (1994). 'Die mythische Wirklichkeit eines Volkes: J. J. Bachofen, das Mutterrecht und der Nationalsozialismus', in Charlotte Kohn-Ley and Ilse Korotin (eds), *Der Feministische 'Sündenfall': Antisemitisches Vorurteile in der Frauenbewegung,* Wien: Picus, pp. 84–130.

Nedelsky, Jennifer (1996). 'Relational Autonomy: Freedom and Choice', Lecture at the Humboldt University 20 May 1996, Berlin.

Offen, Karen (1993). 'Defining Feminism: A Comparative Historical Approach', *Signs* 14: 119–57.

Prokop, Ulrike (1995). 'Elemente des weiblichen Autoritarismus: Die Sehnsucht nach der "Volksgemeinschaft" in der bürgerlichen Frauenbewegung vor 1933', in Christel Eckhart *et al.* (eds) *Sackgassen der Selbstbehauptung: Feministische Analysen zu Rechtradikalismus und Gewalt,* Kassel: Jenior & Preßler, pp. 57–74.

Rommelspacher, Birgit (1992). *Mitmenschlichkeit und Unterwerfung: Zur Ambivalenz weiblicher Moral,* Frankfurt: Campus.

Sanders, Dietke (1995). *Frauen und Behinderung. Zum Verhältnis zwischen nichtbehinderten und behinderten Frauen,* Dipl. Arbeit, Berlin: ASFH.

Sarka, Tanikar and Butalia, Urvashi (eds) (1995). *Women and Right-Wing Movements: Indian Experiences,* London: Zed Books.

Shrage, Laurie (1994). *Moral Dilemmas of Feminism,* London: Routledge.

Willems, Helmut, Stefanie Würz, and Roland Eckert (1993). *Fremdenfeindliche Gewalt: Eine Analyse von Täterstrukturen und Eskalationsprozessen,* Forschungsbericht des BMFJ, Bonn.

Yuval-Davis, Nira (1994). 'Women, Ethnicity and Empowerment', *Feminism and Psychology,* special issue on 'Shifting Identities, Shifting Racisms', 4, 1: 179–95.

CHAPTER 4

'It Works Both Ways': Belonging and Social Participation among Women with Disabilities

Judith Monks

Citizenship, Disability and Stigma

Disabled bodies cause problems for both legislature and executive in polities founded on liberal ideology. On the one hand, the state is responsible for compensating for and to an extent preventing the difficulties posed by bodily limitations. In this case competitive relations between individuals are mediated by statutory rights and obligations. On the other hand, responsibility to maintain freedom of the market demands that contract relations between individuals are free from state interference (Wright and Shore 1995: 31). The British welfare system, for example, since 1945 has adopted assumptions and practices of two forms of citizenship which are in some respects contradictory (Scott 1994: 154–5). The first is the liberal mode, which links the rights and obligations of citizenship to market relations and an obligation to work. Minimal statutory provision would be the ideal from this standpoint, together with a large contribution from voluntary organisations and private insurance. The second is the social democratic mode, which supports statutory contribution schemes in the context of public commitment to provide full employment. The contradictions become apparent at the point of contact between citizen and statutory agent where the civil implications of acts, claims and failings are realised. In the present context there is formal scrutiny of 'ability' and 'disability' with respect to rights and obligations relating to performance. An outcome of formal categorisation as 'disabled' carries not only rights to compensation but also the stigma of classification as 'different' and 'lesser'; that is, compensation is awarded on grounds which are far from neutrally valued.

The reality of stigma for those whose livelihood and social participation depend on public provision came persistently to my attention in my recent research on the meaning of personhood for people with multiple sclerosis (MS).[1] Compensation clearly entailed dilemmas relating to the propriety of some kinds of special treatment and, more fundamentally, to what special provision meant for one's value as a person. One young woman, for example, told me how she had been 'very depressed' by the speedy success of her application for Attendance Allowance.[2] She recognised that she needed help but 'in her head and in her heart', she said, she was *not* a disabled person. Another of my research participants worked for an organisation which practised positive discrimination in favour of disabled people and she was concerned about the doubt this practice threw on the capability of those singled out for special treatment. At the same time, she said, most disabled people had limited job opportunities. 'It works both ways', she reflected: compensation itself entails confirmation of reduced capacity to contribute. Below, I explore the significance of this two-way dialectic for the social participation in liberal democracies of people with long-term and potentially disabling bodily impairments. I suggest that where disability throws doubt on the generalised capacity of those affected to the extent that their moral standing as human beings is also in question, a discourse of civil rights, with its connotations of exclusive interests and identity, may be less welcome than one of inclusion, mutuality and belonging. This raises the question, as Meekosha and Dowse (1997: 65, 67) have pointed out, of what kind of civic involvement is open to people in these circumstances.

In exploring these issues, I refer especially to a self-help group of people with MS which I visited twice during my fieldwork as well as interviewing some of the members. I note the importance to the membership of their MS group identity, but as an *inclusive* symbol of their generalised sameness. I also point out how this symbolisation was gendered: disability and gender were mutually reinforcing symbolic practices of generalised social belonging. This is an aspect of group identity which is neglected in accounts of contemporary citizenship which focus rather on the exclusivity of 'communities' and the need for dialogue to explore commonalities of interests. In the public arena also, the value placed on 'collectivising' symbols (Wagner 1981: xv, 42) which categorise individuals according to ascribed characteristics, works against the full participation of those for whom a particular social identity is problematic. I suggest that the study of inclusive processes may contribute to our understanding both of resistance and of alternative forms of citizenship which provide for flexible kinds of participation.

What follows, therefore, is a discussion of one aspect of substantive citizenship (Michailakis 1997: 25, drawing on Weber; Runciman 1996: 55); that is, of the practical realisation of opportunities for and limitations of civic involvement. I begin by considering in more detail the relevance of intersubjectivity to the study of citizenship, particularly in relation to the collectivised identities which inevitably emerge in the course of civic participation. I outline two modes of intersubjectivity which Crossley (1996: 23) has called egological and radical. Egological intersubjectivity is the kind of shared understanding which interactionists claim arises from our ability to 'take' the other's point of view through an imaginative transfer of our own experience. In contrast, in the radical mode, awareness of self and other as distinct beings is dissolved in openness towards mutual purpose and understanding. I illustrate this discussion with reference both to the disabled people's movement in Britain and, more specifically, to the MS Group's concerns about their identity and their attempt at civic participation. Finally, I draw on some recent writing which has explored, on the one hand, a radical democratic citizenship and, on the other, a radical and feminist disability politics, to interpret the Group's activities as a resource for conceptualising an inclusive form of citizenship.

To frame this discussion I draw on Wagner's (1981) analysis of collectivising symbolisation – the collective identification of individuals whose autonomy and similarity, according to particular characteristics, is taken for granted. Thus people may be identified as women or disabled, or as disabled women, when sub-groups differentiate as they contribute to the group in their various ways. The process of differentiation involves another kind of symbolisation, akin to that of metaphor, which assumes a ground of similarity rather than of difference. The two kinds of symbolic practice, of identity and difference, are dialectically related, particularity thus being produced simultaneously with the collectivity (*ibid.*: xv, 42–50). In the present context, the knowledge and practices of disability as particular ways of being are simultaneously those of 'the disabled' and 'women' as structural categories. Wagner (*ibid.*: 50, 59–60, 116) suggests that in societies where symbolic practice is dominated by the naturalising categories of science, collectivising symbolisation takes precedence with little or no popular awareness of the dialectical process or of a ground of sameness against which particularity is highlighted. My own research participants, however, were all too aware of the stigmatising consequences of their collectivised difference and thus also of how this may be challenged through practices which construed them as *particular* people. That these particularising practices were necessarily the same as those which categorised them and identified their difference was a problem which, as we have already seen, opened up symbolic practice to their critical reflection. I draw on their insights further in what follows and suggest that they help us to see beyond the collectivising spatial and temporal representations of identities and interests of many current discussions of contemporary citizenship, to the dynamics of repression and resistance, as well as to the nature of the intersubjective grounding of dialogue.

Intersubjectivity and Civic Participation

The problem of welfare provision for disabled people with which I began, though simply stated, is a complex one. It glosses moral judgements about appropriate compensation, assessment and eligibility, as well as the practicalities of effective distribution. In other words, the procurement of rights as a disabled person involves both social and moral action. This dual nature of civic participation, the distributive and the moral, may be identified in contemporary writing on citizenship as relating to one or both of two dichotomies: the public *vs* private social spheres and universalistic *vs* particularistic discourses. These dichotomies, and the relationship between them, have been interpreted in slightly varying ways when used to illuminate different substantive issues and to highlight specific ways of conceptualising possibilities for civic action. Below, I discuss the public/private distinction in connection with concerns about the limits of social structure, practical politics and interests, and the universal/particular dichotomy with respect to issues of moral positioning, normative action and identity. This is to clarify how a concept of intersubjectivity is implied through both perspectives and how the conceptualisations, which are different in each case, may be understood to support each other.

Egological intersubjectivity and public and private spheres

At the heart of liberalism is the idea of society as a collectivity of individuals who relate on the basis of socially recognised rights and obligations. At the very least this philosophy requires a notion of shared understanding of what social commitment involves: of the nature of rights and obligations; of what one's rights and obligations are and of an intersubjective unity in which social expectations make sense. Thus Crossley (1996: 49–7) identifies egological intersubjectivity as a necessary ground for civic motivation and relations. He derives the notion of egological intersubjectivity ultimately from Husserl's discussion of how we know others also to be conscious beings. This, according to Husserl, is through our imaginatively transferring to others our own experience (*ibid.*: 6). In his discussion of citizenship, Crossley draws on G. H. Mead's development of this general thesis to stress that a sense of self as citizen arises, like all self-knowledge, from social experience. Through social interaction we learn not only symbols of communication but also to reflect on the point of view of individual others and on that of the 'generalised other' representing a particular group (Crossley 1996: 156–8; Mead 1962: 152–8). Notwithstanding the emphasis on the social nature of selves, however, egological intersubjectivity ultimately treats society as a network of interacting individuals, separable from and able to manipulate their social encounters (Rose 1962: 7–8, 12–15).

The resonance of egological intersubjectivity with liberalism is clear. However, the perspective carries two conceptual implications which link it with a distinction which has been commonly proposed in feminist critiques of citizenship in liberal democracies: that between public and private social spheres. The public sphere encompasses the competitive pursuit of individual interests or, alternatively, the search for common concerns among interest groups. The private sphere, often equated with the family and intimate relationships, is the arena of affect, reciprocity and of relational attributes and needs. The first implication of egological intersubjectivity for the public/private dichotomy is that of the social positioning and relationships of power which pertain between individuals or groups in pursuit of interests or in the establishment of 'common' concerns. An egological perspective would recognise not only shared understanding of rules of engagement and knowledge of others' perspectives but also misunderstandings, stigmatising values and differential resources on which participants may draw to manipulate knowledge for their own advantage. Crossley (1996: 116) considers a truly civil public sphere to be an ideal. Young (1995: 184–5) provides an empirical example of the actuality in her discussion of Jane Mansbridge's research on decision making in a New England Town Meeting. Mansbridge reported that certain people – women and black, working-class and poor people – were effectively unheard in spite of their formally equal right to participate.

This brings me to the second implication of egological intersubjectivity for a public/private distinction: the exclusion from civic participation of people recognised to have different – the 'wrong' – *kinds* of interests and abilities, or to lack those which are publicly valued. The notion of an ideal sovereign subject supports an understanding of exclusionary practices as necessary to the definition of self, or of 'we' and other. 'Second-class citizens' are those who are formally or in practice denied full public recognition by contradistinction to normatively more acceptable subjects and groups. Associated sexist and ablist practices may be embedded in social institutions, at once excluding sections of the population and facilitating their dependence, subservience or more generally their stigmatisation (Crossley 1996: 167; Vogel 1994: 76–7). Disabled people, specifically, may be rendered dependent and passive through their very contribution to a disability industry incorporating, for example, social service, planning, engineering, educational and biomedical sectors. In addition, they give sustenance to an active, charitable citizenry (Meekosha and Dowse 1997: 50, 53, 57; cf. Fagan and Lee 1997: 146). Thus the 'cared for' may be denied recognition not only through relegation to a private sphere, but also within that sphere itself.

Egological intersubjectivity relies on a notion of the fundamental distinctiveness of social actors, whether the latter are conceived of as individuals or as groups. Thus Crossley (1996: 156) identifies the egological mode as the most appropriate for thinking about dialogue between the disparate groups which in his view make up contemporary polities. That he calls such groups 'island communities' (*ibid.*: 160) underlines how egological intersubjectivity supports a spatialised conception of the public and private and of their constituent elements, albeit with an assumption of an integrated whole. For Crossley, the motivation for dialogue derives from a shared valuing of citizenship in the general sense of a participatory politics and from a practical need to deal with the distribution of resources. Thus group representatives do not need to like or understand each other but they do need to 'take the citizen role' in Meadian terms and to recognise others' ability to do likewise (*ibid.*: 158, 162). Even the precise meaning of citizenship need not be shared. Debates on the issue will keep alive the relevance of the symbol and, together with regular opportunities for practical civic involvement, sustain the 'artificial community'[3] which is the public site of inter-group dialogue and decision. Crossley admits to the ideal nature of the scenario he is depicting here, acknowledging that even the intersubjective valuing of the citizen role cannot eliminate asymmetries of power and influence (*ibid.*: 161).

Other scholars have been more specifically concerned than Crossley with the position of historically oppressed groups, especially women but also disabled people as well as others. The seminal work of both Phillips (1993) and Young (1995), for example, recognises asymmetric group difference as fundamental to contemporary pluralism. Group membership, they argue, is increasingly defined in opposition to 'other' groups, often drawing on shared experience of domination. This has the dual effect of producing stigmatised identities and of reducing possibilities, as well as the motivation of dominated groups for mutual understanding and compromise. There are differences in the detail of their programmes, but both Phillips and Young emphasise the central role of practical dialogue itself in determining outcome. They attribute motivation for dialogue, as does Crossley, to a perceived need for policy decisions. However, they understand the guiding principle of dialogue to be the recognition, if not celebration, of difference itself. For Phillips and Young, 'difference' grounds dialogue although, as Phillips (1993: 161) argues, particular differences will be in flux and dialogue will stretch and realign solidarities. For this to occur, however, the relative strength of marginalised groups must be protected. Otherwise members will see little virtue in shifting their own position (Phillips 1993: 158; Young 1995: 191).

Implicit in the work of Phillips and Young is an assumption of the possibility of mutual respect and cooperation. Also implied is a shared understanding of ground rules for the procedure of dialogue itself. Similarly, Yuval-Davis (1997: 19) suggests that the common knowledge produced through what she calls 'transversal dialogue' is sustained by the compatibility of the values of participating groups. All these frameworks for pluralist politics are radical compared with that of Crossley: they recognise difference as the guiding principle of dialogue and emphasise praxis and shifting alliances. Furthermore, something beyond a common commitment to policy making is seen to be driving this process. There is the production of difference and solidarity themselves. There are more radical accounts yet, but before introducing these I must outline an alternative, radical mode of intersubjectivity, identified by Crossley as fundamental to the egological mode but not developed by him in relation to citizenship. This articulates especially with debates about universality and particularity in that it provides for an understanding of difference as grounded ultimately in a mutual differentiation of self and other, and hence in an appreciation of social inclusion and exclusion as moral discourse and practice.

Radical intersubjectivity and universalistic and particularistic discourses

We have seen how groups which comprise the contemporary pluralist order may be conceptualised without recourse to universalistic notions of citizenship. This not only takes account of empirical divergences in meanings attributed to citizenship but also avoids the normative and hence socially exclusive tendencies of universal standards in general. In other words, exclusion from full substantive citizenship may concern more than denial of access to significant social relations and an equitable share of resources, important though these matters are. It will also involve moral judgements about social acceptability. This is implied in the relational definition of second-class citizen which I noted above. Significantly, Yuval-Davis (1997: 17) refers to such people as 'moral aliens'. Universalising moral discourses create alien categories, the members of which are often in some way socially controlled and dependent. Vogel (1994: 77, drawing on Pateman) provides a detailed discussion of this general idea with respect to conceptualisations of the private sphere of marriage and the associated subservient role of women. She argues that historically it was through marriage that women *became part of* the public domain, albeit in a subordinate position. Vogel's achievement is to show the interdependence of social and moral discourses of citizenship and gender, as well as the power of cultural practice to limit the actual participation of people with formal citizen status. I return to her work later.

People who are socially excluded or oppressed, and who are often also defined as lacking qualities of a normative social being, may find solidarity in the shared experience of exclusion itself (Phillips 1993: 17, 145; Young 1995: 186). The 'communities' which emerge may become politically active, being potential contributors to the dialogic process discussed above. Experience of the interdependence, mutuality and solidarity which arise from shared activities and communication is an important part of membership, even of direct political action (see, for example, Bristo 1995: 100–2). It is in connection with social solidarity that radical intersubjectivity is most obviously relevant to issues of pluralism and civic involvement. After outlining the basic premises of radical intersubjectivity, I will return to the radical tendencies in conceptualisations of pluralist politics by Phillips, Young and others to discuss its relevance for the participation of people whose social identity is stigmatised and in itself a barrier to full participation.

The 'radical' quality of radical intersubjectivity lies in the associated communion of face-to-face situations and in the notion that mutuality of being is prior to all reflective awareness of self and other. This gives a fundamental symmetry to social interaction, though one pregnant with possibilities for dominance through forms of objectification (Crossley 1996: 13). The existentialist philosopher Merleau-Ponty is perhaps the most cited exponent of radical intersubjectivity. His major work, *Phenomenology of Perception* (1962), develops his ideas as a critique of the perceptual process assumed in empiricist accounts of scientific knowledge. For Merleau-Ponty, our perception of material objects does not occur by means of discrete stimuli which are interpreted by our brains. Rather, he argues, we disengage from objects through apprehending their particular qualities, at the same time becoming aware of our own sensual and material integrity (1962: 302–4, 314–21). Where the apprehended other is a human being, this disengagement involves recognising our own part in gesture–response reciprocity (1962: 351–5). In his essay, 'The Child's Relations with Others', Merleau-Ponty makes an unusually succinct reference to this process:

> In perceiving the other, my body and his are coupled, resulting in a sort of action which pairs them.... Reciprocally I know that the gestures I make myself can be the objects of another's intention. It is this transfer of my intentions to the other's body and of his intentions to my own, my alienation of the other and his alienation of me, that makes possible the perception of others. (Merleau-Ponty 1964a: 118)

This differs from Mead's account in that our knowledge of others does not involve an imaginative (egological) leap from our own into their own conscious awareness. Instead, Merleau-Ponty suggests that one's very awareness of one's own consciousness depends on a pre-reflective awareness of mutuality.

Crossley presents Mead's and Merleau-Ponty's accounts of intersubjectivity as complementary in two major ways. First, he looks to Mead for a broader sociological perspective for Merleau-Ponty's phenomenology. He suggests that Mead offers a perspective on self-awareness in the context of community, through his ideas of role-taking and of the generalised other. For Mead, selfhood and citizenship coincide (Crossley 1996: 65, 157). Merleau-Ponty, on the other hand, barely examines the nature and sustenance of the subjective bonds which unite people through space and time (Langer 1989: 160). As Langer (*ibid.*: 160–7, 174) points out, *Phenomenology of Perception* was a preliminary working of ideas which were developed in later writings with respect to an ontology of meaning. It was not a sociological project.[4] Second, and drawing also on Buber, Crossley proposes that we shift back and forth between egological and radical intersubjectivities in social practice, sometimes 'deeply engrossed with others', then 'stultified by a reflective block, only to be undermined later by a genuine spontaneous communication which collapses the reflective barriers of self and other' (Crossley 1996: 71). While Crossley stresses that the radical mode is foundational to these reflective episodes, in that people remain aware of and responsive to others at a pre-reflective level (*ibid.*: 32, 71), he privileges the egological notion of individuals with their own place in space and time. This emphasis supports his conception of isolated times of engrossment and of reflection. We may push the implications of radical intersubjectivity further, in a way which offers some insight into processes of inclusion and exclusion in civil society.

Merleau-Ponty's phenomenology provides a radical account of the nature of social relationships which dissolves any primordial space between subjectivities. Instead, it posits a continuous dialectic of communion and difference. Perception of time and space, from this perspective, is also a matter of differentiation: times and spaces exist because we mark them out, one against the other. This means we may interpret Merleau-Ponty's reference to the 'pre-reflective' in its constitutive sense: the tension between pre-reflective and reflective modes of intersubjectivity is constitutive of all social practice. While this insight does not explain a sense of belonging to a widely dispersed social group, it does suggest how dialogue between members of different groups may be inherently inclusive. Indeed, part of the achievement of Merleau-Ponty's critique of objective rationality was to provide a philosophical basis for a morality grounded in the dual perception of self and other:

> the perception of the other founds morality by realizing the paradox of an *alter ego*, of a common situation, by placing my perspectives and my incommunicable solitude in the visual field of another and of all others. Here as everywhere else the primacy of perception – the realization at the very heart of our most personal experience, of a fecund contradiction which submits this experience to the regard of others – is the remedy to skepticism and pessimism. (Merleau-Ponty 1964b: 26)

This provides for what Langer has called a 'basic harmony' in dialogue and makes conflict contingent and open to critique (Langer 1989: 153–4). It is a view which grounds identity and difference in dialogue itself.

Radical intersubjectivity and citizenship

We may now appreciate how a radical perspective on intersubjectivity may help to develop the feminist critiques of citizenship which I introduced earlier. These critiques propose that participants in dialogue may find common ground because of their commitment to, and cultural understanding of the process of dialogue itself. They also propose that at the same time as participants clarify their commonality, they reciprocally confirm their difference. In other words, they recognise dialogue as symbolic practice through which collectivities are simultaneously produced and differentiated. The concern of writers such as Phillips, Young and Yuval-Davis is with the possibility of common understanding in pluralist society. 'Difference' is their starting (and finishing) point, while their attention focuses on how commonality may be achieved. The acknowledged dialectical quality of dialogue, and the mutual understandings which ground it, receive less attention. Returning first to Vogel's work, I suggest how these critiques may be sharpened using the insights of Merleau-Ponty. I also draw on my earlier introduction to Wagner's work on symbolisation and show how this helps to take the implications of radical intersubjectivity beyond those for face-to-face interaction.

With respect to women's civic participation and following Vogel (1994), we may say that there are no 'gender neutral spaces' (*ibid.*: 86) of citizenship through which women might begin to achieve equal involvement. This is because the very institutions of citizenship, as well as the concept of the private individual, were founded on a gender distinction which assigned women a 'proper' place and mode of conduct. In most democracies women are now formally full citizens. In practice, however, there are still relatively few women in spheres of significant social and political influence. Vogel (*ibid.*: 83–5), drawing on contradictions in Tocqueville's work, attributes this to the simultaneous production of social and moral distinctions. Her own perspective collapses spatial and temporal distinctions between public and private: women in the public sphere are vulnerable to definition as out of place, for example, or to finding themselves in 'feminine' occupations. Vogel's programme is to encourage a pluralist rather than hierarchical structure which recognises the social (not biological) particularity of women. She aligns herself in this with Iris Young (1995: 87) although her work implies an account of the current situation which contrasts with that of Young, at least in relation to gender and citizenship. We may see her perspective on the differentiation of genders as analogous to Merleau-Ponty's account of the constitution of self and other. My phenomenological reading of Vogel (1994) is as follows: if collectivities of women and men in any way constitute pluralist society, then this is not as 'island communities' but as identities which are continuously and ubiquitously produced. In addition, these identities are both moral and social, being constituted through different though mutually dependent kinds of symbolic practice, in which the social structural identity predominates in public discourse over the moral. Implicit cultural beliefs and practices relating to gender constitute men and women as particular kinds of fundamentally similar social beings. At the same time, the social differentiation of men and women reinforces the collectivising symbols of masculinity and femininity which define gender categories as fundamentally distinct.

The principle of radical intersubjectivity is that of differentiation from a pre-reflective mutuality. The process of differentiation is embodied rather than intellectual; that is, the experience of difference is primarily through that of agency and resistance. This process is not open to our reflective awareness; we cannot experience ourselves experiencing. At best, we may gain insight through the paradox of the attempt itself (Langer 1989: 165–6). We are aided, however, by the critical awareness of people who have experienced contradictions in their daily practice. Women are well represented here, as we have seen. As women differentiate from men, they may experience aspects of their identity which do not resonate with their experiences with other women, for example, or with formal discourses on citizenship rights, equal opportunities and so on. This may lead them to question the assumptions of collectivising representations of genders or citizens and to ponder on their sustenance and possible resistance. Such reflections, and especially the subversive practices to which they give rise, provide some insight into the kinds of embodied cultural practices which ground the gendering of public and private social life. I shall suggest that the experience of people who, in a similar process of differentiation, are identified as 'disabled' may in the same way help us to conceptualise practices and assumptions to do with fundamental social acceptability and competence. It is these qualities of personhood which give participants in dialogue a basic common ground while, simultaneously and paradoxically, construing disabled participants as incapable (cf. Crossley 1996: 158).

The position of people whose social identity is both 'woman' and 'disabled' is instructive. The former identity, through illuminating particularly relationships between public and private social spheres, illustrates how we may think of the pursuit of interests by individuals and groups differentially located with respect to social and material resources. A disabled identity encourages us to consider how social distinctions are moralising discourses in which particular individuals and groups may be rendered less acceptable with respect to shared values. In public discourse, both identities relate to collectivised categories with connotations of social exclusion. However, disabled women are necessarily realised in social engagement. This contradiction means that reflections on and by disabled women, and disabled women's treatment in the public sphere, are resources for understanding how collectivised identities and interests necessarily imply possibilities for a generally shared identity and purpose, albeit with particular emphases. Two examples will help to clarify this.

The first example[5] is that of the emergence of a category of 'disabled women' within the British disabled people's movement and the way disabled women's particular experience has been conceptualised by disabled feminist writers and by other disabled scholars. The emergence of gender as an issue was part of a wider tendency within the disability movement for members to unite around 'experience' which they shared with members of other movements or organisations, for example those for people with particular sexuality as well as women. In the 1980s, the 'social model of disability' had provided a focus for the movement, through its definition of disability as a singular experience of a particular kind of social oppression (Oliver 1990). With the increasing opportunities for social contact between disabled people, both formal and informal, the notion of singularity could not be sustained. By the early 1990s there was undeniable differentiation of the movement motivated by claims of *particular* experience of disablement. A current major dilemma for the movement, then, lies in the membership's recognition of peculiarities of experience being coupled with a commitment to collective political action.

A similar tension between particular and collective has arisen for disabled women in their relationship with both the disability and feminist movements. They have challenged, for example, the neglect of gendered stereotypes of disabled people by the mainstream disability movement (Lonsdale 1990: 64–

83; Morris 1991: 96–101 and, for a North American context, see Asch and Fine 1997: 241–50 and Thomson 1997: 228) and the social exclusionary meanings of choice and rights embedded in campaigns, by non-disabled feminists, related to abortion and informal care (Keith 1992; Lonsdale 1990: 160–1; Morris 1991: 64–83, 146–68; Thomson 1997: 284–6). However, disabled feminists have not argued for their severance from the mainstream movements. Neither have they always supported the mainstream goals of personal empowerment and independence, pointing out that these are unrealistic for many disabled women. They present their particularity as relative, not absolute, drawing on a relational view of society which their impairment facilitates.

We may draw on Wagner's analysis of symbolic practice to contextualise disabled feminists' insights with respect to the fundamental common identity from which differentiation arises. Wagner's (1981: 31) general thesis is that where there is cultural emphasis on collectivising symbolic practice, this produces incessant fragmentation and multiplication of particular minority demands. He also points out, however, that this mode of thought and practice obscures how fragmentation involves only a *partial* differentiation from a cultural ideal. Thus, he says, we 'invent' our non-conventionality dialectically as we become aware of our social limitations (*ibid.*: 47, 116–17, 125). For Westerners, the demands of rationality inhibit celebration of this aspect of our identity. Thus, when we organise as women, disabled people or as citizens, for example, we tend to be conscious of our collective sameness and attribute factional tendencies to 'natural' personal or biographical differences. We may come to recognise these attributes as symbols of smaller collectivities, which may themselves fragment in turn. The moral project of the early disabled feminists, to counter the exclusionary tendencies of both mainstream feminist and disability movements, gave them a sensitivity to the reciprocal, inherently inclusive aspects of particularity. Their voices, however, are becoming submerged in a growing disability literature which interprets collective action in terms of personal empowerment, consumerism and choice of partial identity (Shakespeare 1996; Findlay 1995: 132–3; Hasler 1993: 282–4). The notion of *personal* experience itself is emerging as a new collectivising symbol.

My second example comes from the self-help group for people with MS which I introduced earlier. For members of the Group, all women, the significance of their diagnosis and disability lay in the doubt these threw on their potential as acceptable and adequate members of society. Like other participants in my research, they had become unusually aware of the values which underpinned daily practice and of how their 'difference' both bounced off cultural ideals and reinforced their collective identity: their very participation paradoxically confirmed and categorised their incompetence. Thus the members consciously strove to emphasise their particularity as disabled women, not in order to claim their collective difference as particular women nor as particular disabled people, but to confirm their belonging to a wider moral community of particularly gendered and embodied persons. I saw this, for example, in the value they placed on the social contact the Group provided. Socialising with people with MS was important to almost all of my research participants. This was because participants believed themselves to have a basic common bodily experience.[6] Within the Group, members explored this commonality and sought others who reflected their own particularity. They would, for example, discuss their symptoms in the context of gendered bodily experience, for example of the menopause. They also debated the merits of different ways of living with MS and did so in my presence in relation to the different circumstances of women and men. *Being* a person with MS through these conversations socialised bodily feelings and linked them with a meaningful biography. It meant a way of being like *everyone* else.

For Group members, 'women' and 'people with MS' were inclusive categories. From their perspective, citizenship was also inclusive, in that both civic action and compensation for disability should recognise a person's fundamental sociality. Thus when a local advisory body on disability invited the Group to submit a statement about members' needs, together with information which might be useful to others with MS, the members provided what they called 'local information', of use to disabled people in general and perhaps to others with specific problems who lived and worked in the surrounding area. However, this seemed not to have been acceptable because it was not presented in terms of 'disability issues' – 'access', for example. Group members seemed to lack interest in this kind of generalised definition of their needs. 'We are all individuals', they told me; that is, they had specific personal problems which they could solve using their own resources.

The problem of the approach used by the Disability Forum was that compensation for disability would involve a 'disabled' social identity. Disabled in this sense was a collectivised category which distinguished disabled people from service providers and from people in other social categories. In contrast, for the MS Group members, 'disabled', 'MS' or 'woman' were metaphors for the particularity of lives. For them, the Group was not an island community in a society of communities or categories, with specific characteristics and associated claims on resources. Rather, through *being* disabled women or women with MS, Group members recognised themselves as an integral part of a relational whole, not just the Group itself but the local community. Their limited attempt at civic involvement on this basis was not successful and their perspective is, on the face of it, incompatible with the pluralist politics in which others were engaged. In this way, the Group's experience indicates some important concerns which a radical and inclusive citizenship would need to embrace.

Towards a Conceptualisation of an Inclusive Citizenship

Disability and womanhood in liberal democracies are both contradictory experiences. Both encourage reflection on the processes of social identity and, especially in the case of disability, on sociality itself. Disabled women are particularly well placed, therefore, to reflect on the duality of social reality; on how the differentiating practices through which we sense ourselves and our belonging necessarily realise characteristics which may ground our social and moral difference. 'It works both ways' is something which may be said of all social life. The insights of disabled women may help to develop a critique of democratic citizenship which goes further than the current focus on pluralism and a search for commonality through dialogue. Women with disabilities, like disabled people in general, are not adequately conceptualised simply as another interest or identity group. The cultural devaluing of disability makes their social identity something they may wish to resist, as well as throwing into relief the interdependence of civic and moral concerns in social participation. I shall discuss how we may theorise disabled women's experience in relation to two issues concerning pluralist politics. The first has to do with the nature of the constituent alliances: that 'groups' may be politically motivated from without and that we should therefore not take them for granted. The second issue relates to the nature and motivation of dialogue: that there are intersubjective aspects of dialogue which relate to the basic processes of human sociality and which may provide a starting point for a conceptualisation of civic participation which is inherently inclusive. Both these issues concern resistance to the privileging of collectivising over particularising practices.

We have seen how feminist writers on citizenship have helped to theorise the constitution and relationship of social groups and movements. However, they have neglected the analytic possibilities of a radical view of intersubjectivity and a fully relational perspective on society. Thus they have tended to conceptualise groups as discrete communities, albeit often with reciprocal identities, which refine their commonality and difference when they come together in dialogue. I noted especially the more radical approach of Ursula Vogel who argues that the production of identity is an ubiquitous and continuous process and one in which, at least in the case of gender, social categorisations obscure moral judgements. Nevertheless, Vogel is committed to a similar kind of pluralism to that of her less radical contemporaries. Women's citizenship, she suggests, 'would evolve from praxis, from the self-organisation of women and from the dialogue between autonomous groups' (Vogel 1994: 87). The more radical aspects of Vogel's work resonate with ideas of contemporary scholars who try to define a radical democratic citizenship. I draw on Mouffe and McClure to provide a link between radical notions of citizenship and recent phenomenological and postmodernist analyses of gender and disability. Together this work begins to provide a framework for civic participation which would take account of the kind of moral concerns show by the women of the MS self-help group.

Mouffe's (1992a: 2–3) project is to define a conceptual framework for what she calls a radical plural democracy; that is, a democracy which incorporates liberalism in a way which values civic participation. In this context, citizenship is not a legal status but a commitment to principles, variously interpreted and contested, of freedom and equality for all (Mouffe 1992b: 231, 235). Mouffe's formulation of pluralism differs from those I outlined earlier in how these shared principles are said to relate to individual and group identities and to dialogue. Briefly, Mouffe (*ibid.*: 236–7) argues that shared identity as radical democratic citizens is a fundamental requirement for successful dialogue and that it arises from common experience of the ubiquitous tension between individual freedom and the demands of civility. In other words, people gain multiple individual identities of gender, ethnicity and so on, through action framed by 'a dialectic of subversion and over-determination' (Mouffe 1992a: 11). This experience may be brought to dialogue, where a similar tension is relevant between group and collective interests. Thus Mouffe suggests that dialogue is concerned not so much with a search for commonality, as with enactments of citizenship in attempts to resolve this tension.

McClure (1992) explores in more detail the nature of political agency within the general context outlined by Mouffe. She does this in a way which helps us to interpret the political significance of, for example, the MS Group members' resistance to a disabled social identity. Of especial interest, from our point of view, is her discussion of the formation of multiple identities and of how these may challenge the notion of a unitary citizen-subject who would recognise state institutions as the proper site of political struggle (McClure 1992: 121–5). McClure, drawing on De Lauretis, sees individual identities as socially and historically situated and as defined relatively, one to another. She suggests that as we enact particular identities we may introduce variations through our other affinities. Our non-conventional performances are challenges to cultural codes, often with political import. For example, the gendering of the 'differently abled', as McClure calls them, may affect their claims in connection with needs and rights, as well as their critique of cultural representations and practices encountered in the course of daily life. These claims are ubiquitous and may be shared among those in similar social positions or made to the 'others' against whom the claims themselves are directed. For Mouffe, they constitute the genesis of the experience and practice of political agency. In other words, members of contemporary democracies are coming to recognise the origins of their political agency neither in exclusive group affinities nor inter-group dialogue, but in the multiple sites of everyday social practice (McClure: 123–4).

In both Mouffe's and McClure's accounts, the intersubjective process is one of the production of political agency through that of relational differences. The significant differences may be between individual freedom and conventional civility or between claims about one's own identity and social representations. As in Wagner's account of social differentiation, the primary experience of agency and identity is seen as a dialectic of social practice. Now, however, we may see the dialectic in the context of civic participation. In this way, Mouffe and McClure help to theorise the MS Group women's sense of subjection *vis-à-vis* the advisory body and to legitimise their practice as a form of political resistance. Questions remain, however, as to how we might think about the sustenance and effectiveness of this kind of practical, disparate resistance in a cultural and political context where a collectivising discourse predominates.

According to the members of the MS Group, their efforts to improve facilities for disabled people in their locality had little effect. I cannot comment from the perspective of the service providers, nor from that of the advisory body, but certainly members themselves felt their contributions were ultimately ignored. The Group had not entered into prolonged dialogue. Members' major concern was not with the specifics of local provision but with their own social legitimacy. From this point of view, the terms on offer for dialogue were inappropriate. We may see this most clearly in the case of the Group's relationship with the advisory body, in which the relationship itself identified members in a way they found unacceptable. Members resisted the exclusivity of the category 'disabled'.

A radical disability politics, now being developed by disabled academics, also questions the exclusivity of the identity politics which has developed in the wake of the social model. This work attempts to deconstruct the concepts of disability and impairment and draws on postmodernist and phenomenological perspectives. One example, which is also feminist in its approach, is the study by Shildrick and Price (1996)[7] of embodied resistance to the collectivised categories and individuation inherent in the assessment for Disability Living Allowance. The authors view such welfare procedures as disciplinary processes, in the Foucaultian sense, which rigidly control the representation of applicants' bodies and behaviour and draw applicants into associated practices of self-surveillance (*ibid.*: 100–4). Shildrick and Price argue, however, that the body's inability to conform provides a continuous source of resistance. This is resistance not only to a unitary disabled identity but also to the gendering of this identity through implicit reference in the assessment to a notion of the healthy male body. Thus, they conclude, a radical politics of disability 'might disrupt the compulsory character of the norms of abled and disabled, not by pluralising the conditions of disability [...] but rather by exposing the failure of those norms to ever fully contain or express their ideal standards' (*ibid.*: 106–7). Bodily practice, then, is a persistent irritant to modernist categories, whether manifest in assessment questionnaires, 'disability issues' or even in the built environment (see Butler and Bowlby 1997).

These explorations of radical citizenship and disability politics provide an understanding of acts of identification as primarily bodily practices which are conditioned by the experience of multiple affinities. Drawing also on my earlier discussion of intersubjectivity and symbolic practice, we may see each act as potentially exclusive or inclusive, either result being necessarily vulnerable to resistance from the other. I have tried to show how the persistent challenges inherent in this process are especially noticeable to people commonly identified as disabled. I have also suggested how disabled people may facilitate challenge by promoting inclusive meanings relating to the particularity of biography. The ubiquity of this process means we must look to the everyday experiences of the socially marginalised to find a vision of what, for them, would be an appropriate citizenship. We need to explore not only the discursive contexts of subjection and resistance but also, and more urgently because they have been neglected, situations where participants sense respect for their social and personal legitimacy. In my own research, participants told me how they would, sometimes successfully, turn around formal situations involving exclusive identification, to produce mutual involvement and outcomes which recognised their particularity and personal agency. One young woman, for example, described her medical assessment for Mobility Allowance[8] as a mutual, though covert, process in which the 'questions on the paper' were somewhat creatively interpreted to her advantage. Similarly, in a political context, the Executive Director of the Spinal Injuries Association, Stephen Bradshaw, has achieved results through appeal to a mutual sense of the ridiculous; by 'exposing how silly something is' (*Disability Now* 1994: 13). Yet another pointer may be found in persistent references in the disability press to the issue of access to polling booths (see, for example, the correspondence in *Disability Now* 1997a, b, c). A postal vote, as an exclusive option, is commonly viewed as an inadequate and inappropriate expression of civic participation.

All these examples draw attention to the meaning of practice: how practice provides opportunities for the expression of inclusivity, even in institutionalised or political contexts. An appropriate citizenship would realise participants' social membership both formally *and* through practice. It would be a reflexive citizenship because practice refers here, not only to procedure but also to *how* procedures are carried out and to the multiple sites in which civic participation may be pursued. Citizenship, then, is a quality of participation just as much as a formal status. Failure to recognise this is to exclude those who question their dominant social identities as appropriate reflections of their personhood.

Notes

1. This research was carried out for a doctoral thesis (Monks 1996). The fieldwork was conducted principally in north and west London and comprised in-depth

interviews with 21 people with MS. These data were complemented through the use of documents, observation and media presentations.

2. Attendance Allowance was introduced in 1970 and was intended for people who required long-term personal care. Eligibility was on the basis of a medical report by a doctor appointed by the Department of Social Security, the final decision being made by the Attendance Allowance Board (Barnes 1991: 107, 110–13). In 1993 the Attendance Allowance was replaced, for people under 65 years of age, by the Disability Living Allowance.

3. Crossley (1996: 161) draws here on Passerin d'Entrèves (1992).

4. In the final chapter on 'Freedom', Merleau-Ponty widened the relevance of his phenomenology to discussions of class, collective identity and action. His account of mutuality in this context is undeveloped in that it does not deal with the mediation between subjects through visual or oral representations. See Csordas (1990) for the use of Bourdieu's notion of *habitus* as a complement to the phenomenology of Merleau-Ponty, where the history of social institutions is of concern. I have referred rather to Wagner because of the comparative cultural perspective he brings to a discussion of the differentiation of social institutions and because of the way he links this process with one of perception of agency (difference) and convention (sameness) as a continuous dialectic of social practice.

5. Additional sources for the early history of the disability movement were Barnes (1991: 217–25), Davis (1993), Findlay (1995), Lonsdale (1990: 156–62) and Oliver (1996: 113–8).

6. That this was in spite of acknowledged variability in the manifestations of MS indicates the power of medical diagnosis as a collectivising symbol.

7. See also the first chapter in Shildrick (1997).

8. Mobility Allowance, as it was during the fieldwork, is officially explained in leaflet NI211 (April 1992), prepared by the Department of Social Security. The following is a brief description of the allowance taken from the *Directory for Disabled People*, published in association with the Royal Association for Disability and Rehabilitation: 'Mobility Allowance is a tax free, non-contributory and non-means-tested benefit for which application may be made by people aged 5–65 years. ... To qualify, the person must be unable or virtually unable to walk through limitations relating to distance, speed, time or the health consequencies of the exertion required.' In addition this state of affairs must be likely to last for at least one year and be incapable of elimination by the use of a walking aid (Darnbrough and Kinrade 1998: 26–7).

References

Asch, A., and M. Fine (1997). 'Nurturance, Sexuality and Women with Disabilities: the Example of Women and Literature', in L. J. Davis (ed.) *The Disability Studies Reader*, London: Routledge, pp. 241–59.

Barnes, C. (1991). *Disabled People in Britain and Discrimination: A Case for Anti-Discrimination Legislation*, London: C. Hurst in association with the British Council of Organisations of Disabled People.

Bristo, M. (1995). 'Lessons from the Americans with Disabilities Act', in G. Zarb (ed.) *Removing Disabling Barriers*, London: Policy Studies Institute, pp. 96–107.

Butler, R. and S. Bowlby (1997). 'Bodies and Spaces: an Exploration of Disabled

People's Experiences of Public Space', *Environment and Planning D: Society and Space* 15, 4: 411–33.

Crossley, N. (1996). *Intersubjectivity: the Fabric of Social Becoming,* London: Sage.

Csordas, T. J. (1990). 'Embodiment as a Paradigm for Anthropology', *Ethos* 18: 5–47.

Darnbrough, A. and D. Kinrade (1988). *Directory for Disabled People,* 5th edition, London: Woodhead-Faulkner in association with the Royal Association for Disability and Rehabilitation.

Davis, K. (1993). 'On the Movement', in J. Swain, V. Finkelstein, S. French and M. Oliver (eds) *Disabling Barriers – Enabling Environments*, London: Sage, pp. 285–92.

Disability Now (1994). 'Scourge From the Laurels: Profile on Stephen Bradshaw', 13 August.

— (1997a). 'Letters to the Editor', 16 August.

— (1997b). 'Letters to the Editor', 16 October

— (1997c). 'Letters to the Editor', 16 November.

Fagan, T. and P. Lee (1997). 'The "New" Social Movements and Social Policy: a Case Study of the Disability Movement', in M. Lavalette and A. Pratt (eds), *Social Policy: a Conceptual and Theoretical Framework*, London: Sage, pp. 140–60.

Findlay, B. (1995). 'From Charity to Rights: a Disabled Person's Journey', in G. Zarb (ed.) *Removing Disabling Barriers*, London: Policy Studies Institute, pp. 131–6.

Hasler, F. (1993). 'Developments in the Disabled People's Movement', in J. Swain, V. Finkelstein, S. French and M. Oliver (eds) *Disabling Barriers – Enabling Environments*, London: Sage, pp. 278–84.

Keith, L. (1992). 'Who Cares Wins? Women, Caring and Disability', *Disability, Handicap and Society* 7, 2: 167–75.

Langer, M. M. (1989). *Merleau-Ponty's 'Phenomenology of Perception': a Guide and Commentary*, Basingstoke: Macmillan.

Lonsdale, S. (1990). *Women and Disability: the Experience of Physical Disability among Women,* London: Macmillan.

McClure, K. (1992). 'On the Subject of Rights: Pluralism, Plurality and Political Identity', in C. Mouffe (ed.) *Dimensions of Radical Democracy: Pluralism, Citizenship and Community*, London: Verso, pp. 108–27.

Mead, G. H. (1962). [1934] *Mind, Self, and Society*, edited with an introduction by C. W. Morris, Chicago: University of Chicago Press.

Meekosha, H. and L. Dowse (1997). 'Enabling Citizenship: Gender, Disability and Citizenship in Australia', *Feminist Review*, 57: 49–72.

Merleau-Ponty, M. (1962). *Phenomenology of Perception*, translated from the French by C. Smith, London: Routledge and Kegan Paul.

— (1964a). 'The Child's Relations with Others', in M. Merleau-Ponty, *The Primacy of Perception and Other Essays*, edited with an introduction by J. M. Edie, Evanston, IL: Northwestern University Press, pp. 96–155.

— (1964b). 'The Primacy of Perception and Its Philosophical Consequences', in M. Merleau-Ponty, *The Primacy of Perception and Other Essays*, edited with an introduction by J. M. Edie, Evanston IL: Northwestern University Press, pp. 12–42.

Michailakis, D. (1997). 'When Opportunity Is the Thing to be Equalised', *Disability and Society* 12, 1: 17–30.

Monks, J. A. (1996). 'Describing Sickness: Talk, Social Relations and Personhood Following a Diagnosis of Multiple Sclerosis', PhD thesis, Department of Human

Sciences, Brunel University, UK.

Morris, J. (1991). *Pride against Prejudice: Transforming Attitudes to Disability*, London: Women's Press.

Mouffe, C. (1992a). 'Democratic Politics Today', in C. Mouffe (ed.) *Dimensions of Radical Democracy: Pluralism, Citizenship, Community*, London: Verso, pp. 1–14.

— (1992b). 'Democratic Citizenship and the Political Community', in C. Mouffe (ed.) *Dimensions of Radical Democracy: Pluralism, Citizenship and Community*, London: Verso, pp. 225–39.

Oliver, M. (1990). *The Politics of Disablement*, Basingstoke: Macmillan.

— (1996). 'Defining Impairment and Disability: Issues at Stake', in C. Barnes and G. Mercer (eds) *Exploring the Divide: Illness and Disability*, Leeds: Disability Press, pp. 39–54.

Passerin d'Entrèves, M. (1992). 'Hannah Arendt and the Idea of Citizenship', in C. Mouffe (ed.) *Dimensions of Radical Democracy: Pluralism, Citizenship and Community*, London: Verso, pp. 145–68.

Phillips, A. (1993). *Democracy and Difference*, Cambridge: Polity.

Rose, A. M. (1962). 'A Systematic Summary of Symbolic Interaction Theory', in A. M. Rose (ed.) *Human Behaviour and Social Processes: an Interactionist Approach*, London: Routledge and Kegan Paul, pp. 3–19.

Runciman, W. G. (1996). 'Why Social Inequalities Are Generated by Social Rights', in M. Bulmer and A. M. Rees (eds) *Citizenship Today: The Contemporary Relevance of T. H. Marshall*, London: UCL Press, pp. 49–63.

Scott, J. (1994). *Poverty and Wealth: Citizenship, Deprivation and Privilege*, London: Longman.

Shakespeare, T. (1996). 'Disability, Identity and Difference', in C. Barnes and G. Mercer (eds) *Exploring the Divide: Illness and Disability*, Leeds: Disability Press, pp. 94–113.

Shildrick, M. (1997). *Leaky Bodies and Boundaries: Feminism, Postmodernism and (Bio)Ethics*, London: Routledge.

Shildrick, M. and J. Price (1996). 'Breaking the Boundaries of the Broken Body', *Body and Society* 2, 4: 93–113.

Thomson, R. G. (1997). 'Feminist Theory, the Body, and the Disabled Figure', in L. J. Davis (ed.) *The Disability Studies Reader*, London: Routledge, pp. 279–92.

Vogel, U. (1994). 'Marriage and the Boundaries of Citizenship', in B. van Steenbergen (ed.) *The Condition of Citizenship*, London: Sage, pp. 76–89.

Wagner, R. (1981). *The Invention of Culture*, revised edition, Chicago: University of Chicago Press.

Wilson, M. (1997). 'Citizenship and Welfare', in M. Lavalette and A. Pratt (eds) *Social Policy: a Conceptual and Theoretical Framework*, London: Sage, pp. 182–95.

Wright, S. and C. Shore (1995). 'Towards an Anthropology of Policy: Morality, Power and the Art of Government', *Anthropology in Action* 2, 2: 27–31.

Young, I. M. (1995). 'Polity and Group Difference: a Critique of the Ideal of Universal Citizenship', in R. Beiner (ed.) *Theorizing Citizenship*, Albany, NY: SUNY Press, pp. 175–207.

Yuval-Davis, N. (1997). 'Women, Citizenship and Difference', *Feminist Review* 57: 4–27.

PART TWO

Exclusionary Citizenships

CHAPTER 5

Female Education and Citizenship in Afghanistan: a Turbulent Relationship

Niloufar Pourzand

Introduction

Female education has been an intensely controversial issue throughout the modern history of Afghanistan, entrenched in numerous internal social divisions, and reflected in conflicts with various external forces. Always a highly political issue, it has reached a point of acute crisis at the present moment in Afghanistan's history, with the Taliban authorities having stopped formal female education altogether. It is thus particularly important to unravel and understand why female education bears such a heavy symbolic load in Afghanistan, especially for members of the Taliban who have become the *de facto* leaders, dominating most of the country since their Kabul take-over of September 1996. In the light of this, the aim of this chapter is to explore why and in what ways discourses on female education have been central to definitions and constructions of gendered citizenship in twentieth-century Afghanistan.

Prior to elaborating upon the specific case of Afghanistan, however, I would like to point to some general and theoretical issues on citizenship, women's role and education. The subject of female education and gendered citizenship will then be analysed as it was developed in the context of two regimes in twentieth-century Afghanistan, both of which attempted to *expand* female education: first, during the monarchical period of Amanullah Khan Durrani in the 1920s, within the framework of a Western-inspired ideology of modernisation and the building of a nation-state; second, in the late 1970s and 1980s, under the regime of the Afghan Communists and their socialist ideology of modernisation. It is against these initiatives that the Taliban directed their more recent campaigns against formal female education.

Concepts of Citizenship, the Role of Women and Female Education

Various discourses exist relating to concepts of citizenship within countries, between different countries and at the international level. Yet most of the numerous definitions of citizenship put forward by Western scholars (for example, Marshall 1950; Turner 1990) appear more relevant to Western societies. Citizenship is, let us recall, according to Marshall,

> a status bestowed on those who are full members of a community. All who possess the status are equal with respect to the rights and duties with which the status is endowed. (1950: 14)

Such conceptualisations have been criticised by progressive academics based in the West (Yuval-Davis 1997; Walby 1994) as being blind to gender, class, race, disability and sexual differences within a country. However, these are not the only reasons which make them inapplicable or less applicable to non-Western, non-liberal or non-democratic systems of rule.

In the West (in spite of all its plurality), citizenship is most frequently used in the context of the rights and duties of citizens *vis-à-vis* an elected government which depends upon their votes and taxes, marked by a strong sense of continuity and accountability. Such governments are elected through a multi-party system (by both male and female citizens). In the West, being a citizen means being the subject of a welfare state which is expected to take care of one's basic needs and to safeguard one's rights. Of course, in the West all citizens are not equal in every respect, nor do they benefit equally from existing resources, but nevertheless there exists at least a minimum set of common understandings regarding the rights and duties of male and female citizens. Inequalities in the West are usually, though not always, more subtly expressed than in those non-Western countries torn by ethno-political struggles.

In a country like Afghanistan, citizenship has a quite different meaning. Being an Afghan man or woman, especially in the past eighteen years of war, has been a very traumatic and insecure experience. It has meant belonging to an almost always contested national entity (either for ideological, religious, ethnic or other reasons, or a combination of these factors); it means being the subject of a non-elected state with its own particular and severely enforced ideology which extends very few if any rights; it means having no non-violent alternative for changing the regime and its instruments of control. It also means being manipulated by state authorities who want to define and redefine what it is to be an Afghan male or female citizen in order to fill its ranks and project its image both internally, within the nation, and internationally.

Citizenship for Afghan men and women has been the equivalent of belonging to a country in which the regime has dramatically, and with almost inconceivable acts of bloodshed and human suffering, changed hands several times in the lifespan of one generation. It has meant belonging to a stateless and divided country interminably at war; being located in the middle of a civil war waged among politico-religious and ethnic groups, each trying to enforce their own particular vision of what it is to be an Afghan citizen (man or woman), each with the support of various regional and international forces. For millions of Afghans it has meant having to spend all their lives in neighbouring countries and being constantly reminded of their non-citizenship in those countries – regardless of having, in many cases, the same language, religion or ethnic affiliation as the citizens of those countries. For many Afghan men and women, it is their citizenship which prevents them from obtaining visas to most countries of the world – though they might never even have lived in Afghanistan!

In addition, there are all the various internal divisions among Afghans which impact upon their concepts of citizenship and add to its fragility – including gender, ethnicity, language, religion, parochial affiliation, politics, ideology, class, disability, marital and family status, urban or rural origin and much else besides. Citizenship in Afghanistan is thus radically unlike its Western counterpart in almost every conceivable sense.

It is in relation to this fragile and yet dramatically contested arena of citizenship in Afghanistan that the pivotal role of female education has to be understood, as defining and redefining concepts of gendered citizenship by the state and political groups vying to control it. This centrality is based on the important role women play as biological reproducers of members of ethnic collectivities, and thus also of the boundaries of ethnic/national groups. As key participants in the ideological reproduction of the collectivity and central transmitters of its culture, women become signifiers of ethnic/national difference – the focus and symbol in ideological discourses used in the construction, reproduction and transformation of ethnic/national categories. They are also participants in national, economic, political and military struggles (see Anthias and Yuval-Davis 1989).

More specifically, women in Muslim societies are perceived as 'metaphors for the integrity of the Islamic community, expressing its purity in an idiom common to Muslim culture, honour and … chastity' (Peteet, 1993: 53). This means that the provision of different forms of education to girls and women has been important to the regimes and political parties or groups in Afghanistan, since at times, including the present, it has been the state which has defined the role of female education in its constructs of citizenship, while at other times it has been the various parties. Often, it has been a struggle between the two over what it means to be an Afghan man or woman subject, with the role of female education constrained by the prevailing definition. Both regimes and political groups have been, and continue to be, almost exclusively controlled by men.

All nations are founded on powerful constructions of social reproduction and hence also of gender. Despite national movements' ideological investment in the idea of popular unity, historically nations have often tended to sanction prevailing institutionalised gender differences rather than abolish them (McClintock 1993: 61). Education is one of the main 'public' institutions where this 'sanctioned' gender difference may be contested. It is one of the first and most important 'public' spaces made accessible to women in the course of 'modernisation' and is therefore important in defining the changing roles of men and women in society. Gender differences may be undermined or reinforced through education in two ways. One is from within the educational system itself, through the curriculum, teacher feedback and extra-curricular activities. The other, which is less common, is in debates about female education *per se,* as is the case in Afghanistan.

Female education in Afghanistan has become the arena in which women's symbolic centrality as bearers of gendered collective identities is expressed and contested, both within the country and in reaction to external forces. It is the transformative potential of education, and its importance in national and international debates on rights and development issues, which makes it so central to definitions of citizenship, in particular for Afghan women. Writing about Turkey and Iran, Kandiyoti (1991) and Najmabadi (1991) have elaborated upon other examples of state-supported female education within the context of nation-state building and 'modernisation'.

Afghanistan

Afghanistan is a landlocked 'nation of minorities' (Jawad 1992) located between Pakistan, Iran, China, Tajikistan, Uzbekistan and Turkmenistan, with a population of about 16 million. Its extreme ethnic heterogeneity as well as its regional and international position has continuously impacted upon local politics. Pashtuns, who speak Pashtu and are the largest ethnic group, have dominated Afghan politics for most of the country's history. The second-largest group is that of the Tajiks, whose language is Dari/Farsi – the *lingua franca* of Afghanistan. Other ethnic groups include the Uzbeks, Turkmens, Hazaras, Aimaq and Baluch. Ethnicity remains a critical issue in Afghanistan and has further strengthened the controversy over female education as respective leaderships take up various positions on this issue. Linked to ethnic affiliations in Afghanistan is tribal affinity. In particular, the Pashtun tribes have played a determining role in Afghan history, their male leaders meeting in *loya jirgas* (tribal councils) to debate and decide about important local and national issues. The Pashtunwali (or tribal code of the Pashtuns) is very conservative in its approach to the role of women in society and has been linked with Islamic ideology, often interpreted in such a way as to discriminate against women.

Another important factor in Afghan history has been the rural/urban divide, with 85 per cent of the population living in rural areas (Centlivres-Demont 1988) while political power has been monopolised by a minority urban elite. The influence of Islam in Afghanistan should not be underestimated. Although various interpretations of Islam have been influential, most predominant have been conservative schools of thought (and their similarly traditional view on women). The majority of Afghans are Sunni Muslims, with a minority of Shiite Muslims, often in conflict with each other. At times, religious and ethnic divisions have been linked in Afghanistan, as is the case with Hazaras who, as Shiites, are an ethnic as well as a religious minority. An ultra-conservative ideological standpoint towards women's position has been forcefully reinforced by most of these various political and religious groups. Virtually all subscribe to concepts of gendered citizenship, underpinned by ethnic power struggles for dominance and articulated through a rejection of what is seen as 'foreign intervention'.

Hence, another crucial factor in contemporary Afghan history has been its turbulent relationship with the outside world, beginning with the British colonialists in the eighteenth and nineteenth centuries. Afghanistan was important to them as a 'gateway to India' and, though it was never directly colonised, British direct or indirect influence over the country was considerable. Afghan traditional mistrust of foreigners and Westerners can be traced to this uneasy relationship. It enables various groups in Afghanistan to revisit female education since it is perceived as a 'Western' phenomenon, as a 'foreign import' and as a threat to what it is to be an 'Afghan' man or woman.

The emergence of modern Afghanistan can be traced back to 1747 when Ahmad Shah Durrani (a Pashtun) extended his influence over most of what is known as Afghanistan today, including its non-Pashtun areas. Abdul Rahman (1880–1901), another Pashtun leader, expanded Afghan territory by forcefully bringing within his jurisdiction areas such as the Hazarajat and Nuristan (known as Kafirestan, 'land of the infidels'). He contributed significantly to Afghanistan's status as a nation-state, building up an army and a state bureaucracy. Rahman introduced formal education for elite men in an attempt to curb the monopoly of religious leaders over education and to develop the required human resources for his army and bureaucracy.

King Habibullah, Abdul Rahman's son, ruled from 1901 to 1919 and is known for his intensive modernising efforts. In these he was influenced by developments in other regional countries, including India, Iran and Turkey, countries which were expanding their education systems in a move to become 'modern'. Habibullah established the first Western-inspired secular schools for boys and declared education obligatory for all boys. A whole generation of Afghan men was educated during his reign, men who would make their impact on Afghan history in the years to come. At the same time, he was denounced by many of the more traditional and conservative forces in society as being a foreign stooge.

It was left to King Amanullah (1919–29), however, to initiate formal female education. Amanullah is known as the great reformer – a title for which he was to pay heavily. He was immensely influenced by his father-in-law, Mahmoud Tarzi, Afghanistan's best-known intellectual reformer of the early twentieth century. Tarzi believed that Islamic countries had to modernise while maintaining their independence and integrity. Amanullah faced serious resistance from the clergy and the more conservative groups in the society, including other Pashtuns, who claimed he was too Westernised. After ten years on the throne, the King was assassinated by a Tajik called Bach-e Saqao, 'the water-bearer'. This assassination no doubt had ethnic and class grievances behind it as well as a concern to maintain conservative values. One of Bach-e Saqao's first steps when assuming power was the closing down of girls' schools!

Bach-e Saqao's reign did not last long and another Pashtun came to the throne – Mohammad Nadir Shah. Nadir Shah was more conservative than Amanullah but, despite this, he gradually reopened and expanded female education. It was during Mohammad Zahir Shah's reign (1933–73) that the largest number of Afghan women were able to be educated; educational institutions expanded throughout the country, as did the social and political activity of urban and elite women (Gauhari 1996). Pashtuns continued to be in positions of privilege, with Tajiks as the second most powerful ethnic group. Ethnic discrimination persisted, however, especially with regard to the Hazara. Class divisions also continued, giving ground to considerable unrest, in particular among the expanding educated younger generation. It was during Mohammad Zahir Shah's relatively peaceful reign that the number of Afghan leftists as well as Islamists (followers of political Islam) increased, emerging from universities, the growing bureaucracy and the military – all responding in their own ways to the various changes and conflicts in society, in the region and at the international level.

In 1973, Zahir Shah was deposed by his cousin and Prime Minister, M. Daoud, who ruled the country until the Communist takeover of 1978. The Communist leaders (Taraki, Hafizollah Amin, Karmal, Najibullah) of Afghanistan were among the recently educated elite of the society. Their predominantly urban and Pashtun backgrounds and Communist ideological commitment (especially their atheism), as well as their clear affiliation to a foreign country (the USSR), immediately discredited them in the eyes of many Afghans. The Communists wanted Afghan citizens (male *and* female) to become socialist cadres and comrades – concepts very alien and distasteful to most Islam-loving, independent and traditional Afghans. The Soviet Union's military intervention and its brutal and evident influence over all aspects of Afghan life – including education – transformed Afghan society forever. Resistance to this invasion seriously impacted upon the upward trend in female education that had occurred during Mohammad Zahir Shah's reign. Consequently, from 1978 onwards female education faced a series of severe setbacks.

Afghan Mujahedin, Islamic fighters, from all walks of life and from all ethnic groups, fought against the Soviets and the Communists. In 1992, after fourteen years of war, the Mujahedin succeeded in taking charge of Afghanistan. This was followed, however, by a period of constant fighting among the various Islamic political groups, each attempting to seize power in Afghanistan. The country has been suffering from war and all its disturbing repercussions for almost twenty years now. Many of these political groups are divided along ethnic as well as religious lines and seem unable to overcome their differences. Most of these groups have taken a conservative view on women's issues and all have, in different ways, restricted women – both inside Afghanistan and in Pakistan's refugee communities.

Since 1994, yet another force has appeared on the scene: the Taliban (religious students), who are predominantly Pashtun and come out of the religious schools or madrassas of Pakistan and southern Afghanistan. Most are from rural backgrounds. Of all the groups contending for power, they have imposed the harshest restrictions on women. Girls' schools have been closed down and women banned from teaching. Men too face many restrictions. They are forced to grow beards and to wear clothing deemed appropriate. The Taliban concept of Afghan citizenship for both men and women is ultra-conservative, and especially so in the case of women; they have been prohibited from working in the non-health sector or going out in public on their own. In addition, the Taliban are pursuing a pro-Pashtun ethnic policy at the expense of other minorities (as, indeed, are most other minority group leaders). Taliban's policies have stirred considerable and heated debates among Afghans and beyond the country, in the region and at the international level. These include a focus on the rights and wrongs of female education. Once again, female education has become a central issue in how a political group struggles to construct and reconstruct Afghan gendered citizenship. To begin to understand the very extremist position of the Taliban on female education, however, it is important to refer back to other periods of Afghan history and the development of the debate on female education. What follows is a preliminary effort towards such an end.

Citizenship and Female Education During Amanullah Khan's Reign (1919–29)

Amanullah had aspired towards establishing a new Afghan national identity which would surpass the various ethnic, religious, tribal and parochial affiliations and differences within the country. His aim was to provide an alternative discourse to that of traditionalists on what being an Afghan man or woman was or could be. His was a vision of a Western-inspired 'modern' Afghanistan. The background against which his policies were implemented has been, in the words of the famous Afghan specialists P. and M. Centlivres-Demont (1988), one in which

> The image of Self and Other, or social identity in Afghanistan, rested not on an idea of nation and citizenship, but on a feeling of appurtenance both to a supranational entity, the Islamic community or *umma*, and to an infranational one, the regional, tribal or ethnic community. (Centlivres-Demont 1988: 142)

Amanullah realised that to achieve his goals for Afghanistan against such odds he needed to change Afghan men as well as women. M. Tarzi, his mentor, put it in the following words: 'only enlightened and educated women could be good wives and mothers, [and] bring up the children in whose hands the future rests' (Olesen 1995: 118). Amanullah wanted to grant citizenship rights to Afghans based on 'liberal Western constitutions', a key tenet of which was 'emancipating women to become equal citizens' (Olesen 1995: 119). 'Free and independent women … on an equal basis with men, would build the new Afghanistan', according to the King's vision (*ibid.*).

Amanullah opened Kabul's first girls' school, Esmat, in 1921. Others were to follow, some sponsored by his wife Soraya and her mother. Girls began to be sent abroad for the first time in Afghan history, though in small numbers and to another Muslim but moderate country, Turkey (Poullada 1973: 73). However, the opportunity to study was not provided to all girls equally. Girls of the urban elite, in particular the Pashtun elite, were in a much more advantageous position to benefit from it. Similarly, it is important to note that secular education began as a state enterprise in Afghanistan and not a civil one. It was thus implemented top-down, especially in the beginning. Foreign educators were used for the purpose of curriculum development and teacher training, much to the distaste of some of the clergy and other prominent leaders or groups. In addition, Amanullah attempted to unveil Afghan women and introduce other 'modern' changes into their lives.

Amanullah began facing serious opposition from various quarters in society which claimed that he was too Westernised and was distancing the country from the true Islam, including its clergy and traditional leaders. One of the most important criticisms levelled at Amanullah was related to his encouragement of female education. The religious leaders 'contended that education for women would lead to the breakdown of the family, sexual anarchy, and ultimately degrade women. The honour of the nation would be lost' (Dupree 1984: 307). Many Afghan traditional leaders felt that Amanullah was 'challenging the full authority of a man over his family and particularly his womenfolk' (Olesen 1995: 136). They questioned his policies with reference to Islam and the Pashtunwali code of honour which stems from tribal and religious notions of the integrity of the family and its women, and the unconditional demand for defence of *ghayrat, nang va namus* – honour, shame and reputation (Olesen 1995: 136–7).

The closing of girls' schools featured prominently in the demands of the leaders of several rebellions (Khost, Shinwari) against the King. The clergy demanded that girls only study the Koran, that they only study until the age of puberty (which was defined as nine) and that their male teachers be at least 80 (Olesen 1995: 135). Others demanded the closing of all girls' schools and the recall of all Afghan girls sent abroad. It was these rebellions that gradually weakened Amanullah until he was finally assassinated by Bach-e Saqao. Nevertheless, Amanullah will remain known as the father of female education in Afghanistan. He firmly believed in the link between female education and the construction or reconstruction of concepts of gendered citizenship, in line with the modernisation of the nation. He was influenced by Western-inspired concepts of progress in his vision of the ideal Afghan man or woman. There is no doubt that his efforts to expand female education were one of the main reasons leading to his fall. These efforts came into conflict with traditional gendered ideologies of other powerful groups in the country. Nevertheless, what he began set a precedent for what was to come, and provided the country with an experience of female education never to be fully erased from Afghan memory – neither by its proponents, nor by its opponents.

In spite of the opposition to Amanullah's female education policy, the trend was gradually and without much fanfare to be continued until 1978. By then, many more Afghan men and women had been educated, reached university and begun work in various fields, some women achieving quite high-ranking social positions. By 1976, the country had 888,800 school pupils and 15,000 university students of both sexes (Kakar 1995: 79). This trend at all times faced opposition from reactionary social forces but did not produce a head-on collision again until after the Communist takeover of 1978, perhaps because until then it was not fiercely enforced or radical in its content.

Citizenship and Female Education under Communist Rule in Afghanistan (1978–92)

The PDPA (People's Democratic Party of Afghanistan) came to power in Afghanistan not through a popular revolution but rather through various power struggles and Soviet Union support, terminating in the Saur Revolution or *coup d'état* of April 1978. The female literacy rate in 1978, despite all the political controversy it had created, was no higher than 4 per cent, against 19 per cent for men (Moghadam 1994: 859). One of the first steps taken by the Communists was to implement an intense and widespread national education and literacy programme, focusing on girls and women. The objective was to re-socialise Afghans to support their 'revolutionary' and 'socialist' country. Anahita Ratebzad, the top female member of PDPA and one-time Minister of Education, in one of her first speeches after the takeover said: 'the duties of women and mothers, who shape the future of the country … is to bring up sons and daughters who are sincere and patriotic'. She called on Afghan women to 'consolidate your revolutionary regime as bravely as the heroic and brave men of the country' (Dupree 1984: 312).

A new concept of gendered Afghan citizenship, as outlined in Article 12 of the Basic Lines of Revolutionary Duties of the government, which called for 'equality of rights of women and men in all social, economic, political, cultural, and civil aspects' (Dupree 1984: 312), was being pursued. According to a Kabul newspaper of the period,

> Education and enlightening women is now the subject of close government attention ... to teach people the aims of the Revolution and how to meet these goals ... An illiterate person stands outside politics ... An illiterate woman cannot carry on the struggle, cannot handle properly the family affairs, and cannot rear properly sound and healthy children. (Dupree 1984: 316)

Literacy continued to be hailed as imperative in reaching the objectives of the revolution and to be carried out at all cost. Often, villagers were coerced to attend classes or men were forced to allow their wives and daughters to attend. According to Moghadam (1994: 864), many refugees who came into Pakistan in 1978 gave as their major reason 'the forceful implementation of the literacy programme among their women. In Kandahar, three literacy workers from the women's organisation were killed.' While the progressive potential of such policies cannot be denied, then, the manner in which they were implemented, as well as their formulation, did not resonate with most Afghans. The PDPA underestimated the potential for resistance against their policies and presence within Afghan society, and this included the issue of female education. According to Jawad (1992: 19), 'The National education system was modeled on the Soviet system, curricula were designed by Soviet specialists, kindergartens were run by Soviet women.' In addition, several thousand Afghan youth, including young girls, were sent to the then USSR for education. All these policies were seen as 'brainwashing' and 'anti-Islamic' by many Afghans and were so presented by the opposition leaders, the Mujahedin – who were fighting against all that the PDPA stood for, including its concepts of (un)gendered Afghan citizenship.

One of the differences between the Mujahedin and the religious opposition to Amanullah was that many of the leaders had themselves received formal and more secular education and presented their opposition to female education as tactical and related to the direction and content of such education, rather than its very existence. What actually happened following their takeover in 1992 proved a far more drastic break, however. In the battle against Communist domination, female education became a site of struggle between the PDPA and its opponents. Resistance and opposition to female education were fierce and much more widespread than during Amanullah's period. They were seen by the public and portrayed by the Mujahedin as integral to the opposition to the Soviet military presence (since 1979), to the non-Islamic and atheistic content of that education, to the dictatorial methods of the PDPA and, in general, to an imposed and alien socialist ideology. Female education was constructed as a threat to traditional concepts of Afghanistan's identity, both as a Muslim country and as a proudly independent nation.

In an interview in 1980, Anahita Ratebzad conceded to errors, 'in particular the compulsory education of women', to which she added: 'the reactionary elements immediately made use of these mistakes to spread discontent among the population' (Moghadam 1992: 435).

> The Mujahedin instigated this national divide on female education by encouraging non-cooperation by girls ... the Mujahedin asked girls to return to their homes in order to protest the Soviet occupation. They promised to reinstate education for girls when they succeeded in expelling the foreigners. (Dupree 1984: 334)

Once again in Afghan history, therefore, female education became a terrain over which ideological and political rivalries were fought. The divide was so serious and the struggle so fierce and intense that it has impacted upon the discourses of female education and gendered citizenship up until the present moment, even after the downfall of the PDPA, the break-up of the USSR and the passage of considerable time since these events occurred.

In the context of the history of female education in Afghanistan, Amanullah's reign will remain known as the period in which formal female education in Afghanistan began, in spite of opposition from conservative forces in society, while the PDPA years will be known as a major historic setback for female education. This resulted from their broader policies and the reaction to them by opposition Islamic groups and their supporters. Both sides were fighting over what it meant to be an Afghan, whether male or female, and who has the right to define this identity, with female education placed in the vortex of the struggle.

Conclusion

The complexity of the situation with regard to female education in Afghanistan arises from its integral connection to political, ethnic, religious and class struggles within a broad opposition between parochialism and foreign intervention. This chapter has demonstrated how female education discourses and views have thus been integral to the construction of Afghan citizenship as a contested status, first in the 1920s and once again in the 1978–92 period. Female education has thus always been a very political issue in Afghanistan. Under Amanullah, it was linked to a Western-inspired modernisation drive, to Islamic reform and to concepts of enlightened gendered citizenship within a newly constituted nation-state. With the PDPA, it was Soviet-inspired socialism, carried out in the name of Communism and linked to concepts of equal citizenship under a socialist Afghanistan, that prevailed. In both cases, female education played a key role in the regimes' efforts to transform society and to constitute Afghan citizens, both men and women, in conformity with a specific ideological framework and political objectives. Not surprisingly, then, female education became one of the main targets of opposition forces during both the periods referred to in this chapter. These denounced the education of women as 'foreign-inspired' and a threat to what it means to be an Afghan woman, and thus to Afghan society as a whole. Women – as informed, enlightened and educated agents, or as pious mothers, daughters and wives confined to the home – became a litmus test of ideological tendencies defining citizenship within the evolving nation-state, the focus and symbol of ideological discourses used in the construction, reproduction and transformation of ethnic/national categories (Anthias and Yuval-Davis 1989: 7).

The struggle over female education, with more liberal and progressive forces supporting its expansion and more conservative forces opposing it, continues today in Afghanistan and among Afghan refugees. Female education in Afghanistan was and remains an arena over which male political leaders fight their wars against each other and against non-aligned outsiders, at the expense of women and children, repeatedly denying them access to a basic human entitlement which all Westerners, men and women alike, take for granted.

Acknowledgements

This chapter is based on library research as well as one short visit to northern Afghanistan in June 1996, and on interviews with Afghan men and women of different ethnic groups, social classes and age groups, as well as Afghan specialists in the UK. A longer version of this chapter became my MA dissertation for the Ethnic and Gender pathway, University of Greenwich, titled Female Education, Ethnicity and National Identity in Afghanistan. I am presently working on a doctoral thesis on the same subject. I thank Professor Nira Yuval-Davis, Dr Elaine Unterhalter, Dr Pnina Werbner, UNICEF and my family for making this work and publication possible.

References

Anthias, Floya and Yuval-Davis, Nira (eds) (1989). *Nation–State–Women,* London: Macmillan.

Centlivres-Demont, Micheline (1994). 'Afghan Women in Peace, War and Exile', in Ali Banuazizi and Myron Weiner (eds) *The Political Transformation in Afghanistan, Iran and Pakistan,* NY: Syracuse University Press, pp. 333–66.

Centlivres-Demont, Micheline and Pierre (1988). 'The Afghan Refugees in Pakistan: An Ambiguous Identity', *Journal of Refugee Studies* I, 2: 141–53.

Dupree, Nancy (1984). 'Revolutionary Rhetoric and Afghan Women', in Nazif Shahrani and Robert Canfield (eds) *Revolution and Rebellion in Afghanistan*, Berkeley: University of California, pp. 121–43.

— (1992). *The Present Role of Afghan Refugee Women and Children,* The Hague: Bernard van Leer Foundation.

Gauhari, Farooka (1996). *Searching for Saleem: An Afghan Woman's Odyssey,* Nebraska: University of Nebraska Press.

Gupta, Bhabani Sen (1986). *Afghanistan: Politics, Economics and Society*, London: Pinter Publishers.

Jawad, Nassim (1992). *Afghanistan: A Nation of Minorities*, London: Minority Rights Group.

Kakar, Hassan M. (1995). *Afghanistan: The Soviet Invasion and the Afghan Response, 1979–1982*, Berkeley: University of California Press.

Kandiyoti, Deniz (ed.) (1991). *Women, Islam and the State*, London: Macmillan Press.

Marshall, T. H. (1950). *Citizenship and Social Class*, Cambridge: Cambridge University Press.

McClintock, Anne (1993). 'Family Feuds: Gender, Nationalism and the Family', *Feminist Review* 44: 61–79.

Moghadam, Valentine (1992). 'Revolution, Islam and Women: Sexual Politics in Iran and Afghanistan', in Andrew Parker, Mary Russo, Doris Samer and Patricia Yaeger (eds), *Nationalism and Sexualities*, London: Routledge, pp. 424–46.

— (1994). 'Building Human Resources and Women's Capabilities in Afghanistan: a Retrospect and Prospects', *World Development* 22: 859–75.

Najmabadi, Afsaneh (1991). 'Hazards of Modernity and Morality: Women, State and Ideology in Contemporary Iran', in Deniz Kandiyoti (ed.) *Islam and the State*, London: Macmillan Press, pp. 48–75.

Olesen, Asta (1995). *Islam and Politics in Afghanistan*, London: Curzon Press.

Peteet, Julie M. (1993). 'Authenticity and Gender: the Presentation of Culture', in Judith Tucker (ed.) *Arab Women: Old Boundaries, New Frontiers*, Bloomington: Indiana University Press, pp. 49–62.

Poullada, Leon (1973). *Reform and Rebellion in Afghanistan, 1919–1929*, Ithaca, NJ: Cornell University Press.

Pourzand, Niloufar (1996). 'Female Education, Ethnicity and National Identity in Afghanistan 1920–1996', unpublished MA thesis, London: University of Greenwich.

Shahrani, Nazif (1984). 'Introduction: Marxist "Revolution" and Islamic Resistance in Afghanistan', in Nazif Shahrani and Robert Canfield (eds) *Revolution and Rebellion in Afghanistan*, Berkeley: University of California, pp. 3–58.

Turner, Bryan (1990). 'Outline of a Theory on Citizenship', *Sociology* 24, 2: 189–218.

Walby, Sylvia (1994). 'Is Citizenship Gendered?' *Sociology* 28, 2: 379–95.

Yuval-Davis, Nira (1997). *Gender and Nation*, London: Sage Publications.

CHAPTER 6

Citizenship, Difference and Education: Reflections Inspired by the South African Transition[1]

Elaine Unterhalter

Education and Citizenship

Education is a particularly complex area to link with a theory of citizenship that is sensitive to difference. This is partly because education is itself so amorphous a terrain. It encompasses concerns with formal institutions of learning, like schools and universities, and the people who work in them, the pedagogical processes that go on in them, and the ways in which they are organised, governed and located in relation to state and civil society. But education is also embedded in a wider set of relationships, and is thus caught up in debates about epistemology, language, nationalism, culture and notions of self. It is also intrinsic to work in economic planning and a wide range of social policy debates. There is a very diverse spectrum of ideas on what education is for. These range from largely economistic concerns with skill formation and preparation for the world of work, generally (though this is often not acknowledged) under capitalist relations of production, to concerns with developing personal autonomy and location within a framework of what John White has called 'our attachment to the experienced world', that is, the social landscape, whether perceived as 'nature' or as collectivity (White 1995: 19). This fluidity concerning a definition of education coexists with the practicality of much of the work of education – a class of students to teach, a specific policy programme to design and implement. As a result, education can never be discussed exclusively in theoretical terms. Thinking about education in relation to debates about citizenship and difference is an exercise in what Mary Maynard has enjoined feminist scholarship to undertake: to move to think of situated relationships, mid-level concepts (Maynard 1995: 271).

This fluidity means that there is no neat set of correlations to be traced between education and citizenship, although some have been posited. In this chapter I look at three ways of thinking about the relationship of citizenship and education, exploring how each has dealt with the problem of difference, and the contrasting meanings assigned by each approach to difference. The first approach to education and citizenship I want to consider is the argument that education enables citizenship to develop and flourish. According to this view education is primarily the servant of, or conduit to, citizenship. A second approach argues that education is a form of citizenship, an acting out, or speaking of citizenship. This approach elides education and citizenship, suggesting that citizenship shares many similar terrains and processes with education, or that education is an articulation of citizenship. The third view suggests that citizenship enables education to take place, according it a relatively autonomous institutional and analytical sphere. Thus citizenship legitimates education and shares many (but not all) attributes with it; but education also has the potential to destabilise present meanings of citizenship and to constantly criticise some of the formalised notions of self and community on which any particular conceptualisation of citizenship might be based. Each view, as I demonstrate below, entails a particular notion of difference, and each view of difference accords gender a different explanatory space.

My thinking about these issues has emerged from reflections on the way South Africa has grappled with the development of a new constitution and the formulation of a transformed education policy. In the 1990s South Africans negotiated a transition to democracy that captured the world's imagination. A society that had been marked by violence, inhumanity, lack of rights and profound division across barriers of race, gender and ethnicity, negotiated and agreed a constitution that sought to heal the wounds of the past and build a new nation on the basis of peace, human rights and equality. After the elections of 1994, an intensive period of constitution making began, probably one of the most democratic processes of constitution writing in history. Feminist activists and lawyers played a key part in this process. The new constitution became law in 1996. Side by side with the formulation of the new constitution, debates took place on the refashioning of education, and an Education Policy Act was passed in 1996. These documents articulate two very different views of the relationship of education and citizenship. The Education Policy Act is an example of the first view I have identified, that is, that education fosters citizenship, and is an instrument of nation building; while the constitution suggests the third position, that citizenship enables education, but that education is a relatively autonomous sphere of culture and difference. While it is beyond the scope of this chapter to discuss these documents, their history and detailed discursive framings in any depth, they provide dramatic examples of the ways in which the relationship of education, citizenship and difference are being struggled over by a society which appears the repository of so many dreams of citizenship, both local and global, evoking images of peace, reconciliation, and ambitious education for democracy.[2]

The policy positions of these South African documents provide a stepping-off point to explore how the connections between citizenship, difference and education have been theorised. I now want to look in more detail at the three formulations of this relationship I have identified.

Education for Citizenship

The role of education in shaping the citizen of the modern polity has been of central concern to theorists of democracy and of nationalism. Gellner's analysis of nationalism sees formal schooling as a pivotal transformative experience which establishes the homogeneous culture and forms of communication that give birth to industrialised nations, which in turn confer specific abstract rights on citizens, different to the localised and tradition-bound rights of non-national polities (Gellner 1983). Foucault describes schooling as instilling the regimented discipline of the body and mind fundamental to modernity and life within the modern state (Foucault 1977). Guttman has pointed out how education not only sets the stage for democratic politics, but plays a central role in it; thus questions of the purposes and distribution of education are central questions for political theory (Guttman 1987). Hogan argues that the two objectives of liberal democratic education – to protect the highest-order interests of individual citizens and to promote a form of political community – mirror the objectives of democracy (Hogan 1997).

In the 1980s and 1990s, side by side with these concerns with liberal education and democracy, a dominant concern of nation-building analyses of education, for both rich and poor countries, flowed from human capital theory.[3] In these formulations the nation became equated with the firm, its citizens with workers, and democracy with the operation of the market. A strand in the critical responses to the development of marketisation in education, both at the theoretical and at the organisational level, has been to posit an alternative vision which centres on the notion of active citizenship and lifelong learning (Whitty 1997; Ranson 1993; White 1996; Carr and Hartnett 1996a). These critiques acknowledge that part of the popular appeal in the rhetoric of marketisation was its apparent acknowledgement of 'active individuals and choice' after decades of social democracy stressing passivity in exchange for the receipt of uniform state allocations. Liberal left critics' elaboration of the notion of citizenship was therefore an attempt to borrow the idea of active individuals. In their work individuals motivated by the wish for private gain and self-advancement in the market (where each possessive individual is pitted against another) were transformed instead into active individuals seeking private and public gain through self-realisation, in partnership with others, in the *civitas* or political community.

The arguments formulated by these writers are interesting and appealing, but fail to engage with the ideas posed by feminist writings on the state and education policy (Kenway 1990; Williams 1993; Kingdom 1996; Foster 1997). These highlight how governments, through an appeal to an abstract concept of the citizen, stripped of all qualities save subjective rationality and morality, have been able to maintain and perpetuate social divisions based on gender, race, ethnicity, sexuality and disability. Denials of citizenship rights to certain racialised or gendered groups, such as was the case in South Africa under apartheid, generally rest on assertions of the irrationality or lack of morality of these groups.

For most of the twentieth century education has been a key site of state endeavour in both what are termed the (developed) minority and the (developing) majority world; it has been central to state formation and intertwined with this has been its implicit or explicit concern with the fostering of values of citizenship with a stress on the undifferentiated rights of the political subject (Green 1990; Harber 1989; Spring 1980). This political subject is represented stripped of its gender, ethnicity or race, without sexuality or physical capacity. The argument put by critics is that the appeal to an abstract notion of citizenship disguises practices of persistent discrimination (Williams 1993; Guttman 1995).

The assumption of much of the writing on education for citizenship is that difference is, at worst, a problem that gives rise to discrimination, and that must be overcome by a Kantian ethic of immanent rights; or, at best, a private sphere of culture, that must be tolerated and lived with because tolerance is one of the markers of citizenship. This assumption is evident in writing within this framework that identifies how education in general and public schooling in particular can educate children for democracy by including special curricular emphases in this direction (White 1995; Harber 1992; Fogelman 1996; Demaine 1996). The approach is typified by the work of Patricia White who has discussed how schools can develop citizenship by developing democratic dispositions which constitute the attributes of citizens (White 1996). White constructs a list of the dispositions which, she argues, inform a flourishing democratic life and discusses how these may be taught in 'real schools'. She acknowledges the ways in which democratic dispositions may themselves be partial – honesty, for example, may not always be the best policy; students might need to understand adversarial relations in real-life politics as well as honest and supportive ones.

But despite this awareness of some ambiguities, White, like many of the other writers within this tradition, has developed a notion of citizenship, and therefore education for citizenship, that fails to recognise and take account of difference. While she is sometimes concerned with the impact of ethnically inscribed divisions on developing democratic dispositions, she, like many others, tends to view citizenship in terms of universals that everyone, despite or because of their differences, should try to recognise and respect.

The strengths of this position are in the ways in which it stresses equality and ties education very clearly to an objective. But there are also a number of problems with this approach. First, it tends to represent both education and citizenship as homogenising processes, where difference is viewed as an obstacle to be overcome. Difference presents a string of problem areas and gender is just one other area on the string, lined up with the other problems. This stance obscures the ways in which difference can be either empowering or a realm of continuing, unacknowledged disempowerment. The response to the public articulation of gendered difference within this position would therefore be to condemn it. The ways in which noting gender difference might be an important part of mobilisation against discrimination are delegitimated. The problem of difference is, according to this view, to be accommodated either through tolerance (and a suspension of critique) or through consultation (and an accommodation of those aspects of different views with dominant paradigms). Neither approach subjects citizenship, education or difference to critical scrutiny; education is always linear, citizenship always the goal and difference always somehow deviant or marginal. The position, expressed thus, does not allow for change or shifting perceptions within any of the major terms. In this position, education is presented as a linear process, which it need not be. Seeking to utilise it as such, even for the worthy objective of citizenship and equality, is both to refuse to explore the richness of education's complexity, and probably to ignore or stigmatise the ways in which linear causality is not achieved. I now want to counterpoint the notion of education for equal citizenship with a second theorisation – education as citizenship – that celebrates the very area of difference and shifting perceptions the first position distances itself from.

Education as Citizenship, Citizenship as Education

The return to an engagement with the political by many feminist and other critical writers worldwide in the 1980s and 1990s has produced a very rich literature on citizenship.[4] This has partly been a response to the ideological attack on forms of the welfare state by neoliberalism, espoused both by governments and supranational organisations like the World Bank. It has also partly been an engagement with questions posed in thinking about the state by the growth of new social movements, and the emergence of new states like South Africa, or those brought into being by the fall of communism. Often the formation of these has been precipitated by the interventions of new social movements. Interest in citizenship has also partly been a reflection on the changing meaning of the nation-state, given the moves towards European and other regional and global forms of integration. Much of this writing has sought to infuse the notion of citizenship with different meanings to those of individual property or rights, which had been annexed in the conservative discourse of marketisation and the minimal state. In stressing the importance of pluralism these new discussions on the left have sought to emphasise a redemptive self-realisation through participation in collectivities, and raised questions of how to conceptualise a notion of the common good. Hannah Arendt's work on citizenship, participation in the public sphere and political agency has been much discussed (Passerin d'Entrèves 1992; Phillips 1993; Elshtain 1997).

Feminism posed a particular critical challenge to older conceptualisations of citizenship because it highlighted that public and private were constructed spheres, acting to legitimate the subordination of women (Pateman 1988; Shanley and Narayan 1997). Discussions of citizenship and the political had often been used to exclude women or other groups, viewed as non-citizens, because of their difference. The malleability of notions of 'public', 'private' and 'rights' were not, according to this critique, unfortunate consequences of a particular conception of citizenship, but constituted the very essence of the mainstream notion of citizenship (Lister 1997; Yuval-Davis 1997a). What this writing put on the agenda was the challenge of engaging with difference, not as a problem to be ironed out, or accommodated, as in the previous framework, but as a constitutive component of theorising.

Chantal Mouffe's writing encapsulates the richness of many of these discussions and the complexity of the issues raised. For Mouffe the achievement of liberal democracies has been in instituting the principle of justice and defending a plurality of rights against the private power of monarchies or oligarchies. She points out, however, that the cost of this achievement has been to relegate morality to the sphere of the private or the individual (Mouffe 1992: 230). In many countries this duality often placed schools in a particularly ambiguous position concerning morality and the ways to teach it: to what extent are values religious, civic, or loosely humanist?

For Mouffe the challenge of current political philosophy is to bridge two dichotomous conceptions of the collectivity. These are, on the one hand, the view of:

> an aggregate of individuals without common public concern and [on the other hand] a pre-modern community organised around a single substantive idea of the common good. [The challenge is e]nvisaging the modern democratic community outside of this dichotomy. (Mouffe 1992: 231)

To achieve this she seeks to formulate an ethics of modern citizenship compatible with pluralism. This entails not a set of abstract principles imposed arbitrarily from without, but a set of rules which she identifies as 'a grammar of political conduct' inscribed in all actions, as I will demonstrate shortly (Mouffe 1992: 231). To be a citizen is to subscribe to these rules of political conduct, to speak and act their language. Citizenship is acted and re-enacted in this language. It is a constant process of identification. Thus citizenship is neither a plurality of interests and identities, as in the classic liberal approach, or an imposed assumption of the singular notion of the common good, as in communitarian critiques.

Mouffe's analysis represents, then, an attempt to reconcile the principles of democracy – liberty and equality – with a reality of constantly changing political identifications. This approach, she notes,

> [can] only be formulated within a problematic that conceives of the social agent not as a unitary subject but as the articulation of an ensemble of subject positions, constructed within specific discourses and always precariously and temporarily sutured at the intersection of those subject positions. Only with a non-essentialist conception of the subject, which incorporates the psycho-analytical insight that all identities are forms of identification, can we pose the question of political identity in a fruitful way. (Mouffe 1992: 237)

Thus for Mouffe active citizenship entails entering a discursive order constituted through language and the acquisition of shifting and different identities, constructed around principles of liberty and equality.

Mouffe's ideas have been interestingly associated with debates about the new constitution in South Africa. In a key article on constitution making in South Africa, Woolman and Davis argue for judges to work within a framework of 'creole liberalism'. They derive this from a rejection of an orthodox liberalism that negates difference, and coin the term creole liberalism after a survey of work, like that of Mouffe, that engages with positive dimensions of difference. According to Woolman and Davis, creole liberalism recognises that

> public difference and some individual and group differences *must be maintained and supported by the polity* if we are to retain a meaningful notion of autonomy and individual freedom. (Woolman and Davis 1996: 396, emphasis added)

While Woolman and Davis argue convincingly that recognition of difference by the state is an important constitutive process of the political, and acknowledge that this position derives from accepting the constructed notion of the self as mediated through membership in a number of different communities, they do not grapple with the implications of that construction. This is the question that Mouffe engages with: that selves are constructed in constantly shifting identifications. Communities are not static, nor are the selves they generate. Woolman and Davis, like many of the lawyers who have helped frame the South African constitution, are silent on the connection between citizenship and education, and the challenge of theorising a link between a realm of public policy and a non-essentialist subject (Van Wyk *et al.* 1994). Albie Sachs, one of the key political activists and theorists in the South African constitution-making process, formulates his discussion of education very much within the framework of the more orthodox position of education for citizenship which I outlined on page 101 (Sachs 1990: 79–89).

Like Chantal Mouffe, Nira Yuval-Davis has also grappled with building a more complex theorisation of citizenship that takes account of difference amongst political subjects and tries to overcome citizenship's sexist, racist and European and North American biases. Yuval-Davis suggests that the notion of citizenship needs to be reconceptualised as a multi-tier construct that is capable of theorising people's membership of a variety of collectivities – state, civil society, family – and explaining the way in which the different tiers shape and are shaped by each other (Yuval-Davis 1997b, Chapter 4).

Yuval-Davis's multi-tier delineation of citizenship is more structured than Mouffe's loose differentiation between the subjective, the social collectivity and the realm of the political and the state. For her, the assertion of active citizenship entails an acknowledgement of the interconnectedness and the difference between these separate yet linked tiers. A notion of active citizenship is also central to Yuval-Davis's theorisation, but is differently inflected from conceptualisations of this that pay no heed to difference (Yuval-Davis 1997b: 83–8). Active citizenship, rather than being an unproblematic engagement with the realm of civil society, is for Yuval-Davis entailed in the process of transversal dialogue. This is simultaneously an acknowledgement of a social actor's specific (if momentary) location and her or his empathy with the different location(s) of comrades, friends, allies or antagonists engaged in advancing specific large or small projects. As in the Gramscian position adopted by Mouffe, transversal dialogue entails the transversal politics of coalition building, in which the specific positioning of political actors is recognised and considered. This approach is based on the epistemological recognition that each positioning produces specific situated knowledges which cannot but be unfinished, and therefore dialogue among those differentially positioned should take place in order to reach a common perspective. Transversal dialogue should be based on the principles of rooting and shifting – that is, being centred in one's own experiences while being empathetic to the differential positionings of the partners in the dialogue (Yuval-Davis 1997a).

It can be seen that this notion of transversal dialogue, like Mouffe's notion of shifting forms of political identification, seeks to bring to discussions of citizenship the notion that difference is not a problem to be overcome or eradicated, as in the first approach outlined here, but an inevitable reality, and discussion is richer for this acknowledgement.

I have quoted Mouffe's and Yuval-Davis's arguments at some length because they both engage with issues of difference and with shifting identities within the formulation of citizenship as a grammar of political conduct (for Mouffe) or a multi-tier construct of different collectivities (for Yuval-Davis). While they are different – in that Mouffe acknowledges universals which Yuval-Davis is suspicious of – they both see citizenship as a process of engagement and reform rather than a system of fixed values. What do these analyses imply for thinking about education?

On one level there are ways in which these analyses of citizenship and political action elide with conceptions of education. Citizenship is achieved through a process of multiple, partial identifications which utilises a grammar of political conduct and entails critical pedagogic processes of learning and teaching. Similarly 'transversal dialogue' as a strategy for political conduct draws explicitly on an acknowledgement of partial and shifting epistemologies, political action through learning, and dialogue.

Interestingly, in elaborating the notion of active citizenship, political analysts like Mouffe and Yuval-Davis have borrowed some of the vocabulary of active learning (like dialogue and codes of conduct) from writers on education. Simultaneously, educational philosophers and sociologists in the 1990s have been very attracted by theories of education and citizenship, often seeing the former not as causative of the latter, as in the first approach I discussed, but as constitutive of it. Unlike the first approach where education can produce citizenship, in this approach education *is* citizenship, seen as an ongoing process.

There are two quite different articulations of this position, one that ignores difference and one that engages with it. For Stuart Ranson, lifelong learning is an expression of active citizenship (Ranson 1993). At the centre of what he terms a new 'moral and political order' is the presupposition of a learning society (Ranson 1993: 341). This learning society is open to new ideas, to listening to a range of perspectives. Citizenship expresses 'our inescapably dual identity as autonomous individuals and responsible members of the public domain' (Ranson 1993: 341). Practical reason provides the epistemology, the mode of knowing and of acting for the citizen, enabling him or her to understand the duality of citizenship and develop a moral capacity to comprehend the particular in the light of the universal. For Ranson, in opposition to the passivities which he believes have been bred out of state interventions, it is important to reformulate citizenship in terms of action and reason and in this new guise to advance education as a human right. Ranson distinguishes between three levels in looking at the ways in which learning is valued – at the level of the self in a quest for self-discovery, at the level of the society in the learning of mutuality within a moral order, and at the level of the polity in learning the qualities of a participative democracy (Ranson 1993: 342).

Ranson, however, elides learning and citizenship in a particular way that avoids dealing with difference. He wishes to preserve the tension between private and public – inherent in discussions of learning – in his thinking about citizenship. Although he is critical of what he sees as a bland concept of human rights, his notion of active citizenship is equally abstract and unsituated, despite its substitution of vigour and action for the passivities, in his view, of the human rights discourse. His notion of citizenship depends on a prior assumption of uniform opportunities – that all can act similarly, all inhabit public and private space with similar ease – that is troubling. It takes no account of difference as limiting and of the ways in which the public and the private are safe or not safe spaces for action for different groups of people. For example, in apartheid South Africa in the 1980s, the white authorities, attempting to destroy black squatter settlements in large cities like Cape Town, would daily flatten houses with bulldozers. Every evening, women and men, returning from work, would try to rebuild them (Cole 1987; Platzky and Walker 1985; Unterhalter 1987). In this encounter, like many that are similar, where the 'private' but subordinate individual encounters the state, the private space of the home is not protected, but demarcated as illegal; any quest for personal autonomy and self-discovery in this context had necessarily to be focused on engagement with this oppressive power of the state. The dual identity of public and private assumed by lifelong learning has to become, at such moments, a single identity. This is a persistent theme in South African literature and visual art from the 1960s to the 1990s. Ranson's celebration of the public–private duality is unable to grapple with such sliding parameters.

There are echoes, in Ranson's presupposition of learning as process, of Yuval-Davis's notion of transversal dialogue, but where her notion is situated in relation to the state, the nation and a range of other collectivities, his appears to float free. It is Ranson's assumption that all ideas are given equal voice that is particularly difficult (Ranson 1993: 341). Much of the post-colonial epistemological critique has been concerned to point out how histories of colonisation have silenced certain languages and perceptions and reconstituted others (Chambers and Curti 1996). Similar points are made by many feminist writers on epistemology (Alcoff and Potter 1993). Although Ranson emphasises openness to new ideas, he does not consider the possibility that certain ideas cannot even be spoken. A learning society needs to develop its capacity to listen to ideas that have been silenced, to be sensitive to forms of learning that have not been dignified by that term. It must be partly constituted around notions of redress – not as a mechanical form of affirmative action but as a constant questioning about who determines what is learning. To do this it cannot have learning as a constitutive condition without critically and constantly addressing the question: Learning for what purpose? Whose agenda for learning is being tabled?

In contrast with Ranson's failure to engage with notions of difference in linking learning and citizenship, Ariana Hernandez's writing about the struggle for democracy in Argentina clearly articulates this connection. Through an analysis of pedagogy as a means to bring together theory and practice with political and ethical concerns, Hernandez theorises a link between education and citizenship that draws on feminist writings about a pedagogy of difference as a political project of democratisation (Hernandez 1997). For Hernandez this entails that pedagogy, democracy and discourse are bound to each other in what she sees as a metonymic relationship (1997: 95).

Hernandez, like Ranson, places learning at the centre of any democratic process. For both, citizenship entails learning. But while for Ranson, the learner is an integrated individual (without race or gender, for example), for Hernandez the learner is always situated within shifting collective identities. For Ranson what is learned is to bring together personal autonomy and public responsibility, while for Hernandez what is learned is to struggle with collective difference in a joint project for emancipation. Ranson's 'practical reason' does not appear to engage sufficiently with collective differences. Difference for him appears always posited as 'the particular', subsumed under the universals. However, one of the achievements of poststructuralism is surely to point out that it is collective rather than just individual difference that is universal, while it is our universals that are particular and constructed.

There are many links between Hernandez's position and those of Mouffe and Yuval-Davis. While learning for all three is part of the process of contestation, identification or dialogue through which citizenship is constituted and reconstituted, always partial and always unfinished, for Ranson learning is much more unambiguously 'good'. However, there are differences between Hernandez, Yuval-Davis and Mouffe. Where Mouffe would place liberty and equality at the centre of a radical democratic process, Hernandez places critical pedagogy and Yuval-Davis transversal dialogue.

All the writers I have discussed in this section are concerned to explore the overlapping spaces or intersections of learning through dialogue and citizenship. All (bar Ranson) acknowledge collective difference both as constitutive of such knowledge acquisition and citizenship and as entailed in their articulation. Difference in this analysis is not a list of deviations from the norm, conceived as the abstract (but, in fact, modelled on a representative of a dominant group). Difference here is a shifting set of identifications in which gender might shape or be shaped by, for example, race, ethnicity or sexual orientation. The connections suggested by these writers between dialogical learning generally, education more specifically, and citizenship constitute, I believe, a very generative space for inquiry. The problem that none of the critics engage with, however, is the nature of education as a particular institutional space. In exploring this third approach. I now want to look at a third way in which the relationship between education, citizenship and difference can be theorised.

Citizenship Enables Education

The third position I want to explore emerges from some of the problems of the two positions I have thus far outlined. According to this third position education will not necessarily advance citizenship, as is claimed by the first view, but rather citizenship (complexly defined) secures (some) education. Hernandez suggests a relationship between education and citizenship that is metonymic; this third position suggests a relationship where one is metaphoric of the other. They are linked, but they are separate.

In contrast to the second view this third position argues that education, like political action, is not only a set of dialogues. Neither Mouffe nor Yuval-Davis discuss the specifics of institutional locations and practices. Both draw most of their examples from new social movements, with unstable and shifting boundaries of action. For Mouffe, institutions must be analysed and engaged with as discursive surfaces rather than empirical referents. Her notion of constantly shifting identity leads her to conclude that there can be as many forms of citizenship as there are interpretations of the ethico-political principles of modern democracy (Mouffe 1992: 237). But what does this multiplicity mean for the teacher or the planner? How is one to act, given particular institutional settings, boundaries and constraints that are not wholly negotiable? Is reflection on the prevailing discourses in terms of the accepted grammar of conduct good enough? Is transversal dialogue, appropriate in developing political strategies, also adequate to a range of other pedagogical settings? What of situations that are complex and ambiguous not only because of the range of meanings of different social actors but also because of different material and institutional conditions? What forms of learning and teaching practice are appropriate to these?

I recently was running an undergraduate seminar on the lessons of the Holocaust for sociology. One of the students, a young British-born man of mixed race, argued that, first, the Holocaust was the 'fault of the Jews' because they failed to resist, and second, that concern about the Holocaust was overstated because it took attention away from the horrors of the slave trade. Throughout the seminar he was churlish and aggressive. He clearly interpreted my engagement with his analysis – first, by pointing to historical work regarding Jewish resistance to the Holocaust; second, by discussing the differences in sociological analyses of the slave trade, and last, in terms of my own response to the Holocaust as a Jew – as a failure to engage with his concerns. Throughout the seminar I was on the brink of tears. I felt utterly deskilled by my inability to connect with a student or to express political ideas in ways that developed rather than foreclosed on learning. Although I was the teacher in a position of institutional authority and my knowledge conferred power, at another level it did not. My failure as a teacher in this instance was painfully confirmed for me when the student did not return to the seminar for the rest of the term.

The moment illustrates two identities in formation, and a sense that one struggle for liberty displaces another, so that they are seen to be mutually exclusive. It suggests that the structuring of an unambiguous grammar of conduct is itself a difficult political process and an even more ambiguous pedagogic encounter. In political confrontations of this type what is learned? What is taught? Where there might have been a transversal dialogue, it appeared to have gone nowhere. Perhaps other members of the class, witnessing the impasse, learned something. But perhaps they too came up against barriers to understanding.

This event indicates for me that while education might overlap with and be entailed by theories of citizenship it also occupies a distinctive realm. It is a space that is simultaneously public, private and intermediate. For education the divisions between these spaces are not clear-cut nor are they loosely intertwined. This is in contrast to the sharp polarity between public and private Arendt demands and the loose collapse of their divisions Yuval-Davis and Mouffe suggest. But the intermediate space of education is not blank. It is marked by global, national, local and micro-political boundaries, strongly invested codes of certain forms of conduct over others. These spaces are partly shaped, but also themselves shape divisions of class, gender, race and ethnicity. All make for a very complex meeting ground of both so-called public and private concerns. While at certain historical moments certain discourses collapse or replace public with private concerns, similar processes might erode the boundaries of education as an intermediate space, making it either entirely the stuff of the personal and subjective, or of the public and objective. At different moments education might be understood as a subset of the political, as an aspect of autonomy and self, or somewhere half-way between, in constant tension with the other discourses like, for example, those of popular culture beyond the classroom, and other processes of political or personal identification that intrude into it. Debbie Epstein and Richard Johnson's work on schooling sexualities brings out this tension with a rich array of empirical detail (Epstein and Johnson 1998). This constant shifting between 'private' and 'public' is precisely what makes education an intermediate space, neither simply 'private' nor simply 'public', but always both in uneasy tension.

In this formulation the role of citizenship, which is entailed both by political action and political interpellation, is to secure an independent intermediate space for education. It is in this space that some of the formulations of difference – conceived as intersecting and 'given' by the political, the economic or the cultural – and indeed the very conception of the political realm itself are critically explored, reconstituted and returned to the public and private spheres for further reconfiguration. I believe that education does not either suppress difference for a greater public good, as in the first position I outline, or celebrate difference in an ever-changing language of collective public action, as in the second position. Rather, I advocate an acknowledgement of a separate space for education, where difference is discursively explored and institutionally framed and reframed.

In this spirit, the South African constitution is premised on a notion that education is a relatively autonomous sphere; it is implied that education and citizenship comprise a converging but different terrain. The constitution guarantees to everyone the right to a basic education, including adult basic education, and further education (beyond four years of basic education) which the state 'through reasonable measures must make progressively available and accessible' (South Africa 1996: 14). It is noteworthy that education is not tied to citizenship, implying that people who are in South Africa as visitors, migrant workers or refugees all have the right to education. But while everyone is guaranteed the right to education, there is no compulsion regarding the necessity to undertake education. The right is an entitlement, not an imperative.

The constitution confers on members of particular cultural, religious or linguistic communities (there are nine recognised official languages) rights to enjoy their culture, practise their religion and use their language, to form associations and other organs of civil society and *to establish their own independent educational institutions*. However, the constitution is explicit that these rights must not be exercised in a manner inconsistent with any provision of the Bill of Rights (*ibid*.: 15). By this means the constitution wishes both to allow particular collectivities the right to continue to exist and conduct educational projects, while wishing to stress that these projects must not enshrine discrimination as outlawed in other sections of the Bill of Rights. It remains to be seen whether, for example, religious and other associations which discriminate against women or non-members can be prosecuted under the constitution, or whether a defence of cultural authenticity can be made and be accepted by the constitutional court.

In some ways the clauses of the constitution dealing with education are quite vague. In contrast with the very tight delimitation of roles and activities outlined with regard to employment, for example, education is left loose and unspecified. Indeed, the constitution suggests that in contrast with the view that education should be used to promote active citizenship, as implied by Gellner for example, the South African constitution sets broad parameters of rights, and devolves education provision to state institutions and culturally identified bodies of civil society. Education in this view will not necessarily advance citizenship, but rather citizenship secures (some) education.

In some respects this is a useful position. Education, like political action, is not only a set of dialogues or a social movement with unstable and shifting boundaries. As a material institutional space that is at once public, private, and intermediate, it needs a measure of autonomy and independence that would allow difference and identity to be discursively analysed and subjected to critical reflection.

Conclusion

The three positions on the relationship between citizenship, education and difference I have outlined each entail a different way of thinking about these terms. In the first position education moulds and integrates the citizen into the polity. Collective difference may be ignored in the interests of equality or tolerated in the interest of harmony. In some contexts certain forms of difference, for example concerning gender or religion, might be more accommodated than other forms of difference, like race for example. But in other contexts the boundaries of tolerance and rejection might be configured differently.

In the second position, I outline how citizenship and education are theorised in terms of their intersections and how part of this theorising entails an acknowledgement of the material and discursive power of difference. Gendered, racialised and ethnic differences are powerful forces shaping the interconnections posited between education and citizenship.

In the third position I outline, which is the position I find most useful, there is an attempt to consider how citizenship enables education and also forms its particular intermediate institutional space. Gendered, racialised, ethnicised and other forms of difference shape and are shaped by the rigidities and the changes in this space. It is in this space, contoured in particular formations at particular moments, that views of citizenship might be imposed or that critiques of particular formulations of citizenship might be articulated. Both entail connections or divisions between collectivities, subsuming or enunciating their difference according to complex readings. The relationship between education and citizenship is not given, nor is it endlessly elastic. It is constituted and reconstituted around material conditions and the languages that frame and reframe these.

Notes

1. A number of the ideas in this chapter emerged in discussion over many years with my father, Jack Unterhalter. Although we often took quite different positions his assistance with sources and his engaged but always sceptical insight were always inspirational. His sudden death in 1997 meant that he could never read a more polished version of many of our long talks, but this article is as much of him as it is of me. My thanks also to Diana Leonard, Valerie Hey, Patricia White, Penny Enslin and Linda Chisholm for comments on earlier drafts of this chapter and to my brother, David Unterhalter, for some guidance on sources. A special note of gratitude to Pnina Werbner and Nira Yuval-Davis for critical and stimulating engagement with these ideas in the process of revising the initial conference paper for publication.

2. For a more detailed discussion of these policy documents and changing conceptions of the South African polity see Unterhalter (1998), Unterhalter and Samson (1998).

3. For some examples of this approach see Psacharapoulos and Woodhall (1985), World Bank (1995), Psacharapoulos (1995), Reich (1991), Hutton (1996), Fukuyama (1995). For some critiques see Escobar (1995), Bennell (1995), Carr and Hartnett (1996b), Lingard, Knight and Porter (1993), Kenway (1995).

4. See for example Andrews (1991), Mouffe (1992), Phillips (1993), Held (1995), Yuval-Davis (1997b), Glaser (1997), Hernandez (1997).

References

Alcoff, L. and E. Potter (eds) (1993). *Feminist Epistemologies*, London: Routledge.

Andrews, G. (ed.) (1991). *Citizenship*, London: Lawrence and Wishart.

Arendt, H. (1958). *The Human Condition*, Chicago: University of Chicago Press.

Bennell, P. (1995). *Using and Abusing Rates of Return: a Critique of the World Bank 1995* Education Sector Review, IDS Working Paper No. 22, Brighton: Institute of Development Studies, University of Sussex.

Carr, W. and A. Hartnett (1996a). 'Civic Education, Democracy and the English Political Tradition', in J. Demaine and H. Entwhistle (eds) *Beyond Communitarianism:*

Citizenship, Politics and Education, Basingstoke: Macmillan, pp. 64-82.

— (1996b). *Education and the Struggle for Democracy: a Politics of Educational Ideas*, Buckingham: Open University Press.

Chambers, I. and L. Curti (eds) (1996). *The Post-Colonial Question: Common Skies, Divided Horizon*, London: Routledge.

Cole, J. (1987). *Crossroads: the Politics of Reform and Repression 1976-1986*, Johannesburg: Ravan.

Demaine, J. (1996). 'Beyond Communitarianism: Citizenship, Politics and Education', in J. Demaine and H. Entwhistle (eds) *Beyond Communitarianism: Citizenship, Politics and Education*, Basingstoke: Macmillan, pp. 6–29.

Elshtain, J. B. (1997). 'Political Children: Reflections on Hannah Arendt's Distinction between Public and Private Life', in M. L. Shanley and U. Narayan (eds) *Reconstructing Political Theory: Feminist Perspectives*, Cambridge: Polity Press, pp. 109–27.

Epstein, D. and R. Johnson (1998). *Schooling Sexualities*, Buckingham: Open University Press.

Escobar, A. (1995). *Encountering Development*, Princeton: Princeton University Press.

Fogelman, K. (1996). 'Education for Citizenship and the National Curriculum', in J. Demaine and H. Entwhistle (eds) *Beyond Communitarianism: Citizenship, Politics and Education*, Basingstoke: Macmillan, pp. 83–91.

Foster, V. (1997). 'Feminist Theory and the Construction of Citizenship Education', in K. Kennedy (ed.) *Citizenship, Education and the Modern State*, London: Falmer, pp. 54–65.

Foucault, M. (1977). *Discipline and Punish*, London: Allen Lane.

Fukuyama, F. (1995). *Trust: the Social Virtues and the Creation of Prosperity*, London: Hamish Hamilton.

Gellner, E. (1983). *Nations and Nationalism*, Oxford: Blackwell.

Glaser, D. (1997). 'South Africa and the Limits of Civil Society', *Journal of Southern African Studies* 23, 1: 5–25.

Green, A. (1990). *Education and State Formation: the Rise of Education Systems in England, France and the USA*, London: Macmillan.

Guttman, A. (1987). *Democratic Education*, Princeton: Princeton University Press.

— (1995). 'Challenges of Multiculturalism in Democratic Education', *Philosophy of Education*: 86–105.

Harber, C. (1989). *Politics in African Education*, London: Macmillan.

— (1992). *Democratic Learning and Learning for Democracy: Education for Active Citizenship*, Ticknall: Education Now Books.

Held, D. (1995). *Democracy and the Global Order: From the Modern State to Cosmopolitan Governance*, Cambridge: Polity.

Hernandez, A. (1997). *Pedagogy, Democracy and Feminism: Rethinking the Public Sphere*, Albany: State University of New York Press.

Hogan, D. (1997). 'The Logic of Protection: Citizenship, Justice and Political Community', in K. Kennedy (ed.) *Citizenship, Education and the Modern State*, London: Falmer, pp. 40–54.

Hutton, W. (1996). *The State We're In*, London: Vintage.

Kenway, J. (1990). *Gender and Education Policy: a Call for New Directions*, Geelong: Deakin University Press.

Kenway, J. (ed.) (1995). *Marketing Education: Some Critical Issues*, Malvern: Deakin University Press.

Kingdom, E. (1996). 'Gender and Citizenship Rights', in J. Demaine and H. Entwhistle (eds) *Beyond Communitarianism: Citizenship, Politics and Education*, Basingstoke: Macmillan.

Lingard, B., J. Knight and P. Porter (eds) (1993). *Schooling Reform in Hard Times*, London: Falmer.

Lister, R. (1997). 'Citizenship: Towards a Feminist Synthesis', *Feminist Review* 57: 28–47.

Maynard, M. (1995). 'Beyond the "Big Three": the Development of Feminist Theory in the 1990s', *Women's History Review* 4, 3: 259–81.

Mouffe, C. (1992). 'Democratic Citizenship and the Political Community', in Chantal Mouffe (ed.) *Dimensions of Radical Democracy: Pluralism, Citizenship, Community*, London: Verso, pp. 225–39.

Passerin d'Entrèves, M. (1992). 'Hannah Arendt and the Idea of Citizenship', in Chantal Mouffe (ed.) *Dimensions of Radical Democracy: Pluralism, Citizenship, Community*, London: Verso, pp. 145–68.

Pateman, C. (1988). *The Sexual Contract,* Cambridge: Polity Press.

Phillips, A. (1993). *Democracy and Difference,* Cambridge: Polity Press.

Platzky, L. and C. Walker (1985). *The Surplus People: Forced Removals in South Africa*, Johannesburg: Ravan.

Psacharapoulos, G. (1995). *Building Human Capital for Better Lives*, Washington: World Bank.

Psacharapoulos, G. and M. Woodhall (1985). *Education for Development: An Analysis of Investment Choices,* New York: Oxford University Press.

Ranson, S. (1993). 'Markets of Democracy for Education', *British Journal of Educational Studies* 41, 4: 333–52.

Reich, R. (1991). *The Work of Nations: Preparing Ourselves for 21st Century Capitalism*, London: Simon and Schuster.

Sachs, A. (1990). *Protecting Human Rights in a New South Africa*, Cape Town: David Philip.

Shanley, M. L. and U. Narayan (eds) (1997). *Reconstructing Political Theory: Feminist Perspectives,* Cambridge: Polity Press.

South Africa (1996). *Constitution of the Republic of South Africa*, Pretoria: Constitutional Assembly Government Printer.

Spring, J. (1980). *Educating the Worker Citizen: the Social, Economic and Political Foundations of Education*, New York: Longman

Unterhalter, E. (1987). *Forced Removal: the Division, Segregation and Control of the People of South Africa,* London: International Defence and Aid Fund for Southern Africa.

— (1998). 'Stakeholding: Promises and Penalties for Educational Transformation', paper delivered at the World Congress of Comparative Education Societies, Cape Town.

Unterhalter, E. and M. Samson (1998). 'Unpacking the Gender of Global Curriculum in South Africa', paper presented at the Symposium on 'Globalization of Education: Feminist Perspectives on Schooling, Family and State', AERA Annual Meeting, San Diego, April 1998.

de Villiers, B., D. Van Wyk, J. Dugard and J. Davis (1994). *Rights and Constitutionalism: the New South African Legal Order*, Oxford: Clarendon Press.

White, J. (1995). 'Education and Personal Well-being in a Secular Universe', Inaugural Lecture, London: Institute of Education, University of London.

White, P. (1996). *Civic Virtues and Public Schooling: Educating Citizens for a Democratic Society*, New York and London: Teachers College Press.

Whitty, G. (1997). 'Consumer Rights versus Citizen Rights in Contemporary Education Policy', in D. Bridges (ed.) *Education, Autonomy and Democratic Citizenship in a Changing World*, London: Routledge.

Williams, P. (1993). *The Alchemy of Race and Rights,* London: Virago.

Woolman, S. and D. Davis (1996). 'The Last Laugh: Du Plessis v De Klerk, Classical Liberalism, Creole Liberalism and the Application of Fundamental Rights under the Interim and Final Constitutions', *South African Journal on Human Rights* 12, 3: 361–404.

World Bank (1995). *Priorities and Strategies for Education, a World Bank Review*, Washington: World Bank.

Yuval-Davis, N. (1997a). 'Women, Citizenship and Difference', *Feminist Review,* 57: 4–28.

— (1997b). *Gender and Nation*, London: Sage.

CHAPTER 7

Producing the Mothers of the Nation: Race, Class and Contemporary US Population Policies

Patricia Hill Collins

In the United States, notions of motherhood influence definitions of American national identity. Just as mothers are important to family well-being, ideas about motherhood remain central to constructing both the citizenship rights of diverse groups of women and American social policy. In a nation-state like the United States where social class, race, gender and citizenship status operate as intersecting dimensions of social inequality, neither families nor the mothers within them experience the equal treatment associated with citizenship. In the 1990s challenges to affirmative action policies, the emergence of increasingly strident anti-immigration rhetoric, and concerted efforts to reinstate 'values' in civic life emerged to preserve racialised and class-specific notions of American national identity. In this politicised climate, women's citizenship rights articulate with questions of their suitability to be 'mothers of the nation'.

In this chapter, I explore this relationship between motherhood across citizenship categories and American population policies. I survey selected contemporary population policies for middle-class White women, working-class White women, African-American women, and undocumented immigrant Latinas. The distinctive social locations of these four groups as first-class, second-class and non-citizens shapes their perceived suitability as mothers of the nation. As a result, population policies applied to each group demonstrate how American social policies are designed to regulate experiences with motherhood of women from different racial, social class, and citizenship groups in defence of perceived nation-state interests.

Motherhood, Citizenship and Population Policies

In the United States, families constitute primary sites of belonging, whether they are kinship groups organised around biological cores, communities composed of families residing in geographically identifiable, ethnically and/ or racially segregated neighbourhoods, so-called racial families codified in science and law, or the nation-state as extended family marked by citizenship and alien status (Collins 1998). Family operates as a fundamental unit of social class structure, whether via affluent and/or middle-class White families' inherited wealth or White working-class assumptions about entitlement to the male 'family wage' (Collins 1997). Grounded in notions of blood ties where who belongs to one's 'blood' or family remains central to issues of responsibility and accountability, individuals feel that they 'owe' and are responsible for members of their families, even when such family members lack merit. In contrast, no such allegiance is extended to outsiders or to those who somehow have been denied citizenship in biological, geographic, racial, ethnic or national 'families'.

Motherhood serves a fundamental gatekeeping function in all of the above areas. Just as mothers are typically central to family well-being, particular versions of motherhood permeating the American 'family ideal' (Andersen 1991) frame American national identity. Ideas about idealised and stigmatised motherhood within family rhetoric contribute to the links among family, race and nation. As a result, the issue of who will control women's mothering experiences lies at the heart of state family planning decisions. When attached to state policy in a racialised nation-state like the United States, this question of controlling the fertility of women within different race, class and citizenship groups becomes politicised (Davis 1981). Eugenics movements illustrate the thinking underlying population policies designed to control the motherhood of different groups of women for reasons of nationality and/or race (Haller 1984). Aiming to increase fertility for more desirable segments of the population and decrease fertility of less worthy citizens, in periods of profound social change eugenics philosophies implicitly shape public policy. Some women emerge as more worthy 'mothers of the nation' than others. In the United States, the civil rights, women's, and other social movements of the 1950s through the early 1970s, because they stimulated widespread social change, apparently created such a climate. American population policies from the late 1970s to the present become more comprehensible when placed in the context of a rhetoric of national family planning.

Based on their racial, ethnic, social class and citizenship status, different groups of women encounter markedly different population policies. Broadly defined, population policies encompass the constellation of social policies, institutional arrangements and ideological constructions that shape the reproductive histories of all women. Social class and citizenship status both affect women's experiences with population policies. Because women who are middle-class and/or affluent American citizens do not depend on government programmes, market-based policies and private sector initiatives more often regulate this group's experiences. While state policy regulates these private sector activities, state involvement is thus less visible as an active agent in structuring population policies for middle-class and affluent women.

In contrast, working-class and poor women with American citizenship rely more overtly on public revenues and as a result are more likely to encounter population policies crafted within and implemented by social welfare bureaucracies.[1]

Depending on their race, region of the country and rural or urban residency, these women experience varying patterns of second-class citizenship. While women lacking citizenship may appear to fall completely outside population policies, reliance on the domestic labour of these undocumented workers makes their mothering experiences more central to population policies than is typically realised.

Moreover, recent technological changes have profoundly altered the very category of mother. The proliferation of reproductive technologies in the post-Second World War era fostered the splitting of motherhood into the three categories of genetic, gestational and social motherhood. Genetic mothers are those who contribute the genetic material to another human being. Gestational mothers are those who carry the developing foetus *in utero* until birth. Social mothers care for children actually born. Traditional views of motherhood promulgated by the traditional family ideal present one White middle-class woman as fulfilling all three functions, assisted in her social mothering by working-class women and/or women of colour. However, new reproductive technologies that have made it possible for two or even three women to each specialise in one of these mothering categories for one particular child further complicate population policies applied to multiple groups of women (Rowland 1987; Raymond 1993).

The following sketches of population policies targeted toward different groups of women outline the differential choices offered to women of varying racial, social class and citizenship groups. The analysis is not meant to be exhaustive but instead suggests an analytical framework that might be applied to all women in the United States. Moreover, within each group, individual women exercise considerable agency. Thus, nothing about the following discussion should be taken to mean that women's experiences are determined by their racial, ethnic, social class or citizenship status. Rather, these categories constrain choices and may foster women's agency in ways that can be quite unintended.

Mothers of the Nation: Middle-Class White Women

Within a logic of eugenics, where the falling birth rate of the dominant group is seen as 'race suicide', women belonging to dominant groups are routinely encouraged to increase their reproductive capacities (Yuval-Davis 1997). In the United States, the value placed on whiteness and its longstanding association with first-class American citizenship links White women's reproduction to American national interests in profoundly important ways. In order to avoid 'race suicide' and meet so-called positive eugenic goals, American

White women of varying social classes are encouraged to become genetic and gestational mothers. Through their genetic motherhood, White women hold the key to notions of racial purity so critical to racial categorisation in the United States. When it comes to social motherhood, however, not all White American women are the same. Through their ability to transmit national culture to the young, middle-class and affluent White women allegedly remain superior to all other groups in socialising White youth into naturalised hierarchies of race, gender, age, sexuality and social class. Moreover, middle-class White women have also been central as symbols of the family, neighbourhood and national territory that must be protected and defended. As a result, middle-class and affluent White women are encouraged to have babies and remain firmly entrenched in both popular culture and scholarship as emblematic of desirable motherhood worth protecting.

Population policies targeted toward middle-class and affluent White women remain less visible than those aimed at less affluent women primarily because such policies remain privatised. One feature of the traditional family ideal is its alleged economic self-sufficiency (Coontz 1992). Idealised motherhood constructed within these parameters demonstrates a similar economic autonomy. Insurance coverage allied with the benefits of full-time employment via husbands' or women's own employment, corporate day care for working mothers, and tuition remission plans for children in families with employed parents, all directly or indirectly subsidise middle-class women's reproductive activities. Moreover, state policies that motivate middle-class women to reproduce remain largely hidden in a complex edifice of tax policies such as the deductibility of home mortgage interest and child care credits for the children of working parents. State policies encouraging middle-class White women's fertility operate less through visible state social welfare policies than through less overt state policies governing taxation, insurance, employment conditions and health care regulation (Ikemoto 1996).

Collectively, the privatisation of motherhood, combined with corporate and public policies, favours middle-class White women as genetic, gestational and social mothers. For example, the construction of infertility as a national tragedy via considerable American media attention reflects a preoccupation with reproducing the White middle class. Infertility is typically presented either as a human tragedy – the case of the unfortunate woman who cannot bear the child she so desperately wants – or, increasingly, as the personal failing of those women who pursued careers, waited too long to have babies, and now find themselves childless because they turned their backs on their rightful roles as women. In most cases, the deserving infertile women are White and affluent – poor infertile women are of little concern. Infertile middle-class women are assisted with a dazzling array of medical advances to foster the genetic and gestational motherhood that leads to social motherhood. Depending on their private insurance carriers, these women may be able to defray part of the enormous costs of infertility procedures (Raymond 1993). New reproductive technologies such as *in vitro* fertilisation, sex predetermination, surrogate embryo transfer, and ability to fund surrogacy are routinely differentially distributed depending on the race and class of women (Rowland 1987; Nsiah-Jefferson 1989).

These new reproductive technologies have been accompanied by a complementary set of social policies targeted towards social motherhood among middle-class White women. Daily and calendar year school schedules, recreational facility hours, medical and dental appointments, and other social institutions remain organised around the assumption of the idealised stay-at-home mother and/or affluent mothers who can pay someone to take up the slack. While working mothers from all social classes stand to gain from child care reforms such as paid or unpaid maternity leave and employer-provided day care, again, such reforms remain disproportionately directed at middle-class White women.

Children born to middle-class and affluent White mothers foster the continuation both of biologically White families and of racially homogeneous neighbourhoods described by sociologists Douglas Massey and Nancy Denton (1993) as 'American apartheid'. Correspondingly, child welfare policies in the United States favour middle-class White children. Education, health care, housing, recreational facilities, nutrition and public facilities such as libraries and police protection all keep this group's interests in mind. Moreover, the privatisation of these services effectively insulates middle-class White children from the perceived harm of contact with all but a handpicked few working-class Whites and children of colour. While the signs of racial segregation have been taken down, racial and social class segregation persists. For middle-class White mothers raising children in planned suburban developments enjoying adequate police protection, safe schools, convenient shopping and private transportation, social motherhood remains an attractive option. For women lacking class privileges of this sort, social motherhood operates quite differently.

Becoming 'Fit' Mothers: Working-Class White Women

Working-class White women's experiences with motherhood reveals how social class affects White women's experiences with first- and second-class citizenship. Because working-class White women can be genetic and gestational mothers of White children, this group becomes 'fit' to produce the biological or population base of the nation. Working-class White women remain less 'fit', however, for passing on national culture, raising academically and economically productive citizens, being symbols of the nation and exploring other dimensions of social motherhood (Yuval-Davis 1997). Within this contradiction, working-class White women are encouraged to give birth to children, but receive much less support in raising them. If married, such women experience the pressure of declining family wages available to their spouses as well as their own vulnerable positions in changing labour markets. In contrast, unmarried women, especially if young, encounter pressures to give birth to White babies in order to relinquish them for adoption.

Reproductive, employment and social welfare policies having disproportionate impact on working-class White women reflect this basic contradiction of encouraging working-class White women to become genetic and gestational mothers while stigmatising their performance as social mothers. With the passage of *Roe vs Wade* in 1973, working-class and poor White women gained access to legal and safe abortions. At the same time, the decreasing stigma attached to single motherhood, coupled with changes in eligibility for social welfare benefits, made it possible for low-income single mothers to procure a steady if inadequate subsistence income for their children. Many White women who formerly would have remained in troubled relationships and marriages, or released their children for adoption, chose to raise their children as single parents. Together, these factors fostered increasing rates of White female-headed households with children, coupled with decreasing availability of healthy White adoptable babies.

Recent efforts to limit access to abortion and other selected family planning services for working-class and poor women, to weaken affirmative action programmes in higher education and the workplace, and the 1996 Personal Responsibility and Work Opportunity and Reconciliation Act (PRWORA) that abolished the federal Aid to Families with Dependent Children (AFDC) programme by placing it under the supervision of fifty individual states, collectively provide working-class White women with a changing constellation of reproductive 'choices'. For example, the 1977 Hyde amendment had the effect of making it more difficult for working-class women, on and off public welfare assistance, to secure safe abortions through Medicaid on the grounds that the state should not 'pay' for abortions from public money. It thus encouraged working-class White women to carry babies to term. Similarly, the work requirements of PRWORA are designed to push even more working-class White women into the labour market, often into part-time work or service jobs that offer less desirable benefits and salaries. The advice that these mothers should find work sounds hollow in a climate where adequate and affordable day care is non-existent, where public schools maintain hours leaving considerable unsupervised time, and where weakening commitment to training, higher education and employment equity make it more difficult for working-class women to procure adequate employment. Cutbacks in support for poor families, described by Katz (1989) as a shift from the war on poverty to the war on welfare, mean that the most impoverished segments of White working-class women receive decreasing levels of support for their children. In political and economic contexts constrained by such limited 'choices', adoption can emerge as the best alternative.

Collectively, these policies suggest that ideological portrayals of working-class White women as mothers must continue to valorise genetic and gestational motherhood yet support the notion that working-class White women are less fit social mothers. When the cost of raising White children can be supported by the family wages of White working-class family units approximating the traditional family ideal, then such children represent few problems for the state. In cases where the state must take a more active role in supporting the children of working-class White single mothers, however, children are wanted only if their cost can be shifted to White, middle-class, married-couple families. Working-class White women thus encounter a specific constellation of population policies. They are denied abortion services. They are denied educational and employment opportunities that would allow them to support their children financially. They encounter increased exposure to cultural messages that encourage them to have their biologically White babies but to become moral mothers by relinquishing their children for adoption to 'good' homes.

'Undeserving' Mothers: Working-Class African-American Women

Controlling the genetic, gestational, and social mothering experiences of working-class African-American women has long been essential to both a racialised American nationalism and Black women's accompanying second-class citizenship. In prior eras, a combination of a need for cheap, unskilled labour and the political powerlessness of Black populations fostered population policies that encouraged Black women to have many children. Since African-Americans themselves absorbed the costs attached to reproduction, a large, disenfranchised and impoverished Black population matched the perceived interest of elites. Black children cost employers little because they required minimal training and could be easily fired. In Southern states, for example, African-American children's public schools closed to allow them to work in the fields while their White counterparts remained in their classrooms. Moreover, because African-American children were denied education and social welfare benefits routinely extended to other groups, they cost the state little.

Two factors in the post-Second World War American political economy changed all this. First, as jobs were mechanised and shifted outside American borders, the decreasing need for low-skilled labour paralleled an increasing reliance on a more highly educated and expensive workforce. Raising children became more expensive, and privatising these costs became increasingly attractive to employers. Second, the social movements of the 1950s and 1960s produced some unintended effects concerning African-American citizenship rights. Blacks began to benefit from entitlement programmes long enjoyed by Whites. For example, the use of 'employable mother rules' by many states from the 1940s through the 1960s worked to deny Black mothers ADC/

AFDC benefits, thereby coercing them to perform agricultural and domestic work (Amott 1990). Gaining access to AFDC, however, meant that African-American women could refuse exploitative jobs and gain social welfare benefits for their children. From the perspective of employers, Black labour became expensive to train and hire, and African-American children in particular became increasingly expendable.

Beginning with the 1965 government report *The Negro Family: the Case for National Action,* also known as the Moynihan Report, African-American women as mothers increasingly came under attack (Coontz 1992). Black women were deemed deficient in all three categories of mothering. Since African-American children were increasingly seen as expendable in the labour market, Black women's contributions as genetic mothers became devalued. African-American women were also deemed poor social mothers to their own children and, following the mother-blaming ushered in by the Moynihan Report, a heightened and more virulent strain of mother-blaming emerged. Black mothers became increasingly condemned for a host of social problems plaguing African-American communities that allegedly resulted from their faulty parenting (Zinn 1989). While African-American women's potential contributions as gestational mothers has yet to be determined, the 1993 *Johnson vs Calvert* case provides some intriguing insights. In that case, Anna Johnson, an African-American woman, was hired as a gestational mother by a married couple consisting of a White father and a Filipino mother. When Ms Johnson changed her mind and sued to keep the baby, she was denied custody. The court had difficulty conceptualising a Black woman as the mother of a White baby (Ikemoto 1996).

Portraying African-American women as unfit mothers generates support for coercive population policies and cultural practices. The 'unfitness' of working-class Black mothers as qualified to pass on national culture has been constructed in opposition to the 'fitness' of middle-class White women. Moreover, these negative controlling images applied to African-American women also work to disqualify Black women from ever being considered as symbolising the nation that merits protection. If anything, working-class Black women have been constructed as the enemy within, the group producing the population that threatens the American national interest of maintaining itself as a 'White' nation-state. Joining longstanding notions of Black women as unfit mothers are newly emerging images of Black women as sexually irresponsible and/or abusive mothers. Portraying Black women as unable to handle rational decision making and choice remains central to constructions of Black women's maternal unfitness. Building on long-standing notions of Black people and women as being less intellectual, more impulsive, and more emotional, such images provide a context for quasi-coercive population policies. Because Black women are 'unfit' mothers they become 'undeserving' of the benefits of belonging to the American national family (Lubiano 1992).

In such a climate, the social institutions that working-class Black women encounter as mothers take on a particularly punitive cast. Working-class and poor Black mothers are often employed yet are severely disadvantaged. Child care remains hard to find and, for those in part-time or seasonal employment, health benefits are limited. Overall lack of job security makes it difficult to plan. Recent figures show that Black women's fertility remains slightly higher than that of White women (2.2. versus 2.0 on average in 1995 – see Bianchi and Spain 1996). But these figures have to be seen against a history of racial segregation that means that working-class Black women encounter limited opportunities in their own education, housing, employment, access to health care, and access to quality schools and recreational facilities for their children. Moreover, population policies search for ways to reduce the size of the Black population. Population policies directed at African-American women typically encourage permanent and/or reversible sterilisation, especially if women receive public assistance. Ongoing debates about the politics surrounding Norplant and Depo Provera as reversible forms of sterilisation illustrate these issues. Even though African-American women often welcome these temporary sterilisation 'choices', this exercise of choice must be viewed in the context of the limited nature of choices that working-class Black women have in areas of sexuality and fertility.

Mothers for Hire: Undocumented Latinas

Historically, the range of reproductive choices available to middle-class White women could not have occurred without the exploitation of the labour of African-American women, among others. As women of the desirable group, middle-class White women have long depended on the labour of poor women and/or racial/ethnic women to fulfil the less desirable aspects of social motherhood. Historically, African-American women served as child care workers and have assumed much responsibility for the domestic labour that allowed middle-class White women to maintain the position of good mother, often at great personal cost to their own children (Dill 1988; Glenn 1992). Recently, the combination of African-American women's physical unavailability due to intensified residential segregation, their access to social welfare benefits and other entitlements of American citizenship, and ideological bashing of Black women as 'welfare queens' have rendered African-American women less attractive as social mothers for middle-class White children.

Currently, undocumented immigrant women from Mexico and other Latin American countries have become one of the newest groups of women who provide social motherhood for the children of more affluent women in the United States. Research exploring the experiences of this super-exploited group of women as genetic, gestational and social mothers to their own children remains in its infancy. Migration literature is just beginning to examine the significance of gender itself (see, for example, Pedraza 1991; and Hondagneu-Sotelo 1996) let alone women migrants' experiences with genetic, gestational and social motherhood. Rather, current concern seems targeted on the employability of undocumented immigrant women, as well as on potential claims on state services of their children.

Through its execution of the Immigration Reform and Control Act (IRCA) of 1986, the Immigration and Naturalisation Service (INS) continued the historical role of the state in using government policies to maintain racial/ethnic women as a low-wage labour force or, in Grace Chang's (1994) words, new 'employable mothers'. Anti-immigration rhetoric demonstrates a new dimension, however: immigrants as economic welfare burdens. Former discussions of immigration that emphasised the fear that male migrant labourers might steal jobs from 'native' workers have shifted to claims that immigrant women may increase welfare spending. 'Men as job stealers are no longer seen as the immigrant problem,' suggests Chang. 'Instead, immigrant women as idle, welfare-dependent mothers and inordinate breeders of dependants are seen as the great menace' (1994: 263).

The invisibility and exploitation of undocumented Latinas as employable mothers speaks to the importance of American citizenship in framing Latinas' experiences with population policies. Because such women exist outside the national family, their experiences as mothers hold little interest to Whites, African-Americans, and other groups with citizenship. Such women appear in the literature primarily as employees fulfilling social mothering functions for other groups. Overall, by standing outside the nexus of family relations, undocumented Latinas reinforce the meaning of belonging.

Closing Remarks

In the United States, intersections of race and social class foster distinctive population policies for women of varying citizenship statuses. If the American nation-state is conceptualised as a racialised national family, with the traditional family ideal structuring normative family values, then standards used to assess the contributions of family members in White, heterosexual, married-couple households with children become foundational for assessing group contributions to national well-being overall. Middle-class White women are encouraged to reproduce and are provided with infertility services and top-notch prenatal care. Working-class White women are encouraged to reproduce only if they absorb the costs of child rearing or relinquish their children to another home. Working-class African-American women, especially those living in poverty, are discouraged from reproducing at all. Finally, as employable mothers, undocumented Latinas remain virtually invisible. Collectively, the experiences of these four groups suggest that when it comes to being 'mothers of the nation', race, class and citizenship status matter greatly.

Note

1. The two-stream approach of the American social welfare state shows clear biases concerning how desirable mothers should be treated and how their less desirable sisters should be handled (Gordon 1994). The first, the social insurance component of Social Security, Veteran's Benefits, Medicare and Disability, contains programmes that are not stigmatised. In contrast, the second stream, social welfare programmes for people in poverty such as Aid to Families with Dependent Children, operate quite differently. The changing recipients of this programme reflect efforts to craft the programme, not to meet the needs of the recipients, but to address the labour needs of the economy overall (Amott 1990; Brewer 1994). Lacking the income to purchase private insurance and health care services, poor women and women of colour are often dependent on local, state and federal government to provide reproductive services.

References

Amott, T. L. (1990). 'Black Women and AFDC: Making Entitlement Out of Necessity', in L. Gordon (ed.) *Women, the State, and Welfare*, Madison: University of Wisconsin Press, pp. 280–300.

Andersen, M. L. (1991). 'Feminism and the American Family Ideal', *Journal of Comparative Family Studies* 22, 2: 235–46.

Bianchi, Suzanne M. and Daphne Spain (1996). 'Women, Work, and Family in America', Population Reference Bureau 51, 3, Washington DC: Population Reference Bureau.

Brewer, R. (1994). 'Race, Gender and US State Welfare Policy: the Nexus of Inequality for African American Families', in G. Young and B. Dickerson (eds) *Colour Class and Country: Experiences of Gender,* London: Zed Books, pp. 115–28.

Chang, G. (1994). 'Undocumented Latinas: the New "Employable Mothers"', in E. N. Glenn, G. Chang, and L. R. Forcey (eds) *Mothering: Ideology, Experience, and Agency,* New York: Routledge, pp. 259–86.

Collins, P. Hill (1997). 'African-American Women and Economic Justice: a Preliminary Analysis of Wealth, Family and Black Social Class', *University of Cincinnati Law Review* 65, 3: 825–52.

— (1998). 'It's All In the Family: Intersections of Gender, Race, Class and Nation', *Hypatia*, 13, 3: 62–82.

Coontz, S. (1992). *The Way We Never Were: American Families and the Nostalgia Trap*, New York: Basic Books.

Davis, A. Y. (1981). *Women, Race, and Class*, New York: Random House.

Dill, B. T. (1988). 'Our Mothers' Grief: Racial Ethnic Women and the Maintenance of Families', *Journal of Family History* 13, 4: 415–31.

Glenn, E. N. (1992). 'From Servitude to Service Work: Historical Continuities in the Racial Division of Paid Reproductive Labour', *Signs* 18, 1: 1–43.

Gordon, L. (1994). *Pitied but Not Entitled: Single Mothers and the History of Welfare,* Cambridge: Harvard University Press.

Haller, M. H. (1984 [1963]). *Eugenics: Hereditarian Attitudes in American Thought*, New Brunswick: Rutgers University.

Hondagneu-Sotelo, P. (1996). 'Overcoming Patriarchical Constraints: the Reconstruction of Gender Relations Among Mexican Immigrant Women and Men', in E. N. Chow, D. Wilkinson, and M. B. Zinn (eds) *Race, Class, and Gender: Common Bonds, Different Voices,* Thousand Oaks, CA: Sage, pp. 184–205.

Ikemoto, L. C. (1996). 'The In/Fertile, the Too Fertile, and the Dysfertile', *Hastings Law Journal* 47, 4: 1007–61.

Katz, M. B. (1989). *The Undeserving Poor: From the War on Poverty to the War on Welfare,* New York: Pantheon.

Lubiano, W. (1992). 'Black Ladies, Welfare Queens, and State Minstrels: Ideological War by Narrative Means', in T. Morrison (ed.) *In Race-ing Justice, En-gendering Power: Essays on Anita Hill, Clarence Thomas, and the Construction of Social Reality*, New York: Pantheon, pp. 323–63.

Massey, D. S. and N. A. Denton. (1993). *American Apartheid: Segregation and the Making of the Underclass*, Cambridge, MA: Harvard University Press.

Nsiah-Jefferson, L. (1989). 'Reproductive Laws, Women of Colour, and Low-Income Women', in S. Cohen and N. Taub (eds) *Reproductive Laws for the 1990s*, Clifton, NJ: Humana Press, pp. 23–67.

Oliver, M. L. and T. M. Shapiro. (1995). *Black Wealth/White Wealth: a New Perspective on Racial Inequality*, New York: Routledge.

Pedraza, S. (1991). 'Women and Migration: the Social Consequences of Gender', *Annual Review of Sociology* 17: 303–25.

Raymond, J. (1993). *Women as Wombs: Reproductive Technologies and the Battle over Women's Freedom*, San Francisco: Harper San Francisco.

Rowland, R. (1987). 'Technology and Motherhood: Reproductive Choice Reconsidered', *Signs* 12, 3: 512–28.

Yuval-Davis, N. (1997). *Gender and Nation*, Thousand Oaks, CA: Sage.

Zinn, M. B. (1989). 'Family, Race, and Poverty in the Eighties', *Signs* 14, 4: 875–84.

CHAPTER 8

Constitutionally Excluded: Citizenship and (Some) Irish Women

Ronit Lentin

Introduction

> I am 60 years of age, born in Ireland, Traveller all my life and was still discriminated against. If you want to go for a drink, won't be served, there's time if you go into a café you won't be served. Children call us bitches.... So there's an awful lot of discrimination, even if you go into a shop you're going to buy a few groceries, you're followed around ... to see what you're doing ... and that's nothing compared to the names we are called at times ... but ... you are born in this country, reared in it, we are the real Irish.... (K, personal communication, April 1997)

This comment by a Traveller woman talking about the exclusion of Irish Travellers, a group which sees itself as 'more authentically Irish' than the settled Irish, illustrates the erasure, by the narrow definition of 'Irishness', of members of minority ethnicities and consequently, of the truly multi-ethnic nature of Irish society. This chapter argues that neither 'Irishness' nor 'Irish women' have been ethnically problematised in discussions of Irish national identity. The chapter links the construction of Irish national identity, the 1937 constitution, citizenship, and racism to the gendered access to citizenship by women members of one minority ethnicity, Irish Travellers – though women of other ethnic minorities, as well as refugees and asylum seekers, share with Travellers a limited access to Irish citizenship.

Traditionally an out-migration country, Ireland is fast becoming an in-migration destination, an integral part of 'Fortress Europe'. Between 1992 and August 1998, 9,449 people applied for asylum in Ireland compared with 39 in 1992 (Nozinic, forthcoming), drawn by Ireland's economic success and the generous welfare payments to asylum seekers, with a resulting increase in racist discourses (for example, Cullen 1997: 11).

Mohanty (1991: 75) argues that claims to the universality of gender oppression are problematic since they are based on the assumption that the categories of race and class have to be invisible for gender to be visible. However, most studies addressing citizenship and Irish women (for example Jackson 1993; Gardiner 1996; Maddock 1996; Walby 1996; Coakley 1997) presume a universality of Irish 'women' and fail to address the impact of racist discourses and the differential access to citizenship on women of ethnic minorities.

My inquiry has auto/biographical resonance: as an Israeli Jewish woman, 'post-nuptially naturalised' and resident in Ireland since 1969, I have experiential, gendered knowledge of exclusion from nationalist constructions of 'Irishness'. I suggest that the ethnocentrism and racism implicit in the narrow definition of 'Irishness' is a central factor in the limited access by minority Irish women to aspects of citizenship. I also argue that the resultant Irish racism interfaces with other forms of exclusion such as those based on class or gender in ways that reflect upon the very nature of Irish national identity.

Irish Nationalism and the 1937 Constitution

In discussions of the construction of Irish political and cultural nationalism (for example, Hutchinson 1987; Tovey *et al.* 1989), 'Irishness' is neither ethnically differentiated nor (en)gendered, despite the 'intensely ethnocentric Catholic identity' of the mass of the people (Hutchinson 1987: 47). During the struggle for independence, Gaelic authenticity, based on the will of Ireland's (Catholic) majority, became equated with political freedom (Hutchinson 1987: 307). Eamonn de Valera, Ireland's first prime minister and author of the 1937 constitution, was attached to the ideal of a pious Catholic, self-sufficient rural Ireland (Hutchinson 1987: 320) and the new Irish state legislated vigorously to preserve Catholic values.

One result of equating Gaelic authenticity with political power was a drive towards ethnic homogeneity, exemplified, for instance, by members of the Protestant community abandoning Ireland to 'return' to Britain (Hutchinson 1987: 311). Another result, less frequently commented upon, is a postcolonial reconstruction of rigid gender roles (cf. Nandy 1983; Meaney 1991). The Irish nation imagined itself as a 'deep horizontal comradeship' (Anderson 1983), which constructed images of suffering Mother Ireland, far from the experience, expectations and ideals of contemporary Irish women (Meaney 1991: 3).

One political discourse through which we can test the homogeneous construction of Irishness is the 1937 constitution, which is worth studying as a manifesto, not merely as a legal document (Kelly 1988: 21), and which, I argue, is not only gendered but also ethnically exclusionary. The constitution is religiously non-inclusive; it is based on sedentary[1] values; it erases ethnic minorities and constructs a monolithic 'woman' as mother and carer whose place is firmly within 'the Family'.

> *Preamble.* 'In the Name of the Most Holy Trinity, from Whom is all authority and to Whom, as our final end, all actions both of men and States must be referred,

> We, the people of Éire, Humbly acknowledge all our obligations to our Divine Lord, Jesus Christ, Who sustained our fathers through centuries of trial, Gratefully remembering their heroic and unremitting struggle to regain the rightful independence of our Nation... Do hereby adopt, enact and give to ourselves this Constitution.' (*Bunreacht na hÉireann*, Constitution of Ireland 1937)

Michael Mann (1997) argues that the 'we the people' who ordain constitutions excludes women and property-less people and is dominated by questions of class, household position and gender. Tovey *et al.* (1989) refer neither to ethnic diversity within the Irish national 'we', nor to its gender implications. Women, however, though often symbolising a collectivity's unity, honour and *raison d'être,* are often excluded from the collective 'we' of the body politic (or incorporated as dependants and minors), and in this sense the construction of womanhood has a property of 'otherness' (Yuval-Davis 1997: 47).

The 1937 constitution, a product of its time, is the highest expression of Irish ethnocentrism. According to Kelly (1988: 211), De Valera 'was unquestionably both courteous and not only just but generous in his approach to minority traditions, but his Constitution seems almost deliberately designed to alienate them'. Minority traditions were conceived in religious terms (cf. Keogh 1988): any notion of difference relates to religious difference, and 'Irishness' derived an uncontested definition from the conflict with Britain and from aspirations to national and territorial unity.

'Irishness' was also derived from a European postcolonial tradition which 'prioritised sedentarism over nomadism and which legitimised the social and cultural values of settled communities and property-owners while undermining the position of the property-less' (MacLaughlin 1995: 28).[2] As indigenous people, Travellers do not share hegemonic value systems with the majority of the Irish population in relation to fixed location, property owning, public and private space, sexual and marital practices (such as 'matched weddings', an important Traveller custom, see O'Malley-Madec 1993; Ní Shúinéar 1994), and are therefore not part of the 'moral community' of the nation (see Yuval-Davis 1997: 71).

This has contributed to the racialisation of 'tinkers' or Travellers, as did the strong sense of 'community' which, while it had its roots in a rural setting, was reproduced in urban environments (McVeigh 1992: 41–2). To be a Traveller has a specific meaning for settled Irish society in the metaphorical sense of the word; movement is understood as an expression of powerlessness, poverty, famine, the social failure of family and community, all of which have deep resonance in Irish history. Travellers, in their insistence on nomadism as a way of life, may invoke negative associations for the settled Irish, reminding them of what some of them used to be and what they do not want to be again. All this may offer a partial explanation of Irish sedentarism (McVeigh 1992; 1996).[3]

The construction of 'Irishness' is also disturbingly gendered, as is evident from the wording of the 1916 Proclamation of the Irish Republic, according to which Ireland organises and trains 'her manhood' through pre-state military organisations.[4] The 1937 constitution is also gendered. Women played no part in framing Bunreacht na hÉireann, though women's organisations protested against the 'assumptions made in the constitution concerning the legal rights, the role and the status of women in Irish history' (Scannell 1988: 122).

> *Article 41.2* (1). 'In particular the State recognises that by her life within the home, the woman gives to the State a support without which the common good cannot be achieved.' (*Bunreacht na hÉireann* 1937)

Although the constitution formally entitles Irish women to become citizens on the same basis as men, the unparalleled Article 41.2 conceives women, in the spirit of patriarchal Catholicism, primarily as mothers. The use of the generic 'woman' erases difference and occludes the material realities of women's lives (cf. Mohanty 1991).

No feminist discussions of the constitutional construction of Irish womanhood differentiate, however, between majority and minority Irish women.[5] Mary Robinson (1993: 104), while arguing that the construction of the family is based upon marriage and thus due state protection, does not interrogate the contradiction between the constitutional promise to protect the family and the reality of life for families of minority ethnicities. One example of this contradiction is the lack of protection for families by government housing policies for Irish Travellers, who, arguably, with 23,000 members,[6] are Ireland's largest ethnic minority. These policies, through evictions and prohibition orders, effectively break up Travelling families, rather than according them state protection (McDonagh 1994: 106).

Irish Travellers: Citizenship and Ethnicity

Anthias and Yuval-Davis (1992) locate women as central to the reproduction of national collectivities, not simply in the biological sense of giving birth to future members of collectivities, but also in symbolic and boundary-constructing terms (Yuval-Davis and Anthias 1989).

Citizenship is one measure of membership in national collectivities. Unlike liberal definitions of citizenship as membership of a state, T. H. Marshall's definition of citizenship as 'status in a community' endowing individuals with civil, political and social rights (Marshall 1950; 1975; 1981), offers the possibility of interrogating multi-tiered access to citizenship by sub-state collectivities and the relationship of these collectivities to the state.

There are two main strands of feminist critique of Marshall's concept of citizenship. Walby (1993; 1996) argues that citizenship is gendered but does not problematise the multi-ethnic nature of the 'community'. This is addressed by the other strand, posited by Nira Yuval-Davis (1993; 1997), who examines 'the differential access of different categories of citizens to the state and the implications this has for relations of domination'. An adequate theory of citizenship should not take the state or the 'community' as self-evident givens, and should develop a notion of difference and different power dimensions of different collectivities within society (Yuval-Davis 1993: 66–7).

There has been a debate in Irish social sciences as to whether Irish Travellers are an 'ethnic group', a 'culture' or a 'sub-culture'. Like Ní Shúinéar (1994), O'Connell (1994), McVeigh (1992; 1996) and MacLaughlin (1995), I regard Travellers as an ethnic group. They are an ethnic group according to criteria of ethnicity posited by Barth (1969) and Smith (1986: 22–32), among others. Travellers see themselves as

> a small indigenous minority who according to historical material have been part of Irish society for centuries. They have a long shared history, value system, language, customs and traditions which make them a group which is recognised by themselves and others as distinct. This distinctive life style based on a nomadic tradition, sets them apart from the sedentary population or 'settled people'. (Pavee Point 1996: 1)

McLoughlin (1994) argues that Travellers are not an ethnicity but merely a distinct class-determined group, but other contributors to May McCann *et al.* (1994) view Travellers as an ethnic group with a distinct culture. Much of the debate centres on the question of origins. If, until recently, Irish Travellers were thought to derive from Irish peasantry dispossessed of their lands and forced onto the road, a more acceptable theory is that they have pre-Celtic origins (as summed up by Ní Shúinéar 1994). Travellers have maintained their ethnic separateness from the surrounding Irish society through the centuries, partly through their language (called Gammon, Shelta, or Cant) and partly through endogamy and through broader cultural differences, maintained by their unwillingness to assimilate (May McCann *et al.* 1994: xv–xvi). They have also maintained their separateness by protesting and, more recently, organising against injustice and seeking to mobilise support for a positive social identity through organisations such as the Irish Traveller Movement, Pavee Point, and the National Traveller Women's Forum. These Traveller organisations have created space for Travellers to come together and highlight and redress the issues they regard as important (Pavee Point 1997b: 6).

Citizenship and Traveller Women

While women have always played important and economically active roles in Traveller society, the inequalities experienced by Travellers in Irish society have a particular impact on Traveller women. Like other women, they have primary responsibility for family and domestic duties, but the lack of basic facilities affects their health and life expectancy. While Traveller women experience sexism within their own community, they also experience discrimination like other Travellers (Crickley 1992: 101; Pavee Point 1997b). Travelling women are the symbolic 'border guards' who embody their collectivity by marrying endogamously. The practice of matchmaking, while a 'positive response to a very difficult problem – getting a husband in an endogamous community' – perpetuates rituals of sexual control serving the interests of elders within an essentially patriarchal social order (O'Malley-Madec 1993: 218-19).

Beyond their community, Travelling women experience a number of barriers preventing their full access to civil, political and social citizenship. The following discussion uses published studies and quotes from a group interview I conducted at the Dublin Traveller Centre Pavee Point with six members of the Cultural Heritage Group, as part of a project on experiences of racial exclusion in Irish society.[7]

Civil citizenship

The liberty of the person, including freedom from violence, is a central civil citizenship right.

> There is violence against Travelling women, but there's more violence against settled women, a lot more.... You can read about a settled woman murdered every week, or every month anyway. Well thank god, Traveller women, the men does not kill them. (K)

Traveller women confirm that racist violence against Travellers causes high levels of stress which in turn affects the level of violence against Traveller women (Kelleher and Associates with O'Connor 1995; McDonagh, cited in McKay 1996: 8). Traveller women share the same refuge spaces with settled women although these do not cater for their cultural needs (Smyth 1996). The report of the Task Force on the Travelling Community (1995: 288) recommends working out together with Traveller women 'culturally appropriate ways to support Traveller women who experience (male) violence within their community'. The Working Party on Violence Against Women and Children (National Women's Council of Ireland 1996), however, while recommending an examination of the needs of Traveller women, did not include a Travelling woman – an indication of the exclusion of Traveller women from important Irish feminist projects.

The right to control one's body is another civil citizenship right. While Irish fertility rates are declining below the replacement rate of 2.1 per woman, they remain high among Travellers, with an average of eight children per family (Pavee Point 1996). In 1996, Traveller women rejected Dáil member Austin Deasy's suggestion that the only way to 'solve' the 'Traveller problem' was to contain their numbers through birth control. Ironically, their objection centred upon their being 'Irish' and 'Catholics' like the rest of the population:

> Travellers are Catholics.... We have the same rights as any woman to make choices. Who is Austin Deasy to come preaching birth control to us? Does he want to wipe us out?' (McKay 1996: 8)

The civil citizenship right to own property sounds hollow in relation to Irish Travellers. National elite assumptions about the 'normality' of sedentary living have resulted in continuous government efforts to 'settle' the Travellers and assimilate them into the ethnically unproblematised 'community'. As a result, nomadism, an important way of life for Travellers, makes access to some public services impossible (Collins 1995: 29). The numbers of Irish Travellers are growing due to early marriages, the rarity of unmarried women of child-bearing age and the high fertility of married Traveller women, but also as a consequence of the return to Ireland of many Travellers because of increasing anti-Traveller racism in Britain (MacLaughlin 1995: 34). One result is that Travellers are being moved constantly by local authorities, local residents and the Gardaí (Irish police). Methods used include forcible evictions, digging trenches around encampments, erecting earthworks and dumping rubbish and used cars around their caravans, threats by officials and residents and formal evictions. This results in large Traveller encampments outside the major cities which, in turn, contribute to anti-Traveller racism and vigilante attacks.

Overcrowding, poor conditions and shortage of serviced sites make more Traveller families take to the road: in 1993 more than 1,100 families out of 3,828 were living on the roadside (O'Kane 1993: 6). In 1994 in the Greater Dublin area no Travellers had access to public phones on site, 50 per cent had no electricity, bath, shower or hot water, 36 per cent had no flush toilets, 28 per cent had no toilets at all, and 60 per cent were without fire precautions (*Still No Place to Go* 1994). The lack of basic services makes life particularly difficult for Traveller women. Many sites are rat-infested, and even better sites are often inappropriately located:

> They build sites in places that they shouldn't build them … there's one in Mullingar, where I come from. And it's built with a graveyard … on one side of it, the morgue is the other side of it, and there's the ... crematorium ... the other side (M) … there's no place for children's safety ... you're above the hill, and you're into the motorway (K).... The site that we're in, Finglas, is a lovely site, but there again, it was built right at the dump. And the smell out of that dump, about three evenings a week, is unbelievable … they give you a clear message that you belong with the rubbish. (M)

Political citizenship

While Irish women were given the franchise at independence, the number of women in public office, at around 15 per cent, is low.[8] Despite the patriarchal nature of the Travelling community, Traveller women play significant leadership roles within their community and also represent their community politically. In the early 1980s, a Traveller woman stood for national elections in response to anti-Traveller campaigns and secured a considerable vote. In 1994, a Traveller woman was elected Town Commissioner in a West of Ireland town. A number of Traveller women have received national awards, yet the central contribution which women make to the well-being of the Traveller community is largely unrecognised (Task Force 1995: 282).

Social citizenship

It is in the areas of poverty, paid employment, social welfare rights, health and education, that Irish women have been deprived of equal access to social citizenship (for example, Daly 1988; O'Neill 1992). Traditional rural Traveller occupations have diminished with industrialisation, and Travellers were forced to migrate to cities in order to make a living. While some continue to be self-employed, many are unable to gain access to the mainstream economy and are dependent on social welfare for survival (Pavee Point 1996). This common argument against them is rejected by Traveller women:

> They're saying Travellers should be in work and we shouldn't be getting the dole; and who in the name of God, discriminating against us, not letting us in to have a drink or into the pictures, or into a café, who, what settled person is going to stand up and give us a job? And they keep telling us we shouldn't be getting the dole. Who is going to give us a job? (M)

Despite all this, Travelling women tend to be excluded from conventional research on poverty and unemployment, which is based on the sample of the Register of Electors, since they are rarely registered (Daly 1988: 19).

Health is another central issue of social citizenship. Only 5 per cent of Irish Travellers reach the age of 50 and a mere 2 per cent live to be 65 (O'Morain 1996: 2). Travelling men's life expectancy is ten years lower than that of settled men and Traveller women's life expectancy is 12 years lower than that of settled women (O'Nualláin and Forde 1992). Traveller women get much less ante-natal care than is recommended and suffer more complications during pregnancy; the rate of immature births is three times the national average and there is a high proportion of low-birthweight infants (O'Nualláin and Forde 1992).

The Irish education system does not cater adequately for Travellers' cultural needs, either (Kenny 1997).[9] Government education initiatives in relation to Travelling children, including visiting teachers, special schools, special classes (not the preferred option for Traveller parents), and special pre-schools, have resulted in 80 per cent of Traveller children attending primary school (Kenny 1997; Pavee Point 1997a). Segregation still exists, however, and it is Traveller mothers who interface with the education system:

> I had a young fellow in a special class myself, but that was done away with because of some of the mothers.... He was 13 when he was in that special class, and all he

> was getting was Peter and Jane … and in some of the lessons the master said, well if you don't sit down, you'll get no jellies … so I took him out ... but he went to a mixed school … and he came out without even knowing [how] to spell his name.... Even though special classes [were] done away with, there's still, in some of the schools … a special roll book for Travelling children. The teacher explained it was for to count to see how many Traveller children were in the school, but I don't think there should be a special roll book. And we didn't know, but they were getting a grant for having that book there.... (N) Some [Travelling children] are seen as stupid. You're seen as lazy, you are a hindrance to society.... (M) The school we were in, like the special class I was in ... they give us jigsaw puzzle ... at the age of 12....(B)

In secondary school levels, the situation is far worse: only one in 20 Traveller children aged 12–15 attends mainstream secondary schools and the majority leave school within their first two years (Pavee Point 1997a). The women I spoke to are disillusioned: 'Because the way it is in primary school, from the teachers and from these [special] classes, they don't want to know about secondary school' (N). Access to education is also gendered: Traveller parents are more reluctant to send girls to school than boys, because of fears about purity and family honour (Kenny 1997).

Irish Nationalism and Racism

I would argue that the civil, political and social exclusions from citizenship outlined above are a form of Irish racism. Though some theorists (for example, Anderson 1983) have proposed that nationalism and racism may be separated as opposing sentiments, Yuval-Davis (1997) has argued with some cogency that the tendency to conflate 'nation' and 'state', and the naturalisation of the hegemony by one collectivity over both state and civil society, is at the basis of the prevalent connection between nationalism and racism.

One way of making sense of Irish nationalism as racially exclusionary is understanding it as what Smooha (1997) calls 'ethnic democracy'. In an ethnic democracy the dominance of the ethnic majority, or 'core nation', is institutionalised and given a structured superior status. In an ethnic democracy the laws of citizenship, naturalisation, immigration and property ownership favour the majority; members of the minority are denied certain individual rights and face institutional discrimination with regard to employment and other resources. These attributes may describe the Irish nationalist project's relation to Travellers. The working ethnic democracy, however, does enable the minority to struggle against discrimination, as is evident in the recent political organisation of the Travelling community and its alliance with other minority ethnic organisations in naming and combating racism (for instance, in the Irish National Committee of the European Year Against Racism, and the Platform Against Racism).

Another way of theorising the relationship of Irish Travellers to the Irish nationalist project draws on Goffman's (1968) theory of stigma as an instrument used by a majority to grade others as 'abnormal' while simultaneously defining itself as 'normal'. Irish nationalism, which constructed itself in opposition to British colonialism, employed stigmatising stereotypes as a convenient weapon for coping with the ambiguous presence of 'strangers', the 'ambivalent third' in the binary opposition between (Irish) 'friends' versus (British) 'enemies' (see Bauman 1991). While this binarism guarantees a neat classificatory opposition, the cosy antagonism is disrupted by strangers, in this instance Travellers (or Jews, and, more recently, Black people) who, according to McVeigh (1992: 41–2), 'have threatened the very nature of "community" in Ireland'. Travellers, above all, threaten the dominant 'we' by their very nearness and, at the same time, their refusal to assimilate. Anti-Traveller racism has several hallmarks in its construction of 'others' in order to exclude and/or exploit: they are inferiorised as unmodern or premodern, they are excluded from material benefits, they are stigmatised by being called names such as 'knackers' and 'Gypsies', a classic stigma strategy, they are denied access to public services and places of entertainment, and they are blamed for social problems, such as crime, or littering, though, as the women I spoke to attest, littering is often caused by settled people and blamed on Travellers:

> There [is] talk about rubbish.... It's the settled people, it's them that throw the rubbish around. Because they are coming with washing machines, and bags, and every type of dirt and they're dumping it off on the side of the road where the Travellers are staying. And the Travellers are blamed. (M)

Travellers are also blamed for their own situation and Traveller women are given the message that their problems can be 'solved' if they cease to be Travellers, although they may be left with little opportunity to address their own situation as women, since challenging their oppression may be seen internally as attacking Traveller culture (Task Force 1995: 284).

A third way of theorising 'Irishness' is through the concept of racialisation, which occurs wherever racism structures particular relationships. Ireland is racialised in different ways: it is empowered by its 'whiteness', its (mostly) Roman Catholic Christianity, its Europeanness, and its access to power blocs such as the USA, but disempowered by its colonial past, its location on the periphery of Europe, and its history of emigration and dependency (McVeigh 1996: 28).

Conclusion

McVeigh (1992, 1996) sees sedentarism and anti-Traveller racism as 'organic' to Ireland. Racist discourses and attacks against Travellers, like those against refugees and asylum seekers and against other 'non-Irish Irish', many of whom have lived in Ireland for decades, are on the increase (Irish Refugee

Council 1996; Maher 1997: 3). Sexist and racist comments, such as the former Junior Minister Emmet Stagg's description of Travelling women as 'effectively slaves' (McKay 1996: 8), homogenise all Travellers, and, as often happens with racialised groups, rally Traveller women to support their men, despite the existence of some sexism within the Travelling community.

The monolithic constructions of 'Irishness' and 'Irish women', which erase the ethnic minority experience, have precluded examinations of the unequal access to citizenship by minority Irish women. More significantly, ethnocentrism and racism inform our understanding of 'Irishness'. Ireland has traditionally regarded itself as a non-racist society, primarily because of its colonial past and diasporic experience. McVeigh (1992: 42–3) argues that 'countering racism is a necessary part of tackling existing inequalities in terms of class, gender, sexuality.... Racialised out-groups have come to represent the presumed chaos which lies outside the protection of the Irish "community".'

Traveller stigmatisation has gendered connotations: when a Traveller woman is followed around a supermarket or refused service by suspicious staff, she has to deal with that discrimination if she is to feed her family. Even when Traveller men are given access to places of entertainment or pubs, women are barred, or men are not allowed in when accompanied by women (Task Force 1995: 284). The stigmatisation is doubly hurtful since Travellers consider themselves 'more Irish than the Irish':

> The funniest part of it is, if tourists from different parts of the world come to Ireland, the Irish are real generous to accept them, to have a drink, and they are brought into hotels and they have bed and breakfast and their dinners, and they can go anywhere they like. Through Ireland. And their own Irish people that was born, reared for generations, for hundreds and hundreds and hundreds of years, up to this day, can't go in and have a drink and can't go anywhere. (M)

Irish feminist and sociological analyses of Irish women's access to citizenship have not problematised the all-inclusive category 'Irish women', nor have they dealt with Irish women of minority ethnicities.[10] Feminist anti-racist critiques of traditional ideologies of citizenship have expanded our understanding of the complexity of the analytical and political issues involved in understanding women's access to their rights as citizens (Yuval-Davis 1993). Toni Morrison (1992: 8–9) suggests that only through a close examination of discourses of 'blackness' can we understand the nature, and cause, of 'whiteness'. Similarly, only through examining racialised discourses and encounters, and the experiences of ethnically excluded groups in Irish society, including the access of Irish Traveller women to citizenship, can we understand fully the implicit as well as explicit nature of majoritarian Irish national identity.

Acknowledgements

Thanks to Nira Yuval-Davis and Pnina Werbner for inviting me to present an earlier version of this chapter at the 'Women, Citizenship and Difference' conference in Greenwich, July 1996. Thanks also to members of the Cultural Heritage Group at the Traveller Centre Pavee Point in Dublin, who spoke to me, and to Bríd O'Brien who set it up, and to Gerry Boucher and Hilary Tovey of the Department of Sociology, Trinity College Dublin, for comments on earlier drafts of this chapter.

Notes

1. I use the term 'sedentary' to indicate the opposition to 'nomadism' in the context of the relationship between Travellers and the settled Irish population.

2. Máirín Kenny (1996: 14) argues against MacLaughlin that there is no evidence that bourgeois Irish nationalists 'required' Travellers or were even aware of them. However, it is precisely this lack of awareness of ethnic difference which I consider to be at the heart of the narrow definition of 'Irishness'.

3. I am indebted to Gerry Boucher for this insight.

4. Paragraph 2 of Poblacht na hÉireann, the Provisional Government of the Irish Republic's Proclamation of the Irish Republic during the 1916 Easter Rising against the British, reads: 'Having organised and trained her manhood through her secret ... and open military organisations ... having patiently perfected her discipline, having resolutely waited for the right moment to reveal itself, she now seizes that moment ... relying in the first on her own strength, she strikes in full confidence of victory' (cited in De Rossa 1991).

5. One notable exception, linking feminism and ethnicity in relation to Travelling women, is Crickley (1992: 101–8).

6. Ironically, although it is difficult to calculate the exact population structure of Travellers, Travellers are the only section of Irish society to be counted on 31 March every year by local authorities on behalf of the Department of the Environment (O'Kane 1993: 6).

7. This project was funded by the National Committee for Development Education, Dublin.

8. This low figure may seem inconsistent with the election of two successive women presidents, one of whom, Mary Robinson, currently the UN High Commissioner for Human Rights, was very much identified with the Irish women's movement.

9. Unlike the religious needs of Protestant, Jewish and Muslim children who are offered denominational state primary and second-level education.

10. With the exception of Lentin (1996 and 1998). See also, though not in relation to citizenship, Crickley (1992) and the Task Force on the Travelling Community (1995). For a discussion of the intersection of racism and sexism, with a short section on citizenship, see Pavee Point (1997b).

References

Anderson, Benedict (1983). *Imagined Communities*, London: Verso.

Anthias, Floya and Nira Yuval-Davis (1992). *Racialized Boundaries: Race, Gender, Colour and Class and the Anti-Racist Struggle*, London: Routledge.

Barth, Frederic (ed.) (1969). *Ethnic Groups and Boundaries*, London: Allen and Unwin.

Bauman, Zigmunt (1991). *Modernity and Ambivalence*, Cambridge: Polity Press.

Bunreacht na hÉireann (Constitution of Ireland) (1937). Dublin: The Stationery Office.

Coakley, Anne (1997). 'Gendered Citizenship: the Social Construction of Mothers in Ireland', in Anne Byrne and Madeleine Leonard (eds) *Women and Irish Society: a Sociological Reader*, Belfast: Beyond the Pale Publications, pp. 181–95.

Collins, Martin (1995). 'The Travelling Community and Ethnic Groups', in Niel Collins (ed.) *Minorities: the Right to Be Different*, Celbridge: The Social Study Conference, pp. 29–31.

Crickley, Anastasia (1992). 'Feminism and Ethnicity', in Dublin Travellers Education and Development Group. *DTEDG File: Irish Travellers – New Analysis and New Initiatives*, Dublin: Pavee Point, pp. 101–8.

Cullen, Paul (1997). 'Images Aimed at Tourists Attract Refugees As Well', *Irish Times*, 19 April 1997: 9.

Daly, Mary (1988). *Women and Poverty*, Dublin: Attic Press.

De Rossa, Peter (1991). *Rebels*, London: Bantam Books.

Gardiner, Frances (1996). 'Women, Citizenship and the Welfare State', paper presented at the Women and Citizenship Spring Seminar Series, Women's Studies Centre, University College Galway, April 1996.

Goffman, Irving (1968). *Stigma: Notes on the Management of Spoilt Identity*, Harmondsworth: Penguin Books.

Hutchinson, John (1987). *The Dynamics of Cultural Nationalism: the Gaelic Revival and the Creation of the Irish National State*, London: Allen and Unwin.

Jackson, Pauline (1993). 'Managing the Mothers: the Case of Ireland', in Jane Lewis (ed.) *Women and Social Policies in Europe: Work, Family and the State*, Aldershot: Edward Elgar, pp. 72–91.

Kelleher and Associates with Monica O'Connor (1995). *Making the Links: Towards an Integrated Strategy for the Elimination of Violence against Women in Intimate Relationships with Men*, Dublin: Women's Aid.

Kelly, John (1988). 'The Constitution: Law and Manifesto', in Frank Litton (ed.) *The Constitution of Ireland 1937–1987*, Dublin: Institute of Public Administration, pp. 208–17.

Kenny, Mairín (1996). Review of Jim MacLaughlin, *Travellers and Ireland: Whose Country, Whose History? Pavee Point Newsletter* 5, July: 14.

— (1997). *Routes to Resistance: Travellers and Second-Level Schooling*, Aldershot: Ashgate Publishers.

Keogh, Dermot (1988). 'The Irish Constitution: an Analysis of the Making of the Constitution', in Frank Litton (ed.) *The Constitution of Ireland 1937–87,* Dublin: Institute of Public Administration, pp. 4–84.

Lentin, Ronit (1996). 'Introduction: the Gendered State(s) of Ireland', in Ronit Lentin (ed.) *In From the Shadows: the UL Women's Studies Collection*, Vol II, Limerick:

Department of Government and Society, University of Limerick, pp. 4–13.
— (1998). '"Irishness", the 1937 Constitution, and Citizenship: a Gender and Ethnicity View', *Irish Journal of Sociology,* 8, 11: 5–24.

MacLaughlin, Jim (1995). *Travellers and Ireland: Whose Country, Whose History?* Cork: Cork University Press.

Maddock, Evie (1996). 'Citizenship, Protection, Control – Resistance', in Ronit Lentin (ed.) *In from the Shadows: the UL Women's Studies Collection,* Vol II, Limerick: Department of Government and Society, University of Limerick, pp. 112–20.

Maher, John (1997). 'Racism Creeping into Dublin with Refugee Influx, Say TDs', *Irish Times,* 26 May: 3.

Mann, Michael (1997). 'The Flip-Side of Democracy: in What Circumstances Has Popular Sovereignty Legitimated Murder?' Paper presented at the Seventh Annual Conference of the Association of the Study of Ethnicity and Nationalism, LSE, London, April 1997.

Marshall, T. H (1950). *Citizenship and Social Class,* Cambridge: Cambridge University Press.

— (1975). *Social Policy in the Twentieth Century,* London: Hutchinson.

— (1981). *The Right to Welfare and Other Essays,* London: Heinemann Educational Books.

May McCann, May, Séamas a Síocháin and Joseph Ruane (eds) (1994). *Irish Travellers: Culture and Ethnicity,* Belfast: Institute of Irish Studies.

McDonagh, Michael (1994). 'Nomadism in Irish Traveller Identity', in May McCann May, Séamas a Síocháin and Joseph Ruane (eds) *Irish Travellers: Culture and Ethnicity,* Belfast: Institute of Irish Studies, pp. 95–109.

McKay, Susan (1996). 'Travellers' Pride Strikes out at Political Prejudices', *Sunday Tribune,* 23 June 1996: 8.

McLoughlin, Dympna (1994). 'Ethnicity and Irish Travellers: Reflections on Ní Shúineár', in May McCann May, Séamas a Síocháin and Joseph Ruane (eds) *Irish Travellers: Culture and Ethnicity,* Belfast: Institute of Irish Studies, pp. 78–94.

McVeigh, Robbie (1992). 'The Specificities of Irish Racism', *Race and Class* 33, 4: 31–45.

— (1996). *The Racialization of Irishness: Racism and Anti-Racism in Ireland,* Belfast: Centre for Research and Documentation.

Meaney, Geraldine (1991). *Sex and Nation: Women in Irish Culture and Politics,* Dublin: Attic Press.

Mohanty, Chandra Talpade (1991). 'Under Western Eyes: Feminist Scholarship and Colonial Discourses', in Chandra T. Mohanty, Ann Russo and Lourde Torres (eds) *Third World Women and the Politics of Feminism,* Bloomington, Indiana: Indiana University Press, pp. 51–80.

Morrison, Toni (1992). *Playing in the Dark: Whiteness and the Literary Imagination,* London: Picador.

Nandy, Ashis (1983). *The Intimate Enemy: Loss and Recovery of Self Under Colonialism,* Delhi: Oxford University Press.

National Women's Council of Ireland (1996). *Report of the Working Party on the Legal and Judicial Process for Victims of Sexual and Other Crimes of Violence against Women and Children,* Dublin: NWCI.

Ní Shúinéar, Sinéad (1994). 'Irish Travellers, Ethnicity and the Origins Question', in May McCann May, Séamas a Síocháin and Joseph Ruane (eds) *Irish Travellers:*

Culture and Ethnicity, Belfast: Institute of Irish Studies. pp. 54-77.

Nozinic, Drazen (forthcoming). 'The Refugee Experience in Ireland', in Ronit Lentin and Robbie McVeigh (eds) *Situating Racisms: The Racialization of Irishness*, Dublin: Irish Academic Press.

O'Connell, John (1994). 'Ethnicity and Irish Travellers', in May McCann May, Séamas a Síochâin and Joseph Ruane (eds) *Irish Travellers: Culture and Identity*, Belfast: Institute of Irish Studies, pp. 110–20.

O'Kane, Paul (1993). 'Who Are the Travellers? How Many Are There?' *Irish Times*, 23 October 1993: 6.

O'Malley-Madec, Mary (1993). 'The Irish Travelling Woman: Mother and Mermaid', in Ailbhe Smyth (ed.) *Irish Women's Studies Reader*, Dublin: Attic Press, pp. 214–39.

O'Morain, Padraig (1996). 'Dr Connell Said 95% of Travellers Die by 50 Due to Poor Conditions', *Irish Times*, 26 June 1996: 2.

O'Neill, Cathleen (1992). *Telling It Like It Is*, Dublin: Combat Poverty Agency.

O'Nualláin, Sinéad and Mary Forde (1992). *Changing Needs of Irish Travellers: Health, Education and Social Issues.* Renmore, Galway: Woodlands Centre.

Pavee Point (1996). *Fact Sheet*, Dublin: Pavee Point.

— (1997a). 'Partnership in Education', *Pavee Point Newsletter* 11, Spring.

— (1997b). 'Racism vs Sexism? Issues Arising in Addressing the Two', *Pavee Point Newsletter* 6, May 1997.

Robinson, Mary (1993). 'Women and the Law in Ireland', in Ailbhe Smyth (ed.) *Irish Women's Studies Reader*, Dublin: Attic Press, pp. 100–6.

Scannell, Yvonne (1988). 'The Constitution and the Role of Women', in Brian Farrell (ed.) *De Valera's Constitution and Ours*, Dublin: Radio Telefis Eireann/Gill and MacMillan, pp.123–36.

Smith, Anthony D. (1986). *The Ethnic Origins of Nations*, Oxford: Basil Blackwell.

Smooha, Sammy (1997). 'The Problematics of Ethnic Democracy as a Third Type of Democracy in Ethnically Divided Societies', paper presented at the Seventh Annual Conference of the Association of the Study of Ethnicity and Nationalism, LSE, London, April 1997.

Smyth, Ailbhe (1996). 'Seeing Red: Men's Violence against Women in Ireland', in Ronit Lentin (ed.) *In from the Shadows: the UL Women's Studies Collection*, Vol II, Limerick: Department of Government and Society, University of Limerick, pp. 15–36.

Still No Place to Go (1994). Dublin: Irish Traveller Movement.

Task Force on the Travelling Community, Liz McManus and Mary Kelly (1995). *Report of the Task Force on the Travelling Community*, Dublin: Stationery Office.

Tovey, Hilary, Damian Hannan and Hal Abrahamson (1989). *Why Irish? Irish Identity and the Irish Language*, Dublin: Bord na Gaeilge.

Walby, Sylvia (1993). 'Is Citizenship Gendered?' *Sociology* 28, 2: 379–95.

— (1996). 'Women and Citizenship: towards a Comparative Analysis', in Ronit Lentin (ed.) *In from the Shadows: the UL Women's Studies Collection*, Vol II, Limerick: Department of Government and Society, University of Limerick, pp. 94–111.

Yuval-Davis, Nira (1993). 'The Citizenship Debate: Women, Ethnic Processes and the State', *Feminist Review* 39: 58–68.

— (1997). *Gender and Nation*, London: Sage Publications.

Yuval-Davis, Nira and Floya Anthias (1989). *Woman – Nation – State*, London: Macmillan.

PART 3

Ambivalent Citizens: Migrants and Refugees

CHAPTER 9

Feminism, Multiculturalism, Essentialism

Aleksandra Ålund

Today's processes of global compression are accompanied by national fragmentation, leading to the construction of new and new-old individual, local, regional and ethnic identities. On the one hand, the sense of national community is weakened or threatened by a homogenising globalisation, the decline or even collapse of the welfare state and the growth of a sense of political anonymity, generated in the shadow of a supranational Europe. Economic and class transformations, along with widespread unemployment and social exclusion, have resulted for many in the unmooring of old certainties. In response to this insecurity, many Europeans seek a confirmation of their political identities and political subjectivies through negative comparisons with incoming 'immigrants' – 'us' and 'them'. The quest for identity is mediated by a symbolic rhetoric of culture, ethnicity, regionalism and community. The notion of community, although problematic (see Young 1990a), evokes an imagined relation between identity and place. But it also celebrates differences and uniqueness in a world of migration, globalisation, cultural borrowings and mergings, thus disclosing the dilemmas and ambiguities of modern society (Ålund 1995).

If the search for roots has become widespread – from national identities to identity politics – so too the multiple expressions of exclusion have also proliferated. The uniting core of different exclusionary practices is often a *rationalisation of social tensions* regulated and controlled through normalising definitions. This involves problematising the cultures of 'other' ethnic groups, or immigrants and refugees – not least 'immigrant women' – as backward traditions that create differences and conflicts with the 'normal' population. Thus, the social deprivation suffered by ethnic minorities tends to be understood in simplistic, culture-related terms. Culturalisation – a culture-related disguise of social inequality and discrimination (Ålund and Schierup 1991; Ålund 1993, 1994b) – occupies a prominent place in the processes of change currently affecting European society.

Cultural differences in this discourse are elaborated within a fundamental polarity. The increasingly common political and popular argument focuses on whether various groups of refugees and immigrants are 'suited' or 'unsuited', more or less 'adaptable' or 'foreign'. Culture becomes the basis on which to differentiate and select among people; a basis for erecting 'Fortress Europe' and the 'Mediterranean Wall'. Immigration and immigrant policies are coordinated or 'harmonised' restrictively in relation to this discourse, via selection at the frontiers of Fortress Europe.

There is a growing interconnection between reinforced external barriers and internal constraints such as discrimination in the labour market, segregation in housing, political marginalisation and racism in everyday life (Essed 1987). Behind the labels of refugee, immigrant and the new underclass, a new kind of second-class citizen, the Stranger, is appearing in Europe (Ålund 1995), leading to what Barker has called the new racism (Barker 1981; see also Ålund and Schierup 1991; Wrench and Solomos 1993; Silverman 1992). Culturalism, differentiated racism or cultural racism have a powerful effect on immigrant policies in Sweden as well as in the rest of Europe. It is therefore important to look critically at the prevalence of this discourse and at the part it plays, so that real social inequalities do not remain hidden in a fog of stereotypical and media images of cultural differences, commonly described as imported 'immigrant problems'.

In Sweden (and elsewhere in Scandinavia) a cognitive ordering system embedded in culturalist 'the Immigrant as a Problem' discourses has even penetrated the theories and practices of apparently progressive organisations such as the trade union movement, the youth movement and the feminist movement. The consequence is a tacit acceptance of open discrimination against individuals with an immigrant background. There has been a move away from the renowned political visions of 'equality', 'freedom of choice' and 'partnership' which in the mid-1970s marked Sweden's proclaimed egalitarian, multicultural ideology, its inclusivist 'immigrant policy' which – in contrast to Germany's guest-worker policy, for example – made it rather easy for the country's immigrants to obtain full (formal) rights of citizenship.

A gradual change occurred in the character of the public debate in the 1980s, especially after 1988 when there was an intense debate about 'refugees as a problem'. Public debate has become increasingly concerned with the alleged criminal behaviour of immigrants and with drawing boundaries between cultures. The dominant ideological trend has been towards culturalising 'problematic immigrants' rather than problematising the structural restraints imposed upon them. Unemployment among 'immigrants' – an official category including both immigrants with foreign citizenship and Swedish citizens with at least one parent born abroad – passed 30 per cent in December 1997. A shift in ideological orientation and institutional practices seems to have taken place at various levels since the early 1990s. This complex process of reorientation ranges from heavy-handed symbolic manifestations by new, ideologically and politically marginal racist groups at street level (burning crosses; leading assaults on refugee camps) to discreet and almost imperceptible reformulations of government reports which in general tend to focus on immigrants as a 'problem'. At the same time, however, a hierarchical 'ethnic division of labour' (Schierup and Paulsson 1994) has developed, the Swedish counterpart to the familiar phenomenon of the 'vertical mosaic' (Porter 1968).

A blanket of obscurity is, however, all too easily cast over social problems such as segregation and discrimination against immigrants by this discursive culturalisation of differences. The residential segregation of immigrants is explained on the grounds of their cultural preference for living together (Andersson-Brolin 1984). Exclusion from the labour market is seen as being due to the immigrants' 'mentality'. Bad health, early pensioning off and long periods of sick leave – especially of immigrant women – are explained with reference to cultural peculiarities (cf. the critical discussion in Ålund 1988; Knocke 1994 and Schierup and Paulsson 1994). Social exclusion, discrimination, stigmatisation and marginalisation evolve in parallel with under-representation in the political system. Residential segregation is a fact which hits immigrants hard.

This is the social context of cultural identity formation. Ethnic identities are firmly anchored in their social contexts and cannot be understood apart from their embeddedness within particular social settings (Ålund 1995). Numerous ethnically mixed communities – such as those in Swedish multi-ethnic suburbs – have become refuges for excluded minorities, social havens in the midst of a hostile world. These structurally isolated and exploited areas of ethnic and class-segregated living have frequently become the basis for political mobilisation. Beyond new inclusive solidarities, however, we can find in the constitution of these new, multi- and transethnic communities a number of exclusivist reactions. The immigrants are the constructed Others who, in turn, construct their own Other. The development of this kind of 'ethnic absolutism' (Gilroy 1987) can thus be understood as a modern reaction to contemporary forms of exclusion from the dominant culture and social order. Social inequalities may generate subcultural differences, but without reflecting on the connection between the two, the multidimensionality will be lost and multiculturalism will be reduced to the cultural, disconnected from the social.

The position of immigrants within the ethnicised societal division of labour, as well as in the cultural status hierarchy, highlights the importance of the relationship between structural positioning and culture. The cultural, however, may acquire in the eyes of observers an independent force in its own right. Hence, in their bare and distorted forms, stereotypical explanations explain away the social as a matter of culture, thus reducing it to a site for the production of identities and difference.

What this fails to recognise is that social struggle is conducted through culture. Ethnicity in this context is to be understood as an expression of specific reactions to the growing experiences of multiple exile among the majority of Scandinavian immigrants. Culture becomes a battlefield, expressing the paradoxes inherent in the politics of multiculturalism (Ålund and Schierup 1991). In the midst of a rhetoric of multiculturalism and a contingent politics of recognition, what tends to be neglected are obvious class divisions and social inequalities; instead, structurally generated differences are explained in terms of cultural stereotypes about the innate 'mentalities' of migrants or refugees which prevent them from escaping poverty or state dependence.

Feminism and the Recognition of Difference

Dominant academic discourses have actually helped to construct such oppositions between Us and Them. The problem of perpetual strangerhood is articulated by forging a series of marginalised social categories through various combinations of racialised, gendered or ethnicised representations. This is a familiar theme in feminist research and political discussion, not least because the excluded, 'the Other', the 'Invandrare', the 'Ausländer', as Nora Räthzel (1995) informs us, are constructed as 'the counterimages of 'Heimat', the Homeland. Thus they threaten to expose internal contradictions in the imagined harmony of the Heimat.

The negative force of an oppressive 'traditional' culture has been a dominant theme in popular as well as academic conceptions of Swedish migrant women, who are otherwise largely invisible in Swedish feminist research. The popular dichotomisation of people into categories like 'Swedes' and 'immigrants', 'modern' and 'traditional', has governed the understanding of women and difference. It is in this spirit that the image of immigrant women has come to be constructed in terms of an opposition between modernity and tradition.

Women of migrant background have continuously been represented as belonging to an undeveloped culture, in contrast to a modern, superior and supposedly homogeneous 'Swedish culture', with connotations of a 'natural order'. The very notion of 'immigrant women' – a discursively created stereotyped category – comprises a significant example of stigmatised 'Otherness' (Ålund 1988, 1996a). With few exceptions, the little that has been published has only contributed to confirming the popular image of 'immigrant women' as largely subordinated, passive and driven solely by tradition (see the critical discussion in Knocke 1991, 1994; Ålund 1991a, 1994a, 1996a).

What is usually not recognised is that cultures are formed within the framework of both pre- and post-migratory antagonisms and related to emergent struggles in the pre-political contexts of everyday life, as well as in wider public arenas (Ålund 1991a). Rather than being passive victims, women who have immigrated actively employ the complex cultural symbolism of their histories to challenge contemporary forms of subordination and, in the process, they create new solidarities. In the Swedish context the role of women in the development of culture and local urban communities is often essential in that they act as the main bearers of informal networks integrating local public life. Centred around the family, the household and local community life, such female networks may nurture boundary-crossing cultural dispositions and give birth to new forms of social organisation. Within the locus of the local neighbourhood and of everyday life, a subtle and complex identity work anchors new forms of consciousness and alternative definitions (Ålund 1991a).

Sustained by the mediating space of female social networks, new solidarities and complex cultural identities can emerge from struggles centred around the power of social definitions. Collectively experienced social injuries (related to segregation, discrimination and political marginalisation) affect the creation of shared values in such a way that, instead of the 'personal' representing the 'political', the political (or communal) position becomes personalised. Dynamic communication linking individual experience with an intimate social circle generates a critical collective as well as personal awareness. Creative resistance to stigmatising institutional labelling is articulated through women's own culturally derived discourse (Ålund 1988, 1991a, Ålund and Schierup 1991).

Among Swedish women from former Yugoslavia experiences of solidarity, cooperation and rebellion against oppression seem to have their historical roots in female practices in spheres such as the household, the fields, handicrafts or trading (Rihtman-Augustin 1984). Embedded in the values and types of social relations found in the rural societies most women emigrated from, informal subcultures have developed and been transformed into networks of 'immigrant women' trying to cope with new dilemmas and conflicts. In so far as they deal with current social problems (of discrimination and ethnic conflicts) that are often expressed in broader forms of solidarity that transgress narrow ethnic boundaries, these emerging forms of consciousness may be defined as 'modern'. At the same time they are grounded in 'tradition' and a socio-cultural 'heritage' in the country of origin. This tradition cannot, however, be reduced to 'patriarchal oppression'. Just as there is a strong element of patriarchal oppression in Western countries of immigration, there has always been, as Dunja Rihtman-Augustin (1984) argues, an element of rebellion embedded in concealed 'female subcultures' flourishing in the interstices of many so-called traditional systems. In *The Structure of Traditional Thought* Rihtman-Augustin (*ibid.*) rejects as static the unidimensional, normative approach to what is conventionally described as 'traditional society'. Instead, she draws attention to the existence of a complex and dynamic duality between the official norms presented by an ideal order and everyday reality, marked by conflicting definitions and resistances.

Rihtman-Augustin's argument concerning the multidimensional aspects of 'traditional' female subculture fits in well with the global approach of

Linda Nicholson's (1986) *Gender and History*. Nicholson claims that 'ignored facts' (*ibid.*: 205) led feminists to adopt Western conceptions of history, which became the general 'norm to which others have been taught to aspire' (*ibid.*: 208). This type of criticism focuses on the tendencies in contemporary feminist research to take Western norms not only as 'given by nature', but also as 'superior'.

Normality, Hegemony and the Other

The current phase of academic debate regarding the growing interest in cultural differences mirrors an ongoing struggle over definitions of the normal that has characterised the feminist debate since its earliest days. The recognition of difference in feminist theory was preceded by criticism of ethnocentricity, initiated by black feminists in the United States and Britain. The essential aspects of this critique concerned the problem both of the 'invisibility' of black and ethnic women in the writings of white feminists and of their 'visibility' only as victims. It was particularly the critique of the 'victim' perspective, linked to the dominant discourse of 'triple oppression' (of ethnicity, class and gender), that opened up a new understanding of the relationship between normalising definitions and colonial and postcolonial imaginaries of resistance – the images and struggles for selfhood mobilised by oppressed peoples.

In his essay 'The Politics of Recognition', Charles Taylor (1992), referring to Fanon, points to the effects that the imposition of the coloniser's inferiorising image has on the colonised. Taylor problematises modernity's limitations and the gap between an Enlightenment-based Utopia of universalism and a political reality which renders women and ethnic minorities invisible and culturally excluded. Non-recognition or misrecognition can be 'a form of oppression, imprisoning someone in a false, distorted, and reduced mode of being', he writes (*ibid.*: 25). In this perspective, the victimisation of immigrant and minority women represents a discursively important form of racism, as was pointed out long before Taylor by several feminists of minority background. It is Taylor's essay, however, that has become the focus of the present debate about multiculturalism, citizenship, and recognition.

The importance of recognising and valorising the 'cultural differences' of black, ethnic and immigrant women in the texts and politics of mainstream feminism has only recently been acknowledged in feminist studies. The perception of diversity as a threat has gradually been replaced by calls to promote a politics of recognition which allows space for differences as well as solidarities.

The evolution of feminism from what Iris Young (1990b) has called 'humanist feminism', focusing on demands for equal status and equal rights, into so-called 'gynocentric feminism', or a woman-centred standpoint

('standpoint feminism'), based on what is distinctively womanly such as maternity and caring, was dominated by a homogenised image of woman as the norm: implicitly, moreover, she was white and middle-class. This marginalisation of black and migrant women and what was called 'the other opinion' in the mainstream feminist discourse met with criticism, exposing the ethnocentricity and political hegemony of feminist 'knowledge'.

Gloria Hull *et al.* (1982) express this pithily with the title of their book *All the Women Are White, All the Blacks Are Men, But Some of Us Are Brave.* In a much-publicised article, 'White Women Listen!', Hazel Carby (1982) argued that to get women to come together to fight for their common interests, it was first necessary to get white women to do something about the racism within themselves. Racism became a white feminist 'problem'. In claiming that race was the primary source of their oppression, black and migrant feminist women 'threw into doubt the universality of the central categories and assumptions of mainstream feminist analyses', as Daiva Stasiulis (Stasiulis 1987) has argued. For black and migrant women, as Ellie Vasta (1992: 14) also claims, to start to identify themselves 'outside the mainstream women's movement was both a political gesture to break the notion of homogeneity and an act of self empowerment'.

This kind of criticism from minority women was followed by self-criticism within mainstream feminism from the mid-1980s, which suggested that, historically, white femininity had been constructed through offensive stereotypes and myths pitting 'European' and 'civilised' against 'non-European' and 'non-civilised' (see, for example, Barrett and McIntosh 1985; Harding 1986; Elshtain 1986; Nicholson 1986). A further evolution of feminist research, particularly since the early 1990s, has begun to recognise and scrutinise difference.

Identity Politics: Its Potential and Traps

To start with, the recognition of a variety of experiences grounding identities – social, cultural and sexual – was met with opposition. An internal feminist identity politics was seen as representing a divisive threat to the political unity and theoretical core of the movement. In response to the impact of French deconstructivism and poststructuralism, however, new orientations became evident internationally, associated with postmodernist discourses which focus on culture and identity (Evans 1995; Farganis 1994). At the same time, critical disputes about the political and theoretical consequences of identity politics have also emerged. In particular, both the theory and politics of difference have been criticised for their culturalising and essentialising impact. A return to a focus on traditional social divisions such as class or institutionally embedded racism is now apparent, one which recognises the close association between social, cultural and identity-seeking processes.

Moreover, several feminists have warned against the reductionist separation of structures of domination. Androcentrism, racism and class oppression both overlap and conflict. According to Floya Anthias and Nira Yuval-Davis (1992), we must address the intersection between gender, class, ethnicity and racialised state practices. A disconnection of ethnicity as 'culture' from an interrelated spectrum of 'structural inequalities' leads merely to competing hierarchisations of oppression and fruitless debate – over whether race, gender or class constitute the greatest oppression.

Internal identity politics within feminism risks creating new 'purified' cultures (Yuval-Davis 1997). One result can be a retreat into ghettoised lifestyles (Parmar 1989). Conceptions of what 'identity' is are frequently based on reductionist assumptions of cultural homogeneity. A conflation of group identities with culture, as Iris Young (1990a) points out, has been associated in the West with inferiorising discourses; of racism, sexism and xenophobia. Young suggests that cultural differences should be recognised within an egalitarian procedural framework. This involves opening up the public sphere to the 'unassimilated Other'. Yet such a position fails to take account of the hybrid and composite nature of identities. Recognition of the culturally different, 'unassimilated' Others risks producing new demarcations and constructions of Otherness. No-one today lives in discrete, 'authentic' and 'unassimilated' cultural worlds. Well-meaning attempts to render Others culturally visible may give rise to just as many problems as does a homogenisation of femininity (Bottomley 1991).

The dilemmas of a politics of recognition are difficult to resolve (Trow 1996). As bell hooks (1991) points out, identities are complex, and their deconstruction can make their heterogeneity highly visible, highlighting shared worlds of experience across difference. The reality of the black experience is, nevertheless, one of racism, and as long as racist practices remain, a politics of identity will remain central to the black political struggle.

The connection between identity politics and social exclusion is directly related to citizenship as a universal discourse. The academic challenge has been to conceptualise analytically 'new modes of articulation between the universal and the particular', as Chantal Mouffe (1993) puts it. Concepts such as 'differentiated universalism' (Lister 1997) and 'transversal dialogue' (Yuval-Davis 1997) express this endeavour. A new politics of feminist solidarity, capable of encompassing the cultural voices and representations of difference, is adduced (Yeatman 1993). With reference to ethnicity, the question has been one of acknowledging cultural specificity without ignoring social inequalities (Lister 1997). The challenge is to analyse the varying conditions for membership in the political community: the right to social justice, to participation in the political process, to welfare (Marshall 1950; Turner 1990). This applies in particular to the political exclusion of refugees, asylum seekers, migrant workers and minorities, including women in general, and the discriminatory practices to which they are subjected within the European Union (cf. Morokvasic 1984, 1991, 1993; Knocke 1995).

Women as independent migrants have to an increasing extent become 'the new helots' (Cohen 1987) of a changing world order. They now constitute well over half of those involved in global migration. A significant example of this development is represented by the thousands of Third World maids and nannies, without any legal rights whatever, forced by economic exigencies to leave their homes in order to go into service with rich families in Asia, the USA or Europe. Since the early 1990s, however, women such as Philippine housemaids have begun organising worldwide against the oppression to which they are exposed (Stasiulis and Bhakan 1997). Discussing political activism of Pakistani diasporic women, Pnina Werbner (1996: 5) argues that 'they have, literally, rewritten the moral terms of their citizenship – from passive to active, from disadvantaged underclass and racialised minority to an elite cadre of global citizens'. Ellie Vasta (1992: 3) writes about Australia that 'migrant women's racially structured gender position has led to the emergence of organisations like the SPEAKOUT and ANESBWA, and has led to their struggles and "cultures of resistance" against marginalisation in economic, state, cultural and political arenas'. From this kind of political platform, migrant women seem to start moving towards broader solidarities, across ethnicities and sexualities. They have recognised that identity politics is not an end in itself but a precursor to further, more broadly based activities and alliances, based on political commitments rather than on discrete cultural identities (*ibid.*).

An increased insight into the internationalisation of racialised boundary-making, as well as into the politics of resistance, alliance and coalition building across ethnic and gender boundaries, has generated new questions for international gender research. In Sweden, an interest in these questions has long been confined to a small group of feminists of immigrant background. This is now changing, with an analytical shift in feminist research towards a more comprehensive understanding of the need to address the conditions of ethnic minority belonging, here and now, and their own experience (Ålund 1991a).

This has become particularly important as the focus of empirical research, and the academic and public debate in Sweden, as well as in the rest of Scandinavia, has moved away from first-generation migrants to so-called 'immigrant youth'. These new Swedes are fighting for membership of a society which still does not regard them as part of it, as 'real' Swedes. Their search for an identity is marked by conflicting experiences of local living in segregated conditions of suburban life, and a generalised feeling of being excluded from the wider national community (Ålund 1996b). This returns us to the question raised earlier of emergent cultures of resistance.

Culture and the Politics of Resistance

Living in complex societies entails participation in multiple, 'more or less discrepant universes of discourses', as Barth (1989: 130) has observed.

People today move between different partial and simultaneous cultural worlds and therefore 'their cultural construction of reality springs not from one source and is not of one place' (*ibid.*). In similar vein, Stuart Hall describes contemporary identities as strategic and positional, 'never singular but multiply constructed across different, often intersecting and antagonistic discourses, practices and positions' (1996: 4). Cultures have a remarkable openness and ability to interact with 'outside' signals and to incorporate them (Sollors 1989). This represents, as Ulf Hannerz argues, not just 'a matter of assimilating items of some distant provenance into a fundamentally local culture' (1990: 238) as in the case of globalised commodities. Much of what 'passes for novel cultural interchange these days is instead', Steve Vertovec writes with reference to Hannerz, a view of 'cosmopolitanism as a perspective, a state of mind or a mode of managing meaning' (1996: 394).

Emergent mixtures of cultures, cultural innovation, a multiplicity of identities (in an individual as well as a collective sense) illustrate the diversity of contemporary multicultural society and its potential for change. Debate in Sweden as in Europe in general has failed to theorise this kind of 'multicultural multiplicity'. As Hall (1993: 361) puts it, cultural multiplicity is the destiny of modern society. This does not automatically mean that multiplicity is always publicly evident; the real risk is that public discourses will continue to presume 'pure' forms of national and traditional identity.

The development of new, distinct aesthetic modes of popular culture which transgress cultural frontiers and express resistance to social marginalisation is generating new forms of solidarity and collective identity. Young people in particular create new transcultural communities grounded in their experiences of living in a multi-ethnic society (Hewitt 1992; Jones 1988). Yet, as Angela McRobbie points out (1994), research into the relation between gender, ethnicity and youth contains many gaps, not least on young women, among whom a thought-provoking kind of resistance and a new cultural language seem to be growing: a new, 'hybrid' ethnicity which expresses the rhetoric of proud young womanhood.

In the multi-ethnic cities of today, young people develop complex life forms, a polyphony of cultural styles in which local, national and global influences fuse. In Stockholm, these new ways of living transcend frontiers, creating cultural amalgamations and successive transethnic urban social movements (Ålund 1993, 1995, 1996b, 1997). Daily living in an ethnically mixed society stimulates young people in particular to create bridges across ethnic boundaries and fuse cultural expressions. This comes along with a heightened social consciousness critical of increasing discrimination, as well as a sense of shared subordination expressed in the lyrics of rap music and in growing social movements against racism and enforced ethnic boundaries (Ålund 1994b). The formation of new voices and new 'hybrid' identities is, as Homi K. Bhabha says (1996: 58), closely related to a construction of visions of 'community and versions of historic memory that give narrative form to the minority positions they occupy, the outside of the inside: the part in the whole'.

The expression of these processes is deeply embedded in the autobiographical stories of young women which I collected in the course of my fieldwork in Stockholm (Ålund 1997). The feeling of outsider identity and the search for a sense of belonging saliently characterise their identity work. The social contexts of their immediate life worlds, with their inequalities and tensions, give rise to conflictual forces of belonging/not belonging, particularly significant for young people defined as 'immigrants' and strangers, from generation to generation. Their often marginal position in the societal division of labour – and that of their parents as well – impacts on the character and role of their felt ethnic identities. These, I found, were by no means self-evident. The individual interviews repeatedly exposed a destabilisation of notions of fixed ethnicity. The young women's experiences were mediated by a variety of social and cultural worlds, and by the experience of intense cultural multiplicity in their daily lives. For the women, diverse cultural elements were mixed and crossed as they formulated new identities for themselves. Their narratives are permeated by a multiplicity of histories and memories, and by dreams of overcoming the experience of not belonging. Behind the individual life stories, a common pattern emerges: the need to connect split worlds and to transgress existing boundaries. A successful way toward 'home' and 'belonging' requires bridges that connect and include.

Against this background I have found it crucial to focus my investigations on the urban politics of similarity and resistance, emerging from a recognition of shared social conditions and cultural expressions across differences.

Conclusion

I have argued in this chapter that the emergence of transcultural identities and new social movements is particularly significant as it finds expression among young people in general, and women in particular, in multi-ethnic urban settings. In defining a multicultural politics of citizenship the notion of transculturalism is central (see Ålund and Schierup 1991). The composite character of modern identities creates the conditions that enable the development of boundary transgressing, new social and political solidarities. The importance of transcultural and transnational conversations, not least on the issues of gender, allows citizens to connect different experiences and historical memories. These advance shared understandings of contemporary forms of oppression as the grounds for a national, even global politics of solidarity.

Yet, as I have argued, a culturalist tendency is still strongly present among Scandinavian feminists. Any classification of people purely in terms of culture – a classification that fails to acknowledge that cultures, identities and ethnicities are hybrid, composite and responsive to structural inequalities and exclusions – will continue to promote a hegemonic social order that legitimises the exclusion of ethnic minorities, not least minority women. The result of such cultural reductionism is apparent in the present deepening divisions of Swedish society along ethnic lines. It underlines the need to develop new critical cultural research on social citizenship, linking it to economic and social rights, which takes account of the richness of cultural diversity and the part it plays in combating a pluralism of oppressions.

Acknowledgement

This is a revised version of an article published in *Sosiologisk forskning* 2, 1997

References

Ålund, Aleksandra (1988). 'The Power of Definitions: Immigrant Women and Problem-Centred Ideologies', *Migration* 4, 88: 37–55.

— (1991a). *Lilla Juga; Etnicitet, familj och kvinnliga nätverk i kulturbrytningars tid,* Stockholm: Carlssons.

— (1991b). 'Ungdom, multietnisk kultur och nya gemenskaper', *Kvinnovetenskaplig tidskrift* 3, 91: 18–31.

— (1993). 'Crossing Boundaries: Notes on Transethnicity in Modern Puristic Society', *Xenophobia and Exile; Rescue* 43, Copenhagen: Munksgaard, pp. 149–61.

— (1994a). 'Det statistiska genomsnittet och bortom – en invandrad kvinnas arbetslivshistoria', in C. U. Schierup and S. Paulsson (eds) *Arbetets etniska delning,* Stockholm: Carlssons, pp. 101–27.

— (1994b). 'Ethnicity and Modernity: on Tradition in Modern Cultural Studies', in John Rex and Beatrice Drury (eds) *Ethnic Mobilisation in Multi-Cultural Europe,* Aldershot: Avebury.

— (1995). 'Alterity in Modernity', *Acta Sociologica* 38: 311–22

— (1996a). 'Vida's Metamorphosis to "Immigrant Women"', Esbjerg: SUC: Papers, *Migration* No. 10.

— (1996b). *Multiethnic Sweden: Youth in a Stockholm Suburb*, Esbjerg: South Jutland University Press: Papers, Migration No. 7.

— (1997). *Multikultiungdom: Kön, etnicitet, identitet*, Lund: Studentlitteratur.

Ålund, Aleksandra and Carl-Ulrik Schierup (1991). *Paradoxes of Multiculturalism,* Aldershot: Avebury.

Andersson-Brolin, Lillemor (1984). *Etnisk bostads-segregation*, Sociologiska institutionen. Stockholm: Stockholms universitet.

Anthias, Floya and Yuval-Davis, Nira (1983). 'Contextualising Feminism: Gender, Ethnic and Class Divisions', *Feminist Review* 15: 62–75.

Anthias, Floya and Yuval-Davis, Nira (1992). *Racialised Boundaries: Race, Nation, Gender, Class and the Anti-Racist Struggle*, London: Routledge.

Barker, Martin (1981). *The New Racism*, London: Junction Books.

Barrett, Michelle and McIntosh, Mary (1985). 'Ethnocentrism and Socialist-Feminist Theory', *Feminist Review* 20: 23–49.

Barth, Fredrik (1989). 'The Analysis of Culture in Complex Societies', *Ethnos* 54, III–IV: 120–42.

— (1994). *Manifestasjon og prosess*, Oslo: Universitetsforlaget.

Bhabha, K. Homi (1996). 'Culture's In-Between', in Stuart Hall and Paul du Gay (eds) *Cultural Identity*, London: Sage, pp. 53–61.

Bottomley, Gillian (1991). 'Culture, Ethnicity and the Politics/Poetics of Representation', *Diaspora* 1/3: 303–21.

Carby, Hazel (1982). 'White Women Listen! Black Feminism and the Boundaries of Sisterhood', in Centre for Contemporary Cultural Studies, *The Empire Strikes Back*. London: Hutchinson, pp. 212–36.

Cohen, Robin (1987). *The New Helots: Migrants in the International Division of Labour*, Aldershot: Avebury.

Elshtain, Jean Bethke (1986). 'The New Feminist Scholarship', *Salmagundi* 70–1: 3–26.

Essed, Philomena (1987). *Academic Racism: Common Sense in the Social Sciences*. Working paper No. 5, Amsterdam: CRES Publ. Series.

Evans, Judith (1995). *Feminist Theory Today: An Introduction to Second-Wave Feminism*, London: Sage.

Farganis, Sandra (1994). *Situating Feminism: From Thought to Action*, Thousand Oaks, London, New Delhi: Sage.

Gilroy, Paul (1987). *There Ain't No Black in the Union Jack*. London: Hutchinson.

— (1993). *The Black Atlantic: Modernity and Double Consciousness*, London: Verso.

Hall, Stuart (1992/1994). 'New Ethnicities', in James Donald and Ali Rattansi (eds) *'Race', Culture and Difference*, London: Sage, pp. 252–60.

— (1993). 'Culture, Community, Nation', *Cultural Studies* 7: 349-63.

— (1996). 'Introduction: Who Needs "Identity"?', in Stuart Hall and Paul du Gay (eds) *Cultural Identity*, London: Sage, pp. 1–18.

Hannerz, Ulf (1990). 'Cosmopolitans and Locals in World Culture', in Mike Featherstone (ed.) *Global Culture*, London: Sage, pp. 237–51.

Harding, Sandra (1986). *The Science Question in Feminism*, New York: Cornell Press.

— (1990). 'Feminism, Science, and the Anti-Enlightenment Critiques', in Linda J. Nicholson (ed.) *Feminism/Postmodernism*, New York and London: Routledge, pp. 83–107.

Hewitt, Roger (1992). 'Language, Youth and the Destabilisation of Ethnicity', in Cecilia Palmgren, Karin Lövgren and Göran Bolin (eds) *Ethnicity in Youth Culture*, Stockholm: University of Stockholm, pp. 27–43.

hooks, bell (1991). *Yearning: Race, Gender and Cultural Politics*, London: Turnaround.

Hull, Gloria, Patricia Bell Scott, and Barbara Smith (eds) (1982). *All the Women Are White, All the Men are Black, But Some of Us Are Brave*, Black Women's Studies. New York: The Feminist Press.

Jones, Simon (1988). *Black Culture White Youth*, London: Macmillan Education.

Knocke, Wuokko (1991). 'Invandrade kvinnor – vad är 'problemet'? *Kvinnovetenskaplig Tidsskrift* 3: 4–15

— (1994). 'Kän, etnicitet och teknisk utveckling', in Carl U. Schierup and S. Paulsson (eds) *Arbetets etniska delning*, Stockholm: Carlssons, pp. 81–107.

— (1995). 'Migrant and Ethnic Minority Women: the Effects of Gender-Neutral Legislation in the European Community', *Social Politics* 2, 2: 225–38.

Liljeström, Rita (1979). 'Invandrarnas barn, skolan och framtiden', in *Svensk invandrarpolitik inför 1980-talet*, Stockholm: Arbetsmarknadsdepartementet 6: 15–58.

Lister, Ruth (1997). 'Citizenship: Towards a Feminist Synthesis', *Feminist Review* 57: 28–48.

Marshall, T. H. (1950). *Citizenship and Social Class*, Cambridge: Cambridge University Press.

McRobbie, Angela (1994). *Postmodernism and Popular Culture*, London and New York: Routledge.

Morokvasic, Mirjana (1983). 'Women in Migration: Beyond the Reductionist Outlook', in Annie Phizaclea (ed.) *One Way Ticket: Migration and Female Labour*, Routledge and Kegan Paul, pp. 13–33.

— (1984). 'Birds of Passage Are Also Women', *International Migration Review* 18, 4: 886–907.

— (1991). 'Fortress Europe and Migrant Women', *Feminist Review* 39: 69–84.

— (1993). 'In and Out of the Labour Market: Immigration and Minority Women in Europe', *New Community* 19, 3: 459–83.

Mouffe, Chantal (1993). *The Return of the Political*, London: Verso

Nicholson, Linda J. (1986). *Gender and History*, New York: Columbia University Press.

— (ed.) (1990). *Feminism/Postmodernism*, New York and London: Routledge.

Parmar, Pratibha (1989). 'Other Kinds of Dreams', *Feminist Review* 31: 55–65.

Peterson, Abby (1994). 'Racist and Antiracist Movements in Postmodern Society: Between Universalism and Particularism', paper presented at the XIII World Congress of Sociology, Bielefeld, July 1994.

Porter, John (1968). *The Vertical Mosaic: Analyses of Social Class and Power in Canada*, Toronto: University of Toronto Press.

Räthzel, Nora (1995). 'Images of Heimat and Images of 'Ausländer', in Aleksandra Ålund and R. Granqvist (eds) *Negotiating Identities; Essays on Immigration and Culture in Present Day Europe*, Amsterdam-Atlanta: Rodopi, pp. 45–71.

Rex, John (1995). 'Ethnic Identity and the Nation State: the Political Sociology of Multi-Cultural Society', *Social Identities* 1, 1: 21–35.

Rihtman-Augustin, Dunja (1984). *Struktura tradicijskog misljenja*, Zagreb: Skolska knjiga.

Schierup, Carl-Ulrik and Sven Paulsson (eds) (1994). *Arbetets etniska delning: Studier från en svensk bilindustri*, Stockholm: Carlssons.

Silverman, Max (1992). *Deconstructing the Nation: Immigration, Racism and Citizenship in Modern France*, London: Routledge.

Simmel, Georg (1994). [1909] 'Bridge and Door', *Theory, Culture and Society* 11: 5–11.

Sollors, Werner (ed.) (1989). *The Invention of Ethnicity*, Oxford: Oxford University Press.

Stasiulis, Daiva, K. (1987). 'Rainbow Feminism: Perspectives on Minority Women in Canada', *Resources for Feminist Research* 16, 1: 5–9.

Stasiulis, Daiva and Bhakan, Abigail (1997). 'Negotiating Citizenship: the Case of Foreign Domestic Workers in Canada', *Feminist Review* 57: 112–38.

Taylor, Charles (1992). *Multiculturalism and 'The Politics of Recognition'*, Princeton: Princeton University Press.

Trow, Martin (1996). 'De universella värdena', *Svenska Dagbladet*, June, 2.

Turner, Bryan S. (1990). 'Outline of a Theory of Citizenship', *Sociology* 24, 2: 189–217.

Vasta, Ellie (1992). 'Immigrant Women and the Politics of Resistance', paper for the Australian Immigrant Women's Speakout Association Conference, 16–17 October.

Vertovec, Steve (1996). 'Berlin Multikulti: Germany, "Foreigners" and "World-openness"', *New Community* 22, 3: 381–99.

Ware, Vron (1992). *Beyond the Pale: White Women, Racism and History,* London: Verso.
Werbner, Pnina (1996). 'Reversing the Moral Terms of Citizenship: Transnational Belonging and Political Activism of Pakistani Diasporic Women', paper presented to the Conference on 'Women, Citizenship and Difference', 16–18 July, London: University of Greenwich.
Wrench, John and John Solomos (eds) (1993). *Racism and Migration in Western Europe,* Oxford and Providence: Berg.
Yeatman, Anna (1993). 'Voice of Representation in the Politics of Difference', in S. Gunew and A. Yeatman (eds) *Feminism and the Politics of Difference,* Sydney: Allen and Unwin.
Young, Iris Marion (1990a). 'The Ideal of Community and the Politics of Difference', in Linda J. Nicholson (ed.) *Feminism/Postmodernism,* London: Routledge, pp. 300–24.
— (1990b). *Justice and the Politics of Difference,* Princeton, NJ: Princeton University Press.
Yuval-Davis, Nira (1997). 'Women, Citizenship and Difference', *Feminist Review* 57: 4–27.

CHAPTER 10

Muslim and South Asian Women: Customary Law and Citizenship in Britain

Samia Bano

Community and the Law

Liberal political theory operates according to the principles of individual choice, personal freedom and religious toleration, grounded in the notion of individual rights. Within this tradition group rights are viewed with suspicion and seen as inherently dangerous and oppressive if they fail to acknowledge conflict and diversity within the group. Recently, however, liberals have begun to argue that group interests may, in fact, be accommodated within the framework of individual rights (Taylor 1994; Kymlicka 1995).

This raises a number of important conceptual and theoretical questions regarding the relation between individual and group rights, how these are to be distinguished and how clashes between individual and group rights may be reconciled. Embedded in these is the key question of what makes a community a community of rights. Does the state, in granting individuals the right to enjoy their culture, have an obligation to foster that culture and ensure its survival?

One kind of critique of liberalism comes from 'communitarians' who argue that liberalism has failed to encompass the concept of 'community' adequately within its analysis of rights. These critics claim that liberalism, by assuming that the individual exists prior to a community, fails to capture the reality of human experience. According to Christian Bay,

> Liberals have persistently tended to cut the citizen off from the person; and they have placed on their humanistic pedestal a cripple of a man, a man without a moral or political nature, a man with plenty of contractual rights and obligations perhaps, but a man without moorings in any real community, a drifter rather than a being with roots in species solidarity. (cited in Dunleavy and O'Leary 1987: 30)

By contrast with liberals, communitarians aim to place the individual within a community, seen to play a defining role in identity formation. According to Sandel, the introduction of 'community' into the liberal conception of rights enhances self-consciousness and individual identification with a wider subjectivity of 'participants in a shared identity, be it family, community, class or nation' through a sense of participation and engagement with others (Sandel 1982: 79). Belonging is central to the communitarian ideal. Human beings are defined as being socially interdependent, connected over their life course through complex social networks. People as subjects are continuously 'made' through their engagement with their society and its institutions (Bay 1978: 45). 'Community' thus provides a sense of social selfhood and identity, a moral biography embedded in the 'story of those communities from which I derive my identity' (McIntyre 1981: 205; Parry 1969: 182). What we are or are able to become depends to an important extent on the wider community in which we live.

The limitations of the 'communitarian' approach lie in its failure to address the issue of difference and diversity within a group. For Hirsch, the communitarians fail to acknowledge the negative dimensions of 'community':

> [b]oth homogeneity and moral education can be politically dangerous in several ways: by encouraging the exclusion of outsiders; by encouraging indoctrination or irrationalism; by compromising privacy and autonomy. (Hirsch 1986: 14)

The notion of community constructs boundaries which involve processes of exclusion as well as inclusion. The development of the individual thus becomes dependent upon the community yet this fails to recognise that individual and group rights may diverge.

The issue is, therefore, how a theory of cultural minority group rights may include a recognition of difference, including gendered difference, within groups. The principle of recognition may open a Pandora's box, as van Dyke points out, 'from which all sorts of groupings might spring, demanding rights' (1995: 234). To avoid this proliferation of 'groups' claiming 'recognition', Fiss identifies two characteristics of a social group which differentiate it from 'mere aggregates': its 'entity' and its interdependence. By entity he means that the group has a distinct existence and identity apart from its members, and that individuals derive their sense of well-being, status and identity from their membership in the group (see Dunleavy and O'Leary 1987: 57).

A similar definition might serve to define 'community'. Communities nest within one another: local, national, global. They also intersect: British Muslims belong to the global Muslim *umma*, for example. Britain as a national community has its own specific legal system, but Britain is also a member of the international community which recognises transcendent human rights. Recognising religious/cultural practices in English law may contravene individual rights as defined by the United Nations Human Rights Charter and other conventions. Indeed, the recognition of a 'cultural/religious' practice may be regarded by some members of a community as a 'right', and by others as a means of oppression. Britain has no written constitution but is a contracting party to two main conventions which set out the rights of minority groups: namely, the 1953 European Convention on Human Rights, including its protocols, and the International Covenant on Civil and Political

Rights. Article 27 of the International Covenant on Civil and Political Rights declares:

> In those States in which ethnic, religious or linguistic minorities exist, persons belonging to such minorities shall not be denied the right, in community with the other members of their group, to enjoy their own culture, to profess and practise their own religion, or to use their own language. (Cmnd 3230 of 1967)

The legitimacy of these conventions has been recognised by Parliament as obligatory in English law (see, for example, Scarman 1978 Q.B. 36, 48).

The Law and Minority Rights

The relationship between the law and the rights of minority groups in Britain is both complex and problematic. Lacey points out that a 'legal commitment to formal equality is insufficient to guarantee the fair treatment of groups which have suffered a history of prejudice and discrimination' (1992: 101). Moreover, anti-discrimination law has a limited scope in a racist and sexist society. Discrimination, she argues, can only be redressed through political action in a world in which white, male and middle-class people have privileged access to the law (Lacey 1992: 105).

Concepts such as 'equality of opportunity' are seen by activists as 'ideologically loaded', providing limited *de facto* protection for members of minority groups. However objective or neutral the apparatus of the law may appear, its implementation will always reflect the norms and values of society. The Race Relations Act 1976 outlaws only those types of acts which it defines as 'racist'. It is significant, therefore, that the meaning of the term 'racism' is constantly being expanded in the UK in response to new precedents (Banton 1991). Critiques of the 'discourse of rights' highlight its individualistic, competitive and anti-social character, and deconstruct its supposed neutrality and objectivity in order to expose its substantive preconceptions and the ways in which it systematically favours certain kinds of interest (Lacey 1992: 107). Thus the law operates to maintain the hegemony of privileged and established elites.

The public/private dichotomy in English law remains central to constructing the boundaries within which the free practice of cultural customs and religious beliefs is deemed acceptable. The law seeks not to intervene in matters which it defines as belonging to the private domain. As Lacey points out, however, this avoidance is not politically innocent as the law tends to intervene selectively in the regulation of the 'private' domain (1992: 108). For many years, for example, it was reluctant to intervene in cases of domestic violence, often leaving women in dangerous situations, as the work of Southall Black Sisters among Asian women has documented (1990). They illustrate how policies of multiculturalism have meant that the 'internal affairs' of the community are often left to be regulated by family/community leaders. This has in many cases led to disastrous consequences for women and young girls of the community who choose not to live according to cultural/religious traditional values and beliefs and therefore become ostracised.

Cultural Pluralism in English Law

There are an estimated 2.75 to three million people from ethnic minority backgrounds in Britain, approximately 4.5 per cent of the population. The 1991 census, although it did not contain a 'religious' question, revealed that 640,000 originated from Pakistan and Bangladesh (Modood *et al.* 1997: 13) and about 50,000 from the Middle East (Al-Rasheed 1997: 209); yet the extent to which Islamic law is practised in Britain remains uncertain.

English law is based on a liberal notion of universal neutrality. The Race Relations Act 1976 aimed to promote equal opportunities and to eliminate discrimination in employment, housing, education and the provision of goods and services. Over time the legal system has recognised certain other demands of ethnic minority groups. For example the Shop Act 1950 exempted Jews from Sunday trading laws. The Slaughterhouses Act 1979 allows the slaughter of animals for the purpose of obtaining kosher and *halal* meat for the Jewish and Muslim communities; and since 1976, under the Motorcycle Crash Helmet (Religious Exemption) Act, a Sikh with a turban may ride a motorcycle in Britain without wearing a crash helmet. In addition, voluntary-aided religious and denominational schools are funded by the state, as are army chaplains and university theology faculties.

The courts have also ruled on what is defined as an ethnic and racial group. For example in *Mandla v Dowell Lee* (1983) a Sikh boy was excluded from carrying any religious symbols in school. Lord Denning argued that Sikhs were not racially distinguishable from other Asians. In the House of Lords, however, a wider view of 'ethnic minority' was taken and seven criteria, including a common religion, were established. Thus the headmaster was found guilty of indirect discrimination under the Race Relations Act 1976, and Sikh children are allowed to carry religious symbols in school. It is important to note that under the Race Relations Act 1976, Jews, Sikhs and Gypsies are defined as ethnic groups but Muslims, Hindus and Afro-Caribbeans have so far been excluded. The present proposed revision of the Act includes a section on religious discrimination for the first time.

Poulter argues that, given liberal principles, we must be clear about the limits of cultural pluralism 'which need to be imposed in support of the overriding public interest in promoting social cohesion' (1992: 156). This view is shared by Lester and Bateman who warn that cultural tolerance must not become a 'cloak for oppression and injustice within the immigrant communities themselves' (cited in Poulter 1992), nor must it endanger the integrity of the 'social and cultural core' of English values as a whole.

Making provision for ethnic minority groups seeking to exercise religious customs and practices has raised the question of the need for 'special treatment'. This is because, as Montgomery argues, 'Provisions providing for formal equality may result in greater restrictions of the freedom of minority groups than is experienced by the majority' (1992: 193). Such restrictions may well arise from the legal commitment to protect rights of religious freedom that make it necessary to devise special rules for particular groups. But does recognising a group right mean compelling all members of the group to partake of the right in question, even against their will?

Montgomery outlines four different types of group rights. The first is where individuals acquire rights by virtue of their membership of the group, once membership is established. This principle has been applied in English law to Quakers and Jews, for example, who are allowed by the Marriage Acts 1949–86 to solemnise marriage acts. Their special privileges date from 1753 and they are not subject to the regulations. English domestic law makes no concessions, however, to other religions or customs, apart from Christianity.

The second type of 'group right' recognises a 'private' space in which 'a self-contained parallel system of rules would operate' (Montgomery 1992: 195). The Ottoman Empire operated with a plural system according autonomy to religious groups or *dhimmis* to manage their family law internally. Drawing on this tradition some sections of the Muslim community in the UK would like to claim legal autonomy in matters of family law, to enable Islamic law to be applied in the 'private' sphere of family relations. If this claim were accepted in Britain, a different system of personal laws would govern Muslim citizens from those applied to the community at large. But this would raise the issue of how to deal with those individuals who do not wish to conform to the traditional customs of their communities. Clearly, such a group right is problematic if it is based on the *exclusive* recognition of a single common identity for all the members of the cultural and religious minority. As Montgomery points out, support for such a right rests on a number of assumptions. First, the group must have some discrete identity which enables its members to be distinguished from outsiders. Second, the group must be essentially homogeneous in respect of its desire for the special treatment. Third, not only must the group generally want special treatment, but the treatment must be of a nature which creates liberties that can be exercised by all. The claim for an exclusive or territorially based separate personal law system remains problematic since the cultural boundaries of groups are rarely unambiguous. This is because, as Verman points out, 'Individual people are likely to feel part of one group in some contexts and of another in relation to different issues' (1982: 32). Boundaries are more easily defined when minorities are concentrated territorially, as is the case with indigenous minorities. A further option, the one adopted in India, is to create two parallel systems of personal law – customary/religious and civil – and allow all citizens the right to choose between them. Of course, as Sara Hossain (1994) points out, the operation of a legal pluralist system in India remains both controversial and problematic. Furthermore, it is far too simplistic an analysis to argue that all citizens have the right to choose which system they wish to adhere to. Women are often denied this choice and risk being ostracised from their community and family if they wish to opt out of the system of religious laws.

The third type of group right is a dispensation or entitlement allowing members of the group, as a collective body, to act in a way which would otherwise be unlawful. For example, the Sex Discrimination Act 1975, section 19, allows qualifications and authorisations to be withheld from one sex 'for purposes of organised religion' in order to comply with the doctrines of that religion or avoid offending the religious susceptibilities of a significant number of its followers.

Finally, the fourth sense of a group right is where the right permits some individual members to have special privileges deriving from their membership in the group. For example, both the Jewish and Muslim communities have designated members of the community who have the right to slaughter animals differently from the rest of society. Furthermore Muslim girls have been allowed to wear headscarves to school, contravening the school uniform, and a similar dispensation exists for Jewish boys to wear religious caps. Prior to changes to the law, Muslims and Jews were exempt from Sunday trading prohibitions.

Clashes between individual and group rights, then, are most likely to occur when full autonomy is granted to a 'community', as was the case in the Ottoman Empire, or under colonial indirect rule. Figgis underlines the paradox that group rights are, on the one hand, powerful in challenging state hegemony and acting to restrict state power; but, at the same time, they also may restrict individual freedoms, as collective decisions and values cannot be guaranteed to coincide with the individual concerns of certain group members (Montgomery 1992: 123).

Despite his strong advocacy of an active and transformative multiculturalism, Parekh (1995) is critical of calls for autonomous group rights from different religious groups. He believes that Britain cannot allow separate legal systems for different communities without violating the fundamental principles of common citizenship and equality before the law. The law, he points out, has evolved and accepted cultural differences in case law without violating these principles. For example, in *R v Bibi* (1980) the Court of Appeal reduced the imprisonment of a Muslim widow, found guilty of importing cannabis, from three years to six months on the grounds that, among other things, 'she was totally dependent on her brother-in-law and was socialised by her religion into subservience to the male members of her household' (Parekh 1994: 200). In *R v Bailey* and *R v Byfield* the moral codes of men brought up in the West Indies were taken into consideration in sentencing them for having sexual intercourse with girls under the age of 16, and in *Malik v British Home Stores* (1980) it was decided that in appropriate circumstances Asian women may wear trousers at work, even though white women may not (*ibid.*).

The Recognition of South Asian and Muslim Customary Laws in English Family Law

It has been argued that in a multicultural and heterogeneous society there must be a commitment to cultural diversity and pluralism in the area of family life, just as in other areas, and that the law should uphold and support a diversity of family arrangements whether or not they are reflective of differences in race, culture or religion (Bainham 1995: 235). This is echoed by Joseph Raz, who argues that 'the phenomenon of a multicultural society goes beyond mere toleration and non-discrimination. It involves recognition of the equal standing of all stable and viable cultural communities existing in a society' (1986: 38). Raz suggests that we need a radical policy of liberal multiculturalism that would transcend an individualistic approach but would at the same time 'recognise the importance of unimpeded membership in a respected and flourishing cultural group for individual well-being' (1986: 44). A redefinition of society would mean there would no longer be majority and minority groups but rather a 'plurality of cultural groups' each of equivalent worth. He accepts that some cultures or some features of them may be unacceptable to the society as a whole, because of their oppressive aspects. Even Raz and Bainham, however, fail to consider the need to take into account power imbalances in the institution of the family: who determines what is considered acceptable or unacceptable behaviour within the institution of the family?

The issue of arranged marriages is a case in point. It is a basic condition of a legally valid marriage that it should be a voluntary union, a principle upheld in *Singh v Singh* (1971). A marriage may be voidable on the grounds of lack of consent. The courts take the view that the cultural traditions of those ethnic groups in which arranged marriage is practised must be respected. A number of cases, however, have examined the issue where pressure to get married has been exerted by parents. In *Singh v Kaur* (1981), a reluctant Sikh bridegroom protested about his arranged marriage to a young woman in India which led to a series of arguments with his parents. The court, however, rejected his petition for nullity on the grounds that the evidence of pressure fell far short of the threat to 'life, limb or liberty' then thought to be necessary to vitiate an apparent consent. Ormond LJ argued that the practice of arranged marriages could not be undermined in the Asiatic and other communities. In *Hirani v Hirani* (1982), however, a 19-year-old Hindu girl succeeded in her petition for nullity. In order to prevent her association with a young Muslim man her parents had forced her into marriage and threatened her with eviction if she failed to go through with the ceremony. Ormond LJ judged this to be a

> classic case of a young girl, wholly dependent on her parents, being forced into marriage with a man she has never seen in order to prevent her (reasonably from her parents' point of view) continuing an association with a Muslim which they would regard with abhorrence. (*ibid.*)

In this case the courts, through the principle of true consent, allowed a young woman to reject a cultural practice which she considered oppressive.

Like English civil marriage, so too in Islamic law marriage is a contract between consenting parties in the presence of witnesses (Pearl 1987). Unlike the civil law, however, Muslim law does not recognise a marriage between a Muslim woman and a non-Muslim man. It does, however, recognise polygamy, prohibited under English law. According to Islamic law men can take up to four wives, even if they rarely do so, with clear repercussions for internal familial power relations.

Problems of power inequalities within the family are also evident in the case of divorce. Under Islamic law, for example, a divorce can be obtained in a number of different ways: through *talaq* (unilateral repudiation by the husband), *khul* (divorce at the instance of the wife with her husband's agreement, and on condition that she will forgo her right to the *mehr*) and *ubara'at* (divorce by mutual consent). In the present, revised English family law there is only one way to obtain a divorce, on the grounds that the marriage has irretrievably broken down, after a two-year separation where the decree is made absolute. The question of recognition of a unilateral divorce (*talaq*) has been the subject of considerable litigation, culminating in the House of Lords judgement in *Quazi v Quazi* (1979). Lord Justice Wilberforce held that:

> (a) No *talaq* which is pronounced in England will be valid in England regardless of the domicile of the parties and also regardless of whether the husband goes abroad to an Islamic country to appear before the Arbitration Council as laid down by the Muslim Family Ordinance 1961 (21 s.16 Domicile and Matrimonial Proceedings Act 1973).
>
> (b) If both the parties are habitually resident in UK for more than one year, the English courts will not recognise a *talaq* pronounced anywhere other than the country of nationality or of domicile of the parties. If only one party, or neither party is habitually resident in the UK for this period, then a *talaq* pronounced in a third country (other than the country of the nationality) will be treated as valid in England only if it is valid by the law of the domicile of both parties.
>
> (c) There is a residual power to refuse recognition of a *talaq* otherwise valid under the provisions of the 1971 Recognition of Foreign Divorces and Legal Separations Act 1971. The discretion operates broadly within the framework of public policy grounds (the House of Lords in *Quazi v Quazi* held that this discretion will be exercised very rarely indeed, however).

After a divorce Islamic law only obliges a husband to support his wife during the three-month period of *idda* during which she is precluded from remarriage (Nasir 1986: 137–8). The husband does have to pay her any deferred dower, however, and the English courts have been prepared to order the payment of such dower (*Shanoz v Rizwan* 1965; *Qureshi v Qureshi* 1972).

Thus we see that religious/cultural traditions can be practised within the private sphere of the family as long as they do not conflict with liberal legal principles of 'equality before the law' and 'common citizenship' (Parekh 1990: 23). However, 'personal religious legal systems' (for example, Islamic legal systems) are not recognised in their extremity as legitimate under English law. Indeed, they are currently critiqued by a growing number of Muslim women scholars and activists (for example, Mernissi 1992 and 1993). Personal laws are defined as 'customs' which, like English common law, are allowed as long as they do not conflict with English statutory law. Thus Muslims can get married in an Islamic way as long as the marriage is registered with the state. For Muslims in Britain, then, voluntary adherence to Islamic Shari'a law and the setting up of Muslim courts on the model of Rabbinical courts is likely to be the preferred solution for those seeking to pursue a fully Islamic way of life (see Shadid and van Koningsveld 1996).

Honour and Shame: the Implications of Recognising South Asian Customary Law

Women in South Asian communities may be affected by the operation of customary personal laws within the legal system in several different ways. As Anthias and Yuval-Davis (1992) have argued, women play a central role in the symbolic reproduction of 'community' and its survival. Women are singled out by the law: 'On the one hand, women, like men are members of the collectivity. On the other hand, there are always specific rules and regulations which relate to women as women' (Yuval-Davis 1997: 22). Furthermore, the role of women among Asians is of paramount importance to those who control communal boundaries, as women are often seen as carriers of the 'collective honour' of the 'community'. The discourse of *izzat* or family honour acts as an important ideological force controlling and limiting women's options and choices within the family structure. It acts as a powerful tool to dictate acceptable standards of behaviour and, like all personal laws everywhere, controls male and female sexuality through the mechanisms of marriage and divorce. For men, the ability to control their wives' and daughters' conduct denotes self-respect, masculinity and conformity to the standards of group behaviour. The role of women as preservers of family honour means that much depends on their willingness to increase the honour of the family through compliant obedience, and they are liable to 'lose' it and thus shame the family by 'disgraceful' public conduct, exposing their husbands' 'failure to exercise proper patriarchal control' (Anthias and Yuval-Davis 1992: 45). Hence, an implicit danger in the operation of customary personal laws in South Asian communities as far as women are concerned is that such an emergent code may seek to legitimise the discourse of *izzat* and, indeed, give it a localised legal backing, with women being the subjects most detrimentally affected by such a development.

Demands for Islamic Personal Laws in Britain

Islamic family law is referred to as personal law. There have been some voices within the Muslim community in the UK demanding that a 'personal regime of law' be adopted for the Muslim community as a whole within the area of family law (Nielsen 1991: 56). Demands for the introduction of some form of Islamic personal laws were first made public by the Union of Muslim Organisations in 1972 at a conference held in Birmingham (Nielsen 1989). This was later reiterated, in 1975, by a number of religious leaders who argued that Muslims must not be prevented from fulfilling their religious duty by obeying non-Islamic laws. The issue, therefore, was one of apparent conflict of laws between two different legal systems. In reference to family law provisions of the Shari'a, the imam of the Regent's Park mosque in London, Sheikh Syed A. Darsh, argued that, 'When a Muslim is prevented from obeying his law he feels that he is failing to fulfil a religious duty. He will not feel at peace with his conscience or the environment in which he lives and this will lead to disenchantment.' For Darsh, Islamic family law provisions are wide in scope and do not contradict English law as 'both aim at the fulfilment of justice and happiness of the members of the family' (Nielsen 1991: 12). The Regent's Park mosque remains central to promoting Islamic affairs in Britain. Its self-appointed Shari'a Council meets regularly to discuss family law issues, acting as a mediator between couples and interpreting Islamic disputes, as do many other *ulama* (Islamic scholars) throughout Britain. Islam is not a centralised religion like the Catholic Church, and religious authority ultimately derives from reputation for scholarship and sound judgement.

In the light of this, the first issue, that of the recognition of Islamic family law in Britain, raises the question of what exactly is meant by the 'Muslim community'. Muslim communities in Britain are diverse, originating from many different parts of the world. The majority of British Muslims, however, come from the Indian subcontinent, most notably from Pakistan, Bangladesh and India. The majority are concentrated in the North of England and the West Midlands, where many were originally employed in the textile industries.

At present it remains unclear which Muslim communities or representatives are calling for the recognition of Islamic personal laws in Britain and what is meant by 'recognition'. There has been debate both at Islamic conferences and seminars, yet such calls are made by Islamic magazines and newspapers such as *Q News* and *The Straight Path* often only in reaction to external events such as the Rushdie affair and the Gulf War. Nielsen points out that it is only the Union of Muslim Organisations which has made this claim with any regularity. Above all, there is no evidence that such calls are coming from members of the communities themselves rather than from religious activist members of Muslim political parties in Britain. We know little about the extent to which Islamic family law is observed in practice (for example in matters of divorce) and if this generates a conflict of laws between the two legal systems.

South Asian Customary Law

Menski's (1994) research into this area and his preliminary findings suggest the emergence of new laws in Britain, which he defines as 'Angrezi' (English) law, with Asians settled in the UK combining the demands and obligations of customary law and English law concurrently. According to Menski, Asian Muslims in Britain, for example, have not simply given up Islamic law but combine Islamic law and English law to form 'Angrezi Shari'a'. He describes a three-fold process generated by internal conflicts within Asian communities and leading, as mentioned, to the creation of 'British Asian Laws in Britain'. The first stage occurred at the time of migration. At this stage ignorance of the legal system meant that customary practices continued to be observed. For example, up until 1970 many Asians did not register marriages and this later resulted in huge matrimonial disputes. Subsequently, however, Asians learnt to adapt to English law – but rather than abandon their customary traditions, they built the requirements of English law into them. The result has been that new British Muslim, Hindu and Sikh law, unique to Britain, has emerged, differing in some important aspects from the Indian, Pakistani or Bangladeshi laws and customs. This was the second phase which created the corpus of precedent law Menski labels 'Angrezi' law. The third stage in this process might involve abandoning ethnic customs and religious personal laws altogether, and practising only state law, but this has not happened and is, indeed, unlikely to happen in the foreseeable future in the case of most Muslims.

Menski argues that English family law must take into account these developments, as failure to do so can result in a misdirection of cases by the judiciary. He remains critical of English lawyers who are not aware of such changes and cites the case of *Kaur v. Singh* (1972) to illustrate the problems caused when an English judge is misled about facts pertaining to an Asian marriage. In this case, the wife managed to obtain a decree of nullity by convincing the judge that it was the husband's duty among Sikhs to make the necessary arrangements for the religious marriage ceremony. The husband was thus held guilty of wilful refusal to consummate the marriage, and the wife had an easy exit out of an unwanted legal marriage that she had entered into because she did not realise that the legal validity of a marriage in English law arises at the point of registration of that marriage. Menski's work is valuable as he demonstrates the ways 'Angrezi' law operates in Britain. For example, if a Muslim couple want to marry they will have a *nikah* (contracting ceremony) and at the same time register in accordance with English law. He argues that if the operation of Hindu, Muslim and Sikh concepts of law within the legal framework of English law is not properly understood, this will lead to distrust of the law among ethnic minority groups, with serious implications for the legal system.

Another important area of concern is the issue of what exactly is meant by 'Hindu', 'Sikh' or 'Islamic' law'. In the case of Islam, the Shari'a law is subject to interpretation by different religious leaders and communities. There is no one comprehensive Islamic legal system but varieties exist according to ethnic or religious affiliations. For example, the Islamic personal laws which exist in the Indian subcontinent vary greatly in comparison with those which exist in Iran or Iraq. There are two main groups of Muslims in Britain, Sunni and Shi'a Muslims, and the practice of Islam within these groups varies in accordance with the different Shari'a schools of thought. There are also many class and sectarian divisions, however, operating according to different Islamic codes of laws; for example, Ismaili Muslims are part of the wider Shi'a group but practise distinct laws applicable only to them. It is therefore difficult to speak of 'Islamic family law' in Britain when it varies so widely according to ethnic and sectarian affiliation. Nielsen notes that the discussion of Islamic family law in Britain in the Muslim magazines centres on the *ethics* of the subject rather than the law (1991: 12). This means that the general principles highlighted in these texts are based on human relations. According to one interpretation, custom is dependent on place, time and circumstances; others regard the role of religious leaders as crucial in defining current Shari'a practice.

Muslim feminists such as Leila Ahmed (1992) argue that there is a fundamental tension in Islam between its ethical or spiritual vision of sexual equality and the unequal hierarchies contained in family laws, instituted in early Islamic society and perpetuated over time by those holding power.

Two important issues must be considered here: first, the extent to which there is compatibility between customary or religious family laws and English statutory law; and, second, the authority and jurisdiction for applying the law. The extent to which South Asian personal law is compatible with English law raises the fundamental question of how two legal systems which draw their legitimacy from opposed sources can operate in conjunction. English law is based upon liberal legal principles of popular sovereignty delegated to Parliament. In the case of Islamic law, Poulter points out that there are a number of Muslim obligations which run counter to international human rights law, such as the practice of polygamy, the right to unilateral male divorce, and under-age marriage. At the same time, although Islamic law is in theory based on divine revelation, the interpretation of the law is delegated to the *ulama*, the learned scholars (even if some Islamists dispute their authority) who may apply it to fit particular contexts. In a sense, then, both Islamic and English law evolve through interpretation and are responsive to current exigencies.

In the past, Muslim groups have come together during Islamic conferences to consider how Shari'a law may be recognised in Britain. The publication by the Lord Chancellor of an 'Interdepartmental Review of Family and Domestic Jurisdiction' brought together a group of English practitioners and Muslim religious leaders in Birmingham in 1990 to discuss how the judicial system might go some way towards meeting Muslim wishes. The discussion centred on procedures for divorce and child custody. It was concluded that neither a separate legal system nor separate legislation were necessary, but a proposal was put forward that religious authorities should take part in the legal process.

Hence, the issue of who interprets Shari'a law and decides which Islamic personal laws should be recognised within the legal system is an important area of concern. As highlighted previously, Muslim communities are not homogeneous nor based around fixed notions of Islamic law. Both the ethics and principles of Islamic law are subject to debate and controversy. Clearly, no one religious leader or religious body in Britain can define which personal laws should become operative in regulating the UK Muslim community. The centrality of women's role within the family and Islamic family law means that different Muslim leaders may define concepts of female roles and status in more oppressive – or more tolerant and liberal – ways, even within the framework of the Shari'a. In the extreme case of legal pluralism of the Ottoman type, this could lead to unlawful female oppression.

Islamic law, like other South Asian religious and customary corpuses of law, defines the position of women in relation to marriage, divorce, child custody, dowry and inheritance. Communal autonomy in matters of personal law would mean that Asian and Muslim leaders would be given legal backing to control female sexuality. It would allow them to define not only the way in which women must behave within the community but who belongs to the community, thereby controlling its boundaries. This would also raise the issue of what constitutes a Hindu, Sikh or Muslim, since many Asians in Britain define themselves in ethnic terms as secular, rather than stressing a religious identity.

Conclusion

The debate on whether Britain should adopt a pluralist legal system to accommodate the practice of South Asian or Islamic customary personal laws must be approached with great caution. Within the English legal system the rights of minority groups have been defined through anti-discrimination legislation. At present the cultural rights of minority groups are recognised and protected in English law as long as they do not violate national and international human rights law. We have seen that this may present problems in the case of South Asian personal laws. The law must also take into account the heterogeneity of South Asian and Muslim settlers in the UK and the many different varieties of religion they practise. Clearly, no single authority can define South Asian personal law, and individuals, in line with liberal principles, would have to be able to opt for a court of their choosing. The danger of a rigid pluralism is evident: it would encourage the creation of separatist politics, ghettoising minority communities outside the mainstream legal system and thus defining them as the 'other'. As a result, instead of enhancing the rights of South Asians or Muslims in Britain, it would serve to curtail their rights and to segregate groups from one another.

The recognition of customary personal laws could limit the autonomy of religious and ethnic minority women, as it would seek to enhance and legitimise their role as 'symbolic reproducers of the community' and allow for more control of their sexuality (Saghal and Yuval-Davis 1992). It might mean the shifting of state regulation to the private domain, thereby giving religious leaders greater power to dictate acceptable patterns of behaviour. The citizenship rights and duties of Asian women as British citizens would thus be undermined by a strictly pluralist arrangement. The adoption and recognition of communal personal laws would, indeed, prove detrimental not only to women but to all members of the community as the concept of 'equality before the law' would no longer be applicable to them. Such a move would involve freezing cultural and religious boundaries according to criteria (ideological, social) which are set, defined and accepted by the current British judiciary, a move that would lead to a reduction of cultural and religious diversity, dynamism and pluralism, rather than enhanced integration.

References

Ahmed, Leila (1992). *Women and Gender in Islam*, New Haven: Yale University Press.

Al-Rasheed, Madawi (1997). 'The Other-Others: Hidden Arabs?', in Ceri Peach (ed.) *Ethnicity in the 1991 Census, Vol II: the Ethnic Minority Populations of Great Britain*, London: HMSO, pp. 206–21.

Anthias, Floya and Nira Yuval-Davis (1992). *Racialized Boundaries: Race, Nation, Gender, Colour and Class and the Anti-Racist Struggle*, London: Routledge.

Bainham, A. (1995). 'Family Law in a Pluralistic Society', *Journal of Law and Society* 22: 234–47.

Banton, Michael (1991). 'The Race Relations Problematic', *British Journal of Sociology* 42, 1: 115–30.

Bay, C. (1978). 'From Contract to Community: Thoughts on Liberalism and Post-industrial Society', in F. R. Dallmayr (ed.) *From Contract to Community*, New York: Marcel Inc.

Dunleavy, P. and B. O'Leary (1987). *Theories of the State*, London: Macmillan.

van Dyke, V. (1995). 'The Individual, the State, and Ethnic Communities in Political Theory', in Will Kymlicka (ed.) *The Rights of Minority Cultures*, Oxford: Oxford University Press.

Frazer, N. and N. Lacey (1993). *The Politics of the Community,* London: Harvester Wheatsheaf.

Galanter, M. (1981). 'Justice in Many Rooms: Courts, Private Ordering and Indigeneous Law', in *Journal of Legal Pluralism* 19, 1: 69–83.

Hirsch, H. N. (1986). 'Liberalism: Constitutional Liberty and the Renewal of Community', *Political Theory* VII: 16–25.

Hossain, S. (1994). 'Equality in the Home: Women's Rights and Personal Laws in South Asia', in R. J. Cook (ed.) *Human Rights of Women: National and International Perspectives*, University of Pennsylvania Press.

Kymlicka, Will (ed.) (1995). *The Rights of Minority Cultures*, Oxford: Oxford University Press.

Lacey, N. (1992). 'From Individual to Group?', in B. Hepple and E. M. Szyszczak (eds) *Discrimination: the Limits of Law,* London: Mansell, pp. 105–10.

McIntyre, G. (1981). *The Limits of Freedom*, London: Blackwells.

Menski, W. (1994). '*Angrezi Shari'a*: Plural Arrangements in Family Law by Muslims in Britain', unpublished paper, SOAS.

Mernissi, F. (1992). *Women and Islam, an Historical and Theological Enquiry*, Oxford: Blackwells.

— (1993). *Islam and Democracy, Fear of the Modern World*, London: Virago Press.

Modood, Tariq, Richard Berthoud, *et al.* (1997). *Ethnic Minorities in Britain: Diversity and Disadvantage*, London: Policy Studies Institute.

Montgomery, M. (1992). 'Legislating for a Multi-Faith Society', in B. Hepple and E. M. Sczyrack (eds) *Discrimination: the Limits of Law*, London: Mansell.

Nasir, J. (1986). *The Islamic Law of Personal Status*, London: Graham and Trotman.

Nielsen, Jorgen S. (1987). 'Islamic Law and Its Significance for the Situation of Muslim Minorities in Europe: Report of a Study Project', *Research Papers: Muslims in Europe* 35.

— (1989). 'Emerging Claims of Muslim Populations in Matters of Family Law in Europe', *Journal of Muslim Affairs* 15: 120–42.

— (1991). 'A Muslim Agenda for Britain: Some Reflections', *New Community* 17, 3: 467–75.

— (1992). 'Emerging Claims of Muslim Populations in Matters of Family Law in Europe', *Research Papers: Muslims in Europe.* No. 13.

Parekh, Bikhu (1990). 'Britain and the Social Logic of Pluralism', in *Britain: A Plural Society*, London: CRE.

— (1994). 'Equality, Fairness and the Limits of Diversity', *Innovation* 7: 289.

— (1995). 'British Citizenship and Cultural Difference', in Will Kymlicka (ed.) *The Rights of Minority Cultures*, Oxford: Oxford University Press.

Parry, G. (1969). *Political Elites*, London: Allen and Unwin.

Pearl, A. (1987). 'South Asian Immigrant Communities and English Family Law 1971–1987', *New Community* XIV, 1/2: 84–105.

Poulter, S. M. (1986). *English Law and Ethnic Minority Customs,* London: Butterworth & Co.

— (1992). 'The Limits of Legal, Cultural and Religious Pluralism', in B. Hepple and E. M. Sczyrack (eds) *Discrimination: the Limits of Law*, London; Mansell.

— (1994). 'Minority Rights', in C. M. Crudden and G. Chambers (eds) *Individual Rights and the Law in Britain*, Oxford: Clarendon Press.

— (1998). *Ethnicity, Law and Human Rights*, Oxford: Clarendon Press.

Raz, Joseph (1986). *The Morality of Freedom,* Oxford: Clarendon Press.

— (1994). 'Multi-Culturalism: A Liberal Perspective', *Dissent* 67: 96–105.

Saghal, Gita and Nira Yuval-Davis (eds) (1992). *Refusing Holy Orders: Women and Fundamentalism in Britain*, London: Virago Press.

Sandel, M. (1982). *Liberalism and the Limits of Justice*, Cambridge: Cambridge University Press.

Scarman, Lord (1978). *Report on Brixton Disorders*, 10–12 April 1981, MND 8427, London: HMSO.

Shadid, Wasif and Sjoerd van Koningsveld (1996). 'Loyalty to a Non-Muslim Government: an Analysis of Islamic Normative Discussions and of the Views of Some Contemporary Islamicists', in W. A. R. Shadid and P. S. van Koningsveld (eds) *Political Participation and Identities of Muslims in Non-Muslim States,* Kampen, Netherlands: Kok Pharos, pp. 84–114.

Southall Black Sisters (1990). *Against the Grain: Southall Black Sisters 1979–1989, A Celebration of Survival and Struggle,* London: Southall Black Sisters.

— (1992). *Domestic Violence and Asian Women: a Collection of Reports and Briefings,* London: Southall Black Sisters.

Taylor, Charles (1994). 'Examining the Politics of Recognition', in Amy Gutmann (ed.) *Multiculturism*, Princeton: Princeton University Press, pp. 25–74.

Verman, F. (ed.) (1982). *Education for All: a Landmark in Pluralism*, 2nd edition, London: The Falmer Press.

Yuval-Davis, Nira (1997). *Gender and Nation*, London: Sage Publications.

Case Law List

Hirani v Hirani (1982). 4 FLR 232, CA.

Kaur v Singh (1972) All ER 292.

Malik v British Home Stores (1982). All ER 189.

Mandla v Dowell Lee (1982). 3 All ER 1108; (1983) 2 AC 548.

Quazi v Quazi (1979). 3 All ER 897.

Qureshi v Qureshi (1972). Fam 173.

R v Bailey (1964). Crim LR 671.

R v Bibi (1980). 1 WLR 1193.

R v Byfield (1972). All ER 174.

Shanoz v Rizwan (1965) 1 QBD 390.

Singh v Kaur (1981). 11 Fam Law 152.

Singh v Singh (1971) 2 All ER 828.

CHAPTER 11

Embodied Rights: Gender Persecution, State Sovereignty and Refugees

Jacqueline Bhabha

Introduction

Refugees crystallise the conflict between two founding principles of modern society – the belief in universal human rights which inhere in all individuals by virtue of their common human dignity, and the sovereignty of nation-states. Legal systems – both national and international – address this conflict in their refugee provisions, and decision makers confront it in judgements on individual cases. As numbers of refugees escalate,[1] the post-1945 international commitment to refugee protection in the West is superseded by a preoccupation with immigration restriction and border fortification (Shacknove 1993), that reveals the ethical limits of the international order. The common dignity supposedly inherent in all human beings is, it emerges, differentially coded for refugees.

This double focus is particularly evident where refugees flee gender persecution – oppression related to 'intimate' norms of one sort or another. For in this context prevalent notions of individual privacy and human rights, in matters of sexuality or reproductive choice for example, clash with equally established conceptions of legitimate state interest in questions of public morals and demography. In the modern state, the duty to produce future citizens inheres in the same subject as the right to sexual privacy, but equally, from the vantage point of international law, the sovereign state's obligation to respect citizens' fundamental human rights is paralleled by its right to address questions of population size.

This chapter explores the conflict and interaction between notions of inherent human rights and state sovereignty as they emerge in asylum cases based on gender persecution. The conflict is clear: human rights arguments are supposed to trump sovereign states' justifications for oppressive or restrictive behaviour, and the international refugee system is a mechanism for translating this theory into practice. If in the process of this translation, however, the content of protected rights is relativised in line with practices prevailing in different states, the system is undermined and the protection accorded individuals is diminished. Intimate behaviour then becomes a legitimated site of state control.

Culturalist arguments offer a particularly persuasive means of justifying the denial of individual protection because they may not entail contradiction of the general principle: though human beings have a common inviolable dignity a given society may impose certain norms of behaviour because it considers them consistent with that human dignity. Norms about quotidian life – the various instances of 'private behaviour' such as dress codes, personal relationships, sexual conduct and initiation – are most amenable to these arguments. Within international law generally, and human rights law in particular, they have traditionally been disregarded as relatively trivial and frivolous, in contrast to the classic grounds of persecution – public political activism and discrimination based on immutable characteristics (such as race or family history). Gender persecution cases, where private choices clash with public expectations of gendered identity, reveal the unresolved tension between individual and state interest in the control of sexuality, and thus provide a fertile arena for investigating arguments qualifying the scope of human rights intervention and denying refugee protection.

Moreover, in the post-Cold War era, when foreign policy (mirroring electoral advantage) is increasingly invoked to mandate restricting access rather than supporting protection, it is clear that there are powerful political reasons why the potential trumping effect of human rights arguments is vulnerable. But this is also the era in which the West is championing one of its prize export products, respect for universal human rights, as part of its new assault on 'the rest' (Huntington 1993: 22) and in tandem with its foreign policy strategy of 'good governance' (Shacknove 1993: 530). To what extent can those same arguments be turned inwards to challenge Western practice? Cases where the very violations invoked to criticise non-Western governments are imported into the domestic arena through asylum applications, and presented as a basis for seeking protection, reveal how refugees become limit cases for the ethics of a given state.

Modern International Refugee Protection – the Postwar Compromise Between Individual and State Rights

The events of the Second World War, and in particular the evidence of mass extermination and unprecedented barbarity of governments against their own citizens, led to the emergence of an international consensus on the importance of recognising and promoting 'the inherent dignity and ... the equal and inalienable rights of all members of the human family'.[2] It was accepted that states could no longer be regarded as the sole arbiters of the needs and entitlements of their citizens and that these might become a legitimate concern of international law (Held 1992: 11). The commitment to universalism in the recognition of fundamental human rights was thus inextricably linked from the start with a challenge to doctrines of strong, national, territorially based sovereignty. This was problematic in two respects.

First, the efficacy of international law depended crucially on the extent to which states had an interest in the new scheme and therefore agreed to implement their obligations. Curtailments of sovereignty could not be wrenched from states, they had to be ceded willingly. Second, loosening the reliance on the territorial state's protection could only increase human rights implementation if alternative protectors were available. This presupposed another challenge to state sovereignty, a requirement that states accept some form of responsibility for individuals or populations originating from outside their territory. But control over the access of non-citizens to the territory is a defining characteristic of the modern state, one jealously guarded by states in the twentieth century.

Recognition of these two major constraints affected the content of the postwar human rights instruments for refugees. No right to asylum was included in the 1951 Convention relating to the Status of Refugees, the instrument central to modern refugee protection, or in any other international instrument. A particular state is thus under no obligation to offer permanent asylum, since the 1951 Convention merely enjoins a state from sending a refugee back to a persecuting country. This obligation can be met by sending the refugee to another, safe country, by keeping the refugee in a temporary status until the risk of persecution ceases, or by forcibly preventing access to the host country's territory, so that no question of expulsion arises.

At the time when the Refugee Convention was being drafted, between 1948 and 1951, the Cold War was in full swing. The states participating in the process were sharply polarised and the Western bloc successfully asserted its greater power. The definition of a refugee incorporated into the Convention reflected liberal political values of non-discrimination and individual autonomy and excluded socialist socioeconomic concerns. Western claims to the protection of universal human rights must be assessed critically in the light of this fundamental, liberal individualistic bias (Hathaway 1991:7).

Scoring ideological successes against the Soviet bloc during the Cold War certainly provided a justification for the limited encroachment on state sovereignty that the refugee system required. The change in world politics following the end of the Cold War disrupted the direct causal link between foreign and refugee policy. Refugees were increasingly viewed as an undifferentiated part of 'foreigners' or 'illegal immigrants', rather than as vehicles for condemnation of enemy regimes. Domestic factors, particularly recessionary tendencies, the resurgence of widespread popular racism and mass unemployment, have combined with the changed foreign policy agenda to set the stage for a growing divergence between human rights and refugee law.

Legal Standards and Ethical Judgements – the Relevance of National Sovereignty

Immigration judges and asylum adjudicators deciding refugee applications have to confront and manage this divergence. The legal standard is set out in the 1951 Convention, which defines a refugee as a person who:

> owing to a well-founded fear of being persecuted for reasons of race, religion, nationality, membership of a particular social group or political opinion, is outside the country of his [sic] nationality and is unable or, owing to such fear, is unwilling to avail himself of the protection of that country; or who, not having a nationality and being outside the country of his former habitual residence ... is unable or, owing to such fear, is unwilling to return to it.[3]

The crucial terms of the refugee definition, 'well-founded fear' and 'persecution', are not defined, compelling decision makers to address the complex interplay between concepts of universal rights and state sovereignty: does this behaviour constitute 'persecution' or give rise to a 'well-founded fear' in this culture? The refugee is defined by the very fact of being outside yet from his or her country. Where issues of intimate behaviour, rather than chosen political opposition and its attendant heroic acts, give rise to asylum claims, the asylum judge is drawn into a high-stakes comparison between opposing normative systems. This is fertile soil for claims and counter-claims about universalism, cultural relativism and cultural imperialism (Donnelly 1984; Pollis and Schwab 1979; Pollis 1996; Kim 1993; Brennan 1991; Gunning 1992). The issue is further complicated by restrictive immigration pressures and partisan foreign policy agendas. Decisions upholding an asylum applicant's claim of persecution may contain 'culturally arrogant', even racist descriptions of the state of origin's policies. Conversely, judgements that dismiss the asylum application, thereby limiting refugee admission numbers, may adopt the language of cultural sensitivity or respect for state sovereignty.

Legitimating Persecution: Respecting Sovereignty or Restricting Refugee Numbers?

Contemporary debates about abortion, gay rights and 'welfare mothers' illustrate the extent to which sexual/reproductive rights uncomfortably straddle the public/private domain within Western political discourse. The same contradictory positioning is evident where non-citizens' rights are at issue. Can a woman successfully claim asylum when her society of origin denied her (and women in general) freedoms considered fundamental according to international human rights norms? (Kelly 1993; Cipriani 1993).

The cases analysed below illustrate the invocation of state sovereignty to define boundaries for international protection. Asylum adjudicators have tended to use simplistic notions of identity when analysing female applicants' complex multi-layered identifications, and to think of political opposition related to gender difference solely in terms of differences between nations rather than in terms of differences within nations, even within ethnic, religious or kinship groupings. By using nationality as a homogenising, essentialising category these decision makers have erased gender difference and domination within the national group.

A clear example of this process is an early case decided in the UK. In 1984 Mashid Mahmoudi Gilani, the finance manager of a chemical company, fled Ayatollah Khomeini's Iran and applied for asylum in Britain on the basis of her fundamental opposition to (and personal experience of) the regime's policies for women. As evidence in her appeal against refusal of asylum she described incidents where she had been reprimanded for her mode of dress by the regime's 'revolutionary guards'. On one occasion she had been threatened with imprisonment for not wearing a veil and clothing which covered her whole body. As a result of these incidents she had suffered a nervous breakdown leading to a skin disease. When asked by the immigration adjudicator what would happen if she went back to Iran she replied: 'I think my nervous breakdown would get worse.... I won't be able to have a social and private life. I will be stuck in my own room or in a hospital.... I need a new life.'[4]

Gilani's testimony was supported by expert testimony detailing punishments for not conforming to the strict dress codes (Neal 1988). The immigration adjudicator held:

> as a matter of common knowledge that women of the Islamic faith are regarded to coin a phrase as second class citizens.... Further that the regime in Iran is regarded with abhorrence in the West and has been roundly condemned by the United Nations.... I fully accept ... women in particular in many instances [have] suffered horrendous treatment.

On the particular circumstances of the asylum applicant, the adjudicator held:

> the appellant, from a middle-class background who has tasted the relative freedom allowed in Iran during the regime of the Shah and *the equality afforded to women in the Western world*, does not wish to return to Iran, *where it is quite clear women in general are seriously underprivileged....* However this is something that applies to women in Iran ... it is clear that a very large number of women in Iran do not agree with the emancipation of women. *It seems to me one is on dangerous ground if you attempt to interfere with a person's customs or religious beliefs and on even more dangerous ground if you do so on a national or world wide scale.*

Yet interference with the applicant's beliefs by the Iranian government was precisely the basis of the asylum application. To make prevalence a qualifying factor in calculating access to rights is to depoliticise majoritarian dominance. By establishing a binary opposition between Westernised and Iranian worlds, this case maps the Iranian state directly onto the woman's body (Sylvester 1995). It also eliminates space for the articulation of difference that the refugee regime was designed to protect and an escape route for a potentially sizeable group of 'Westernised' Iranian women fleeing the excesses of the Khomeini revolution.

Five years later, similar issues were addressed in an American case concerning an Iranian woman appealing the refusal of asylum. The Board of Immigration Appeals rejected her appeal on the basis that she would merely be subjected to the 'same restrictions and requirements as the rest of the population'.[5]

The Next Stage: Feminism and the Islamic Threat

In the post-1945 era, the Iranian revolution was the first major precipitator of refugees from Islamic fundamentalism to the West. As the perceived threat of fundamentalism spread beyond Iran, a more complex agenda has intervened, creating space to validate dissidents and question state legitimacy. A clear example concerns a US immigration judge's decision about a Jordanian Muslim asylum seeker fleeing domestic violence. The asylum seeker based her claim on the persecution to which she had been subjected by her husband and the unwillingness or inability of the Jordanian state to protect her from it.[6] She established that her powerful and wealthy husband was well-connected to the royal family and had subjected her to severe physical abuse over a thirty-year period; and that her attempts to resort to legal remedies for protection had been unsuccessful because of the husband's prominence.

The immigration judge found that the woman had established a well-founded fear of persecution based on her having '*continued to express her belief in Western values through her actions*'. In granting asylum, the judge concluded:

> The respondent is among *the group of women who are challenging the traditions of Jordanian society and government. The respondent's challenge of these traditions is threatening the core of Jordanian society, and because of this, the respondent is beaten to achieve her submission into the society's mores.* The respondent should not be required to dispose of her beliefs.

By characterising her dissent as 'Western' the court perpetuates the earlier essentialised dichotomy that elides social and political complexities in Jordan and 'the West'.[7]

In the aftermath of the Iranian Revolution many Western jurisdictions considered whether Iranian women fleeing their society's Islamic norms qualified for a grant of asylum. The general pattern of decision making reflects a shift towards a gradual but growing judicial acceptance of gender persecution as a valid ground for the granting of refugee status. This mirrors more far-reaching geopolitical changes, coinciding with the fall of Communism as the prime target of Western foreign policy, and the rise of Islamic fundamentalism as a movement of increasing concern to Western governments (*New York Times* 1996; Huntington 1996). The latter development may contribute to a climate of opinion in refugee decision making where feminist arguments concerning women's rights are used (abused?) to defend an undifferentiated concept of 'Western values', to attack an over-simplistic, homogenised notion of Islam and therefore to serve a new foreign-policy-inspired agenda. More complex understandings of the intricate, often non-linear interactions between racial, cultural, class and other social differentiations have yet to find their way into judicial thinking. Meanwhile non-'Western' women may now have increasing scope, at least in the refugee adjudication context, for defending their decisions to break away from certain socially imposed norms. Whether this will significantly affect their overall prospect of success in gaining refugee status is not clear, given the continuing decline in access to refugee procedures and the increasing hostility to non-Western immigration generally.

Intimate Violence: the Territory of Women's Bodies

The incommensurable claims of individual human rights, on the one hand, and policy-motivated considerations regarding state sovereignty, on the other, have surfaced in another group of gender-related asylum cases. These concern women's rights to control their own bodies, specifically their reproductive or genital organs, in opposition to prevailing norms. Whereas Western preoccupations with Islamic fundamentalism may coincide with a more receptive climate towards refugees challenging Islamic norms (much as the Cold War gave anti-Communists relatively easy access to the West), conflicting views on the relative importance of 'non-interference' with state norms (and its correlative impact on keeping refugee numbers down) as against human rights interventionism have produced a contradictory body of refugee case law. Human rights arguments have been used vociferously to critique 'barbaric' or 'primitive' practices occurring in non-Western states, but less consistently to protect victims of those practices seeking refuge in the West. A double standard is often apparent.

A substantial part of this body of law arises out of China's recent population control programme. Its inconsistencies mirror the Western, particularly American, complex policy towards China as a valued trade partner though human rights violator. Evidence of enforced abortions and sterilisation of women has featured prominently in asylum litigation and has been the locus of the opposition outlined above. The arena of conflict is clear: China's right and need to control its population has been endorsed by many policy makers and refugee adjudicators. At the same time there is widespread international agreement that involuntary sterilisation and coerced abortion constitute basic human rights violations. In 1993 both the Canadian Federal Court of Appeals and the US Board of Immigration Appeals reviewed cases challenging the refusal of refugee status to Chinese applicants fleeing their country's coercive population policies. The cases had opposite outcomes.

The Canadian case concerned Ting Ting Cheung and her daughter Karen Lee.[8] In 1984 Cheung gave birth to a son, following which she used an intrauterine device. Medical complications caused by the device forced her to abandon its use, and over the next two years Cheung had three abortions. She refused sterilisation urged upon her by her doctor, apparently because of her husband's opposition to that procedure. In 1986 she became pregnant again and, having decided against another abortion, moved away from her home. The evidence presented was that this child, Karen Lee, was ineligible for normal medical attention and food subsidies, and might not be registrable for school. Shortly after her return home, Cheung was forcibly taken by the Family Planning Bureau to be sterilised. Because she happened to be suffering from an infection at the time, the operation was postponed by six months. During that period Cheung fled to her in-laws to avoid compulsory sterilisation. While there she became pregnant and had another abortion. In the course of these visits in 1989 she participated in three Pro-Democracy Movement demonstrations. Shortly afterwards, having been sought by the public Security Bureau, she fled to Canada with her daughter.

The asylum applications of mother and daughter were dismissed by the Refugee Appeals Board who nevertheless accepted that Cheung would be sterilised if forced to return to China. According to the Board the evidence indicated

> simply a desperate desire [on the part of the Chinese authorities] to come to terms with the situation that poses a major threat to its modernisation plans. It is not a policy born out of caprice, but out of *economic logic*.... The possibility of coercion in the implementation of the policy is not sufficient ... to make it one of persecution. *I do not feel it is my purpose to tell the Chinese government how to run its economic affairs.* [emphasis addded]

The woman's body was considered a legitimate site of state control in China though such control would be considered unlawful in Canada.

The Federal Court of Appeal reversed the Board's decision.

> Under certain circumstances, *the operation of a law of general application can constitute persecution*.... If the punishment or treatment under a law of general application is so Draconian as to be completely disproportionate to the objective of the law, it may be viewed as persecutory. This is so regardless of whether the intent of the punishment or treatment is persecution. Cloaking persecution with a veneer of legality does not render it less persecutory. *Brutality in furtherance of a legitimate end is still brutality.* [emphasis added]

Confronted with the conflict between China's demographic goals and individual human rights enforcement, the Canadian appeal court adopted an interventionist stance privileging private choice.[9]

Contrast this decision with the US case.[10] It concerned a 29-year-old married Chinese man, G, one of approximately 300 passengers aboard the cargo freighter *Golden Venture* that ran aground off the coast of New York in

1993 after a three-month voyage from China, with all the passengers hidden in the ship's cargo hold. Seven of the passengers died attempting to swim to land. G managed to reach the shore, where he was eventually arrested and subsequently imprisoned.

In support of his asylum application G claimed that his problems with the Chinese authorities started in 1990 when his wife was fitted with an intrauterine device after the birth of their first child, a son. The authorities monitored the couple's use of contraception by monthly physical examinations. In 1992, G's wife became pregnant with their second child; to conceal this the couple left home. The authorities appropriated their possessions and interrogated G's parents; when they feigned ignorance of the couple's whereabouts the authorities threatened the parents with imprisonment and destroyed their home. G fled China fearing retribution for having had more than one child. A letter from G's wife in China after his departure described how the authorities had imposed a fine on him, were requiring her to undergo mandatory sterilisation and had prevented registration of the second child's birth until these measures were complied with. In rejecting G's appeal, the Board of Immigration Appeals (BIA) held that the Chinese government's implementation of its family planning policies was not on the face of it persecutive, '*even to the extent that involuntary sterilisation may occur*'. According to the Board

> to prevail on a claim premised on China's one couple, one child policy, it is incumbent upon the applicant to come forward with facts that establish that *the policy was being selectively applied against him* .... [emphasis added]

According to this judgement, a national norm is invoked to delimit the space for international protection. This reasoning has been applied in numerous Chinese asylum cases decided in the US. Over the past eight years, there have been at least nine inconsistent US administrative pronouncements regarding the effect of opposition to coercive population control policies on asylum eligibility. An immigration judge characterised them thus: 'they amount to an administrative cacophony, undeserving of judicial deference. To hold otherwise would be judicial abdication, not principled judicial deference.'[11] The political indecision and ambivalent foreign policy stance towards China are reflected in inconsistent judicial decision making. Though the overwhelming majority of US decisions have rejected asylum claims, several cases[12] have been decided the other way.

The double standard referred to earlier, where Western states – with a marked absence of self-critical awareness – term certain gendered norms imposed on women 'barbaric' or 'primitive', and yet fail to accord protection to individuals seeking to challenge and flee those norms, is also evident in the recently developing jurisprudence on female genital mutilation (FGM) as a basis for asylum. This 'culturally challenging practice' (Gunning 1992: 193), a traditional norm that concretises – even epitomises – gender inequality, has been the subject of considerable critical attention from within the societies affected and the wider international community since the late 1970s.[13] Human rights and feminist activists and health professionals have stressed the irrefutable and dramatic health hazards associated with FGM, its short- and long-term painfulness and its place in a gendered system of oppression and domination; opponents of 'homogenising normativity', on the other hand, critical of the cultural myopia, arrogance and racism through which the critique of FGM is often articulated, have emphasised the practice's embeddedness within a complex web of social and political structures, the vulnerability of communities practising FGM, particularly as immigrants in Western countries, and the need to evolve a non-punitive, culturally sensitive and consensual approach to modification from within the affected group.

FGM is increasingly entering the legal arena in the West as an alleged persecutory practice grounding an asylum claim. As with the Chinese cases, judicial attitudes have been characterised by an overall inconsistency. Some adjudicators, mindful of the immigration risks in opening a potential 'floodgate', have refused refugee status, on occasion conveniently defending this gate-keeping in the language of cultural relativism despite the applicant's explicit rejection of the cultural norm. In other cases an affirmation of universal human rights norms has been coupled with an arrogant, even racist willingness to critique local custom and justify international normative inference. The task of defining a just, humanitarian standard for granting refugee status in such cases is urgent. As in earlier sections, two contrasting judgements are briefly considered.

A 37-year-old woman from Sierra Leone, who had overstayed her period of lawful permission to reside in the US, claimed asylum, *inter alia* because of her fears relating to female genital mutilation for herself and her three minor daughters; she feared imposition of the custom on her daughters and retribution against herself for having publicly critiqued her own, earlier mutilation. The immigration judge found the applicant's fears unfounded and refused asylum:

> Her greatest fear is of the tribes back in Sierra Leone. She disagrees with FGM, refuses to submit her children to it and fears retribution and isolation from her tribe because of her differing views. The Court does not find this to be an adequate showing of fear of political persecution.... In this situation, the respondent cannot change the fact that she is female, but she can change her mind with regards to her position towards the FGM practices. *It is not beyond the respondent's control to acquiesce to the tribal position on FGM.* [emphasis added][14]

This statement should act as a warning to dogmatic cultural relativists of the dangers of uncritical, opportunistic relativism.

An opposite conclusion was reached in the highly publicised and precedent-setting case of Kasinga.[15] This concerned a 19-year-old woman from Togo who had fled her place of origin to escape the imposition of

FGM following the death of her influential father, himself an opponent of the practice. Her evidence was that her paternal aunt had assumed the authority position in the family following the father's death, forcing Kasinga, then aged 17, to enter into a polygamous marriage with a 45-year-old man. Following tribal custom, aunt and husband planned to enforce the young woman's FGM before the marriage was consummated. With the help of her mother and sister, Kasinga managed to flee. On arrival in the US she was detained in oppressive conditions by the immigration authorities for over a year and a half, pending an appeal against the initial refusal of her FGM-based asylum application. The compelling facts of her case, including her horror of the practice and a tearful photograph of her on the day of her marriage, were headlined in the *New York Times* and as a result became the subject of TV talk shows and web discussion pages. The publicity resulted in a political outcry which reached the White House. Suitably shamed, the Immigration and Naturalisation Service (INS) promptly released Kasinga and detailed its senior general counsel to argue the government's case at the appeal. This was presented as a balancing act between 'providing real protection for those seriously jeopardised if returned to their home countries' and attempting to avoid damage to US sovereignty in the form of 'the broad fabric of governmental immigration control'. In a strongly worded and confident decision, the BIA found that FGM, as practised by Kasinga's tribe, constituted persecution, and that as a young woman in the tribe, she had a well-founded fear. No balancing of competing policy concerns was required. They referred to anthropological and medical literature detailing the extreme form of FGM involved and reiterated the legal point that 'punitive' or 'malign' intent is not required for harm to constitute persecution. No doubt the sustained public attention contributed to the BIA's sanguine application of universal human rights principles to this important case.

Conclusion

Western decision makers adjudicating asylum applications based on opposition to oppressive cultural, social or legal norms confront the conflict between notions of fundamental rights and of state sovereignty in terms of the choice of an appropriate human rights standard applicable to non-citizens. The unresolved tension between private choice and public control over matters of sexuality or reproductive rights carries over into an inconsistent body of case law. Moreover, the ethical stance associated with a commitment to refugee protection and membership of the 'international community' may collide with domestic and foreign policy concerns relating to immigration control or international diplomacy. Iranian and Chinese refugees are clearly caught up in this process. In this context the debate about the competing merits of universalist as opposed to relativist conceptions of human rights takes on a very particular set of implications.

Critics of the Western universalist conception of human rights must bear in mind that in the asylum context the application of a uniform standard can provide the basis for a defence of the right to differ and a critique of persecutory practices that a relativist perspective may preclude. It can also provide the consistency in the application of basic international protection that undermines narrowly nationalistic, anti-immigrant, even racist standards for public and foreign policy. In the current, post-Cold War world, the relation between particular conceptions and applications of human rights and Western foreign policy goals is complex. As the analysis of the gender persecution asylum cases above shows, feminist arguments resulting in a more gender-inclusive human rights climate can become allied with the articulation of simplistic anti-Islamic positions.

Relativist conceptions of human rights, while anti-imperialist in intent and rhetoric and sensitive to the need to contextualise social and cultural norms, in the asylum context easily become vehicles for a discriminatory hierarchisation of human rights protection and an uncritical reinforcement of exclusionary state practices. Deference to the sovereign powers of state governments can parallel anti-imperialist claims to regional autonomy and readily translate into a justification for exclusionary policies that effectively withdraw human rights protection from unwanted new migrants. Rights are not ends in themselves. They are instruments to facilitate interventions in the political and social arena. The context in which they are invoked crucially determines their potential effect. Paradoxically, protection of individual asylum seekers' right to differ, of their right to challenge the norm, is best served by articulating and upholding notions of human rights which do not accommodate to the particular.

September 1997.

Acknowledgements

This chapter is based on an article published in *Public Culture* 9 (1996): 3–32. I am very grateful to Kara Points for her help on the manuscript.

Notes

1. Recent estimates suggest that there are about 20 million refugees worldwide and at least the same numbers of people internally displaced. In a world population of 5.5 billion, this means roughly one in every 130 people has been forced into flight, see United Nations High Commissioner for Refugees (1993).

2. Universal Declaration of Human Rights, UNGA, Res. 217 A (III) of 10 December 1948. Preamble.

3. (1951) *United Nations Convention Relating to the Status of Refugees.* Art. 1 A (2).

4. *Gilani v Secretary of State for the Home Department*, Immigration Appeal Tribunal (1987) TH/9515/85 (5216): 3. All subsequent quotes in this section are from this

case. Over the last few years, several jurisdictions, most notably the Canadian and more recently the US, have adopted a more sympathetic approach to women's asylum claims. See Immigration and Refugee Board 1993; Kelly 1994: 813.

5. *Fatin v INS,* 12 F.3d 1233 (3rd Cir. 1993), 1237.

6. *In the matter of A and Z* (1994) A72-190-893, A 72-793-219. All subsequent quotes are from this case. It is accepted that domestic violence can amount to persecution by the state in cases where the state is unwilling or unable to prevent it. See Bower 1993: 173; Goldberg 1993: 565. Canadian courts have granted asylum on this basis in numerous cases; see for example *Mayers v MEI* (1992) F.C.A. No. A-544-92. Both the Canadian Immigration and Refugee Board Guidelines (see note 8) and the United States guidelines (INS 1995: 9) recognise domestic violence as a form of persecution.

7. For example he suggests that domestic violence is defended in Jordan.

8. *Cheung v Canada (Minister of Employment and Irrigation.)* Federal Court of Appeals, (1993) 102 D.L.R. 4th 214.

9. A later Canadian decision reached the opposite conclusion. *Chan v Canada* (1993) 3 F.C. 675. For an interesting discussion of the relationship between population policies and human rights, see Boland 1995: 1257.

10. *Matter of G.* BIA Interim Decision 3215, No. A-72761974 (1993) 8 December.

11. *Guo Chun Di v Carroll,* 842 F. Supp. 858, (US Distr. 1994) Lexos 394.

12. *Xin-Chang v Slattery* 859 F. Supp. 708, 711-13 (S.D.N.Y.); *Zhang v Slattery* No. 94 Civ. 2119 (S.D.N.Y. 1994); *Guo* 842 F. Supp. At 865-70.

13. In fact the first examination of FGM by a UN body took place in 1952, when the Commission on Human Rights addressed the issues. Since then the Commission has explicitly criticised the practices as not only dangerous but a serious attack on the dignity of women. Commission on Human Rights, *Report on the Second United Nations Regional Seminar on the Traditional Practices Affecting the Health of Women and Children.* (1994) E/CN.4/Sub.2/1994/10, 42.

14. *Matter of J.* (1995) No. A72 370 565 (IJ, Baltimore, April 28) reported in *Interpreter Releases* 72 (1995).

15. In *Re Fauziya Kasinga,* Interim Decision, 3278 (BIA 1996).

References

Boland, R. (1995). 'Civil and Political Rights and the Right to Nondiscrimination: Population Policies, Human Rights and Legal Change', *American University Law Review* 44, 4: 1257–78.

Bower, K. (1993). 'Recognizing Violence Against Women as Persecution on the Basis of Membership in a Particular Social Group', *Georgetown Immigration Law Journal* 7, 1: 173–206.

Brennan, K. (1991). 'The Influence of Cultural Relativism on International Human Rights Law: Female Circumcision as a Case Study', *Minnesota Journal of Law and Inequality* 7, 3: 367–98.

Cipriani, L. (1993). 'Gender and Persecution: Protecting Women Under International Refugee Law', *Georgetown Immigration Law Journal* 7, 3: 511–48.

Donnelly, J. (1984). 'Cultural Relativism and Universal Human Rights', *Human Rights Quarterly* 6, 4: 400–19.

Dutch Refugee Council (1994). *Female Asylum Seekers: A Comparative Study Concerning*

Policy and Jurisprudence in the Netherlands, Germany, France, the United Kingdom, Amsterdam: Dutch Refugee Council.

Goldberg, P. (1993). 'Anyplace but Home: Asylum in the United States for Women Fleeing Intimate Violence', *Cornell International Law Journal* 26: 565–604.

Gunning, I. (1992). 'Arrogant Perception, World-Travelling and Multicultural Feminism: The Case of Female Genital Surgeries', *Columbia Human Rights Law Review* 23, 2: 189–248.

Hathaway, J. (1991). *The Law of Refugee Status*, Toronto, Vancouver: Butterworth.

Held, D. (1992). 'Democracy: From City-States to a Cosmopolitan World Order?' *Political Studies* 40: 10–39.

Huntington, S. (1993). 'The Clash of Civilizations?' *Foreign Affairs* 72, 3: 22–49.

— (1996). *The Clash of Civilizations and the Remaking of the World Order*, New York: Simon and Schuster.

Immigration and Naturalisation Service (INS) (US) (1995). 'Considerations for Asylum Officers Adjudicating Asylum Claims from Women', 26 May 1995, p. 9.

Immigration and Refugee Board (1993). *Women Refugee Claimants: Fearing Gender-Related Persecution*, Guidelines issued by the Chairperson Pursuant to Section 65 (3) of the Immigration Act (Ottawa, Canada, 9 March 1993).

Kelly, N. (1993). 'Gender-Related Persecution: Assessing the Asylum Claims of Women', *Cornell International Law Journal* 26: 625–74.

— (1994). 'Guidelines for Women's Asylum Claims', *International Journal of Refugee Law,* 6: 517–30.

Kim, N. (1993). 'Toward a Feminist Theory of Human Rights: Straddling the Fence Between Western Imperialism and Uncritical Absolutism', *Columbia Human Rights Law Review* 25: 49–105.

Neal, D. (1988). 'Women as a Social Group: Recognizing Sex-Based Persecution as Grounds for Asylum', *Columbia Human Rights Law Review* 20, 1: 203–57.

New York Times (1996). 'The Red Menace is Gone. But Here's Islam', 21 January 1996, Section 4: 1.

Pollis, A. (1996). 'Cultural Relativism Revisited: Through a State Prism', *Human Rights Quarterly* 18: 316–44.

Pollis, A. and P. Schwab (1979). 'Human Rights: a Western Construct with Limited Applicability.' in A. Pollis and P. Schwab (eds) *Human Rights: Cultural and Ideological Perspectives*, New York: Praeger, pp. 1–18.

Shacknove, A. (1993). 'From Asylum to Containment', *International Journal of Refugee Law* 5: 516–33.

Sylvester, C. (1995). 'African and Western Feminisms: World Traveling and the Tendencies and Possibilities', *Signs* 20, 4: 941–69.

United Nations High Commissioner for Refugees (1993). *The State of the World's Refugees: The Challenge of Protection*, London: Penguin.

CHAPTER 12

Refugee Women in Serbia: Their Experiences of War, Nationalism and State Building

Maja Korac

The aim of this chapter is to compare state-imposed constructions of the status and role of refugee women in Serbia (Federal Republic of Yugoslavia) with these women's lived experiences, and to explore the complexity of the problems they face in the new nation-state.[1]

An assumption inherent in the politics and policies of exclusionary ethnic-national identifications, exemplified by the recent conflicts in the post-Yugoslav states, is that an ethnic-national collectivity represents an organic wholeness. These collectivities are perceived as 'natural', and membership in them is dichotomised: one belongs, or one does not. This assumption leads to 'political nihilism' (Kaldor 1993: 108) when claims to power are based on a concept of citizenship in which ethnicity is defined as the primary source of identity and belonging. In such a context no political debate or movement is possible and there is no space for political ideas or political parties to gain real social influence (*ibid.*: 108–9). As one Serbian 'patriot'[2] stated, 'Let Serbs be Serbs, not citizens' (*Vreme*, 27 April 1996). This 'political nihilism' thus suppresses all forms of non-ethnic political voluntarism and is easily transformed into the unrestrained power of state bureaucrats in dealing with refugees.

This chapter explores the patterns of state intervention affecting the roles and status of refugee women in Serbia, and the ways in which these interventions have resulted in and reflect an essentialised, male-defined concept of the nation. The discussion examines state-imposed divisions among refugee women along and within ethnic-national lines, and their broader social and political implications.

The Political Context: Implications for Refugees' Safety

Before examining the specific problems of women refugees in Serbia, there is a need to evaluate 'the relationship of the host country to the refugee producing country', since, as Moussa (1993: 177) points out, the reception refugees encounter in the countries where they seek refugee status largely depends on this relationship.

The central element which crucially shaped the situation of refugees in the recent conflict in post-Yugoslav states was a political context in which almost all of the regional host governments were involved in wars – the exceptions being the governments of Slovenia and Macedonia. By August 1995, the effect of these conflicts and the politics of ethnic nationalism was to uproot every fourth or fifth citizen of the region. A large majority of these four to five million 'ethnically cleansed' persons[3] are refugees in the neighbouring post-Yugoslav states (ISHR 1994). They fled predominantly to Croatia and Serbia, and to a lesser extent to other post-Yugoslav states. In such a political context, two basic refugee rights – the right to enter a country of asylum and the right to remain – have been breached by host governments acting according to their political objectives. The USCR reports (1993b: 8–9, 21; 1995: 131, 173) indicate that the refugee policies of the governments of Croatia and Serbia were coloured by events in the war zones.

These political conditions imposed a number of restrictions on refugee safety and well-being. The problems have legal, social and political – as well as psychological – implications for refugees and for their adaptation to new life situations. In such a political context, the position of refugee women is particularly difficult as a result of gender-specific issues. Their situation is generally framed, in Indra's words (1993: 763), by an asymmetry of power and voice between the state, on the one hand, and the refugees on the other. As Indra (1993: 763) further argues, however, this asymmetry is gender-specific, since those who are both refugees and women may be subjected simultaneously to two overlapping silencing processes. How this gender-specific asymmetry originates in the relation between individuals and the state may be explained in terms of Pateman's (1988) analysis of the Western social and political order more generally. Pateman argued, it will be recalled, that the state's construction of relationships in the private domain (including marriage and the family) has determined women's status as citizens in the public domain. Thus, the emergence of the notion of citizenship was constructed in terms of the 'Rights of Man'.

The ways in which this gender-specific asymmetry of power between the state and refugees operate in a particular context will be examined below.

Ethnically Homogeneous States and Refugees: the Question of Gender Implications

The point of departure for discussing the particular relations of refugee women with the Serbian state is to be found in ethnic nationalists' claim to ethnically homogeneous territories and states. One of the main characteristics of this form of nation-state building in the region has been the construction of boundaries according to various exclusionary and inclusionary criteria on the basis of ethnic-national divisions. This has clear gender implications, as we shall see. Both women and men participate in ethnic-national struggles and are victimised by ethnic-national ideologies and politics. Nonetheless, there is a difference between their experiences as participants or victims.

Whenever the creation of boundaries between ethnic-national collectivities involves violent conflict, it is inevitably accompanied by militarisation. As Enloe (1993) emphasises, militarising transformations are embedded in 'changing ideas about manliness – manliness as it supports a state, and manliness as it informs a nation' (Enloe 1993: 247). These changes in ideas about masculinity imply complementary transformations in ideas about femininity. The interdependence, as Enloe argues, is a social construct that usually privileges masculinity (Enloe 1993: 248).

The critical element of an aggressive ethnic-nationalist ideology is, as stated elsewhere (Korac 1993), the violence embodied in militant masculinity. Violence-oriented masculinity becomes the main means of recruiting individuals who are capable of committing insane atrocities because their masculine militant collectivity is the ultimate determinant of good and evil (Korac 1993). A counterbalance to such violence-oriented masculinity is an emotional, committed, supportive but passive femininity. These differentiated roles of women and men within militarised ethnic-national collectivities result in various forms of violence with gender-specific meanings.

Violence-oriented masculinity, as discussed elsewhere (Korac forthcoming), does not victimise women alone. It implies forms of victimisation of men too, from killing to torture and mutilation. Women are commonly victimised through rape, expulsion and forced migration. This gendered difference in experiences of violence stems from the symbolic significance women bear in the relations between ethnic-national collectivities, as analysed by Enloe (1989). She points to a tendency to construct women as precious property of the 'enemy'. As such, they represent symbolic markers of the community and culture to be 'cleansed', and their bodies become territories to be seized and conquered.[4] By contrast, men have a more active role in war and, as a rule, most often enter 'history' as victors.

The massive gendered population transfer in the region of post-Yugoslav states, where over 70 per cent of refugees in some regions are women and children (USCR 1993a), has operated, I propose, as a crucial symbolic and material element in (re)constructing boundaries between ethnic-national collectivities. Of course, instances of women becoming 'special targets' in conflict and war zones are not new. In the context of post-Yugoslav state-building, however, it has a specific meaning.

In this conflict, uprooted women become symbolically and strategically important in the destruction of opposed ethnic-national collectivities. The role women play in this process is intrinsically related to their role in the ideological production and biological reproduction of their ethnic-national collectivities. As several studies have already pointed out (Yuval-Davis and Anthias 1989; Walby 1992; Brah 1993; Yuval-Davis 1993), women are conceived as cultural embodiments of collectivities and their boundaries, as well as participants in ethnic-national struggles. Moreover, Copelon (1994: 207) argues that women who are seen traditionally as caretakers, guardians of their children, men and homes, and hence as pillars of a society in a 'time called peace', represent these roles even more starkly in a time of war. Hence, a forced migration of women in wars expressing ethnic-national oppositions is both practically and symbolically the most effective way to (re)shape the boundaries of an ethnic-national collectivity. Forcing women to flee their homes is, however, just one of the critical elements in this process. The process of (re)shaping boundaries continues in the place of women's exile.

Divisions among Refugee Women along Ethnic-National Lines

According to the official estimates of the High Commission for Refugees and the Red Cross of Serbia (April 1994), the total number of refugees in Serbia is estimated at 400,000: 77 per cent are Serbs, 9 per cent Muslims, 2.6 per cent Croats, and 11.4 per cent 'others' (Albanians, Bulgarians, Hungarians, Jews, Romanians, Yugoslavs, etc.). Women aged 18 years and over compose 85.2 per cent of the refugee population (*Refugees in Serbia* 1994: 6–7).

Exile in Serbia produced a range of individual, social and political problems for women refugees of minority ethnic nationalities. Although the government grants a temporary refugee status to refugees who are not of Serbian ethnic-national background, this officially and legally equal treatment of all refugees is undermined by the everyday problems faced by refugees from minority ethnic nationalities.

In the context of the conflict in the region, Serbia/FR Yugoslavia was a country actively involved in a war in which people from 'other' ethnic nationalities were marked as enemies. Even though these refugees have escaped the immediate danger of the war zone, the host country can hardly be perceived as a 'safe place'. The majority of these non-Serbian refugees are accommodated in 'collective centres'.[5] Nermina,[6] a Bosnian Muslim refugee woman, explains the situation in these centres:

> I'm in an environment where the women are traumatised. They have lost their husbands, children; their husbands are at the front. They take sides, they are nationally oriented, committed. When they listen to the news they comment, they support these stands.... One of the women said to me: 'But you're in Serbia, you must support this here.' In other words, I have to support this policy, such as it is.

The experience of a second Bosnian Muslim refugee woman reveals an individual strategy that refugee women from non-Serbian ethnic nationalities commonly use in their struggle to survive in a hostile environment:

> I only had some minor problems with a woman here [she moved out recently] over the national issue. She kept on raising it, although I never raise it in my

> conversation. She provoked me a little, she even told some people here I hated Serbs, Milosevic [president of Serbia] and other things. Which is completely untrue: I don't hate Serbs and Serbia. I don't hate them, but I don't like Milosevic ... I don't agree with his politics.

Women refugees from minority nationalities tend not to initiate discussions of sensitive political issues. Given the context of their flight, their very presence represents a 'grave breach' of the aggressive Serbian nationalist cause for war. They have to silence and suppress their political views and beliefs; unless absolutely necessary, they tend to make themselves 'invisible'. This 'strategy of silence' is a common element in women's resistance to 'gendered workings of power' (Enloe 1993: 246) in 'a time called peace'. As social and political power shifts radically, however, this strategy becomes a central form of resistance both between and within genders. Consequently, fear endures and a real problem remains in dealing with a collectivity to which these women represent a demonised ethnic-national group. In this respect, the place of exile carries the characteristics of a war zone.

Divisions among Refugee Women within a Single Ethnic Nationality

The politics of ethnic nationalism produces yet another set of problems, this time for women refugees of the majority ethnic nationality. Although ethnic nationalists, in theory, should treat refugees of the same ethnic nationality 'naturally', the pragmatic interests of the state cause internal rifts and struggles over boundary definitions of ethno-national collectivity. Hence, even the rights of the refugees who are of the same ethno-national background as the majority population in their host country are seriously threatened.

For example, Serbs born on the territory of one of the new 'Serbian states' in Croatia or Bosnia-Herzegovina do not have the right to citizenship in the FR Yugoslavia. Moreover, since the government wanted to ensure a sufficient Serbian population in these 'liberated' territories once the war had ended, the government imposed restrictions on maintaining refugee status in Serbia (FR Yugoslavia). As of the spring of 1994 (USCR 1995: 173) these refugees became ineligible for refugee status in Serbia and were being forced to return to their 'liberated' territories, though not necessarily to the homes they had lived in before their flight.

In this move, which the Serbian government considered imperative for 'national security', it was crucially important, both materially and symbolically, to force women to return. A Serbian refugee woman explained the problems these women faced:

> They called me, it was April 19, 1994, to report to the Red Cross. I got there, one young person and an old woman were there. 'Where are your papers, your refugee

> ID...? Where do you come from?' she asks. I said Sarajevo. 'Would you live in Srbinje?'[7] I didn't need to hear any more.... I said: Where's that? 'Formerly Foca,' she said. And then she went on to tell me what state that's in, that it's the Bosnian Serb Republic. Where's that, I asked. In Africa?... And on whose bloody doorstep were you thinking of settling me? 'Well, Madame, the mujahedin killed the Serbs.' Wait a minute, you can't talk to me like that.... How dare you, a clerk, settle me in a state I don't belong to?... 'Well,' she said, 'Mira's[8] your name.' So what if my name is Mira? 'Well you're Serb.'... Then I went mad. Me? Dear Lord, no. 'What are you?' Jewish. 'Oh, sorry.'... And then I quarrelled with her. And they took away my refugee ID and pushed this in front of me and said: 'Here are your papers and go to room 16, they'll put a stamp on them and report every fifteen days.' That's the way it was then and that's the way it is today.

Although the majority of refugee women in a similar situation whom I interviewed were not as vocal as Mira, and were not usually prepared to argue directly with state bureaucrats, they do resist the oppression in as many ways as possible. The methods of resistance depend primarily on women's education, age and place of residence before the flight.

Better-educated, mature, professional women from urban areas, such as Mira, are more likely to have skills and resources with which to demand protection of their rights. The experience of a Croatian Serb refugee woman demonstrates the use of these skills:

> They [the state bureaucrats] said I didn't have the right to stay in Zvezdani Gaj [a collective centre in a Belgrade suburb] any longer, that I had to return [to 'liberated' territory in Croatia], and that I was not a refugee but an economic immigrant. I asked them to put that in writing. I said, 'I cannot deal with you any longer, I will hire a lawyer, pay someone to represent me, and let him fight you, I can't anymore. Put it in writing that I am an economic immigrant. I, with a seven-year-old child, don't have to be the first to return.'

A number of refugee women have become politically conscious and bitter when faced with knowledge of others' victimisation. In such a context, the opportunity to return home seems incomprehensible because of this new consciousness. A refugee woman from a Serb-controlled town in Croatia that is one of those most devastated in the war described her sense of revulsion:

> I can't live in a place in which so many people were killed.... How can I pass by that kindergarten where ... that Italian journalist ... filmed all those slain children in nylon bags? When I pass by that kindergarten, I freeze, I can't even look at it, let alone live there.... I don't want to go to the Bosnian Serb Republic. Why did they banish the Muslims from there? It's awful what's happening.... Let those who liberated, who razed, let *them* be there, live there.

This political consciousness, however, can hardly be translated into an articulated political action. The social ideology which 'naturalises' the ethnic-national collectivity and constructs women's roles does not tolerate a social space for women's autonomous political agency and mobilisation. Instead, the ideology of ethnic nationalism values a 'natural' (that is, biological) role for women and thus imposes restrictions on their space of action. Whenever women fail to meet these criteria they are redefined as 'traitors' to their ethnic nation.

Women as Traitors

The 'naturalisation' of the ethnic-national collectivity thus has clear gender implications. It rests upon the naturalised role of women *qua* mothers and upon the institution of motherhood which defines the 'appropriate' social role of women *vis-à-vis* the family and the nation. Accordingly, the state imposes policies facilitating this institutionalisation and controlling women. If they transgress these roles they are typically seen as traitors or potential traitors to the nation. If a refugee woman of the 'right' ethnic-national background has children in an ethnically mixed marriage, she cannot pass on her citizenship (that is, the 'proper' nation-state membership) to her children unless they first give up their 'improper' citizenship inherited from their father. This particular intervention by the new nation-states is intended to return 'women traitors' to their nationally important role as bearers of culture or to exclude them from the ethnic-national collectivity and the nation-state.

Refugee women who wish to resist giving up their children's second citizenship thus try to resettle in a third country. Although they may have a better chance of a normal life in one of the countries of resettlement, in this context resettlement represents one of the strategies of the new nation-states to create further 'ethnic cleansing' and to strengthen the ethnic-national homogeneity of their collectivities.

The state's promotion of divisions along ethnic-national lines is easily translated into popular discourse in which 'women traitors' are stigmatised. This is commonly accompanied by the woman's rejection by her family, creating a situation where women suffer all the more. One Serbian refugee woman, born in Serbia, who lived in Sarajevo for eleven years after marrying a Bosnian Muslim, revealed:

> Some neighbours and friends blame me, they say 'Go to Alija, [Izetbegovic, president of Bosnia-Herzegovina] ... Take your Muslim children away ... You should all be slaughtered, killed', and more ... It even went so far that my parents said 'Let your husband die,' or 'We wish him dead.' That hurt me a lot.

In a social and political context where state officials prefer to govern the 'Serbs as Serbs, not citizens', the line which differentiates between 'good' and 'bad' Serbian women (or women traitors), is rather fragile.

In sum, it is clear that uprooted women, once exiled in a new nation-state, continue to be marked by their ethnic nationality in a rather ambiguous way, an ambiguity stemming from the essentialist definition of the nation-state.

Ambiguities of Women's Ethnic-National Belonging

The new nation-states construct the roles and status of women through an ideological discourse which promotes 'the centrality of gender hierarchy in processes of identification and group reproduction' (Peterson 1996: 7). The public/private dichotomy in both popular and policy discourse, therefore, strengthens and shapes gender distinctions within and between ethnic-national collectivities. The ambiguity of a woman's ethnic-national identification as a result of gender hierarchy is revealed by the words of this young refugee woman from an ethnically mixed family:

> I think I'm Serb, I don't 'think', I know. My father is, so I am, and that's it, no getting around that.... The most important thing is not what I am, it's that I was very close to my mother's side, to relatives. We were closer to them than father's side.... If I thought long and hard about it, I don't know where I'd get to. Where would I go? My father has very strict views, he held the reins.... When I left I didn't decide who I was, what I am, where I'm going.

New nation-states promote this hierarchy through ideological discourse. The narratives of ethnic-national belonging and identity constructed and imposed by states are based, as we have seen, on essentialist ideas of 'common origin' and 'common destiny'. Even further, the essential relationship *between* such imagined communities (Anderson 1983) is seen 'to be one between irreconcilable polarities, as a relationship between 'right' and 'wrong', 'superior' and 'inferior' competitors' (Korac 1996b: 141). As members of ethnic-national collectivities and as participants in ethnic-national struggles, women tend to take part in and to further generate these narratives. The ambiguities of their ethnic-national belonging, however, as well as the experience of their exile, may render women refugees' locations debatable.

This contested location of refugee women is indicated in an interview with Vera,[9] a Bosnian Serb refugee woman. She expressed a profoundly strong sense of ethnic-national belonging, as well as a certain moral justification of the 'Serbian cause for war': 'Well, my place is somewhere where Serbs live. I would never ever again go, God forbid. Never, d'you understand the meaning of a word? Never.' However, minutes later Vera continued:

> Here [in exile in Serbia] one runs into all sorts of things every day. D'you understand? We weren't aware until the war broke out. D'you know that literally nobody helped me?... Serbs didn't help me. If I'd gone to a Muslim, I would've got accommodation easier than from those at the High Commissioner.

Experiences of exile expose the hollowness of essentialist beliefs in the 'common destiny' of ethnic-national collectivities and related narratives, creating counter-narratives of women's belonging. These counter-narratives challenge the totalising, overwhelmingly male-defined, and reifying boundaries of the ethnic nation and construct alternative imagined communities. A Bosnian Serb refugee woman explained:

> There are refugees [in collective accommodation] … from various regions. There are Serb, Croat and Muslim women.... We're linked by a common fate.... I share a much better understanding with Croat and Muslim refugees than with the people here [in Serbia]. I live here, if this can be called a life. They don't understand me, I don't understand them. There are frequent disputes and I think that I prefer to talk to refugees of any nationality, that we understand each other better.

I do not want to argue that all refugee women have articulated their experience of exile and belonging in the same way. Here is a contrasting account of a Bosnian Muslim refugee woman, married to a Bosnian Serb:

> Masses of refugees cannot understand me. If I were here with my mother, my sister, if we were the same nationality, maybe I'd view things differently too.... Everyone says our fate is the same. But I can't say it's been the same for everyone.... This war has only limited me, narrowed me down, reduced me to merely my children, my husband and his family. And it separated me from my mother, sister. I really feel I've been damaged a lot in this war, as a human being. I'm not aching for those things I had, I'm only aching for the people.

These accounts convey that experiences around belonging cannot be fitted into a single mould, but rather that 'all identity is constructed across difference' (Hall 1987: 44). In a political context where essentialist ethnic-national identification based on patriarchal right is informing the nation and is central to the claim for power, however, any form of transgroup coalition is a challenge to the power structure. What emerges in this context is the political significance of divisions among women along seemingly explicit ethnic-national lines. By contrast, women's multiple and fluid identifications and transgroup solidarities among them tend to disrupt singular identifications with an essentialised, male-dominated group: the nation.

A Concluding Remark: Alternative Politics

The discussion in this chapter has aimed to reveal the complex realities of women refugees at the moment when power in Serbia radically shifted along unified ethnic-national lines. This movement was buttressed by state policies, the public media, and education, all of which defended the power structures supporting a male-centred conception of the nation in which the control over women became a priority. In this context, the state-imposed ethnic-national division among exiled women, combined with their own diverse experiences of conflict and war, tended to reduce the differences among them based on age, class and place of residence before the flight, and to overshadow similarities of their lived experiences regardless of their ethnic nationality. This analysis, I believe, has a potential to uncover 'gendered workings of power' (Enloe 1993) in similar contexts of violent nation-state building, and has wider implications than the region of post-Yugoslav states, as ethnic nationalism reasserts itself worldwide.

The analysis has also aimed to identify potential spaces for a transformation of the totalising, male-defined, and reifying boundaries of the ethnic nation. Refugee women, marked by ambiguous ethnic-national identifications, have the potential, I have suggested here, to become catalysts for change. This potential is realised through women's organised effort to form coalitions 'in which the differences among women are recognised and given a voice, without fixating the boundaries of this coalition in terms of "who" we are but in terms of what we want to achieve' (Yuval-Davis 1994: 189).

Seeds of this organised politics are already extant in the political and humanitarian efforts of some local women's groups. These women's groups were active in anti-nationalist and anti-war campaigns from the very beginning of the conflict which erupted in what once was Yugoslavia. Women's groups have also initiated and established centres to work with women refugees and women who were victims of sexual violence in war. The process and outcome of this effort are explained by a woman activist, a Bosnian Serb refugee:

> They [refugee women] have every right to their bitterness.... However, in some of those talks, I would talk about my friends who were of other nationalities, we'd read a letter from Sarajevo which we got from a Muslim woman. In time they got used to being able to talk about neighbours of other nationalities – because they came here thinking they could never talk about them, that they have to say that 'they are genocidal', that 'they should all be killed', in order to make some friends here. Then, in time ... out of the blue ... friends emerged, daughters-in-law, neighbours, they all emerged out of the blue, who didn't exist up to then.

This politics of the local women's groups has led to a bridging of the differences between women, as well as to a process of healing. A Bosnian Muslim refugee woman, who became a volunteer in the Autonomous Women's Centre in Belgrade, explained the context in which other refugee women in the collective centre accepted her:

> It took me a long time, but they've accepted me finally. I think, I might be wrong, but since I've started working here in the Centre, they treat me differently, because they've seen that other women respect me.

A real potential of this politics of local women's groups, and consequently, a threat to the power relations within and between the new nation-states, is best illustrated by the words of a Bosnian Muslim refugee woman who fled to Croatia:[10]

> The Centre for Women War Victims of Violence became my Embassy. And when you say that, that means that someone is representing you, that it's yours. The Centre became my Embassy. The Embassy of Bosnia- Herzegovina wasn't mine at all. I was there a couple of times and I got so angry with them, and I sent them

> to hell.... At the Centre I really feel that I am on my own territory, those 70 square metres became my lost homeland.

This politics and effort challenge not only the notion of generic 'woman' but also the notion of ethnic-national 'sameness' stemming in large part from a male-dominated discourse. They enable women to stand and speak up for themselves as women and as the female representatives of their nation, rather than solely as mothers, sisters and wives of men who represent the nation.

The organised support of the local women's groups and the success of their efforts to communicate and work across ethnic-national lines is essential in initiating a process of reconstruction and change of the nationalistic politics of exclusion in post-Yugoslav states. The forms of women's organised work and help to refugee women discussed in this chapter represent the ways in which women gain subjectivity and can become more autonomous political subjects. If successful, these efforts can become the avenue to more inclusive or gender-sensitive notions of citizenship.

Notes

1. The complex realities of the women's lives as refugees depicted here are based on data collected during my research in Serbia. The sources for the research ('Women Refugees in Serbia: Ethnic-National Identity and Perceptions of the Conflict in the Former Yugoslavia') include: observations made during fieldwork, in-depth interview data with 18 refugee women from various ethnic nationalities, newspaper articles, papers, newsletters and journals. The fieldwork was conducted in the summers of 1994, 1995 and 1996. The first phase of this research was funded by the Centre for Refugee Studies, York University, Canada. The support is gratefully acknowledged.
2. The speaker is one of the Serbian volunteers to the 'White Eagles', the Serbian paramilitary group responsible for the most brutal atrocities in Bosnia-Herzegovina and in Croatia.
3. The total population of Yugoslavia before the war was 22 million. The four to five million 'ethnically cleansed' persons include refugees, internally displaced persons, as well as approximately 700,000 people who left the country between 1991 and 1995 seeking political asylum in European countries. The data include the UNHCR's report of July 1995, as well as the instances of 'ethnic cleansing' in Srebrenica and Zepa (Bosnia-Herzegovina) and in the Krajina region of Croatia in July and August 1995 (*Nasa Borba,* 10 August 1995). The war in Kosovo has, of course, added another estimated million refugees.
4. Discussion of the meaning of rape in these wars, and the nation-states' response to this form of violence against women, is beyond the scope of this chapter. However, the importance of this issue for a more complex analysis of the relation of women and nation-states is acknowledged. This issue is addressed in 'Ethnic Conflict, Rape, and Feminism: the Case of Yugoslavia' (Korac 1996a).
5. 'Collective centres' or refugee camps in Serbia accommodate 6 per cent of the refugee population. The remaining 94 per cent of the refugees are accommodated by families (relatives, friends, etc.) (*Refugees in Serbia* 1994: 6–7).
6. A pseudonym.

7. A town in eastern Bosnia-Herzegovina, formerly Foca, with a majority Bosnian Muslim population before the war. Currently, it is a Serb-held town, called Srbinje. All Bosnian Muslims in Foca were 'cleansed'.

8. A pseudonym.

9. A pseudonym.

10. This interview was given for the documentary *A Balkan Journey,* directed by Brenda Longfellow, Canada. The documentary was filmed in Belgrade and Zagreb in the spring of 1995. Permission to use the interviews is gratefully acknowledged

References

Anderson, Benedict (1983). *Imagined Communities,* London: Verso.

Brah, Avtar (1993). 'Re-framing Europe: En-gendered Racisms, Ethnicities and Nationalisms in Contemporary Western Europe', *Feminist Review*, 45: 9–30.

Copelon, Rhonda (1994). 'Surfacing Gender: Reconceptualizing Crimes against Women in Time of War', in Alexandra Stiglmayer (ed.) *Mass Rape: the War Against Women in Bosnia-Herzegovina,* Lincoln and London: University of Nebraska Press, pp. 197–219.

Enloe, Cynthia (1989). *Bananas, Beaches and Bases: Making Feminist Sense of International Politics*, London, Sydney, Wellington: Pandora.

— (1993). *The Morning After: Sexual Politics at the End of the Cold War*, Berkeley: University of California Press.

Hall, Stuart (1987). 'Minimal Selves', in *Identity, the Real Me,* London: ICA Document 6, p. 44–6.

Indra, Doreen (1993). 'Some Feminist Contributions to Refugee Studies', paper presented at 'Gender Issues and Refugees: Development Implications', Conference at York University, Toronto, Canada, 9–11 May. Conference papers, Vol. II, pp. 757–66. Toronto: Centre for Refugee Studies.

International Society for Human Rights (1994). *Human Rights Worldwide* 4, 1, March. ISHR, Frankfurt.

Kaldor, Mary (1993). 'Yugoslavia and the New Nationalism', *New Left Review* 197: 96–112.

Korac, Maja (1993). 'Serbian Nationalism, Nationalism of My Own People', *Feminist Review* 45: 108–113.

— (1996a). 'Ethnic Conflict, Rape, and Feminism: the Case of Yugoslavia', in B. Wejnert and M. Spencer (eds) *Women in Post-Communism: Research on Russia and Eastern Europe*, Vol. 2, Greenwich: JAI Press Inc.

— (1996b). 'Understanding Ethnic-National Identity and Its Meaning: Questions from Woman's Experience', *Women's Studies International Forum* 19, 1/2: 133–45.

— (forthcoming). 'Ethnic-Nationalism, Wars and the Patterns of Social, Political and Sexual Violence against Women: the Case of Post-Yugoslav Countries', *Identities – Global Studies in Culture and Power*, 5, 2: 153–81.

Moussa, Helene (1993). *Storm and Sanctuary: the Journey of Ethiopian and Eritrean Women Refugees*, Dundas: Artemis Enterprises Publication.

Nasa Borba, 10 August 1995, Belgrade daily newspaper.

Pateman, Carol (1988). *The Sexual Contract*, Cambridge: Polity Press.

Peterson, V. Spike (1996). 'The Politics of Identification in the Context of Globalization', *Women's Studies International Forum* 19, 1/2: 5–17.

Refugees in Serbia (1994). 17/18, April, Belgrade: High Commissioner for Refugees of Serbia.

US Committee for Refugees (1993a). *World Refugee Survey*, Washington DC: US Committee for Refugees.

— (1993b). 'East of Bosnia: Refugees in Serbia and Montenegro', *Issue Paper*, September, Washington DC: US Committee for Refugees.

— (1995). *World Refugee Survey*, Washington DC: US Committee for Refugees.

Vreme, 27 April 1996, Belgrade weekly magazine.

Walby, Sylvia (1992). 'Woman and Nation', *International Journal of Comparative Sociology* XXXII, 1–2: 81–100.

Yuval-Davis, Nira (1993). 'Gender and Nation', *Ethnic and Racial Studies* 16, 4: 621–32.

— (1994). 'Women, Ethnicity and Empowerment', *Feminism and Psychology* 4, 1: 179–97.

Yuval-Davis, Nira and Floya Anthias (eds) (1989). *Women–Nation–State*, London: Macmillan.

PART FOUR
Feminist Citizenships in a Global Ecumene

CHAPTER 13

Globalisation and the Gendered Politics of Citizenship

Jan Jindy Pettman

This chapter aims to bring critical globalisation literature into productive conjunction with feminist critiques of the gendered impact of globalisation; and to ask whether feminist notions of citizenship can be utilised to think about, and organise in, these globalising times. Feminist critique and politics have revealed that citizenship, both as a status and as a basis for claim, has historically been problematic for women and for men outside dominant groups. Now, in the wake of intensifying globalisation, state transformations and rising exclusivist identity politics, citizenship needs to be rethought as a possible tool for feminist use within a global frame.

Citizenship constructs a public status and identity – long presumed to be male – that rests in ambiguous ways on the private support world of family, home and women. It has always been a difficult construction for women, much debated in feminist literature and conferences (Jones 1993; Phillips 1993; Eisenstein 1993). But it *has* provided spaces for feminist politics. While first-wave feminists and anti-colonial nationalist women struggled for suffrage and legal rights (Jayawardena 1986), later movements used formal citizenship rights as a platform to actualise rights promised to them as citizens. Debates around formal citizenship enabled feminists to expose the contradiction between states' constitutional declarations of equal citizenship and treatment of women as the possessions of their husbands or communities, relegated to the ambiguous space of personal law, for example. These debates also demonstrated that women's and men's memberships of other collectivities, including racialised, ethnic, religious and sexual minorities, continue to affect their access to and experience of citizenship (Yuval-Davis 1991).

Citizenship claims are most often made against 'the state'. Indeed, one way of understanding citizenship is to define it as a person's (or individual's) relationship with their state. But the state has always been an ambiguous and difficult issue in feminist politics. Feminists have revealed *gendered* states, and it seems that state consolidation projects, earlier in Western and more recently in Third World states, frequently reinforced masculinist power (Afshar 1987;

Peterson 1992; Rai and Lievesley 1996). Feminists continue to debate the possibility of a woman-friendly state, and note the irony of appealing to a masculinist state for protection from, for example, male violence (Jones 1993; Brown 1996). Yet feminists continue to address all kinds of claims towards the state, and articulate these claims in terms of women's formal citizenship and social rights. And while many feminists are ambivalent about approaching the state, the state that feminists address is itself changing dramatically (Leech 1994). In recent decades, intensifying globalisation processes have been accompanied by a transformation of states, which have, willingly or unwillingly, disowned many obligations to their citizens. Might we be looking to sites of state which are now vacated, or fundamentally changed, as a consequence of globalisation processes?

To devise effective feminist politics, then, we need to ask where power is located these days (Peterson 1995). Fears of global power and its blatant unaccountability underlie some feminist attempts to reclaim the state, and citizenship, as still difficult, but more accessible than global power. What possibility is there to argue for an inclusive state-based rights collectivity which extends to all those resident in it? What do we make of citizenship when we shift our focus beyond state boundaries, in a search for transnational and transformative feminist alliances?

Globalisation

'Globalisation' is a shorthand for many different and often contradictory shifts in relations of power, wealth and identity (Mittelman 1996). A helpful distinction is between globalisation as process and as ideology. As process, it refers to transformations in relations between politics and economics, capital and labour, states and markets, and international and state ('domestic') politics (Scholte 1996; Tooze 1997). These transformations were ushered in by the rising fortunes of East Asian states, the floating of the US dollar in the 1970s, the oil shocks as OPEC states flexed their muscles, and the steady growth in indebtedness of many Third World states, which allowed increasing intervention by international financial institutions. The transformations were accelerated by developments in technology and communications, enabling instantaneous and deterritorialised organisation and decision making. They were effectively universalised in 1989, with the collapse of state socialism as a practised or imagined alternative to capitalism.

There is much in contemporary globalisation literature detailing deregulation of trade, finance and banking, and the remarkable growth in 'the "symbol" economy of capital movement, exchange rates and credit flows' (Tooze 1997: 224). Financial transactions now massively outpace trade in goods and services. A key feature is 'quicksilver capital' (Douglas 1996) – the hypermobility of capital. Transnational production is increasingly spread over different sites and states, and new corporate management strategies now instantaneously link different parts of the globe, independently of state boundaries and agents.

Whereas the twentieth century has witnessed a growing density of international relations (meaning between states), many of the new transactions or relations bypass states or cross borders beyond state control. Time, place and space are all reconfigured. National economies deregulate and liberalise trade and investment. It is not so much that there is a free market; rather 'almost every aspect of national economic activity is now subject to international supervision' (Tooze 1997: 225). It is increasingly difficult to demarcate boundaries between the international and the national. Almost nothing is simply 'domestic' anymore: the globalised market impacts on individuals as well as states. Feminist politics, too, must be played out in the increasingly contradictory spaces between the supposedly still sovereign 'nation-state' and the powerfully generative global 'system'.

There is considerable dispute in the literature concerning the extent and nature of globalisation, including between 'hyperglobalists' who perceive globalisation as a massive, irresistible force which will result in homogenisation, McDonaldisation or the total integration of the world into a single hierarchically organised set of domination–subordination relations; and the 'globalisation sceptics', who argue the continuing significance of national and international economy, and note the rise in regionalism rather than globalism (Perraton *et al.* 1997). Clearly, though, globalisation is not a uniform, unilinear or inevitable process. It impacts unequally and differentially on different regions, classes and people. It is currently marked by growing disparities of wealth within and between states. Power and wealth are concentrated among the 'triad' of North America, Western Europe and East Asia (Cox 1996). Within these states, too, many experience increasing poverty and reduction of (already inadequate, or conditional) social welfare. Many of those most severely affected are women, including women who are racialised, migrantised and/or without access to formal citizenship. In the process, class becomes an increasingly transnational phenomenon: a tiered hierarchy of new transnational elites, middle classes who service or are rewarded by global servicing, and a vast transnational underclass. While no region or state can escape the impact of the capitalist world market, whole states and regions, notably in Africa, are bypassed, except as suppliers of raw materials or of migrant labour for the rich states and regions. In these new configurations of power, we might expect class to have become a more powerful – rather than, as appears, a less effective – basis for mobilising. So we need to ask what class means in view of the changing global division of labour – and, more particularly, what class means to feminists – these days.

An effect of globalisation as ideology is to naturalise the process, to impute magical qualities to 'the market' (Hamilton 1997: 25), to depoliticise and so distract from the myriad political and economic decisions and practices that propel it. Economic rationalism or neoliberalism is the carrying card of the current phase of globalisation. Shifts in the nature and location of power generate a new political geography, within which transnational companies, international financial institutions and some state elites are now major players.

Globalisation as ideology reminds us of the politics, power relations and material interests that underpin the process. Globalisation as process reminds us that globalisation is always *in* process, is still becoming: and that it is a contradictory and contested process. Critical globalisation literature stresses the importance of recovering agency – and sometimes class – as spaces for resistance to globalisation (Mittelman 1996; *New Political Economy* 1997). Much of this literature makes reference to but does not pursue as central the gendered effects of globalisation, and only hints at or roll-calls women's movements or feminism as resistance. Bringing these writings into productive conjunction with feminist critiques which document the gendered effects of globalisation (Afshar and Dennis 1992; Bakker 1994; Peterson 1995; Kofman and Youngs 1996) can generate strategies that politicise, denaturalise and gender globalisation – rather as feminist critiques politicised, denaturalised and gendered 'the private' in previous and ongoing struggles.

Transforming States

Globalisation signals the transformation of the state, to the point where it now plays a near-universal role as local manager or facilitator for global capital. Many political leaders are either unable or unwilling to direct the national economy, or to abide by the national social contract which guided different states in the postwar years. Samir Amin (1996) notes that the 'three ways' of this contract – Keynesian managed capital with its safety net, Sovietism with its worker citizen, and the Bandung or national development state – all assumed some state responsibility for economy and society. Western states have now begun to re-privatise those responsibilities which worker and women's struggles had exacted. The collapse of European state socialism means 'the market' rules. In the residual Third World, post-developmentalism (McMichael 1996) flourishes in debt-ridden states, now dominated by international financial institutions, conditionality and structural adjustment policies. Even states still formally Communist like China and Vietnam have opened their economy to 'the market'.

States appear to have lost crucial aspects of their sovereignty. It is a mistake, however, to imagine states as yet another victim of globalisation. Particular state elites in the West/North (Reagan's US, Thatcher's Britain, now Howard's Australia, for example) embraced neoliberalism with glee, and others too became active agents in their own state's transformation (Cerny 1996). Some states, especially in East and Southeast Asia, historically welcomed integration into the global economy while simultaneously attempting to maintain control over the direction of national economies, leading to capitalism*s*, or at least to state or regional variants (Cox 1996: 28; Dirlik 1997). The futility of these attempts only became clear in the late 1990s. Thus today neoliberalism takes a somewhat different form in different states. East and Southeast Asian states embraced growth and 'the market', but in more authoritarian or interventionist ways than their Western counterparts. They were held up as models of growth, until the sudden and unexpected 'Asian crisis' spread, from mid-1997. Ideas about cultural difference and Asian values, until recently deployed to explain success, were rapidly mobilised to explain failure,[1] allegedly caused by distortions and the feeding of 'crony capitalism'.

The crisis in a number of Asian economies was triggered by the devaluation of the Thai baht in July 1997, followed by currency crash through most Southeast Asian states. Capital flight from the region was accelerated by harsh IMF intervention, which had the effect of spreading a sense of panic, along with bank and company failures and rapidly rising unemployment (Bello 1998). Indonesia was the most severely affected: there the crisis wiped out three decades of growth, reducing some 17 million families to poverty and threatened starvation (*Canberra Times*, 15 September 1998). The dislocations generated political unrest which saw the overthrow of the Suharto regime and rioting, including rape, in which the primary targets were ethnic Chinese. The crisis demonstrated the power that resides in the IMF and other financial managers of global capital; it also confirmed that scapegoats will be found, most likely those who are perceived as not really belonging within the state, even if their families have been citizens for generations.

While states appear to be giving up on aspects of their sovereignty, or having these taken away from them, they are simultaneously charged with implementing those very policies that facilitate openness and competition, and are approved of by international capital and its managers. They must also manage internal dissent and contain the pain, for 'political instability' will also frighten off investors, and risk further disciplining from the outside. Across the globe, the lure of neoliberal ideology and the power of globalising interests mean that states seek to facilitate the best fit possible with the global market, becoming more open and cutting back on 'unproductive social expenditure' – precisely those sites and roles of state that were pushed and prodded into action by feminist mobilisation.

While interrogating globalisation and state transformation of course requires specificity – Which state? Which women or men within that state? – there is a global trend towards a redefinition of political economy, away from a nation-state base. This trend is characterised by a renegotiation of relations between state and society, as, often, the latter becomes more economy than society; a shift in language from social rights to competition, productivity, and efficiency; and a shift from public to private and from social to family or individual responsibility. These changes dramatically reduce the political space for citizenship or social rights, including rights for women. And they are profoundly gendered in their consequences.

Gendered Transformations

Intensifying globalisation processes and state transformations are highly gendered – in part because women were already positioned in relation to the state, citizenship and the labour market differently from men (though different women are, of course, differently positioned, too; Pettman 1996).

Women are especially hard-hit when the state reduces, or withdraws from, or charges for, social support. Women are disproportionately represented among state workers in those areas most under attack, like health and education. The withdrawal of food subsidies and focus on production for export rather than subsistence or local consumption generate a massive crisis in reproduction, where the conditions necessary for sustaining everyday living are unavailable to so many (Afshar and Dennis 1992). Women in their domestic and reproductive roles must compensate for state retreat, or for state failure to provide social infrastructure and support. In many states, too, girl children are more likely to lose chances and choices as education, for example, becomes much more expensive.

Feminist critics of citizenship have long argued that active citizenship requires material conditions which support and enable women's participation in the public/political sphere. In recent decades, feminists have publicised private lives and family secrets, challenging the public/private boundary line in the process (though the boundary takes different forms in different states, Kandiyoti 1991). They have insisted on expanded notions of the political. Feminist activism in very different forms and places convinced states to assume some responsibility for women's safety or interest, though often with conditions of heightened surveillance or dependence. But even where resources or choices were conceded, they were never beyond question. Now hard-won feminist gains are under renewed attack almost everywhere, under the impact of neoliberalist state ideologies. This is especially marked in formerly state socialist countries, and in states where fundamentalist movements dominate or influence the state, but it is painfully evident, too, in Western states.

Global deregulation and restructuring reprivatise tasks and spaces (Brodie 1994). These forces push women figuratively and sometimes physically back 'home', even though some one third of households do not have a male breadwinner, and more women than ever before officially work outside the home. Alongside this 'return' of women to their presumed place as wives, mothers and carers of citizens, and reduced state attention to their needs, another kind of privatisation – marketising – further undermines women's gains and claims. These shifts accompany the growing dis-organisation of labour, and a 'new mythology' which identifies private power with personal freedom (Wilkin 1996: 227). States appear to be seeking a new kind of citizen, a consumer whose roles and expectations fit better with global capital and state transformation (Chin and Mittelman 1997: 29).

Women as workers have long been caught between their productive and reproductive roles, in ways that disadvantage them in the labour market. That market is segmented along lines of nationality, race/ethnicity, gender and often age, as well as class. International processes, including colonisation and migration, have informed these divisions within states. Now globalisation compounds these dis/connections, and makes access or not to citizenship a crucial determination of difference. And globalisation of the labour force makes it more likely that workers must negotiate state borders and join transnational flows in search of work.

Gender and the Global Division of Labour

The changing global division of labour is marked by a predominantly male core of skilled workers, and a vast global assembly line of casualised, feminised labour (Mitter 1986). Transnational corporations (TNCs) are 'on the global prowl' for cheap labour, or more accurately for 'labour made cheap' (Enloe 1992). The vast majority of workers in export processing zones (EPZs) are young women. Women in First and Third Worlds (though often women from the Third in the First) work in flexibilised, low-paid, risky conditions, in factories and sweatshops and outwork. They have become part of a globalised feminised working class. Maria Mies uses this to argue against 'the limited view of cultural relativism which claims that women are divided by culture worldwide, whereas, in fact, they are both divided and connected by commodity relations' (1986: 3), by their positioning within the global economy.

Women's labour has long been cheapened through ideologies of femininity. Women's work is seen as temporary, filling in before marriage; as supplementary, as if only men are family providers; and natural, as women are expected to have caring and domestic skills already. Women are also constructed as patient, pliant and less trouble, in ways that deny them politics and agency. Gender is racialised, too; commodifying 'Asian women', for example, in ways that launch many of them into particular kinds of work along transnational circuits of exchange – as workers in the EPZs or sex tourist sites, or as international domestic workers (Tolentino 1996; Pettman 1998b).

Women as labour migrants participate directly in globalisation flows, even as their decision to move often reflects the impact of restructuring or other aspects of global change on their and their families' lives.[2] They may be seen to be out of place: beyond the protection/control 'the community' expects, or as transgressors of other spaces. They may be subject to harassment or violence (Pettman 1996). Yet the globalisation of labour and the feminisation of the global division of labour mean that more and more women move across state boundaries in search of work. This places them beyond their state's legal reach, and means they often lack even formal citizenship or legal rights. This is more so where they enter another state illegally, or become illegals through, for example, overstaying a work or tourist visa.

Globally, migration is increasingly in the form of labour migration, including the strictly policed worker contract system of oil-rich Middle Eastern and growing East and Southeast Asian states. For example, more than four million people, close to one in six of the Philippines' workforce, are working overseas. Between one and 1.7 million women from poorer South and Southeast Asian states are employed as domestic workers in a lucrative regional trade. There is an internationalised service class of female employees (Tinsman 1992) and an extraordinary transfer of reproductive labour across state borders (Truong 1996). Home states are often unwilling defenders of citizen rights, when they are dependent on remittances from overseas work, and often on employer states' foreign aid and investment, and when they have little regard for women's or workers' rights at home.

This is a reminder that both citizenship and one's state (as defined through citizenship) still matter. Globalisation has reconfigured but not reduced the hierarchies of states, whose reputation or standing might support or reduce a citizen's claims against another state. So recent reports of abuse against nationals as international domestic workers have become a focus for anxiety and protest in the Philippines. This focus expresses resentment of the exploitation and frequent sexual imputation of the nation's women, whilst also being symbolic of reaction against the international construction of the Philippines (along with Sri Lanka and Indonesia) as a 'nation of servants'. The transnational labour trade thus marks a racialised and inter-national hierarchy of states, as well as a racialised and sexualised hierarchy of women (Pettman 1998b).

While women are especially hard hit by globalisation processes and state transformation, different women are affected differently. Not all women are poor; although nowhere are women as well off or well paid as men are. And rising neotraditionalist and familialist movements impose more 'traditional' family and gender roles on many women, subjecting them to renewed surveillance and control. That particularist identity movements are on the rise in an age of globalisation is less a paradox than it might at first appear. Indeed, they reflect in part reactions against modernisation, the secular state, and the dislocations of power, wealth and meaning that accompany contemporary social change (Moghadam 1994). States' unwillingness, or inability, to 'deliver', their close association with particular interests and/or exclusion of others, trigger reactive politics that mobilise along other associational lines. In migrant-receiving states, migrants or racialised/ethnic minorities become targets in old industrial heartlands, as competition or threat. 'Besieged' majority members mobilise against 'outsiders' and claim the state as theirs only (Yuval-Davis 1991).

These identity politics have especially bad consequences for women. As markers of community boundaries, signifiers of cultural difference and as reproducers both physically and culturally (Yuval-Davis and Anthias 1989), women become vulnerable to boundary policing by both in-group and other men – and women. Here we need to distinguish between the symbolic uses made of women in identity politics, and the ways in which actual women negotiate identity; not forgetting too those women who are agents in exclusivist politics.

These gendered identity politics are often transnational, engaging diasporic networks and using new global technologies to transmit meanings, grievances and funds. Within these deterritorialised identity politics, women can also become the territory (Bloul 1993). Policing women's mobility, relations and bodies becomes part of a national project of boundary maintenance. Culture, identity, difference and community are mobilised, making it even more difficult to give *feminist* accounts of difference that do not become complicit with the uses that masculinist states and identity movements make of women and cultural difference.

Boundary Defence/Boundary Transgressions

While states almost universally continue to liberalise in terms of production, trade and finance, and communications and new electronic technologies override borders, states at the same time act to maintain or reinforce their control of people flows. Border police refuse entry, residence, state services and access to citizenship as their sovereign right (Zolberg 1989). State 'protection' against other people ironically makes illegals and labour migrants unprotected. So we need to ask of each state: Who has trouble getting in, staying in, accessing work and belonging?

The sovereignty story is built upon the nation-state, presuming a coincidence of people, territory, authority and identity that migration disrupts. Citizenship is a territorially based identity, one that rests on state sovereignty, and on the state as container of its citizens' identities. Globalisation erodes sovereignty and territoriality, further confusing the inside and the outside, and making citizenship seem in some senses anachronistic. As we have seen, one dimension of change is the massive transfers of population which have characterised recent decades (and long before that marked the making of 'the world', Castles and Miller 1993). Well over 100 million people now live outside their country of birth or citizenship. Millions of women are resident in countries where they have no citizenship rights, and either no or uncertain residence and work rights. Every state assumes the right to treat citizens and non-citizens differently. So it is a test of the possibilities of feminist politics to take seriously the rights of non-citizens too. In these days of rising racism and anti-immigrant feelings, citizen-based claims which do not attend to the many people in the state who are not citizens easily become complicit with exclusivist or racist politics.

But why, in these days of transnational and global power, of new market citizenship, do states still expect a singular, primary loyalty from 'their' citizens (Appadurai 1993)? So many people are out of place, living, travelling along diasporic or other circuits; identities, too, are often transnational, mobile, and hybrid. Why is it still that most of us do not give 'global citizenship' a thought, unless we have some green or universalistic idealist streak? Can we only imagine a citizenship tied to a state, or a collection of states?

Some states posit a multicultural policy, unsettling the hyphen between the nation and the state, while continuing to 'man' the gates of entry, residence and citizenship against most would-be migrants. Multiculturalism has been described as a top-down labour import and management strategy (Miyoshi 1993); though such policies have usually also emanated from mobilised migrant and social rights movements from below, and sometimes from foreign policy and other state pressures, too. But multiculturalism usually imagines difference in terms of home state and new home. Increasingly, postmigratory identities are more multiple, fluid and multinational, and are negotiated within complex transnational webs of association and communication. Thinking about home, and about citizenship, becomes much more complicated as globalisation processes recast the relationship between people, place and identity (Scholte 1996; Brah 1996). Nevertheless, ideas of place and home live on in the imaginings of many diasporic collectivities, and these ideas have very real implications for notions of self and citizenship.

Resisting Identities/Resisting Globalisation

Capital has been a lot more successful at globalising than labour, or feminism, has. But globalisation impacts directly on people everywhere, in gendered effects. Most globalisation analyses and narratives still invisibilise women, and do not admit their experiences as evidence. How do different women understand, and respond to, global power? Is it possible to use transnational spaces for feminist resistance against the devastation of globalisation and state transformation?

Chin and Mittelman ask, 'What is the meaning of resistance in the context of globalisation?' (1997: 25). Part of the power of globalisation as ideology, as we have seen, is to naturalise the process, to contribute to its own production through making market domination seem not only desirable but inevitable. Part of the politics of resistance is to challenge this market-imposed 'death of politics' (Gill 1996: 12): to put the politics back into 'economics', to trace the power relations, including gender relations, that are embedded in these processes. This means exposing the myth of government and state powerlessness in the face of global forces, and insisting on notions of public accountability and political responsibility. It means reactivating the possibility of a more inclusive political economy, and of a revitalised civil society within states. It also means extending notions of radical and participatory democracy to include global politics, while never losing sight of power relations, of class, gender and other axes of difference, that shape global politics too.

Does citizenship have a role to play in enabling resistance, in particular feminist resistance, to market domination and neoliberal states? Citizenship's two-edged nature – simultaneously inclusive and exclusive – and its long association with dominant group masculinist power make it a difficult concept to utilise. Furthermore, its close association with the state, and with territory and place, make it almost impossible to imagine a citizenship which is deterritorialised.

Is seeking global civil society hopelessly idealistic? Transnational social movements do now imagine, and act within, the world as a political field (Scholte 1996). Intensifying globalisation and state transformation have proceeded at such a pace that it can now be argued we live in post-nation-state times. Transnational power demands – and produces – transnational resistance. There are now extensive networks, conversations, organisations and alliances within international fora, in international NGOs, and in transnational conversations, conferences and campaigns. Interrogating these agents, sites and discourses that are resisting globalisation reveals many that are not progressive, and may be overtly anti-feminist. It is necessary to forge alliances beyond feminism, though feminists themselves are by no means united in their understandings or strategies of resistance in the face of global power.

Feminists have been organising transnationally – for women's rights, for peace, for example – for more than a century. Now, gendered analyses and feminist politics contest the complex power/wealth/identity of the new global gender regime. There are many examples of good feminist transversal practice (Yuval-Davis 1997), like Women Against Fundamentalism and Women Living Under Muslim Laws, whose members include women who have crossed borders as migrants, dissidents or refugees. Others more specifically address globalisation effects, for example the South-based DAWN group. Feminist politics in the processes around international conferences, especially the 1993 Vienna human rights conference, the 1994 Cairo population and development conference, and the 1995 Beijing women's conference, produced connections, contests and writings which reveal something of the difficulties and opportunities of transnational feminist alliances (Sen *et al.* 1994; Otto 1996; Eisenstein 1997).

Feminist theories and practices around difference have generated many insights into intra-state, or First World/Third World, or Eastern/Western European divides (Mohanty *et al.* 1993). Feminists have delved deep into questions of identity and subjectivity (Jones 1993; Zalweski and Enloe 1995; Eisenstein 1996); and self-recognised difference remains a key site for negotiating power and other relations between women, as well as between men and women. Nationality and citizenship, and whether or not we reside in the state where we have at least formal claim to citizenship, are crucial aspects of women's identity, too. The contemporary revival of interest in citizenship, including among some feminists, reflects in part a reaction against global power and state assaults on social, including women's, rights. It is also a reaction against the mobilisation of exclusivist citizenship politics against racialised and minoritised 'others'. But what can we make of citizenship as a tool for feminist resistance to the damaging effects of globalisation processes, state transformations and exclusivist identity politics, especially in our focus on international or transnational feminist politics?

Acknowledgement

An earlier version of parts of this chapter appears in Pettman 1998a and 1998b.

Notes

1. Writing from Australia, I am stunned by the speed of the turn-around from pleas for the Asian miracle/exceptionalism to be emulated, to revisionist smugness which suggests 'they' weren't really up to it after all.
2. This construction reminds us that women often move as labour migrants as part of a family income-earning strategy, rather than as autonomous individuals.

References

Afshar, H. (ed.) (1987). *Women, State and Ideology: Studies from Africa and Asia*, Albany: State University of New York Press.

Afshar, H. and Dennis, C. (eds) (1992). *Women and Structural Adjustment Policies in the Third World*, London: Macmillan.

Amin, Samir (1996). 'The Challenge of Globalization', *Review of International Political Economy* 3, 2: 216–59.

Appadurai, A. (1993). 'Patriotism and Its Futures', *Public Culture*, 5, 3: 411–29.

Bakker, I. (ed.) (1994). *The Strategic Silence: Gender and Economic Policy*, London: Zed Books.

Bello, W. (1998). 'East Asia: On the Eve of the Great Transformation?', *Review of International Political Economy* 5, 3: 424–44.

Bloul, R. (1993). 'Engendering Muslim Identities: De-territorialization and the Ethnicization Process in France', *Gender Relations Project*, Australian National University, Canberra.

Blum, M. (1997). 'Bringing Class Back Into a Changing Capitalist World Economy', *Identities* 3, 3: 413–20.

Blumberg, R. *et al.* (eds) (1995). *Engendering Wealth and Well-Being*, Boulder: Westview.

Brah, A. (1996). *Cartographies of Diaspora: Contesting Identities*, London: Routledge.

Brodie, J. (1994). 'Shifting the Boundaries: Gender and the Politics of Restructuring', in I. Bakker (ed.) *The Strategic Silence: Gender and Economic Policy*, London: Zed Books, pp. 46–60.

Brown, W. (1996). *States of Injury: Power and Freedom in Later Modernity*, Princeton:

Princeton University Press.
Castles, S. and M. Miller (1993). *The Age of Migration*, London: Macmillan.
Cerny, P. (1996). 'What Next for the State?', in E. Kofman and G. Youngs (eds) *Globalization: Theory and Practice*, London: Pinter, pp. 123–37.
Chin, C. and M. Mittelman (1997). 'Conceptualising Resistance to Globalisation', *New Political Economy* 2, 1: 25–38.
Cox, R. (1996). 'A Perspective on Globalization', in J. Mittelman (ed.) *Globalization: Critical Reflections*, Boulder: Lynne Reinner.
Curthoys, A. (1993). 'Feminism, Citizenship and National Identity', *Feminist Review* 44: 37–59.
Dirlik, A. (1997). 'Critical Reflections on "Chinese Capitalism" as Paradigm', *Identities* 3, 3.
Douglas, I. (1996). 'The Myth of Globali[z]ation: a Poststructural Reading of Speed and Reflexivity in the Governance of Late Modernity', International Studies Association conference paper, San Diego.
Eisenstein, Z. (1993). *The Colour of Gender: Reimagining Democracy*, Berkeley: University of California Press.
— (1996). *Hatreds*, London: Routledge.
— (1997). 'Women's Publics and the Search for New Democracies', *Feminist Review* 57: 140–67.
Enloe, C. (1992). 'Silicon Tricks and the Two Dollar Woman', *New Internationalist,* January: 12–14.
Gill, S. (1996). 'Globalization, Democratization, and the Politics of Indifference', in J. Mittelman (ed.) *Globalization: Critical Reflections*, Boulder: Lynne Reinner.
Gills, B. (1997). 'Editorial: "Globalisation" and the "Politics of Resistance"', *New Political Economy* 2, 2.
Hamilton, C. (1997). 'Workers in the Globalised World', *Australian Quarterly* 69, 2: 25–38.
Jayawardena, K. (1986). *Feminism and Nationalism in the Third World*, London: Zed Books.
Jones, K. (1990). 'Citizenship in a Woman-friendly Polity', *Signs* 15, 4: 781–812.
— (1993). *Compassionate Authority,* London: Routledge.
Kandiyoti, D. (ed.) (1991). *Women, Islam and the State*, London: Macmillan.
Kofman, E. and G. Youngs (eds) (1996). *Globalization: Theory and Practice*, London: Pinter.
Leech, M. (1994). 'Women, the State and Citizenship', *Australian Feminist Studies* 19: 79–91.
McMichael, P. (1996). 'Globalization Myths and Realities', *Rural Sociology* 61, 1: 25–55.
Mies, M. (1986). *Patriarchy and Accumulation on a World Scale*, London: Zed Books.
Mittelman, J. (ed.) (1996). *Globalization: Critical Reflections*, Boulder: Lynne Reinner.
Mitter, S. (1986). *Common Fate, Common Bond: Women in the Global Economy*, London: Pluto Press.
Miyoshi, M. (1993). 'A Borderless World? From Colonialism to Transnationalism and the Decline of the Nation-State', *Critical Inquiry* 19, 4: 726–51.
Moghadam, V. (ed.) (1994). *Identity Politics and Women: Cultural Reassertions and Feminisms in International Perspective,* Boulder: Westview Press.
Mohanty, C., A. Russo, and L. Torres (eds) (1993). *Third World Women and the Politics of Feminism*, Bloomington: Indiana University Press.

New Political Economy (1997). Special issue on Globalization and the Politics of Resistance, 2, 2.

Otto, D. (1996). 'Holding up Half the Sky, but for Whose Benefit?' *Australian Feminist Law Review* 6: 7–28.

Perraton, J., D. Goldblatt, D. Held and A. McGrew (1997). "The Globalisation of Economic Activity', *New Political Economy* 2, 2: 279–98.

Peterson, V. S. (ed.) (1992). *Gendered States: Feminist (Re)Visions of International Relations*, Boulder: Lynne Reinner.

Peterson, V. S. (1995). 'Reframing the Politics of Identity: Democracy, Globalisation and Gender', *Political Expressions* 1, 1: 1–16.

Pettman, J. J. (1996). *Worlding Women: a Feminist International Politics*, London: Routledge.

— (1998a). 'Transnational Feminisms', in Caine, B. *et al.* (eds) *Oxford Companion to Australian Feminism*, Sydney: Oxford University Press.

— (1998b). 'Women on the Move: Globalization and Labour Migration from South and Southeast Asian States', *Global Society* 12, 3: 389–403.

Phillips, A. (1993). *Democracy and Difference*, Cambridge: Polity Press.

Rai, S. and Lievesley, G. (eds) (1996). *Women and the State: International Perspectives*, London: Francis and Taylor.

Scholte, J. A. (1996). 'The Geography of Collective Identities in a Globalizing World', *Review of International Political Economy*, 3–4: 565–608.

Sen, G., A. Germaine and L. C. Cohen (eds) (1994). *Population Policies Reconsidered: Wealth, Empowerment and Rights*, Boston: Harvard University Press.

Tinsman, H. (1992). 'The Indispensable Service of Sisters: Considering Domestic Service in Latin America and the United States', *Journal of Women's History* 1, 4: 37–59.

Tolentino, R. (1996). 'Bodies, Letters, Catalogs: Filipinas in Transnational Space', *Social Text* 14, 4: 49–76.

Tooze, R. (1997). 'International Political Economy in an Age of Globalization', in J. Baylis and S. Smith (eds) *The Globalization of World Politics*, Oxford: Oxford University Press, pp. 212–30.

Truong, T-D. (1996). 'Gender, International Migration and Social Reproduction', *Asia and Pacific Migration Journal* 5, 1: 27–52.

Wilkin, P. (1996). 'New Myths for the South: Globalisation and the Conflict between Private Power and Freedom', *Third World Quarterly* 17, 2: 227–38.

Yuval-Davis, N. (1991). 'The Citizenship Debate: Women, Ethnicity and the State', *Feminist Review* 39: 58–68.

— (1997). 'Women, Citizenship and Difference', *Feminist Review* 57: 4–27.

Yuval-Davis, N. and Anthias, F. (eds) (1989). *Woman–Nation–State*, London: Macmillan.

Zalweski, M. and C. Enloe (1995). 'Questions about Identity in International Relations', in K. Booth and S. Smith (eds), *International Relations Theory Today*, Cambridge: Polity Press, pp. 279–305.

Zolberg, A. (1989). 'The Next Waves: Migration Theory for a Changing World', *International Migration Review* 23, 3: 403–30.

CHAPTER 14

Political Motherhood and the Feminisation of Citizenship: Women's Activisms and the Transformation of the Public Sphere

Pnina Werbner

Political Motherhood

Beyond individual rights, citizenship may be grasped as a historically specific embodiment of the legitimate authority of the political community. Struggles over citizenship are thus struggles over the very meaning of politics and membership in a community. Paradoxically, perhaps, it is marginal or non-citizens, those excluded from active participation in the political community, who have had the most impact on citizenship as a historically evolving imaginary. To effect the redefinition of citizenship, non-citizens must first move into the public sphere. Indeed, they have often to redefine what that public sphere is, and its very limits. Hence in this chapter I deploy the private/public distinction as a powerful deconstructive, and yet essential, analytical tool for comprehending 'motherist' social movements both as they developed during the early phases of feminism in the Anglo-American West, and as they currently exist in postcolonial nations and in ethnic diasporic communities. My central argument is that women's active citizenship starts from pre-established cultural domains of female power and rightful ownership or responsibility. These culturally defined domains, or the attack upon them, create the conditions of possibility for women's civic activism which, in the face of male resistance, comes progressively to challenge authoritarian structures of power, usually controlled by men.

The term 'political motherhood' is taken from Jennifer Schirmer's article on 'motherist' movements in Latin America (Schirmer 1993). Distinctively, such movements are always conjunctural: they valorise maternal qualities – caring, compassion, responsibility for the vulnerable – as encompassing and anchored in democratic values. They thus deny dualistic theories of gendered opposition between male and female as embodiments of exclusive qualities. Second, political motherhood is a process of unfolding consciousness, as women progressively move into the public sphere.

Historically, political motherhood challenged, I argue, established notions of civic legitimacy and created the conditions for the feminisation of citizenship: the reconstitution of citizenship in terms of qualities associated with women's role as nurturers, carers and protectors of the integrity of the family and its individual members. These qualities came increasingly to be defined as critical to the continued legitimate authority of the political community. Hence the chapter draws on exemplary case studies to show processes of emerging synergy between motherhood and democracy and of women's radicalisation in the face of male authoritarianism and exclusion.

Perhaps one of the most outstanding examples of the move by women, *en masse*, from pre-established, culturally defined women's power bases into the public sphere was the emergence of political motherhood as a large-scale social movement in the nineteenth century, first in England and the United States and later in the Near East and Asia (Jayawardena 1986).

Political Motherhood and First-Wave Feminism

The army of female philanthropists who invaded the public sphere in Britain and the US during the nineteenth century could little have imagined that by the end of the twentieth century, their particular concerns – with poverty and deprivation, the protection of children, health and education, as well as human rights, alcoholism or male versus female sexuality – would dominate state budgets and run into hundreds of billions of pounds annually. Nor did most of them, when they initially began their activism, anticipate that it would lead them to join the demand for women's suffrage. As Prochaska has argued,

> The interest of philanthropic women in female suffrage emerged, not inevitably, but quite naturally out of certain of their activities.... [E]arly female suffrage societies were seen by them as another branch of philanthropy; the means were political but the end philanthropic.... (Prochaska 1980: 227–8)

Quaker women ministers who initially worked for abolitionist causes in the anti-slavery movement reacted to their exclusion from the World Anti-Slavery Conference held in London in 1840 by calling the Seneca Falls Convention of 1848 – a convention which, declaring that men *and* women are created equal, was the beginning of organised American feminism as a social movement (Banks 1981: 22–3). In 1833, 80,000 women in Britain had signed an anti-slavery petition *(ibid.:* 22). Banks argues that attempts to exclude women from public office in the anti-slavery movement, despite their leading role, forced women such as the Grimke sisters

> to defend their behaviour and it led them into a much more self-conscious articulation of women's rights, which became in time a specific demand for equality between the sexes. (Banks 1981: 22)

Similarly,

> the humiliation of the exclusion [of Lucretia Mott and Elizabeth Cady Stanton]

> from the convention seems to have deepened the feminist consciousness already developing in both women. (Banks 1981: 23)

This radicalisation of women's demands for legal rights was not limited to rights activists; it arose equally among evangelical women working, in the name of Christian virtue and moral purification, to reform the miseries of prostitution, child labour and the conditions of workhouses, or to advocate temperance as men's duty to their families, and the end to double standards of sexual morality.

Walby proposes, against Banks's critiques of the welfare orientation of much women's activism in the inter-war period, that such women,

> while maintaining a theoretical adherence to a division between 'women's sphere' and 'men's sphere,' *sought to enlarge what was encompassed by women's sphere.* Tasks which were performed by women in the household, such as caring for the sick and raising the young, were argued to fall still in women's sphere when carried out in public institutions outside the household, such as schools and hospitals. This claim ... stretched the notion of separate spheres while not challenging it. (Walby 1990: 167; emphasis added)

Hence the institutions of the welfare state, according to Walby, 'were overwhelmingly led by women' (*ibid.*).

One of the remarkable features of first-wave feminism, little noted by social historians, is the enormous expansion of a specifically women's print capitalism in the nineteenth century. If, according to Benedict Anderson, print capitalism enabled the imagination of the nation as a community (Anderson 1983), then *women's* print capitalism, a major feature of the liberal public sphere in Britain and the US in the nineteenth century, reflects the emergence of an imaginary sisterhood and a feminised public sphere. Women published not only women's newspapers and journals, edited by some of the leading feminists of the century, but diaries, biographies and autobiographies, exposés and reform books advocating new welfare policies, political tracts, essays, articles, letters to newspapers and pamphlets. Indeed, these form the basis for most of the historical research on the early emergence of the women's movement (e.g., Prochaska 1980; Eisenstein 1981; Banks 1981; Scott 1996). A parallel development of women's print capitalism occurred in countries beyond the West, such as Egypt, China and India (Jayawardena 1986: 17–18, 51–2). In 1885 Ellice Hopkins, who founded the White Cross Army of men against prostitution,

> addressed meetings of up to 2,000 working men at a time; and she wrote most of the pamphlets which made up the 'White Cross Series,' which sold over two million copies in England and America by the end of the century. One of her effusions, 'True Manliness,' sold 300,000 copies in its year of publication. (Prochaska 1980: 215–16)

It was not just that charitable women ventured beyond the home and familial domestic space, often in the face of male opposition, to assume public roles and offices in voluntary organisations. Women publicised their point of view in a multitude of ways, not only spectacular ventures into dens of iniquity, brothels and pubs, or into the hospices and homes of patients dying of cholera and other contagious diseases, but also by testifying before Select Committees of the House of Commons or the House of Lords, by lobbying and petitioning, by campaigning on a variety of moral causes through the press, and by publishing the intimate details of their activism and daily lives in personal novels, diaries and autobiographies. The imagination of sisterhood and its special (often essentialised) qualities, across classes and even national boundaries, was a powerful message which men, however positioned, could not ignore.

The Political Community and the Constitution of Citizenship

The importance of these developments for the feminisation of citizenship needs to be spelled out. I start from the fact that the legitimacy of the political community is often grounded discursively in certain human qualities, regarded as foundational for the constitution of citizenship and the public sphere, here defined broadly as encompassing both civil society and the state. In opposing the entrenched privileges of the Church and the aristocracy, the philosophers of the Enlightenment stressed individual rationality, autonomy and equality as the central sources of legitimacy for the democratic political community and its public sphere. Historically, these human qualities came to be defined as masculine. Indeed, one of the central paradoxes of modernity has been that the moment of male emancipation was also the moment of gender reification and exclusion (of course, not all men were emancipated either). This was nowhere more evident than in France where, as Joan Wallache Scott has recently demonstrated (Scott 1996), the naturalisation of male privileges in the name of universal rights sexualised the public/private divide in almost pornographic terms. Whereas in England and America attempts were made to confine women to the domestic sphere by constructing them as virtuous mothers and carers, in need of protection from a dangerously sexualised male world, in France women were constructed not only as irrational but as sexually rapacious and violent. Before the French revolution,

> women were very much a part of the opposition to absolutism, and their activity took more or less overtly political forms. The salons, run by elite women, sponsored the discussions that contributed to what became a critical and dissenting 'public opinion.' This public included women but only those of wealth, education and social grace. (Scott 1996: 31; see also Habermas 1989 on the evolution of the public sphere)

Women were active in oppositional journalism. Indeed, with the exception of Rousseau who was strongly anti-feminist (Eisenstein 1981), many of the

French Enlightenment male philosophers such as Montesquieu, Diderot, Voltaire and Concordet were sympathetic, or actively supported, women's rights (Banks 1981: 28). Some women, at least, were no longer confined to domestic spaces – so much so that Sombart proposed that one of the defining features of post-Renaissance developments in Europe was the rise in consumption linked to the secularisation of women (Sombart 1967/1913), a change spearheaded by single courtesans attending the court.

By contrast, following the Revolution and its declaration of equality, liberty and fraternity, a rigid separation of the sexes into two spheres became embodied in a sexual imagery,

> establishing the physical boundaries of masculine and female bodies. Crossing the threshold from the hearth to the forum led to hermaphrodism, they [men] charged, the loss of distinguishing features of male and female. The danger of androgyny was a sexually indecipherable, hence monstrous, body.... [P]olitical women [were depicted in caricatures] as ugly, comical, funny-looking, masculine imitators.... [W]omen with monocles, cigars and beards; and men in skirts.... [T]ransgression was depicted as castration – as a threat to the sign of men's difference and the symbol of his power, now equated with political rights ... rested on segregated spaces. (Scott 1996: 80–1)

At the end of the nineteenth century, women for French thinkers such as Le Bon became a metonym for the crowd, the loss of self, the unconscious, the emotionally shallow, lacking in creativity (*ibid.*: 131–3). They were constructed as violent furies or superstitious handmaidens of priests (*ibid.*: 101–2). Emile Durkheim used morphological evidence to argue that 'women evolved through civilisation to have smaller brains than in primitive societies' (*ibid.*: 96). All these qualities excluded women, naturally and essentially, from active citizenship in the public sphere.

Of course, France was a democracy only intermittently and partially in the years following the Revolution, and women suffered badly under repressive and authoritarian regimes. The law of 28 July 1848, for example, excluded women from participation in clubs, whether as observers or members (*ibid.*: 77). This was at a time, it should be noted, when Anglo-American women's philanthropy was reaching new heights, with hundreds of thousands of women participating in organised charitable works or mobilising for political rights campaigns. In the very year of the Seneca Falls Convention, the Constituent Assembly in France agreed that women must be barred from political activity (*ibid.*: 64). Violent attacks on female meetings were condoned (*ibid.*: 81). The French government undertook welfare reform top-down. All this meant that a fully fledged women's movement never developed in France. Women finally got the vote in 1944. Yet in the USA, too, the process of democratisation, of full adult emancipation, was only achieved in the late 1960s, following the civil rights movement.

Under these circumstances it is hardly surprising that leading French feminists from the very beginning stressed their 'difference' as legitimising grounds for their participation in the public sphere. They drew upon the exemplary figure of the Virgin Mary as mother, an epitome of autonomy, duty and obligation. Jeanne Derrain, a leading French feminist in the mid-nineteenth century, 'turned the trait that constructed the symbolic and distinctive meaning of womanhood in her time into a justification for political rights' (*ibid.*: 70).

The point is, however, that without the philanthropic army of indefatigable women charitable workers, with their spectacular fund-raising capacities, evident organisational skills, ability to hold office and deliver public speeches; without the pamphleteering and parliamentary lobbying, such sentiments lacked political force. In England, by contrast, women moved into the public sphere at the same time that they legitimised their inclusion as full citizens in the political community in terms of their special qualities as mothers. While some continued to espouse radical Enlightenment ideas about gendered equality, there was also a move among Christian evangelicals such as Catherine Beecher to promote the 'notion of female superiority that was accepted not only by women but by many of their male supporters' (Banks 1981: 84, 46). This led many later feminists 'to believe that it was woman's mission to re-shape the whole society' (*ibid.*: 46). This stress on difference and uniqueness was usually based on notions of gendered complementarity. As Ellice Hopkins put it:

> May we not find in the larger family of the State, that the work of the world is best done by the man and the woman together, each supplying what is lacking to the other, the man the head of the woman, the woman the heart of the man. (cited in Prochaska 1980: 219)

For her, as for others in her camp,

> votes for women were simply a means by which society might be made more compassionate, by which the relations of men and women might be made equal and holy. In a world in which women had political power men might be made to rise to the standard which women set them. (*ibid.*)

This stress on difference and complementarity has been transformed, of course, by second-wave radical feminists into an argument *against* 'masculine' individual rationality and 'abstract' universalism. Privileged are the 'unique' qualities of women: compassion, particularism, sociality, obligation. In some instances, this latter feminism represents, however, a move *away* from political motherhood. Political motherhood as conceived here rests on an *encompassing* relationship: women are responsible to their families and the political community in its entirety, *including* men, with regard to issues of universal and humanitarian concern. In line with this, Sara Ruddick (1989) defines maternalism as a protective relationship open to men as well, and rejects an *a priori* 'mythical division between women's peacefulness and men's wars' (1989: 135). Nevertheless, even as they deny so-called 'abstract', 'masculine' universalism (*ibid.*: 128, 135–6), Western maternalists and peace activists take for granted what Third World political mothers cannot: the existence of a stable, liberal democracy; freedom of speech and association; *habeas corpus*, the rule of law. Moreover, as Yuval-Davis perceptively argues, to create peace with the enemy, motherhood must transcend its own particularities (Yuval-Davis 1997: 112).

The strength of political motherhood as an evolving social movement has been to introduce new human qualities into the public sphere, and to define them as *equally* foundational in the legitimation of the political community. The point is not thus whether men are compassionate and loyal or women rational and objective; the point is that *all* these qualities embody and objectify the ideal of citizenship and their *absence* delegitimises the state and its political authority. It is in this sense that I speak, somewhat ironically (without subscribing to essentialist definitions of intrinsic male and female qualities), of the 'feminisation' of citizenship. Arguing against the existence of two contrasting, gendered ethics, Susan Okin proposes that the qualities they jointly espouse are inseparable:

> The best theorizing about justice ... has integral to it the notions of care and empathy, of thinking of the interests and well-being of others who may be very different from ourselves. (Okin 1989: 15)

Similarly, Carol Gilligan speaks of a convergence of 'male' and 'female' ethics which recognises the dual contexts of justice and care (Gilligan 1982: 166–7). Not only feminism but socialism, anti-racism or multiculturalism introduce new human qualities – of economic egalitarianism, tolerance or the right to cultural recognition – into the discourses of legitimation that permeate the public sphere. These new values continuously reconstitute what it means to be a citizen.

Political Motherhood and Postcoloniality

The discussion so far has underlined the fluidity of the private/public divide as a constantly shifting and contested demarcation. As Lister remarks perceptively,

> the public–private divide can be understood as a shifting political construction, under constant renegotiation, which reflects both historical and cultural contexts as well as the relative power of different social groups. The public and private define each other and take meaning from each other. (Lister 1997: 42)

The semantic fuzziness and terminological confusion arising from the widespread deployment of concepts such as private and public in scholarly and public discourses has undermined, it might be argued, the analytic rigour of these terms, and hence their usefulness (Yuval-Davis 1997: 78–9). A further criticism, by Partha Chatterjee, is that

> the line between public and private is a completely inadequate tool for analysing constructions of civil societies in post-colonial nations and that a non-westocentric

analysis of gender relations cannot assume the boundary between private and public as given. (Yuval-Davis 1997: 5–6)

It is sometimes necessary to hold on to a distinction while continually questioning its very possibility. This strategy, of writing against the grain from within a discourse (or 'reading', see Spivak 1987, Chapter 12), displaces discursive certainties by highlighting the instability and multivocality of conceptual distinctions, and revealing the implicit ideological baggage they carry. In line with this, recent feminist philosophers draw on Habermasian discourse ethics to argue against any substantive division between the private and public spheres. The point is elegantly put by Seyla Benhabib in a re-evaluation of Hannah Arendt's thought and of overly juridical or static liberal theorisations of citizenship (Benhabib 1992, Chapter 3). Benhabib defines the public sphere as, very broadly, a political space of discursivity in which contested issues are addressed. It is a permeable arena continuously responsive to new issues, moral challenges and new modes of discourse. Feminism as a social movement and mode of active citizenship has forced certain issues, such as familial power imbalances, into the public sphere. While recognising the basically liberal framework which allows discourse to flourish, Benhabib argues against a topographical or spatial definition of the division between public and private. Any site, however unlikely, can become a site of discourse, and hence part of the public sphere. Moreover, against the liberal view that sees the constitutional framework as basically fixed, she argues that even procedural and constitutional frameworks are open to ethical scrutiny and moral debate.

Benhabib's work points to the fact that the public sphere is a complex and stratified political space, only partially and sometimes implicitly oriented towards the state and state policies. This is particularly evident in motherist movements which often start from very local concerns, and expand their vision and sphere of publicity in the context of a broadening struggle.

In coining the term political motherhood, Jennifer Schirmer highlights the ability of 'motherist' movements in Latin America not only to break into the public sphere, but to create transnational links beyond the nation-state. Motherist movements in Latin America are united in FEDEFAM, the Organisation of Latin American countries for Relatives of the Disappeared, one of the most powerful indigenous transnational networks and human rights lobbies in the world (Schirmer 1993). FEDEFAM includes 17 countries and has support groups throughout the West carrying out fund raising and acting as political watchdogs for human rights abuses (Stephen 1995: 814). Schirmer shows that the organisers of the movement began as mothers whose maternal role as protectors of their homes and family had been violated, and who sought restitution from the state. As the women moved into public political activism, however, they became targets of state violence: they were jailed, kidnapped, raped and tortured; their headquarters were bombed and their lives threatened. Many of the women started in Christian groups espousing liberation theology, a holistic ideology which promotes both economic well-being and political equality and freedom. Hence, Schirmer argues, the political consciousness which the women developed was transformed *in action,* to encompass many different dimensions of their activism, some of which could be defined as 'feminist' (campaigns against rape, domestic violence, the struggle for equal rights in the home and in the public sphere), some as economically pragmatic or class-oriented (such as women's education) and some as universalist (such as fighting for human rights alongside men).

Importantly, the women, Schirmer argues, rejected radical Western feminisms that start from sharp gender oppositions, even while they recognised that militarism and state terror were forms of domination and torture perpetrated by (some) men. She thus rejects the evolutionary distinction posed by feminist scholars such as Kaplan (1982) and Molyneux (1985) between 'female' consciousness (practical and traditional) and 'feminist' consciousness (radical and strategic), with its implication that the latter is more 'advanced' than the former (*ibid.*: 60). Instead she proposes that women's consciousness is contingent and contextual, arising from the articulations of different dimensions of their activism and their long-term ideals and goals. Women's collective experience, in other words, evolves through and in action, determining the specificity of their feminism (see also Radcliffe and Westwood 1996).

Moreover, feminist consciousness responds to the broader national and civil context in which the battle for women's specific citizenship rights takes place. As others, too, have argued (e.g., Johnson-Odim 1991: 315, 321; Basu 1995), in the face of poverty, underdevelopment and severe abuses of human rights, women outside Western democracies have been able, despite the multiple oppressions they suffer, to transcend their narrow interests as women and work for wider and more complex causes, creating alliances by drawing upon all their multiple identities: as mothers, wives, democrats, peasants, workers and patriots, *as well as* women united in a global sisterhood. During the colonial era, women mobilised against specific cultural practices that were particularly oppressive: polygamy, child marriage, widow burning, feet binding or female seclusion, while fighting for the right to property, education and divorce, much like their counterparts in the West (Jayawardena 1986). Indeed, extensive networks of women activists between Asia, the Middle East and the West developed during the nineteenth century. Asian and Middle Eastern women were influenced by missionary women and theosophists while, simultaneously, they also joined the anti-colonial and independence movements (*ibid.*: 20–1, 91). They fought with and against colonialism. Mahatma Gandhi, in his espousal of non-violent resistance, developed his own version of political motherhood, exhorting women to 'extend their hearts and interests beyond the narrow confines of their homes' and arguing that the principle of 'non-violence' (*ahimsa*) and political non-violent resistance were suited to women by nature, that women's courage and self-sacrifice were superior to men's and that, as one women's journal put it,

> Because the qualities which this new form of warfare is displaying are feminine rather than masculine, we may look on this life and death struggle of India to be free as a women's war. (Everett 1979: 76, cited in Jayawardena 1986: 97, who also cites Mies 1980: 125, and Mazumdar 1976: 56, 59)

Following independence, women's organisations in postcolonial nations have differed, however, in the extent to which they have chosen to work for specifically women's interests or understood these to be embedded in broader struggles. In Pakistan during the Zia military rule period, for example, the Women's Action Forum, an urban middle-class organisation of academics and professional women, chose to focus exclusively on combating the regime's Islamicisation programme. The women channelled their energies to fight the proposed introduction of radically discriminatory laws against women in the name of Islam. WAF judged that political parties and organisations in the past had failed to come to grips with specifically feminist issues and had often abandoned women once their struggles were won. Reflecting critically on this choice, however, leaders of the movement recognised that

> Where the initiative has been taken by either peasant or working class women in Pakistan, the issues have notably not been feminist in content. At grass roots, women have acted to save their homes and villages from landlord terrorism, to destroy narcotics dens or to demand justice in criminal cases. (Mumtaz and Shaheed 1987: 151)

By contrast to WAF, in Bangladesh during the same period, women's organisations broadened their alliances. In the face of police intervention and threats, they decided to join forces with the wider movement for democracy rather than focusing exclusively on women's issues. Jahan cites the secretary of one organisation which had successfully spearheaded an anti-dowry signature campaign that collected seventeen thousand signatures:

> I became convinced that authoritarian governments will never let us have the space necessary for effective social action. Therefore, joining the movement for democratization seemed as important as running the campaign for violence against women. (cited in Jahan 1995: 100)

The organisation nevertheless continued its vigorous campaign against gender violence (*ibid.*).

In connecting different struggles, women reach towards a feminist consciousness rooted in particular places at particular historical junctures (Schirmer 1993: 61). Under military rule or dictatorship, such as Palestine under Israeli occupation (see Mayer 1994; Jad 1995), women have had to battle in public for human and democratic rights in the name of incarcerated or 'disappeared' husbands, lovers, sons or brothers, and to create alliances across national boundaries, an issue I will return to below.

The need is thus to avoid 'dualistic theories' which posit an implacable opposition between men and women (Stephen 1995: 824; on such dualisms see, for example, Eisenstein 1981). Third World women sometimes reject the label 'feminism' because it opens them up to the accusation of being Western sellouts (Charles and Hintjens 1998: 20). Reflecting on the possible reasons why 'feminism' is rejected by so many Third World women activists, Basu suggests that

> Resistance to feminism may reflect a fear that it demands a total transformation of the social order. A popular rendition of this anxiety is the notion that feminists are 'man haters.'... Contrast this notion of feminism with the possibility, aired in more than one chapter of this book, that feminism may be an incremental, hidden form of subversion enacted *to protect families and communities, rather than undermine them.* (Basu 1995: 7, emphasis added)

While women's resistance takes multifarious forms, some of them hidden, political motherhood is, by definition, overt; a move into the public domain which challenges the confinement of women to domesticity. As such it necessarily transforms the social order without undermining it. Motherist movements advocate defence of the integrity of family and the autonomy of persons within its ambit of responsibility, and stress the centrality of values associated with motherhood for shaping the wider order of the political community. They work for women's causes while advocating a transcendent world view.

The ability of women to work for, and at the same time transcend, their shared sisterhood derives, Stephen suggests, from a more unitary vision: the women activists in COMADRES whom she interviewed did not perceive themselves simply as opposed to their husbands and sons, but rather as key actors in the family which they grasped organically as a primary source of identity, a corporate unit to be defended and protected, and especially so because their husbands, fathers or sons were absent or subject to state terror (Stephen 1995).

Women's activism defies the imaginary which regards women as the vulnerable objects of male protection (Anthias and Yuval-Davis 1992; Yuval-Davis 1993), or of the 'nation' as a woman to be protected from external violence. In another kind of symbolic analogy, the nation is imaged as an expanded 'family' and it is the task of men to defend its women and children. Both imaginaries – that of woman as 'the nation' and that of the nation as an extended 'family' – are rooted in traditional notions of male honour and shame. But, as we have seen, this very same imagery can be subverted to stress women's superior moral qualities: evangelical women's movements in nineteenth-century England and America invoked the nation as a family in which women and men play a complementary, but equal, civic and public role.

The Passionate Dimensions of Citizenship

There is constant leakage between the passions of nationalism and the moral sentiments constituting human rights and the rights of citizenship. Women's peace movements have attempted to reconstitute citizenship in terms of sentiments of motherhood, justice and compassion. In an early article on the women's peace movement in Israel (Gabriel 1992), Ayala Gabriel-Emmett considers emotions as political forces, as discourses which are located in social relations, and as an ethos which combines ethics and emotions. Contemporary Israeli politics *vis-à-vis* the Palestinians is, she proposes, a 'politics of collective vulnerability'; that is, a politics in which the different political actors all perceive themselves as victims of past suffering. They transcend the memories of this collective suffering by giving vent to different kinds of collective emotions – grief and rage – as expressions of mourning and revenge. Hence, she argues, national vulnerabilities are 'rooted in Jewish and Arab ancient histories, in past glories and distant defeats'. The vigil held every Friday in towns and cities throughout Israel by Women in Black, an Israeli–Palestinian women's peace organisation, and the aggressive opposition to it, 'unveil', she claims, 'the articulation of grief and rage in contesting perceptions of transcending collective vulnerabilities'. The opposition between these two collective emotions represents an opposition between two opposed world views, two opposed visions of the future, and two opposed ethics of political action.

In addition to national vulnerabilities, the vigils also express gender vulnerabilities. Through the vigil Israeli women demand the right not be marginalised. Paradoxically, because they are not combatants in the Israeli army, it is easier for them to reach out to Palestinians. This brings about an intersection or articulation between the politics of gender and the politics of peace.

The politics of gender, Emmett tells us, are a subtext of the vigil, which is explicitly about the occupation of Palestinian lands conquered in the 1967 Six Day War. Through the vigil the women transform political powerlessness into the power of mediation in the peace process. Mothers, sisters or wives, they demonstrate not merely as protected and vulnerable dependants but as protectors. They appeal to Jewish traditions of mourning; they mourn and grieve for the losses of both sides – Israeli and Palestinian. They refer to the Jewish saying that the loss of one human life equals the whole world. They evoke the Jewish image of the mother of Zion, that is, of the nation who mourns for the whole collectivity, for Zion. Hence, they reconstruct grief as autonomous, as not linked to rage and future revenge. They demand that the cycle of death, mourning and revenge be broken. They do this by dislocating nationalism, by creating a transnational women's community which cuts across nationalism. They transnationalise and universalise grief and mourning, the experiences of being a mother and a wife, and of losing fathers, husbands and sons in an endless cycle of war, rage and revenge. Their demonstration underlines internal political divisions and cross-cutting boundaries within Israeli society.

In her more recent book, *Our Sisters' Promised Land: Women, Politics and Israeli–Palestinian Coexistence* (1996), Emmett extends her narrative historically and puts Women in Black in the wider context of Israeli and Palestinian peace and women's movements. Historically, what is interesting is that a projected image from the margins, of mourning women protesting against atrocities perpetrated by men, has been widely exported and internationalised. There have been Women in Black vigils in Belgrade during the Bosnian war, and in various other European cities. As I show below, diasporic Pakistani women in England organised a Women in Black march to protest against atrocities in Bosnia and Kashmir. Unlike the broader Israeli peace movement, Women in Black are concerned not just with a settlement of the Israel–Palestinian dispute, but with justice – a real end to the occupation and all the atrocities associated with it.

Emmett demonstrates the difficulties women's groups face in uniting for peace and suppressing other divisions. There are divisions, for example, between Western European Jewish women, who dominate the peace movement, and Jewish women from Middle Eastern countries (*Mizrahim*) who refuse to join, claiming themselves to be marginalised and orientalised, constructed as 'uncivilised' or lacking 'culture'. So, too, there are divisions between secular and religious women peace activists. The religious activists accuse the secular of holding most events on Saturday, and of lacking roots in Jewish tradition. These religious women are fighting for a different interpretation of the biblical text from that suggested by religious extremists and settler zealots; one that stresses the memory of slavery in Egypt, and the injunction to respect strangers in memory of that experience. Finally, there are divisions between Jews and Palestinian Israelis who suffer racism and discrimination within Israel, and Palestinians on the West Bank. These difficulties are greatest when atrocities occur, as when 21 Palestinians were massacred in the Mosque of Al Aqsa and hundreds wounded, this being followed by revenge killings of Jews. At such times, it is particularly hard to sustain alliances across the Palestinian–Israeli divide.

Another division in the Israeli women's peace movement is between organisations which combine political motherhood, peace politics and feminism, such as Women in Black, and members of women's organisations who attempt to influence the peace process as mothers, without calling themselves feminists. Writing about such movements in Israel, Yael Azmon (1997) stresses the significance of their entry into the public arena (1997: 110). Drawing on Benhabib's theorisation of the plural public sphere as a site of discursive ethics, she argues that the very movement of women peace activists into the public sphere has led them to universalise maternal sentiments, from protecting particular children to protecting any child. Azmon describes how women who started off as passive citizens embarked on a process of discovery and information gathering through which they learnt to mobilise the media on their side and to organise spectacular letter-writing campaigns, to publish articles, lobby government ministries, and petition army commanders. Both movements described by Azmon, although dominated by women, called themselves parents' organisations, thus avoiding the risk of being branded radical feminist and losing support in the wider public. She analyses the way the aporias of war create contradictory universal and 'tribal' discourses, even among ethically concerned parents.

Despite their non-feminist agendas and their adoption of 'masculine' modes of persuasive political action, the movements did in the end transform gendered ideas dominant in the political community, legitimising the right to protest even during times of war, and the right of women, as parents equal with men, to participate in the national debate about war.

Hence, just as in Victorian England slavery, exclusion and immiseration brought about by capitalism impelled women into the public domain, so too developments in and beyond the West in the second half of the twentieth century have impelled women into new forms of activism. The collapse of the protective shield around women and children, and their growing vulnerability to capitalist exploitation, civil war and state terror in many postcolonial nations have forced women to act in their own interests, appealing for support from beyond state boundaries, or, in the case of Western or diasporic women's organisations, mobilising to support vulnerable women and children suffering deprivation or oppression elsewhere in the world or in a mythical or real homeland. In the next section I examine this movement towards autonomous activism through a detailed discussion of the specific case study of diasporic Pakistani women in a British city.

Diasporic Women and Transnational Citizenship

The case study, based on ongoing research during the 1990s in Manchester, examines the battle of diasporic Pakistani women for the right to act and speak in the diasporic public domain in Britain (see also Werbner 1998). Their emergent activism signalled the radical transformation during the 1990s of this political arena, during which the authority of Pakistani male elders and their monopoly of communal public space, of the right to fund-raise, demonstrate and meet British and Pakistani state representatives, was openly contested by women. The clash has to be understood as a clash of discourses, of legitimised ideologies and of postcolonial cultural worlds around the central issue of the position of women in Islam. It also highlights the way an emergent transnational Muslim consciousness is changing the face of British Muslim diasporic politics. I argue that critical to the empowerment of Pakistani women in Britain has been the creation of autonomous women's public arenas, while their ability, despite being a marginal group (women) within a marginal group (Muslim immigrant settlers) to reach out with relative ease to high-ranking British politicians underlines certain general features of contemporary British politics.

This reaching out became evident in a series of meetings. During the first week of February 1994, members of the Al-Masoom Trust, a Pakistani women's organisation in Manchester, met with three British Members of Parliament in quick succession.[1] The meetings, it has to be stressed, were unprecedented; they were a first for members of the Al-Masoom Trust and a first official meeting between British MPs in Manchester and representatives of a women's organisation in the city.

To understand the significance of these meetings and of the narratives articulated in them requires an understanding of past political struggles in the Manchester Pakistani diasporic public sphere. We need from the start to recognise, however, that we are dealing with a moment of transition, a moment in which, in Ricoeur's terms, a new 'text' is performed, a moment of history in the making (Ricoeur 1981).

By the time of the meeting with the third MP the story of Al-Masoom, the moral narrative of its collective identity, its representational reality, had been established. Mrs Khan, the president and leader of the association, rehearsed and perfected her tale from one encounter to the next. The centrepiece of the narrative was a heroic tale of courage and sacrifice. The women had twice undertaken the arduous and risky journey overland from England through Europe to the border of Bosnia, bringing medical supplies, food, clothing, bedding, toys and even an ambulance to the refugee camps on the outskirts of Zagreb. This heroic narrative, retold anew in every encounter with each new MP, was not simply verbal – it was an embodied narrative. It was objectified by the women themselves who gathered around the MPs in Mrs Khan's living room, all of them elegantly dressed in splendid *shalwar qamiz* outfits, the founding members of the older generation seated alongside the 'youth wing'. It was objectified by the large room packed with goods ready to be sent on the next trip to Bosnia: crates of clothing, sacks of rice, large tins of ghee piled high, individually wrapped and sealed parcels of clothing and toys, each to be given away as a gift parcel for *eid* to a refugee child. The parcels had been prepared by the women with loving care. Embodying the heroic tale was also the picture album which proved the reality of earlier trips to Bosnia. There were pictures of the refugee camps, of the children and women crowded around the Al-Masoom workers who had braved the icy cold weather and risked their lives for the sake of their beleaguered Muslim sisters and their children.

The women had prepared certain demands to make to the MPs: they wanted the issue of Kashmir raised in Parliament, and they wanted if possible permission to send a delegation from their organisation to Kashmir. They wanted the local council to allocate them premises from which to work. Mrs Khan's house was their current base – the front room stacked high with the contributions to Bosnia or Pakistan, the cupboards bursting with electrical goods given as part of 'dowries' (personal trousseaux) to poor young Pakistani brides. Every few months the organisation sends a container to Pakistan packed with these trousseaux. Each includes a jewellery set, an electrical good, several outfits, shoes and a bag. These are distributed in Pakistan.

To the critical anthropologist, certain dimensions of this encounter are evident: the women are relatively affluent and the meeting is a symbolic one: the three MPs, official representatives of Her Majesty the Queen, are legitimising by their very presence the right of Al-Masoom to exist. But whereas the first observation, in recognising the class origins of the women, seems to deny their representativeness, the second observation problematises that sociological evaluation by raising the possibility that the women are, in fact, representative in a critically important sense: they are agents of change in a gendered war of positions. The women have been accused by male members of the Pakistani community in Manchester of all manner of cheating and chicanery. It has been said that they confiscate funds supposedly raised for charity; that, despite their claims, they never did go to Bosnia; that Mrs Khan, their leader, is merely masquerading as a philanthropist working for the common good.

At stake, in other words, is the right of diasporic Pakistani women to act and speak in the public domain in Britain, and particularly in its diasporic public sphere. Pakistani women traditionally control costly ceremonial gift exchanges between families and manage most of the celebrations 'for happiness' associated with rites of passage, and especially weddings. Their authority thus extends from the domestic and familial to the inter-domestic domain (Werbner 1990). In claiming a legitimate place in the public sphere, women have used their position as wives, mothers and guardians of family and domestic life, embedded in a female world of popular culture and gift exchange, to create a space of solidarity and a discourse of legitimation. In doing so they have had to overcome the contradiction between their perceived role as living embodiments of a threatened Islamic authenticity – of traditional values under attack from external colonial and postcolonial forces and ideas – and their desire to act as modern subjects (see also Badran 1991: 207). In this latter struggle they deploy precisely the modernist ideas and modes of action which their role as symbolic embodiers of 'tradition' denies. The result of this aporia has been the discursive production by women in the Muslim world of a wide range of intersecting and often inconsistent discourses. These range from an Islamist feminism which advocates strict veiling and separation, and yet at the same time espouses feminist public activism against the secular state (see Göle 1996) to a strong secular women's anti-fundamentalist movement. In between these extremes is a liberal modernist Islamic discourse, represented, for example, by the work of Fatima Mernissi, who, like the Islamists, goes back to the early Islamic sources but does so in order to prove the liberal message of Islam which is denied by the Islamists.

Running like a thread through these different, contradictory and cross-cutting discursive formations is a singular slogan and (in the Sunni world) a single exemplary figure. The slogan is that Islam accords equal (if according to some, complementary) rights to men and women. The exemplary figure is that of Ayesha, the Prophet's young wife who outlived him by some 40–50 years and was, at one time, the commander of an Islamic army in its battle with a dissenting Islamic faction. Ayesha is known for her boldness and her wisdom – she is a source of many of the authentic traditions (*hadith*) about the Prophet's life and his sayings – and also for her courage and independence. She never remarried and hence lived her whole adult life as an authoritative actor in her own right.

Al-Masoom started its life as just another philanthropic organisation. The trust was motivated by the Islamic notion of *khidmat* and *sadaqa* – selfless communal work and charitable giving. As part of its activities it collected clothing to be distributed to the poor in Pakistan. These were sent in containers and distributed there personally by Mrs Khan or the voluntary workers of a Pakistani-based trust in Rawalpindi. She explained:

> Our ambition is to help the truly poor, the street boys and girls left behind, abandoned. We collect money and clothes to give to people who have never been given anything, dowries for girls whom no-one knows are there. We have an organisation in Rawalpindi. I myself go there – I sit in villages with the very poor, I live with them. We collect clothing from various parts of Britain through our networks of friends.

Al-Masoom represents one very familiar narrative in the array of Muslim discourses – a syncretic Muslim feminism which does not deny the traditional role of women as mothers and wives, but nevertheless demands the safeguarding of women's rights along with a demand for equal rights of participation in the national arena and the public sphere. This particular discursive strand has, both in South Asia and in the Middle East, been the platform of primarily urban middle-class women who enjoy all the privileges of their class. Their positioning in the elite has led one critic, Ayesha Jalal, to attack their lack of radicalism, and to argue that they collude *de facto* in their own disempowerment, even though, as she also recognises, these elite urban women have been in the forefront of struggles for women's familial rights and for the right to greater participation in the public sphere (Jalal 1991).

Mrs Khan has built up a circle of devoted women voluntary workers. Most of them come from urban middle-class professional or small-business backgrounds in Britain or Pakistan, in which *noblesse oblige* (that is, *khidmat* in

Urdu) with its associated philanthropic work for the poor is an established tradition (see Caplan 1985).

Why has Al-Masoom emerged at this historical conjuncture? The reasons for this appear to be both local and global. The rise of political Islam worldwide has been associated in Britain with the formation of young women's associations. One attraction of such groups appears to be that they draw on Islam to support legitimised resistance to traditional parental authority and mores (see Lyon 1995). In effect, a return to a pristine Islam has desacralised 'custom' and 'culture', and has thus opened up a whole new discursive space for women to define their rights *vis-à-vis* men as well as their parents. Within this new discourse, the subordination of women is constructed by them as merely a further instantiation of male ignorance of the real and true tenets of Islam. The struggle is around the meaning of Islam and what constitutes religious authenticity. Such a struggle can be conceived of as a struggle for the control of symbolic space, voice and identity (Werbner 1996; on symbolic space see Bourdieu 1985).

The need to legitimise their activities and hence their very presence in the diasporic public sphere has pushed Al-Masoom to perform increasingly spectacular acts of mobilisation and to reach out beyond the community to the legitimate representatives of the British state. Perhaps the most spectacular capturing of public space so far has been the coordination by Al-Masoom of a Women in Black march through the city streets to protest against the continuing violence in Kashmir and Bosnia. The women who participated came from several different women's organisations in the city. Dressed in black, their heads covered with thick black scarves, the women marched through the streets of Manchester, from its immigrant commercial centre some three miles to the Town Hall, shouting slogans such as STOP THE RAPE IN KASHMIR and STOP THE TORTURING OF WOMEN IN BOSNIA, their banners in Urdu and English advertising their organisations and the reason for the procession. At the Town Hall the women were welcomed by the Lord Mayor of Manchester. Gerald Kaufman, MP, joined them midway through the march and addressed them outside the Town Hall.

This march, like the trip to Bosnia, points to another kind of reaching out – the reaching out beyond the specifically national diaspora of Pakistanis, to beleaguered Muslims everywhere. This transnational consciousness, the very real and immediate awareness of the global predicaments of Muslims, is also a feature of Pakistani male politics and the politics of the mosque.

What has been striking about the transformation in the status of Al-Masoom is the naturalness with which the community has shifted from a male-dominated diasporic public sphere to a *gendered* public sphere. While some leaders and groups were still questioning the legitimacy of the organisation, most others were already allocating space for women's organisations in their communal ceremonies and celebrations as a matter of course. No longer rejected by the business community, the diasporic public space came to be reconstructed, at the height of Al-Masoom's activism, *by homology to the private, familial space,* as a gendered space. During ceremonials and public meetings, the women sat in groups and had their own spokespersons.

In order to mobilise support, women drew on their multiple identities – as Punjabis, with a tradition of dance, music, laughter and popular drama; as Pakistani nationalists, raising funds for welfare projects and good works in Pakistan and meeting with Pakistani dignitaries and politicians; as Muslims who identify with the plight of fellow Muslims in Bosnia or Kashmir, mobilise substantial donations for refugees and demonstrate against the atrocities suffered by women and children; and finally, as British subjects who demand equality and reject the aggressive male Pakistani style of politics of the diasporic public sphere.

The ability of ordinary citizens in Britain to make contact with the top echelons of the political leadership is a feature of the British constituency system which expects MPs to bear personal responsibility for the welfare of their constituents. Arguably, the success of Al-Masoom reveals the way Muslim feminist emancipatory politics are facilitated in Britain by the relative openness and pluralism of civil society. In this context, there is no closure of ethnic minority communities. They cannot speak with a single monolithic voice. Their subjectivities – and hence subject positions – are multiple: Pakistani women can align with other women, they can appeal to liberal journalists, to humanitarian activists, to people concerned about human rights. So too Muslim socialists reach out to other socialists, Muslim democrats to other democrats. The political imaginaries of diaspora are thus multiple and the aspirations of diaspora Muslims diverse and often conflictual.[2]

The women of Al-Masoom did not ask for money from the British state. On the contrary, they demanded that fellow Pakistanis donate money to Islamic transnational causes. By avoiding the kind of dependence politics in which many ethnic organisations are enmeshed, they succeeded in capturing the moral high ground and thus opened up a space for women as equal actors in the public domain. Nevertheless, their public status remained precarious. They occupied the boundary zone where Islam, nationalism, feminist activism and popular culture meet; but whereas their political voice could ring out loud and clear, their femininity and sexuality remained closely guarded. Their celebrations and parties, in which the women danced sensuously, expressed their sexuality and joked and clowned, satirising men and celebrating romantic love, were closed to men. Yet it is precisely this conjuncture of the popular and the religious, the patriotic, feminist and humanitarian, the civic and the private, which has enabled the women to forge their own distinctive Muslim political imaginary of maternal and feminine – as well as feminist – politics.

Conclusion: the Power of Political Motherhood

Philanthropic women's organisations and motherist movements are often mocked as being collusive in the perpetuation of capitalism and patriarchal oppression. Such a view denies the impact such movements can have on the state and its legal system. Although often espousing piecemeal reform rather than revolution, historically the impact of political motherhood both on women's consciousness and on the law has been, cumulatively, quite revolutionary. Many welfare-oriented reforms in Victorian England preceded women's suffrage: the Children's Act, the age of consent, licensing rules, access to education, married women's right to own property, to divorce and to child guardianship, work laws, maternity allowances, and a host of other legal reforms.[3] Women have been in the forefront of peace and democratisation movements. This chapter has spelled out some of the synergies between the fight for suffrage or democracy and the struggle for social and civic rights. In some of the cases presented here, women have been concerned with the plight of impoverished or violated others. In other cases, the attack on women's own immediate families created the basis for a wider solidarity. Either way, women translated their compassion into ideological agendas articulated in the public sphere.

In general it may be said, as far as women's citizenship is concerned, that the battle for social citizenship has complemented and reinforced the battle for political and civic rights rather than succeeded it. This has led Walby to critique Marshall's evolutionary model of citizenship rights (from civic to political to social) for ignoring women's and minorities' tortuous route to full citizenship (Walby 1994). The circuitousness of this passage is even truer of the postcolonial world in which women have often had to struggle alongside men for fundamental national, democratic and economic rights, and against them on issues of family violence and economic exploitation. Above all, they have had to fight everywhere to gain a legitimate and authoritative voice in the political community and its public sphere, and to sustain it, once democracy is restored (see Jaquette 1994 and Vargas and Olea, in Chapter 15 of this volume, on this challenge in Latin America).

It is impossible, I have suggested, to separate women's struggle on behalf of oppressed others, immiserated by poverty, illness or hunger, or on behalf of their own families, husbands, fathers and sons, from women's 'rights' struggle for human rights, individual equality and personal liberty. Writing about Turkish women and the rise of a feminist Islamism, Nilüfer Göle evokes Toqueville's view that

> Democracy is fuelled by the 'passion for equality' ... rather than by the phenomenon of equality. In other words, society aims to transcend and change itself depending upon egalitarian utopias. (Göle 1996: 52)

So too, Chantal Mouffe cites Toqueville to argue that

> Once begun, the democratic revolution has had, necessarily, to undermine all forms of power and domination, wherever they might be. (Mouffe 1988)

Benedict Anderson writes about the independence movements in the Americas that they became as soon as they were printed about, 'concepts', 'models' and indeed 'blueprints' which ultimately challenged entrenched institutions, such as slavery, even if this was not the original intent of the Creole nationalists (Anderson 1983: 81, see also 80, 49).

The power of motherist peace or philanthropic movements is, first, that the women who lead them capture the moral high ground by virtue of their public display of compassion, generosity and a sense of justice. Second, their mixed agendas and embeddedness in local traditions enable them to mobilise ordinary women on a vast scale. Third, they attain a measure of autonomy and influence through their fund-raising activities or through international support from women's networks. Perhaps most important of all, such women dare to cross class boundaries to acquaint themselves personally with the sufferings of women and children (and sometimes men) beyond their everyday world. All these factors increase their ability to influence a male-dominated public sphere and, as I have argued here, to introduce new values of legitimate authority into the public domain.

Political motherhood in postcolonial nation-states has to be understood, this chapter has shown, as a process of discovery rather than a specific feminist movement or intellectual 'approach'. It draws on a hybridised variety of quite disparate discourses, some of them close to first-wave feminism, others quite contemporary and radical; some exclusive, others encompassing men too. Chantal Mouffe has argued that

> the subjectivity of a given social agent is always precariously and provisionally fixed or, to use the Lacanian term, sutured at the intersection of various discourses. (Mouffe 1988: 90)

It is the generation of a 'totalising effect' from this discursive hybridity that allows the establishment of a

> chain of equivalence among the different democratic struggles so as to create an equivalent articulation between the demands of women, blacks, workers, gays and others. (Mouffe 1993: 77)

The 'identity' of citizenship arises from a political subject's positioned interpretation of the principles of democracy (liberty, equality). A radical democratic vision stresses 'the numerous social relations in which situations of domination exist that must be challenged if the principles of liberty and equality are to apply' (*ibid.*: 84).

Like other post-liberal feminists such as Dietz (1992) or Phillips (1991, 1995), Mouffe thus stresses the principle of diversity in equality, or 'differential universalism' (Lister 1997: 39), while arguing for a kind of constitutional patriotism (Habermas 1994: 135). Historically, the principle of equality was interpreted so as to exclude women, defined as essentially different, from the public sphere. At the same time, liberalism's espousal of freedom of association and freedom of the press enabled women (and some men), first in Britain and the US and later in colonial and postcolonial nations, to organise to challenge this false universalism. It can be said, then, that along with the stress on the autonomous individual, liberalism in its Anglo-Saxon version also, from the very start, advocated the value of social diversity as against homogeneity, and denied the possibility of an encompassing definition of a single 'common good'. It was, as Taylor has argued, 'procedural' rather than substantive (1992). But the historical paradox of modernity, namely, the reification of women as 'private' at the very moment of male emancipation, and more recent tensions between welfare protection and equal rights feminist activists, have highlighted the *rhetorical* need to stress that equality is not tantamount to a denial of social difference. It is a rhetoric directed against an understanding of 'the universalism of basic rights as an abstract levelling of distinctions, a levelling of both cultural and social differences' (Habermas 1994: 116). On the contrary, Habermas argues, the need is to increase the subtlety of context-specific protective legislation in order to recognise difference without thereby generating new forms of discrimination (*ibid.*: 114–16).

The feminisation of citizenship discussed in this chapter has for the most part not been achieved by women intending from the start to reform the basic liberal-democratic institutions of the political community. But in the course of their particular campaigns as women, mothers and conscientious or pious subjects, they have radically transformed the interpretation of universalism, human rights and the kind of human qualities and sentimental passions fundamental to citizenship and to the legitimate authority of the political community.

Notes

1. All three were members of the British Labour Party and all were representatives of constituencies with relatively large Asian populations.
2. In this sense my interpretation of diaspora is radically in disagreement with Anthias (1998) – who argues that the notion of diaspora precludes cross-ethnic and other transversal alliances.
3. For excellent surveys of a literature addressing the relation between maternalism, gender and the welfare state see Ross (1995) and Bursh (1996). Bursh raises the interesting question as to whether maternalism is not a 'feminism for hard times' which arises in response to an anti-feminist backlash (1996: 431). Her sceptical conclusion is that maternalism has not worked but may work if mixed with a broader agenda for citizens, workers and sexual autonomy (1996: 453–4).

References

Anderson, Benedict (1983). *Imagined Communities,* London: Verso.

Anthias, Floya (1998). 'Evaluating Diaspora: Beyond Ethnicity', in *Sociology*, 32, 3 (August): 557–80.

Anthias, Floya and Nira Yuval-Davis (1992). *Racialised Boundaries: Race, Nation, Gender, Colour and Class and the Anti-Racist Struggle*, London: Routledge.

Azmon, Yael (1997). 'War, Mothers, and a Girl with Braids: Involvement of Mothers' Peace Movements in the National Discourse in Israel', *ISSR: Israel Social Science Journal*, 12 1: 109–28.

Badran, Margot (1991). 'Competing Agenda: Feminists, Islam and the State in 19th and 20th Century Egypt', in Deniz Kandiyoti (ed.) *Women, Islam and the State*, London: Macmillan, pp. 201–36.

Banks, Olive (1981). *Faces of Feminism: a Study of Feminism as a Social Movement*, Oxford: Martin Robertson.

Basu, Amrita (1995). 'Introduction', in Amrita Basu (ed.) *The Challenge of Local Feminists: Women's Movements in Global Perspective*, Boulder, Colorado: Westview Press, pp. 1–24.

Benhabib, Seyla (1992). *Situating the Self: Gender, Community and Postmodernism in Contemporary Ethics*, Cambridge: Polity Press.

Bourdieu, Pierre (1985). 'The Social Space and the Genesis of Groups', *Theory and Society* 14: 723–44.

Bursh, Lisa D. (1996). 'Love, Toil and Trouble: Motherhood and Feminist Politics', *Signs: Journal of Women in Culture and Society* 21, 2: 429–54.

Caplan, Patricia (1985). *Class and Gender in India: Women and Their Organisations in a South Indian City*, London: Tavistock.

Charles, Nickie and Helen Hintjens (1998). 'Gender, Ethnicity and Cultural Identity: Women's "Places"', in Nickie Charles and Helen Hintjens (eds) *Gender, Ethnicity and Political Ideologies*, London: Routledge, pp. 1–26.

Dietz, Mary (1992). 'Context Is All: Feminism and Theories of Citizenship', in Chantal Mouffe (ed.) *Dimensions of Radical Democracy: Pluralism, Citizenship, Community*, London: Verso, pp. 63–88.

Eisenstein, Zillah R. (1981). *The Radical Future of Liberal Feminism*, New York and London: Longman.

Emmett, Ayala (1996). *Our Sisters' Promised Land: Women, Politics, and Israeli-Palestinian Coexistence*, Ann Arbor, Michigan: University of Michigan Press.

Everett, J. M. (1979). *Women and Social Change in India*, Delhi.

Gabriel, Ayala H. (1992). 'Grief and Rage: Collective Emotions in the Politics of Peace and the Politics of Gender in Israel', *Culture Medicine and Psychiatry* 16: 311–35.

Gilligan, Carol (1982). *In a Different Voice: Psychological Theory and Women's Development*, Cambridge, Mass: Harvard University Press.

Göle, Nilüfer (1996). *The Forbidden Modern: Civilisation and Veiling*, Ann Arbor, Michigan: University of Michigan Press.

Habermas, Jurgen (1989). [1962] *The Structural Transformation of the Public Sphere*, trans. Thomas Burger with the assistance of Frederick Lawrence, Cambridge, Mass: MIT Press.

— (1994). 'Struggles for Recognition in the Democratic Constitutional State', in Amy

Gutmann (ed.) *Multiculturalism: Examining the Politics of Recognition*, Princeton NJ: Princeton University Press, pp. 107–48.

Jad, Isla (1995). 'Claiming Feminism, Claiming Nationalism: Women's Activism in the Occupied Territories', in Amrita Basu (ed.) *The Challenge of Local Feminists: Women's Movements in Global Perspective*, Boulder, CO: Westview Press, pp. 226–48.

Jahan, Roushan (1995). 'Men in Seclusion, Women in Public: Rokeya's Dream and Women's Struggles in Bangladesh', in Amrita Basu (ed.) *The Challenge of Local Feminists: Women's Movements in Global Perspective*, Boulder, CO: Westview Press, pp. 87–109.

Jalal, Ayesha (1991). 'The Convenience of Subservience: Women and the State in Pakistan', in Deniz Kandiyoti (ed.) *Women, Islam and the State*, London: Macmillan, pp. 77–114.

Jaquette, Jane S. (1994). *The Women's Movement in Latin America: Participation and Democracy*, 2nd edition, Boulder CO: Westwood Press.

Jayawardena, Kumari (1986). *Feminism and Nationalism in the Third World*, London: Zed Books.

Johnson-Odim, Cheryl (1991). 'Common Themes, Different Contexts: Third World Women and Feminism', in Chandra T. Mohanty, Ann Russo and Lourdes Torres (eds) *Third World Women and the Politics of Feminism*, Bloomington: Indiana University Press. pp. 298–313.

Kandiyoti, Deniz (ed.) (1991). 'Introduction', in *Women, Islam and the State,* London: Macmillan, 1991.

Kaplan, T. (1982). 'Female Consciousness and Collective Action: the Case of Barcelona 1910–1918', *Signs* 7, 3: 545–66.

Kumar, Radha (1995). 'From Chipko to Sati: the Contemporary Indian Women's Movement', in Amrita Basu (ed.) *The Challenge of Local Feminists: Women's Movements in Global Perspective*, Boulder, CO: Westview Press, pp. 58–86.

Lister, Ruth (1997). 'Citizenship: Towards a Feminist Synthesis', Special Issue on 'Citizenship: Pushing the Boundaries', *Feminist Review* 57: 28–48.

Lyon, Wenonah (1995). 'Islam and Islamic Women in Britain', *Women: a Cultural Review* 6, 1: 46–56.

Mayer, Tamar (ed.) (1994). *Women and the Israeli Occupation: the Politics of Change*, London: Routledge.

Mazumdar, Vina (1976). 'The Social Reform Movement in India from Ranade to Nehru', in B. R. Nanda (ed.) *Indian Women from Purdah to Modernity*, New Delhi: Vikas Publishing House.

Mies, Maria (1980). *Indian Women and Patriarchy*, New Delhi: Vikas.

Molyneux, M. (1985). 'Mobilisation without Emancipation? Women's Interests, the State and the Revolution in Nicaragua', *Feminist Studies* 11, 2: 227–54.

Mouffe, Chantal (1988). 'Hegemony and New Political Subjects: Towards a New Concept of Democracy', in Cary Nelson and Lawrence Grossberg (eds) *From Marxism to the Interpretation of Culture*, Urbana: University of Illinois Press, pp. 89–103.

— (1993). *The Return of the Political*, London: Verso.

Mumtaz, Khawar and Farida Shaheed (1987). *Women of Pakistan*, Lahore: Vanguard.

Okin, Susan Moller (1989). *Justice, Gender and the Family*, New York: Basic Books.

Phillips, Anne (1991). *Engendering Democracy*, Cambridge: Polity Press.

— (1995). 'Democracy and Difference: Some Problems for Feminist Theory', in Will

Kymlicka (ed.) *The Rights of Minority Cultures*, Oxford: Oxford University Press, pp. 288–99.

Prochaska, F. K. (1980). *Women and Philanthropy in Nineteenth-Century England*, Oxford: Clarendon Press.

Radcliffe, Sarah and Sallie Westwood (1996). *Remaking the Nation: Place, Identity and Politics in Latin America,* London: Routledge.

Ricoeur, Paul (1981). *Hermeneutics and the Human Sciences*, Cambridge: Cambridge University Press.

Ross, Ellen (1995). 'New Thought on "The Oldest Vocation": Mothers and Motherhood in Recent Feminist Scholarship', *Signs: Journal of Women in Culture and Society* 20, 2: 397–413.

Ruddick, Sara (1989). *Maternal Thinking: Towards a Politics of Peace*, London: the Women's Press.

Said, Edward W. (1983). 'Travelling Theory', in *The World, the Text, the Critique,* London: Vintage.

Schirmer, Jennifer (1993). 'The Seeking of Truth and the Gendering of Consciousness: the COMADRES of El Salvador and the Conavigua Widows of Guatemala', in Sarah A. Radcliffe and Sallie Westwood (eds) *'Viva': Women and Popular Protest in Latin America,* London: Routledge.

Scott, Joan Wallache (1996). *Only Paradoxes to Offer: French Feminists and the Rights of Man*, Cambridge, Mass: Harvard University Press.

Sombart, Werner (1967). [1913] *Luxury and Capitalism*, Ann Arbor: University of Michigan Press.

Spivak, Gayatri Chakravorty (1987). *In Other Worlds: Essays on Cultural Politics*, New York: Methuen.

Stephen, Lynn (1995). 'Women's Rights Are Human Rights: the Merging of Feminine and Feminist Interests among El Salvador's Mothers of the Disappeared (COMADRES)', *American Ethnologist* 22, 4: 807–27.

Taylor, Charles (1992). *Multiculturalism and the Politics of Recognition*, Princeton NJ: Princeton University Press.

Walby, Sylvia (1990). *Theorizing Patriarchy*, Oxford: Basil Blackwell.

— (1994). 'Is Citizenship Gendered?' *Sociology* 28, 2: 379–96.

Werbner, Pnina (1990). *The Migration Process: Capital, Gifts and Offerings among British Pakistanis*, Oxford: Berg.

— (1991). 'Factionalism and Violence in British Pakistani Politics', in Hastings Donnan and Pnina Werbner (eds) *Economy and Culture in Pakistan,* London: Macmillan, pp. 188–211.

— (1996). 'Fun Spaces: On Identity and Social Empowerment among British Pakistanis', *Theory, Culture and Society* 13, 4: 53–79.

— (1998). 'Diasporic Political Imaginaries: a Sphere of Freedom or a Sphere of Illusion?', *Communal Plural: Journal of Transnational and Crosscultural Studies* 6, 1: 11–32.

Yuval-Davis, Nira (1993). 'Gender and Nation', *Ethnic and Racial Studies* 16, 4: 621–32.

— (1997). *Gender and Nation*, London: Sage Publications.

CHAPTER 15

An Agenda of One's Own: The Tribulations of the Peruvian Feminist Movement

Virginia Vargas and Cecilia Olea

In recent decades women's movements promoting feminist perspectives have contributed to democracy by making visible processes of inclusion and exclusion – both within states, and in society more generally. The scenario in which most of the struggles, experiences, forms of resistance and proposals have taken place, however, has changed dramatically.

Processes of globalisation have impacted differently at regional and local levels. Although increasingly interrelated, their economic consequences have been most alarming locally. The restructuring of the world economy in ways that privilege the market over and against the citizen has resulted in serious social exclusions at all levels and the weakening of state control and its leadership role. At the same time these processes have also created a new dynamics leading to greater democratic connections and articulations between the global and local spheres. One of the main effects of the technological revolution has been a broadening of the basis of citizenship for both men and women.

The dramatic global changes during the 1990s have also led to a radical transformation in the lives of women: in their organisations, in their theoretical orientations, in the nature of their struggles and also in the ways in which they negotiate their interests. The period has witnessed the energetic expression of a variety of voices and interests traditionally excluded even from the movements themselves. The certainties of the women's movement in the 1980s regarding the changes needed to combat gender oppression in the public and private spheres have been replaced by uncertainty and introspection. The tendency now is to question grand utopias, to be more realistic, and to connect the movement's struggles and practices with other transformational tendencies within democratic civil societies.

These developments have brought about changes in the emphasis such movements accord to certain areas of activity. One of the most difficult and evident of these is the acknowledgement of the theoretical, epistemological and political complexities implied by individual and collective 'difference'. This is an aspect of feminist and other struggles which has come to be critical for reflection and action. The rediscovery of the global sphere as an arena for struggle, alongside the rediscovery of the historically internationalist character of the movement, are further examples of the changes occurring in this period. The appropriation of the United Nations world conferences by the women's movement, especially the 1995 women's conference in Beijing, have made a fundamental contribution to the evolution of a broader, trans-national and international public sphere.

There is also a change in the emphasis on and selection of issues around which mobilisation occurs. Democracy and citizenship now appear as the main axes of articulation for present struggles. There are various reasons for this. The most obvious is the recognition that political authoritarianism restricts women's self-expression and, with it, the possibility of building alternatives for the transformation of the social order. Democracy continues to be the best arena for the development of diversity, negotiation of different interests and the making visible of inequalities. With respect to this last point, democracy allows an exposure of inequalities including those of power, class, race, ethnicity, age, disability and sexual options. Democracy continues to be the best weapon against continual attacks by fundamentalist and conservative forces threatening advances made by women.

Citizenship encompasses many of the contradictions and tensions in current political and feminist thought; in particular, the tension between the universality of rights and cultural pluralism, individual and collective rights, the principle of equality and the right to be different. On the other hand, the struggle to change a restricted or passive citizenship into a more active one raises the issue of what kind of citizenship we want. Is our goal a 'male' model of citizenship? Or are we adopting a far more flexible notion that encompasses different dimensions – the rights and advances that women and other actors have achieved and strengthened in these last decades? In addition, for women, the concept of citizenship contains three important and interrelated characteristics.

First, it allows us to view successful demands and advances not as the product of the goodwill of governments but as a right (Fraser and Gordon 1992). This raises major new questions concerning how we should express demands for sexual rights, for example. In the same spirit, we have reached a new recognition that the poverty that affects women does not imply welfare-ism but is a matter of economic justice and therefore of social citizenship.

Second, the concept of citizenship allows for a reciprocal recognition of rights and responsibilities as a fundamental basis for democracy. Hence citizenship can articulate our struggles with those that other democratic movements are developing against any form of exclusion. Citizenship, together with solidarity, can provide the basis for equality among different actors.

Another important emphasis relates to the instruments of change. Without neglecting the micro level, the democratisation of daily life and of intimate relations, the women's movement has strengthened both its ability to make proposals and to be present at the state level as well. This has been achieved, as Anne Phillips (1994: 94) proposes, by appointing women representatives in the political community, by exploring the societal processes of inclusion and exclusion, and by subjecting the universalistic pretensions of modern political thought to scrutiny and criticism. In this manner women open – every day – a wider space for the construction of a different kind of citizenship, thus enriching democracy – democracy in the home and in the bed, as the Chilean women say, and also, as Beijing showed us, in global spaces.

In the following pages we examine the challenges of the movement as revealed by the particular case of Peruvian feminism.

The Tribulations of Building an Agenda of Our Own

Fifty years ago, Simone de Beauvoir argued that the recent discovery of contraceptives implied a fundamental revolution in women's lives. Even if some women were not interested in their use, the very fact of their existence ended the 'physiological fatalism' of maternity: since women were no longer fated to be mothers, they would have to look for new ways of being. This search for additional destinies has shaped our generation. Fifty years after this discovery, and close to the beginning of a new century, important new trends appear.

In the last thirty years we have been witnesses as well as actors in the development of one of the most powerful and significant social movements of this century: the women's and feminist movement. This movement – and many others that are looking for additional ways to overcome exclusion, marginalisation and the tyranny of dominant sexual norms – has given rise to what José Nun has called 'the rebellion of the chorus': of those speaking when they should not, escaping from the place where the chorus should be, placing themselves centre stage and demanding to be heard. The women's liberation movement, says Nun, is the symbol of this rebellion (Nun 1989: 3).

The achievements of the women's movement in Peru have been obvious. We have changed commonsense assumptions, gaining strength and visibility. We have also struggled for laws that acknowledge women's citizenship. Our main achievement has been to make evident that relations of inclusion/exclusion are the organising principles of power within our society.

Old and New 'Knots'

'Knots' represent the contradictory development of the movement. We can try to eliminate them with a sword, as Alexander the Great did with the Gordian knot, putting an end to any search or discussion. We can also try to disentangle them, separating the threads, looking for the ends, following their interwoven strands. Through feminist knots we shape feminist politics (Kirkwood 1985: 62).

What Is the Feminist Movement in Peru Now?

The feminist movement in Peru has been one of the most visible and developed in the region. Its development has resembled those elsewhere: it has gradually become pluralistic, going beyond, as Sonia Alvarez (1998) says, the space called 'autonomy' to install itself in multiple spaces: the academy, popular culture, public institutions, high culture and the mass media. The two other original streams with which second-wave feminism developed and interacted – rebellious mothers and women in the official political arena – have become more complex and have enhanced the recognition, weak in the past, of women's subordinate condition and of their demand for full citizenship rights. New streams have also developed, expressing for the very first time the multicultural and multi-ethnic character of Peruvian society: peasant women, indigenous women and *ronderas* (women defending the community against terrorist assault) have started to gain visibility. They are also impacting on the old streams, which are more urban, and tended in the past to have a low awareness of the country's ethnic and cultural diversity even when they incorporated this same diversity.

Out of all these different streams and spaces, our analysis will focus on the modifications of strategies and sites of action of the original feminist stream, which has preserved a separate existence and a certain sense of belonging to what is considered the historical feminist core. This stream, the feminism articulated since the late 1970s, has been the visible face of feminism in Peru. It locates itself historically within the broad spectrum of the left, confronting and questioning not only anti-democratic gender arrangements but the partial and exclusive ways in which Peruvian democracy has developed. It is basically, but not exclusively, an urban movement, largely middle-class, having strong links to grassroots women's movements forged at a time when both were strong and visible, before terrorists assassinated their best-known leaders and before the country itself was paralysed by terror. It has also been a pluralistic movement, with differences, diverse degrees of confrontation and competitiveness, but with no great conflicts, ruptures, or substantial changes in orientation. At present the tendency towards fragmentation, the legacy of years of terror, is being overcome in different ways and with different strategies.

Feminism has also waged significant battles against the Fujimori government over such political personal issues as his use and abuse of presidential power in his relations with his wife. Fujimori's government – authoritarian proponent of neoliberal politics, violator of human rights (including women's reproductive rights due to its sterilisation-oriented policy) – has designated more women ministers than any other in history, has generated a greater institutionalisation around women (the Ministry of Women, amongst others), and more legislation for the defence of women's rights.

For publicly self-declared feminists to concentrate on democracy and citizenship as their fundamental line of action has meant a double strategy. On the one hand, they have attempted to broaden the negotiating space with government and to negotiate specific issues fundamental to women. On the other hand, they have aimed to create spaces of democratic confluence with other women, such as the recently created Women for Democracy alliance. On 8 March 1998 feminists and women from various political parties and the parliamentary opposition, from trade unions and popular women's organisations, organised a national march for the defence of democracy, demanding a referendum on the issue of Fujimori's attempt to stand for re-election for the third time. The emphasis each of these groups places on aspects of a shared orientation highlights the differences within feminism. These are sharpened at present because many issues remain implicit. Thus the current knot, related to feminist autonomy, is plagued by tensions arising from our attempt to preserve a radical questioning feminism while negotiating with an authoritarian government.

There have been many achievements of Peruvian feminism in these two decades of its existence. Not only are we beneficiaries of historic changes – the access of women to education, to the universities, to the use of contraceptives – themselves resulting from the modernisation of the country. The confrontational strategies adopted by feminism have also been fruitful: they are reflected in legislation, in a new institutionalisation around women's concerns, as well as in modifications of traditional commonsense views regarding the division between the sexes, and particularly towards women as 'worthy' of rights.

Different actors emerge from civil society in defence of human rights and citizenship agendas – from peri-urban settlements, the mass media, the university and the culture industries. Feminism has a greater presence in the struggles for human and citizenship rights, and in relation to women from the popular sectors, but less influence on women working in the mass media, culture industries and youth.

The presence of women leaders in different social and political fields is undoubtedly important as they make visible women's demands, thus widening democracy. It is also true that being a woman is not a guarantee of thinking like a woman (as obvious cases show). By 'thinking like a woman' we mean – essentialism aside – a will to democracy that includes women as full citizens, acknowledging their rights and diversity at all levels. With such women it is possible to build a 'critical mass' to ensure sustained and permanent activity.

All this means that 'women's issues' are already established in the public domain, but this achievement is now placed in a different context than that which gave rise to it. New situations and strategies also result in certain 'knots' and tensions within the movement that need to be explored. Hence, the feminist movement is going through a process of transition, looking for forms that might express the multiple changes of the present period. This process presents us with many challenges: how to extend the feminist project to other democratic sectors of society? How to restore the political quality of gender relations? How to maintain dialogue and negotiation with the state, while avoiding fragmentary and *ad hoc* responses and cooption?

We are particularly interested in the analysis of one of these challenges: that is – as Feijóo puts it – how to preserve radical thought and feminist action at the same time that we enlarge our democratic alliances by actively involving ourselves in political and governmental bodies in order to negotiate a women's agenda (Feijóo 1995). This challenge generates many knots, in which are entangled the new meaning of autonomy, ways of relating to the state and women's ways of being political.

In setting an agenda, we need to recognise the fact that the long road towards political autonomy cannot be kept apart from a concern with physical, economic and sociocultural policies, even if these appear to be separate. Nor can we lose sight of the fact that in a country as racist, centralised and male-chauvinist as Peru some dimensions of individual autonomy – economic and even sociocultural – are harder to achieve.

Autonomy

We start with political autonomy which – always a complex concept and practice – continues to provide the parameters for alliances and negotiations with the state and wider society. The strategy of preserving autonomy has allowed the movement to shape its boundaries, to form an identity and from this position, as José Nun has put it, to 'demand to be heard' (Nun 1989: 3).

The beginnings of the autonomy process within the Peruvian movement were part of the learning process of recognising ourselves in a feminist 'key'. Considered in relation to political parties, this strategy of autonomy was undoubtedly defensive. But it was also justifiable and necessary in the process of learning how to assert a public presence without depending on external institutional support, and thus to assume the right to exist and develop independently as a movement

The pursuit of identity politics – so powerful during this period – was a key element within social movements, including the feminist one. It was fundamental in shaping political autonomy since it inaugurated the right to exist out of difference itself. It also helped to make visible the private realm, thus challenging homogenising visions of our condition. In spite of this, as Jodi Dean says, identity politics can limit democracy because it expresses and responds to predetermined demands without necessarily considering the multiple connections people establish in constructing their relations. As such, it is an obstacle to the understanding of politics as the art of living in a community.

Autonomy is not a static political principle, nor a fixed datum of reality, but a flexible and dynamic concept, as it should be within a vital movement conscious of changing economic, political and sociocultural conditions. The context within which autonomy has been exercised has changed dramatically over time. The autonomy of the early movement – undergoing the process of forming a distinctive identity, seeking a language of its own, having limited negotiations with the state and in serious tension with political parties – was completely different from that of the present movement, commanding a whole universe of interrelations and a variety of interests. This present movement has more flexible identities and new relations with the state, achieved mainly through the experience of negotiating at national and global levels. That process opened up new discourses and possibilities of action as well as the need to build alliances with other 'autonomies'. Autonomy, more than ever, confronts us with the tension between freedom and responsibility. For this reason it is an essential principle in learning whom to negotiate with, and when. It is also a privileged domain for the exercise of democracy. It is, therefore, difficult to define autonomy solely as defence of one's own discourse and practice.

The question is how to understand autonomy at a time in which the movement's boundaries are diffuse and when the multiple identities of women question the validity of a single gender identity. Feminism built its autonomy on the basis of a strong political identity as a movement that questioned existing gender arrangements. Advances in the understanding of the complexities of women's lives, and the multiple interrelations contained in 'gender', add more elements and intricacy to this identity.

From an identity of 'resistance', necessary at that time, there are new notes within the feminist project that include not only a generic identity but, in the words of Castells (1997), 'identity as a project'. In this way, and within the perspective of identity as project, the movement's autonomy is built on the tension between identity and rationality. We struggle and act to make visible the exclusion of women and to transform power relations – including gender arrangements – not from a closed identity but from one open to conflict and negotiation. In this way, we organise proposals for social transformation. Rationality, in this case, lies in a democratic construction that can contain human passions and subjectivity. In these terms, identity can be understood as a principle of change in the relations of exclusion.

From such a position, and following Held (1995), the principle of autonomy can be seen to lie at the very heart of the liberal-democratic project for modernity, a project concerned with people's capacity to determine and to justify their own actions, with their ability to choose among alternative political programmes, and with the need to create parameters that can shape the democratic process. In line with Held we argue that governments are entrusted with the capacities of the state only to the extent that they uphold the rule of law which guarantees, protects and improves the autonomy of citizens. If these ends are systematically violated by the authorities their legal status can be put into question or even confronted by citizens. Conversely, to the extent that these ends are denied or boycotted by citizens they become opponents of the existing democratic culture. A legally democratic state is a condition for democracy but it is not the only guarantee for it. A 'democratic will' and a democratic culture are essential.

There are two main ideas in this conception of autonomy: people's self-determination, and the existence of limited government that can exercise a legally defined structure of power. Held concludes that this form of autonomy can be considered democratic autonomy – including the requirement of responsibility – in relation not only to the state but to civil society as well. This process of building autonomy relates both to feminist movements and/or agendas and to those of others involved in the building of a democratic civil society – one that includes alternative actors.

Feminist Politics

The Peruvian feminist movement's contribution to politics is due, in part, to its mere existence. This expressed a confrontation over the distribution of power in society, and denunciation of gender arrangements and of the primacy of a male perspective in all aspects of political and personal life. It implied a demand for the democratisation of personal relations and the questioning of an existing division between the public and the private, which relegated women to the family or, even when they participated in political organisations, to welfare roles. It was expressed in the mobilisations, struggles, and theoretical reflections referred to in the first section of this chapter. 'The personal is political' summarised this particular approach to politics – the construction of the private realm as a means to social change.

Recently the movement's politics has witnessed significant changes. We have already overcome the 'essentialist self-satisfaction' implied by an identity politics that assumes that 'feminists do politics differently': that women are more ethical than men, more democratic. But some of this remains. One example is the consideration of feminism as a 'politics of women for women', denying the benefits of gender equality for society and democracy, with the consequent risk of isolating the achievements made from other, more global transformations.

What is implied by the prioritisation of building democracy? Not simply the potential contribution of women as political actors, since all the various movements aim to achieve this, from an ethnic, racial, sexual, or generational perspective. It implies taking on, from an autonomous perspective, the role of criticising and modifying a national politics that does not respond to women's claims for citizenship. Following Dietz, we need also to affirm that the political concern of feminists is not restricted to familial issues but is more broadly oriented to who determines ends, and how (Dietz 1994).

This goes along with another growing concern in recent years, which is to demand – together with other social actors – new ways of doing politics. As Giddens suggests, it is essential to reinvent democracy: to establish new rules of the game for political struggle. This implies changing existing rules to take into consideration new issues and actors, both in civil society and the state (Giddens 1994).

The new rules are based on mutual responsibilities. The state has the responsibility of guaranteeing rights and their enforcement. From the perspective of rights and duties, civil society and social movements are responsible for putting in question anti-democratic arrangements, exposing them to public debate. Beyond that, our aim is to widen the application of rights, to defend them, and to create pressure to establish public policies and legitimate new rights. Civil society is the realm where passive citizenship turns into active citizenship, which includes the civic virtue of responsibility.

This perspective implies at least one requirement basic in any advance: democratic institutionalisation. A more profound level of institutional life in the country would support dialogue and negotiation and, in particular, respect for agreements reached. This condition can only be met through democratic institutions and movements with the capacity to establish mechanisms of accountability, and introduce political proposals shaping a public agenda. The state needs not only strong but democratic institutions, independent of passing or particularistic interests.

How Is This Expressed at Present?

As mentioned already, the feminist movement arrived on this new scene significantly changed, internally and externally. Not only have some of the basic demands for women's political participation been achieved – more women in decision-making processes, quota systems, new institutions for women's issues. There has also been a modification in the movement's mode of existence and manner of expression. Historically, as mentioned, feminist organisations adopted a 'double mode of existence', as feminist workplaces and as feminist movements. This implied a considerable audacity, which supplied the movement's spontaneity, mobilisational effect, and basis for production of knowledge and agendas. This initial audacity, however, appears to have been replaced by a more effective mode of existence in the shape of feminist non-governmental organisations (NGOs). Sonia Alvarez ironically calls this the 'ngoisation' of the feminist movement (Alvarez 1997). In this transformation the movement lost much of the flavour of the creative, the audacious, the irreverent forms of mobilisation, and of visibility as a movement, without really knowing how – in feminist terms – both to make ourselves visible and to negotiate our proposals within this new scenario.

The search for new forms of existence and new alliances has also come into collision with the 'disenchantment' and fragmentation of democratic civil society, and with lack of experience in addressing an authoritarian state. At present governmental authoritarianism in Peru exceeds the imagination, which is why some analysts have characterised the country as a 'dictatorship'; a semi-closed authoritarian government has concentrated power at the executive level, controlling with relative success other state sectors, with no reference to citizens. But it is still a government that allows political opposition.

In intervening in public policy the movement has used different strategies such as pressure, confrontation, and negotiation. The market-oriented perspective of efficiency and cooperation has also influenced the movement's strategies and the manner of its engagement with the state. Negotiations, alliances and appeals are undoubtedly good for democracy. But, as Pringle and Watson (1994) argue, these can be risky if there are no clear answers to the questions of *how, in what terms, with which tactics, with which results* such strategies towards the state – given an unequal relationship of power – are devised.

Recent research by Rosa Maria Alfaro about the ways in which feminist NGOs relate to the government supports this view. She concludes that these relationships are discontinuous and lacking in stability. The NGOs have no strategic alliances and they are not based on autonomous proposals generated by the organisations: the positions they take up are thus dispersed around themes emanating from the state (Alfaro 1997).

This places the movement on difficult ground. The terms of the relation are determined by one side – that of the state – without any clear intervention from civil society. Under these conditions, sectoral support could mean that the movement is legitimating much more than it really intends – for example, an authoritarian government.

Clearly, then, the movement is searching for autonomous and positive positions from which to approach public authorities. From a perspective of rights, one of the main new issues that the movement is claiming is *citizenship*, asking itself how to avoid Wollstonecraft's dilemma, as pointed out by Carole Pateman (1988): that to demand equality is to accept the patriarchal conception of citizenship, which implies that women should be like men; whilst to insist on the recognition of women's characteristics, capacities and activities is to demand the impossible, because this is precisely what patriarchal citizenship excludes (on this see Mouffe 1996: 9).

The challenge of overcoming this dilemma is nonetheless attractive and promising, because even though citizenship can be seen as what Carlos Franco (1997) calls 'a true lie', it is not only a goal but provides a 'space of democratic dispute', where it is possible to incorporate more flexible and subversive models, based on what women and other excluded actors have discovered and conquered. Citizenship currently appears as a space of dispute partly because of its restricted, partial, exclusive character, and partly because of attempts by those excluded to demand not only their inclusion but the widening of their rights. It is thus a space of struggle for the political autonomy of the movement in its attempts to incorporate new agendas such as sexual and reproductive rights.

A citizenship perspective provides legitimate grounds for negotiations with public authorities, whose action in relation to women is expressed through new, recently created institutions. The Ministry of Women is a product of this position, though it also answers certain clear political needs of the government (Fujimori was the only president who participated in the Beijing conference, possibly hoping to gain the support of women for his re-election). This is also part of the process of state reform. Theoretically, a gender proposal meshes with this need for reform because 'it demands a horizontal treatment of themes, because it is based on intersectoral patterns, because it demands integrated approaches to reality and contributes to making sense of fragmentary knowledges and views within the state' (Valenzuela 1995: 9–10).

In fact, as we know, capitalist modernisation can lead to either democratic or authoritarian institutionalisation. The democratic outcome is expressed through clear channels for consultation and participation between the state and civil society. That is why important sectors of the movement's demands *vis-à-vis* public institutions are oriented towards two issues: democratic mechanisms and a citizen perspective.

In relation to democratic mechanisms, the main goal is to create institutions that advance processes and policies of decentralisation, and that benefit every woman across the country (taking account of the cultural, ethnic and geographic diversity of Peruvian women). Additionally, the need is for clear rules and mechanisms of accountability, citizen participation in decision making, and modes of monitoring governmental commitments that prioritise investment in justice and democracy.

A citizen perspective is based on the assumption that rights belong to people because they are theirs and not from charity. This perspective implies the participation of civil society in the design, implementation and evaluation of government action, keeping a balance between public and civil powers. Finally, it recognises that civil society's autonomy in relation to the state is what guarantees concrete political, economic and social institutions.

An Agenda of Our Own

Feminist discourse has been partially adopted in official political places, sometimes quite rapidly, as Sonia Alvarez (1998) points out. This does not mean that feminists have been coopted; it means that there has been an adaptation of a part of our discourse – a selective adoption. Some critical feminists note that successive Peruvian governments have failed to take on board our most radical proposals, especially those relating to such matters as sexual rights or alternative parenthood. It is therefore important to stress that a public policy is not a feminist policy. Following Gloria Bonder (1995), we need to recognise that we are not building a governmental agenda; we are building a feminist public policy agenda. This means negotiating from a feminist position in order to influence public policies, anticipating that only parts of our agenda, those that fit government plans, will be adopted. The development of democratic state institutions will greatly influence this process.

What is the relation between the movement and the state's partial agenda? Undoubtedly, some government policies also interest feminists. They allow debate on proposals put forward by the movement a long time ago – quotas, action around reproductive rights, the Ministry of Women itself. Another important factor is that these proposals move from 'basic needs' to real citizenship rights that favour processes of empowerment and autonomy for women through the provision of information, responsiveness to public opinion and the ability to participate in decision making.

In this respect, the movement's agenda continues to develop, on the one hand, because movements cannot give up a democratic agenda which brings more rights to men and women. If, for example, it proposes a quota system as a temporary mechanism, to give women access to public political positions, it is well understood that this measure will not change traditional political structures; that it is only by questioning a sexual division of labour which makes women responsible for the private domain that change will be promoted. On the other hand, while the movement may acknowledge as an advance the adoption by the government of 'reproductive rights', it is aware of the risks inherent in family planning programmes under which an increasing number of women are 'accepting' sterilisation. This constitutes a violation of the right to information, as well as the right to knowledge and self-determination.

It follows that everything related to 'body politics' is central to the present feminist agenda: this includes the struggle for a healthy environment for men and women; the struggle for freedom from violence against women – both at home and in the street, in public and in private; and the struggle not only for the recognition of women's rights as human rights, but also for an acknowledgement that there are no human rights without the presence and defence of women's rights.

A fundamental part of this agenda is the emphasis on economic rights, or social citizenship, that aims at the elimination of the primary cause of inequality. The problem is particularly acute at a time when neoliberal policies dominate the public agenda. The lack of economic justice these imply not only affects the majority of the population – women and men – in all the countries of the region; it also exacerbates current discriminations based on gender, ethnicity, age and other factors. Women continue to be the poorest of the poor and they are the ones with fewest options for coping with this situation.

It is important to remember that an awareness of rights is also a means for fighting against poverty. That is why there is a need to emphasise the construction of social citizenship based on the principle of rights and economic justice. Within this framework the women's movement can develop proposals alongside other democratic sectors, challenging the prevalent idea of competitive individualism as the highest virtue.

The agenda, however, also includes issues and proposals that are less consensual, even within civil society, because they go against traditional religious beliefs and stereotypes. They constitute, therefore, a 'space of dispute' within civil society and in relation to the state. We refer to reproductive rights as expressed in debates on abortion and to sexual rights as expressed in sexual preferences.

The aim of the movement is not to defend abortion as a contraceptive practice; nor to demand its acceptance by society as a whole. Abortion is still, however, a symbol of the current feminine condition because it captures the irrationality of women's subordination as well as their resistance and transgression. On the one hand, it is a symbol of the archaic and dark associations that still surround feminine sexuality; and, on the other hand, it is an expression of resistance, without concessions, to a hypocritical sexuality.

Although these issues are still waiting to be recognised by the state, they have already gained an important place within democratic civil society. Regarding abortion, the discussion has been limited, and it is up to the feminist movement to promote a public debate, looking for dialogue and negotiation both with other actors in civil society and with the state. Regarding sexual preferences, the situation has changed from the years when homosexuality was in the closet; it has been outed by homosexuals and lesbians themselves, exposing their option as a right to be different.

The present agenda of the women's movement also includes attempts to incorporate an active concern for culture. The aim is to generate a permanent interest in understanding, using and working with mass media, and engaging with identifiable decision makers – especially with a new generation of women and men having different aspirations. This younger generation has experienced the achievements already gained by Peruvian women and it has other concerns and forms of expression that are important to acknowledge and to explore.

Finally, our agenda also refers to the international realm, seen not only as a space of dispute but also as a place of global solidarity in which to build global citizenship. Global perspectives are basic in a country used to looking permanently inwards at itself, during the long period of terror and the divisions that terror generated. It is important because it allows for the shaping and widening of civil society's orientations as these become less national and more cosmopolitan.

Towards the New Millennium: Is the Feminist Agenda Adequate?

Most of these dimensions of the feminist agenda are part also of the incomplete processes of modernisation of our country. Where do we position an agenda that explicitly points to the need to extend real political and critical spaces, expressions of opinion and cultural differences? It is hard to answer these questions at this transitional moment from one form of existence to another, from one millennium to another, when the feminist movement is trying to redefine its position and to re-elaborate its utopias while attempts to generate autonomous proposals collide with democratic weakness and an authoritarian political culture.

Perspectives

> [We] need to share knowledge about how the movement expresses itself in a democracy, and to explore the impact of democracy on women's organisations. The movement must start from the assumption of diversity, which recognises the multiple positions of the subject. In this sense, the concept of networks as a new principle of coordinating different expressions has the virtue of not rejecting any of the collective and individual profiles which make up its components. (Molina 1998: 98)

Our agenda is based on acknowledging, from an anti-authoritarian position, a diversity of voices, themes, faces and ethics in relation to the exclusion of women. This is a key point that integrates these different expressions of feminist perspectives with the necessary strengths of an autonomous civil society in the face of an authoritarian regime.

Obviously, a truly democratic view should anticipate that these interrelations also carry within them exclusivist dynamics. This fact highlights the need for a democratic practice within the movement itself, by opening itself up to new actors and expressions in order to avoid creating a closed space.

How can we achieve this when the movement is also going through a process of social division, the product of a transition period as it moves towards new forms of organisation and new agendas? How to advance on the earlier achievements of minimal conditions of citizenship, and in spite of all the advances already made? Theoretically, it is impossible for a movement like the feminist one not to negotiate, here and now, better conditions for women by influencing public policies. To reject this option in the present context of democratic weakness, such as prevails in Peru, is to isolate women's interests and perspectives once again, denying the possibility of interaction across differences in order to modify power relations in the political community.

The first reform needed is constitutional: a strengthening of the 'democratic pole' within civil society. This would diminish the risks of authoritarianism. To achieve this, it is necessary to resist any attempt to separate gender from democracy. Feminist struggles need to forge alliances with democratic forces because this is the only way to resist authoritarianism and because there are common interests shared by women regarding the democracy we aim for. It is also important to define autonomy so as to take account of these democratic alliances in civil society, given that there is a struggle within civil society to encompass diversity.

Feminists have supported this democratic pole with an agenda that is against exclusion and stresses the right to be different. This agenda is also a 'feminist pole' from which the movement can negotiate, put pressure, propose and question anti-democratic practices, both in civil society and in official politics. Through this dynamic we strengthen the construction of democratic voices and spaces, at the same time as we strengthen ourselves as feminists, interacting with other actors in society and asserting a feminist identity aimed at global transformation.

Acknowledgement

This chapter is a shorter version of a longer article that includes a section on the historical development of the Peruvian feminist movement during the last 25 years.

References

Alfaro, Rosa Maria (1997). *Mundos de renovacion y trabas para la accion publica de la mujer* (Worlds of Renovation and Obstacles for the Public Activity of Women), Lima, Peru: Asociacion de Comunicadores Calandria Publications.

Alvarez, Sonia (1997). 'Latin American Feminisms "Go Global": Trends of the 1990s and Challenges for the New Millennium', in Sonia Alvarez, Evelina Dagnino and Arturo Escobar (eds) *Cultures of Politics, Politics of Culture: Revisioning Latin American Social Movements*, Boulder, CO: Westview Press, pp. 293–324.

Beauvoir, Simone de (1997). *The Second Sex*, London: Vintage.

Bonder, Gloria (1995). 'La agenda feminista para una política pública', *El Estado y el Movimiento de Mujeres: Retos y Posibilidades*, Foro de ONGs sobre la Mujer, Beijing 95, Coordinadora Regional de ONGs de América Latina y El Caribe, Lima, Peru: FLASCO Publications (Latin American Faculty of Social Science), p. 5.

Castells, Manuel (1997). *The Power of Identity*, Oxford: Blackwell.

Dean, Jody (1996). 'Struggling for Recognition: Identity Politics and Democracy', in *Solidarity of Strangers: Feminism after Identity Politics*, Berkeley: University of California Press.

Dietz, Mary G. (1994). 'Ciudadanía con aire feminista', *Debate Feminista* 10: 30–6.

Feijóo, María del Carmen (1995). 'El Feminismo y el Estado', working paper presented to the NGO Forum of the 4th World Women's Conference, Beijing (unpublished).

Franco, Carlos (1997). 'Ciudadania, una mentira verdadera', *Cuestion de Estado* (Special Issue: *Ciudadania en el Peru y detras de la moda que?*) 20, April, Instituto de Dialogo y Propuestas, Lima, Peru.

Fraser, Nancy and Linda Gordon (1992). 'Contrato versus caridad: Una reconsideración de la relación entre ciudadanía civil y ciudadanía social', *Isegora* 6, November, Madrid.

Giddens, Anthony (1994). *Beyond Left and Right: the Future of Radical Politics*, Stanford, CA: Stanford University Press.

Gramsci, Antonio (1998). *Selections from the Prison Notebooks,* London: Lawrence and Wishart.

Held, David (1995). *Democracy and the Global Order: From Modern States to Cosmopolitan Governance*, Stanford, CA: Stanford University Press.

Kirkwood, Julieta (1985). *Ser Política en Chile,* Lima, Peru: FLACSO.

Meynen, Wicky and Virginia Vargas (1994). 'La autonomia como estrategia para el desarrollo desde los multiples intereses de las mujeres', in Maruja Barrig and Andy Wehkamp (eds) *Sin morir en el intento. Experiencias de planificacion de genero en el desarrollo*, NOVIB/Red Entre Mujeres, Lima, Peru: Flora Tristan Publications.

Molina, Natacha (1998). 'Women's Struggle for Equality and Citizenship in Chile', in Geertje Lycklama, Virginia Vargas and Saskia Wieringa (eds) *Women's Movements and Public Policy in Europe, Latin America and the Caribbean,* New York and London: Garland Publishing.

Mouffe, Chantal (1996). 'Feminismo, Ciudadania y Politica Democratica Radical', in Elena Beltran and Cristina Sanches (eds) *Las Ciudadanas y lo Político*, Instituto Universitario de Estudios de la Mujer, Universidad Autonoma de Madrid, Spain, pp. 1–20.

Nun, José (1989). *La rebelión del coro,* Buenos Aires: Ed. Nueva Visión.

Pateman, Carole (1988). *The Sexual Contract,* Stanford, CA: Stanford University Press.

Phillips, Anne (1994). 'Must Feminists Give up on Liberal Democracy?' in David Held (ed.) *Prospects for Democracy: North, South, East, West,* Standford, CA: Stanford University Press, pp 93–111.

Pringle, Rosemary and Sophie Watson (1994). 'Women's Interests and the Post-Structuralist State', in Michelle Barrett and Anne Phillips (eds) *Destabilizing Theory: Contemporary Feminist Debates,* Cambridge: Polity Press.

Valenzuela, Maía Elena (1995). 'La Legitimidad de la Agenda de las Mujeres', *El Estado y el Movimiento de Mujeres: Retos y Posibilidades*, Foro de ONGs sobre la Mujer Beijing 95, Coordinadora Regional de ONGs de América Latina y El Caribe, Lima, Peru: Flora Tristan Publications, pp 9–10.

Vargas Valente, Virginia (1989). *El Aporte de la Rebeldía de las Mujeres*, Lima, Peru: Flora Tristan Publications.

INDEX